An Historical Geography
of England and Wales

An Historical Geography of England and Wales

Edited by

R. A. Dodgshon
Department of Geography,
University College of Wales,
Aberystwyth, Wales

R. A. Butlin
Department of Geography,
Queen Mary College,
University of London,
London, England

Academic Press
Harcourt Brace Jovanovich, Publishers

London   San Diego   New York   Berkeley
Boston   Sydney   Tokyo   Toronto

ACADEMIC PRESS LIMITED
24–28 Oval Road
London NW1 7DX

United States Edition published by
ACADEMIC PRESS INC.
San Diego, CA 92101

Reprinted 1987
Reprinted 1989

Library of Congress Catalog Card Number: 78-18021
ISBN Casebound edition: 0-12-219250-8
ISBN Paperback edition: 0-12-219252-4

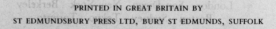

PRINTED IN GREAT BRITAIN BY
ST EDMUNDSBURY PRESS LTD, BURY ST EDMUNDS, SUFFOLK

Contributors

R. A. BUTLIN *Department of Geography, Queen Mary College, University of London, Mile End Road, London, E1 4NS, England.*

H. CARTER *Department of Geography, University College of Wales, Llandinam Building, Penglais, Aberystwyth, Dyfed, SY23 3DB, Wales.*

R. A. DODGSHON *Department of Geography, University College of Wales, Llandinam Building, Penglais, Aberystwyth, Dyfed SY23 3DB, Wales.*

D. GREGORY *Department of Geography, University of Cambridge, Downing Place, Cambridge, CB2 3EN, England.*

I. HODDER *Department of Archaeology, University of Cambridge, Downing Place, Cambridge, CB2 3EN, England.*

G. R. J. JONES *Department of Geography, University of Leeds, Leeds, LS2 9JT, England.*

J. LANGTON *Department of Geography, University of Liverpool, Roxby Building, P.O. Box 147, Liverpool L69 3BX, England.*

R. LAWTON *Department of Geography, University of Liverpool, Roxby Building, P.O. Box 147, Liverpool L69 3BX, England.*

A. MOYES *Department of Geography, University College of Wales, Llandinam Building, Penglais, Aberystwyth, Dyfed, SY23 3DB, Wales.*

E. PAWSON *Department of Geography, University of Canterbury, Christchurch 1, New Zealand.*

B. K. ROBERTS *Department of Geography, University of Durham, South Road, Durham City, England.*

R. M. SMITH *Cambridge Group for the History of Population and Social Structure, University of Cambridge, 27 Trumpington Street, Cambridge, CB2 1QA, England.*

J. R. WALTON *Department of Geography, University College of Wales, Llandinam Building, Penglais, Aberystwyth, Dyfed, SY23 3DB, Wales.*

J. YELLING *Department of Geography, Birkbeck College, University of London, 7–15 Gresse Street, London W1P 1PA, England.*

... ...

R.J.S. Department of Geography, University of Durham, South Road,

... SMITH Cambridge Group for the History of Population and Social
Structure, University of Cambridge, 27 Trumpington Street, Cambridge, CB2
1QA, England.

J.R. WALTON Department of Geography, University College of Wales,
Llandinam Building, Penglais, Aberystwyth, Dyfed, SY23 3DB Wales.

J. YELLING Department of Geography, Birkbeck College, University of London,

Preface

The historical geography of England and Wales has never boasted a wide range of text books. To some extent, this reflected justified satisfaction with those available. However, the last decade has witnessed important changes in the content of historical geography. Stated simply, there has been a shift towards a more interpretative approach to the past. No longer concerned solely with the reconstruction of past spatial patterns, or historical map-making, more and more geographers are showing an equal if not greater concern for the processes which helped structure such patterns. Assisting this transition has been the marked increase in the number of practising historical geographers since the early 1960s, an increase now manifest in the growing volume of published work and organized conference activity. With these developments has come a changing evaluation of past problems. Previously neglected issues have suddenly been cast into sharp focus, sometimes via energetic, multi-sided debates which have injected a new vitality into the subject.

As the impact of these changes has grown, there has emerged an urgent need for a textbook which takes stock of what has been achieved so far in respect of the historical geography of England and Wales. This volume of edited essays seeks to fulfil this need. A series of broad syntheses dealing with the periods before 1500 is followed by a series of detailed discussions of systematic themes within the early modern (1500–1730) and modern (1730–1900) periods. The greater space devoted to the periods after 1500 matches the balance of current work and interest. Their organization on a systematic basis is consistent with the growing tendency amongst historical geographers to identify themselves more by theme (i.e. urban, population) than by period. The editors have not tried to impose a formal structure or format on the discussion. In deference to the fact that once the weight is shifted from description to interpretation, a variety of differing or even conflicting viewpoints is admitted, contributors have therefore been allowed, within limits, to be the architects of their own houses. The editors feel the result is a text that should stimulate the student's mind rather than just fill it, and that will convey many of the ideas and conclusions embodied in much recent literature. Indeed, most contributions would have been substantially different had they been written ten years ago. In short, they demonstrate the progress which has been made in recent years. Above all, they highlight the areas of the subject which have responded most to the challenge of 'new' geography by articulating their ideas or interpretations through concepts, theories or models. However, they also show that this response has not been a slavish application of modern spatial theory to historical data. Whether we talk in terms of historicism or in terms of what E. P. Thompson called 'the discipline of context' whereby each fact or event is given meaning only within 'an ensemble of other meanings', so that we can never totally abstract them from the context of the past, historical geography will always have claim to problems and processes that are distinctly its own. Herein will always lie the originality of its contribution to the wider subject of geography.

Inevitably, a book of this nature cannot be compiled without the editors building up a network of debt. Needless to say, we have a special debt to all the contributors for making the book possible and for working to very strict and tight deadlines. We are also indebted to Anthony Watkinson of Academic Press for his constant help and guidance in the production of the book. Finally, we would like to express our thanks to the technicians in the Departments of Geography at both the University College of Wales, Aberystwyth and Queen Mary College, University of London, who have helped re-draw and re-photograph maps and diagrams, especially D. D. Griffiths and D. Williams of Aberystwyth and D. Shewan of Queen Mary College.

R. A. DODGSHON   R. A. BUTLIN
                          March 1978

Contents

11
The Process of Industrial Change 1730–1900

12
Population and Society 1730–1900

13
Towns and Urban Systems 1730–1900

14
Transport 1730–1900

List of Illustrations

List of Tables

1
Perspectives on Prehistory

B. K. Roberts

Introduction

In an old country like Britain the beginnings of settlement are rooted deeply in the past and this is in itself a sufficient justification for beginning this book with a review of the centuries before the Roman conquest. An answer to the basic question concerning the extent and importance of this contribution to the historical geography of England and Wales is at once simple and complex. It is simple in that the thousands of years represented by the word 'prehistory' saw the exploration and exploitation of most, if not all, environments and the occupation of many; it saw the introduction of those basic supports of all economic life, foodcrops and domesticated animals, and the creation of very large areas within which the primitive, pristine environment had been substantially altered, either by relatively temporary occupation or by permanent settlement. All this is qualitatively demonstrable even if not quantitatively assessed, but the question becomes more complex when one turns to the character of those threads linking such remote times with the present, and attempts to evaluate the degree to which each successive society created discrete patterns of sequent occupance, entirely new beginnings, or, by means of grafting new features onto old, established conditions for continuity.

A single chapter is too limited a framework within which to attempt a neat overall summary of the historical geography of the prehistoric period: what follows is a brief overview of the evidence, the problems and certain re-orientations occurring because of new discoveries, new attitudes and a new understanding of the chronological framework. Any treatment on this scale must be rigorously selective, and the account adopts a simple tripartite framework: a review of the basic evidence, a discussion of changing perspectives, and a single brief case study emphasizing the interpretational problems.

1

Evidence

The special problems of archaeology within the prehistoric period derive from the fact that the evidence for reconstructing the cultural scene is, in the absence of documentary evidence, 'mute'. Men do not always write the truth, but only through documents do we get direct insights into the workings of the mind. Only in the later part of the Iron Age in one part of the British Isles, Ireland, do the tales of the Ulster cycle, of the Cattle Raid of Cooley, of MacDatho's Pig and their like, tell of society's perception of itself, a precious 'window on the Iron Age'. [1] By definition the study of prehistory involves an almost complete reliance upon material remains for the study of pre-literate communities (even the folk tales were committed to paper centuries later) and is therefore subject to all the limitations that this bias imposes. One cannot dig up the tenurial obligations linked to an Iron Age hill-fort or farmstead. Furthermore, while it is theoretically possible to distinguish clearly between (i) archaeological facts, the collection of hard data concerning artifacts, tools and tombs, dwellings and ritual sites, their relative and absolute chronological relationships and their distributions within space and time; and (ii) inference, derived from these facts, about the organization of sites, the implications of the level of material culture present, possible types of social organization and relationships with other cultures, this is in practice far from easy. [2]

Some of the problems of archaeology derive from the circumstance that the more thoroughly a site is studied and the more completely it is excavated, the more thoroughly is that particular body of evidence totally destroyed. For all archaeologists this is a challenging and uncomfortable situation; on some sites, Stonehenge for example, it is an awesome responsibility. This total destruction is probably the basis of those elements of acerbity which notoriously colour many archaeological debates. Mackie, nevertheless, makes an important point when he states his belief that fields of science and scholarship are never in a really healthy state unless argument and debate are constantly going on over the evidence being amassed, indeed he goes as far as saying that 'the existence of at least two alternative explanations for a given set of data is essential if the true scientific spirit of enquiry is to flourish'. [3] To these problems must be added those inevitable tensions caused by period bias: 'found nothing yet, still ploughing through medieval layers' is of course the apocryphal note on a postcard from a Roman archaeologist, but the geographical world should perhaps remember those soil scientists who have reputedly dug through tessellated pavements, oblivious to their existence! There is a serious point here: all observation is selective, we see what we are trained to see and what we expect to see, and the advent of a 'flint-person' upon a local scene, adept at seeing these, can dramatically increase the incidence of such sites. This is an old problem, in a new guise, of an 'active archaeological society' distorting distribution maps.

Archaeology evolved from the systematic study of surviving, visible structures, Stonehenge, hill-forts, megalithic tombs and round barrows, together with chance finds of objects, stone and metal implements, ornaments, ritual items, and more rarely, organic remains. The development of excavation, to search for objects buried in *significant* locations upon undisturbed sites went hand in hand with the development of systematic field-work to find and identify, but not necessarily excavate, new sites. Contemporary archaeology rests upon these two foundations, which provide most of the hard data. To these, however, must be added a third vital element, the library and laboratory work, which support field-work and follow up excavation and are an important part of making the results available. These three techniques produce a body of factual material, evidence, which it is necessary to organize within spatial, temporal and conceptual frameworks. However, the non-archaeologist should be under no doubt concerning the importance of those critical boundaries between fact, reasonable inference, preconceptions based upon *a priori* reasoning, and hypotheses attempting social explanations by analogy.

Figure 1.1 has been designed to illustrate the problems. The first section (Fig. 1.1(a)) maps a series of stones which project through the turf of a gentle hill-slope in upper Weardale, forming what appears to be a significant pattern. Each stone is plotted, and the errors involved are errors of measurement: the pattern on the ground appears on the map. To go further is to infer, to interpret, yet the observations so expressed are hardly satisfactory. Fig. 1.1(b) is based upon the survey of a similar site by Jobey, a very accomplished field worker. This plan, however, already incorporates a substantial degree of interpretation—the surrounding rampart and ditch are noted (the ditch was either absent or merely missed in Fig. 1.1(a); I drew the plan and believe the former alternative!) and the homesteads are plotted. Already the presence of the interpretational element is sufficient to make a direct comparison between the surviving remains at these two sites difficult, even though both are stone-built. Fig. 1.1(c) records features discovered during excavation, and interpreted by

Metres

0   20

N

Track

a

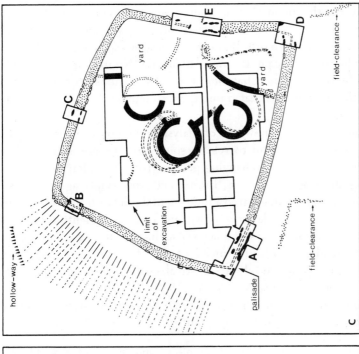

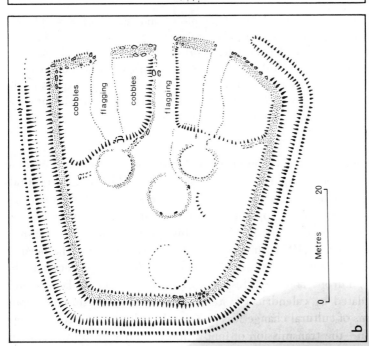

Fig. 1.1. Three Northumbrian homestead enclosures: (a) is after a survey by B. K. Roberts of a site at Bollihope, Weardale, Co. Durham, Grid. Ref. NY 977352; (b) is derived from G. Jobey, in A. L. F. Rivet (ed.) *The Iron Age in North Britain* and is the homestead at Riding Wood, Northumberland, Grid. Ref. NY 818846; (c) is derived from G. Jobey, *Archaeologia Aeliana*, 5th ser., **I** (1973), pp. 55–79, Grid. Ref. NY 662894.

the excavator as the foundations of a succession of circular huts. Let it be emphasized that I in no way question Jobey's interpretations. [4] Nevertheless, the point has to be made that archaeological 'facts' reflect the archaeologist. Clarke put this more formally: 'No archaeological study can be any better than the reliability of the observations upon which it is based and the assumptions that frame the development of its analysis and interpretation.' [5]

The problem of the frameworks of analysis and interpretation is in part historical. It will be helpful to restate some basic premises and earlier concepts before turning to changing perspectives. The identification by Thomsen of three ages, of Stone, Bronze and Iron, implying a universal technological progression created a fundamental temporal and conceptual outline still in use today, and within this the identification of stratigraphically associated assemblages of artifacts, some of which can be used as type-fossils, provided the means of identifying cultures which are, as Childe pointed out, largely a statistical concept. [6] In his book, *The Prehistoric Communities of the British Isles* (1940), he argued that this total assemblage of material was ultimately related to the life-style of a social group or community, going on to point out:

> Did we know the homes, working places and graves of a prehistoric community, together with a large selection of its tools, weapons, ornaments and cult objects, we should be able to form a fair idea of its social structure, religious and artistic ideals. By plotting on maps the distribution of its distinctive products we could trace the peoples' territorial expansion. By comparing these products with those of precursors, neighbours and successors we could evaluate the group's role in local and British history. [7]

These are bold claims, a vision of the past which ultimately touches upon all of the questions and perspectives to be considered below. He reminds us, however, that these conditions are never satisfied, for time, that capricious filter, wreaks appalling havoc with all mans' handiwork.

Childe's views, first put forward in his great synthesis *The Dawn of European Civilisation* (1925), hinged upon two ideas: the first, the need to establish an absolute as opposed to a relative chronology between the cultures of Europe and the Mespotamian and Egyptian artifacts which could be dated by calendrical systems; and second, his thinking upon mechanisms of cultural change was powerfully influenced by the concept of diffusion—the transmission of innovation from one group to another, either by actual folk movement or by the spread of ideas, skills and attitudes. Thus Childe's 1940 study of Britain envisages successive waves of colonization, by Neolithic farmers, who took over from hunter-gatherers, bringing causewayed camps and various types of communal collective tombs, by Beaker folk and other warriors and traders in bronze, by land-seeking peasants of the late Bronze Age Deverel Rimbury culture, and finally by three main waves of Iron Age peoples. There was indeed a place for fusion, between Mesolithic hunters and the Neolithic agriculturalists, between stone-using farmers and bronze-using immigrants, but essential innovations came from without, and even the splendid Wessex culture was not seen as an entirely indigenous flowering for there were, following Piggott, hints of invaders from Brittany. [8] The essential chronological framework for these happenings was summarized in 1951, in a volume involving several scholars, as shown in Table 1.1. [9]

Table 1.1: A basic chronology of British prehistory, 1951 (see Table 1.2 for 1974 version)

Palaeolithic Age	? —B.C. 10,000
Mesolithic Age	B.C. 10,000–2500
Neolithic Age	B.C. 2500–1850
Bronze Age	B.C. 1850–450
Iron Age	B.C. 450–43 A.D.

Piggott in his book on *The Neolithic Cultures of the British Isles* (1954) shortened this chronology, concluding 'it should be possible, in fact, to contain the whole of the British Neolithic cultures described in this book within the first half of the second millennium B.C.' i.e. between B.C. 2000 and 1500. As Atkinson noted all archaeologists must be prepared to have their 'most cherished theories rudely controverted by subsequent research' and this particular conclusion has indeed had to be subjected to drastic revision. [10]

To conclude this review reference must be made to two areas in which rapid developments have occured since the 1950s: the discovery and recovery of hitherto unimagined quantities of basic archaeological evidence and an increasing appreciation of the complex role of later centuries of development in providing the filter mentioned by Childe. Undoubtedly the single most important factor revealing new archaeological sites is the air photograph, and since the late 1940s these have become increasingly available. Broadly three categories of evidence can be culled from such photographs: [11]

(i) Where earthworks remain as upstanding features these, subject to correct lighting and vegetational conditions, can be detected as *shadow* or *shine* marks. When linked with fieldwork and excavation this reveals new details of known sites or the presence of new ones, and in particular allows the relocation of relict landscapes, involving settlements, fields, pasture areas, roads and burial grounds. Rather than individual point sites whole landscapes emerge.

(ii) Where sites have been ploughed out they are often visible as *soil marks*, where changes in colour and texture reveal the presence of buried structures.

(iii) Where such ploughed-out sites are under a standing crop, depending upon the nature of the crop, the state of growth, the lighting, and the groundwater conditions, then the buried structures are often revealed, sometimes with startling clarity by differential growth or parching. One simple point must be stressed: all sites are not always visible and even a known site can appear, disappear and reappear quite unpredictably. The details of a site can also vary enormously from time to time, from photograph to photograph, so that what seems to be a single enclosure when first sighted, can, following study, be seen to lie at the centre of a great complex of ploughed-out earthworks. In short, a known, unexcavated site is always worth re-photographing.

A steady succession of discoveries by St Joseph have appeared in the pages of *Antiquity* and other publications and their volume attests the value of such work. There are few areas of lowland Britain, under crop, which in the six weeks before harvest, will not reveal at least some signs of earlier occupations. In the space available one detailed example must suffice: Fig. 1.2 is derived from maps published in 1974 in a survey of the sites revealed in the previous 50 years along the river gravels of the upper Thames. [12] The original maps were published at a scale of 1:10,560, and reveal incredible quantities of earlier occupation embracing, if pottery scatters and limited excavation be a guide, all periods from prehistory to the eleventh century, by which stage the present landscape structures began to evolve. The point is that these remarkable discoveries do not stand alone: published work reveals similar densities in the Severn-Avon Valley, the

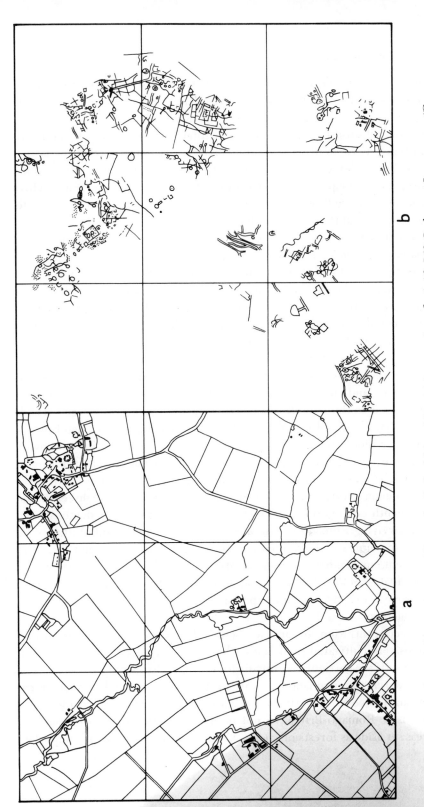

Fig. 1.2. Cropmarks near Stanton Harcourt, Oxfordshire. Map (a) is a portion of a 1:10,560 Ordnance Survey map (Crown Copyright Reserved) with a grid of kilometre squares; map (b) (after Benson and Miles, *The Upper Thames Valley*, pp. 47, 49) shows all known cropmarks.

upper Nene, the Welland and the Trent, while work in progress in many areas, the north-east, to the west of the Pennines, on Dartmoor, Bodmin Moor, the Mendips and throughout the Midlands is demonstrating the presence of unsuspected quantities of total landscape survival, on many soil types. Ford, writing of south Warwickshire, suggests that the layout of medieval open-field landscapes of strips and furlongs often reflect older lines, such as the presence of farmsteads, field boundaries and tracks. How many of these are Romano-British and how many are prehistoric has yet to be resolved, but this does introduce a rather daunting problem: the extent to which many of the details of medieval and later landscapes are subtly related to more ancient landscape structures. There are certainly hints from the upland peripheries of north-eastern England which suggest that 'medieval' irregular fields may reflect older prehistoric layers of occupation. An archaeological site every quarter of a square mile becomes a real possibility, and the implications of such a conclusion has enormous repercussions for those engaged in research, rescue and preservation. Taylor has called this the true 'quantitive revolution' in archaeology. [13]

A second, more complex problem, has been touched upon in this last paragraph, and concerns not so much the way in which evidence can be discovered as the context in which it survives to be discovered. Lands which have been subjected to continuous ploughing (with attendant soil drift), erosion, stone-picking and (presumably) casual artifact recovery will show fewer archaeological features than those marginal pastoral areas, be these chalklands, heathlands or uplands, where upstanding earthworks still remain clearly in evidence, even if degraded by eighteenth and nineteenth-century improvements. Fowler and Bowen have demonstrated that surviving Romano-British field systems in Dorset and Wiltshire lie *above* the limits of local medieval open-field cultivation, and in a very different environment a similar relationship can be seen at Grassington in Wharfdale. Below the medieval head-dyke the earlier systems were destroyed or, as is more probable, subtly integrated with new arrangements. [14]

A concentration of archaeological discoveries may occur within intensively cultivated field lands where these lie upon river gravels, as these soils are particularly suitable for cropmark sites. Of particular value in preserving ancient landscapes are the parklands, created throughout the lowlands since Norman times. Recent work is also producing evidence for extensive Romano-British, if not prehistoric settlement, beneath those areas set aside as forests or chases. [15] Such fossil landscapes are important in that they show what formerly could have existed in other, more intensively exploited areas. A distribution map then, seen as record of hard archaeological evidence, contains many problems. Two in particular are significant when developing hypotheses and arguments: first, within any map there will always be two zones, what Taylor has termed a 'Zone of Survival' and a 'Zone of Destruction', affecting the reliability of the primary observations concerning the presence or absence of data. Furthermore our

> inability to recover the total pattern is made worse by the fact that we have no idea of how complete our evidence is. If we knew that any given pattern was 75 per cent or even 50 per cent complete it would help, but we never do. The recoverable number of settlements may be only 1 per cent of the original total, or it may be as much as 90 per cent. It is very difficult to draw valid conclusions from such evidence.[16]

Atkinson emphasizes a second point,

> all archaeological maps . . . represent the projection onto a single plane of sites which will in general not have co-existed. The effect of such maps is therefore to exaggerate the level and density of human activity, or for that matter population size in the area concerned.

This conclusion, applicable directly to Fig. 1.2, has particularly sharp repercussions within the Neolithic period when radiocarbon dating has extended the time span involved by a factor of four or five (cf. Tables 1.1 and 1.2). Atkinson continues,

> an increase in the duration of a *period* does not produce a concomitant increase in the duration of an individual site . . . . What happens is that a fixed number of sites (and the populations they represent) have to be spread out over a longer period, so that the density of sites in use at any one point in time will be smaller than was previously supposed.[17]

These are simple points, but they warn of the dangers inherent in elaborate exercises based upon distribution maps of questionable and variable validity. Nevertheless, as Hodder and Orton point out, 'the more quantified information which is upon a map or which pertains to spatial patterning, the better that map can be discussed and interpreted'.[18] This is a solution which is relevant both at the scale of the scholar creating national or international generalizations and at the scale of the individual field worker, indeed initially the difficult questions raised by temporal sequences, successive occupations and continuity may be better tackled in terms of very detailed local studies, where a small region forms a laboratory for the accumulation of polychronous data and the testing of hypotheses, the technique of 'terrain' or 'total' archaeology. The work by Fowler at Fyfield Down, where the history of a chalkland landscape is being traced, provides an example, while a recent paper by Simmons and Spratt shows how even within a period as remote and difficult as the Mesolithic, 'amateur' and professional knowledge concerning a limited area can be combined to give new insights. [19]

Perspectives

Changes in the amount of hard archaeological data available and in our understanding of the factors affecting survival and destruction have been paralleled by changes in the temporal, spatial and conceptual frameworks which affect the inferences which can be drawn from that data. Quite obviously, in a brief review, it is not possible to develop arguments concerning all of the real worlds of the prehistoric past. Accordingly in the discussion which follows concerning several systematic themes examples will be drawn primarily from the Neolithic period and will provide sufficient background to permit a brief case study in the final section. The basic cultural assemblages of the British Neolithic were described by Piggott in 1954, drawing together the hard facts of pottery and other artifact types, both small finds and field monuments. It was clear that these communities of stone-using peasants had many features in common, including the same types of agricultural economy, based upon the cultivation of wheat and barley and the raising of domesticated cattle and sheep. Whatever the impact of Mesolithic man upon the environment, whatever his relationship with red deer and the aurochs, there is a general consensus of opinion that agriculture, involving both grain production and stock rearing, developed earliest in the Middle East and that both the idea and the domesticates were diffused throughout Europe, [20] although a recent discussion does suggest, with particular reference to sites in Ireland, that 'both archaeologically and environmentally there may have been no clear distinction between the Mesolithic and Neolithic communities of the fourth millenium B.C.; nor should we try to define one'. [21] The date given here is sufficiently discordant with that given in Table 1.1 as to require explanation.

Changes in Chronological Perspectives

Excavation frequently establishes a relative chronology using the principles of statigraphy, x is older than y, y is older than z, z is younger than x, but in 1951 a revolutionary breakthrough emerged which brought a radical change in temporal perspectives. During the lifetime of all living organisms a small part of the carbon in their tissues is converted, by means of cosmic radiation, into radioactive carbon. On death this radioactivity is gradually lost, and after about 5500 years the original proportion of radiocarbon is reduced by one half—the half-life. This constant can be used as the basis for calculating the absolute age of stratified organic remains from archaeological sites, and by the early 1950s some dates were becoming available: these often proved to be *earlier* than had been expected and more recent work has suggested that the dates so far accepted are not in fact entirely accurate. Correlations between radiocarbon dating systems and the wood of the incredibly long-lived bristlecone pine of California (up to 4000 years), whose age can be counted using the annual growth rings of both living and dead trees, suggests that dates in the third millennium B.C. should be some 500 years older than radiocarbon dating was suggesting. Details of these calibrations are still open to some dispute, but as more results become available, and if they show signs of being internally consistent then the calibrated dates will become more certain. All dates are qualified by the statement of one standard deviation ± so many years, i. e. there is a 66 per cent chance of the date falling within the given time period, and it is now recognized that it is desirable (but expensive) to have several dates from one context. In practical terms this results in a more complex situation which may be tabulated as shown in Table 1.2.[22]

Table 1.2 records the earliest and the latest dates considered by the authors contributing to Renfrew's study to fall within each cultural phase. Two things are immediately evident: first, there is a considerable overlap between the temporal span of each age, while secondly, the dates are precise enough, even with their *known* limits of uncertainty, for their geographical context to become significant, indeed this tabulation has no practical significance, and the strength of radiocarbon dates derives from their temporal and spatial distributions. One needs to know that the date of B.C. 4580, the earliest for a Neolithic cultural context, is from a hearth found at Ballynagilly in Co. Tyrone in Ireland and that the radiocarbon date b.c. (before Christ, in radiocarbon years) using a half-life of 5568 years

Table 1.2: The earliest and latest dates[a] assigned to an archaeological period

Mesolithic Age	b.c	8415 ± 170	2670 ± 140
	B.C		(3480/3400)
Neolithic Age	b.c.	3795 ± 90	1430 ± 120
	B.C.	(4580)	(1670)
Bronze Age	b.c.	2100 ± 50	420 ± 95
	B.C	(2670–2540)	(480)
Iron Age	b.c.	1560 ± 180	A.D. 43
	B.C.	(2050–1750)	

[a] Expressed in radiocarbon years before Christ (b.c.) and approximate calibrated dates (B.C.). Data published 1974.

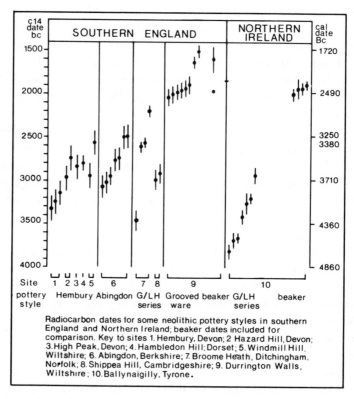

Radiocarbon dates for some neolithic pottery styles in southern England and Northern Ireland; beaker dates included for comparison. Key to sites 1. Hembury, Devon; 2. Hazard Hill, Devon; 3. High Peak, Devon; 4. Hambledon Hill; Dorset; 5. Windmill Hill. Wiltshire; 6. Abingdon, Berkshire; 7. Broome Heath, Ditchingham, Norfolk; 8. Shippea Hill, Cambridgeshire; 9. Durrington Walls, Wiltshire; 10. Ballynaigilly, Tyrone.

Fig. 1.3. Radiocarbon dates for some Neolithic pottery styles in southern England. (After Smith, in Renfrew, *British Prehistory*, p. 107.)

was 3795 $\pm$ 90, and that the laboratory numbers of this date is UB 305. One is, once again, brought face to face with the precise nature of the site, the conditions of deposition and the precise value of the basic data involved. Figure 1.3 shows the temporal and spatial distribution of the radiocarbon dates available up to 1973 associated with certain distinctive Neolithic pottery styles: those with the earliest dates. The Grimston/Lyles Hill vessels, simple round-based pots, are clearly linked with an early phase, and significantly have the widest spatial distribution, occurring throughout the British Isles in a wide range of environments. [23] Their long survival, however, warns against any simplistic interpretation in terms of a rapid initial diffusion. All phases of prehistory are affected by this more precise dating and increasing numbers of new dates will enormously enhance our understanding of the chronological significance of regional cultures and encourage more sophisticated hypotheses. However, the repercussions extend further: prehistoric European cultures, particularly those of the third millennium B.C. are all earlier than was once thought. In practical terms this means that the great chambered megalithic tombs of Western Europe are *earlier* than their supposed antecedents of the Mediterranean, a conclusion which demands a re-assessment of the nature of western Neolithic communities and their achievements, indeed it destroys the essential premise that culture change in Britain (and here one must talk of Britain rather than of England and Wales) was brought about by a series of invasions bringing higher levels of culture derived ultimately from European and Mediterranean contacts. [24]

Perspectives on Continuity

This carries the argument to a key problem, the nature of culture change, implying the adoption of new skills, of metallurgy, of organization and of agriculture, new customs, of decoration, of personal adornment, of burial, of settlement and of warfare, and new social patterns, modes of organization to focus wealth and energy for private and public purposes. With prehistory viewed in terms of a series of invasions, with immigrants arriving from the continent, it was possible (as Fox did in 1952) to talk of new cultures being imposed upon 'kindly' lowlands, whose deep rivers and shallow estuaries 'invited' penetration, only to be seriously slowed at the hill wall of the uplands and more slowly absorbed into the sturdy, rugged cultures of the difficult and demanding terrains of upland Britain. This is a gross oversimplification of such views, and Fox's essay, a bold synthesis, is still worth reading. The Highland and Lowland Zones are a fact of life, as any agricultural atlas will show, but it is easy to overemphasize their importance, particularly when dealing with more primitive economies and localized scales of exploitation. [25] In a closely reasoned paper in 1966 Clark challenged the 'invasion hypothesis': while not ignoring folk movements, the Neolithic colonists, the Beaker people of the early Bronze Age, and some during the Iron Age, he was able to demonstrate the extent to which cultural tracts which developed most fully in the Iron Age were already present during the Bronze Age. Thus the great round houses of the early Iron Age of England and Wales, classically seen at Little Woodbury, are now seen to have Bronze Age antecedents, while the complex roots of hill-forts, pastoral, military, social and religious, have their origins in patterns of territoriality extending back, in certain areas at least, to the farmers of the Neolithic Age. [26]

Continuity, however, is a difficult concept to define: it is a word which begs definition. Continuity of what? Settlement sites, institutions, population, territorial organization, burial customs, agricultural practices or inheritance customs? A practical illustration is provided by the great communal tombs of the Neolithic period, some constructed of timber and earth, others of massive stones and rubble, and which show marked regional differentiation. They are clearly a product of much effort and if the regional variations and the small locality distributions are a guide they were constructed by local population groups within larger regional groupings, as may have been the case with the ritual sites known as 'henges'. These tombs were clearly used throughout a long period of time, often with successive additions to their structures, and invariably with successive internments. Piggott is of the opinion that the great longbarrow at West Kennet, Wiltshire, a member of the Severn-Cotswold tomb group, was built in the middle of the third millennium B.C. but the chambers were not fully sealed until the seventeenth century B.C. and produced pottery ranging from primary Neolithic to early Bronze Age types. [27] Such discoveries must be set in the context of plough marks found beneath the barrow at South Street, Avebury, Wiltshire, where the barrow could be *at least* 30, possibly 100 or 200 years later than the agricultural activity. The recognition that many barrows are indeed composite structures, incorporating several earlier and distinct monuments into a final overall conception opens many perspectives. Here we are at one and the same time faced with several distinct types of continuity, of use, of belief, of sacredness of site, of territorial occupation, and of population. Atkinson believed that at Lanhill in the Cotswolds nine out of the nineteen burials, because of distinctive bone-deformations, could all belong to one family. [28]

This hint that such tombs were built by local communities leads to further questions: the people who built them presumably lived within the adjacent landscapes and even though Neolithic settlements are singularly elusive, Renfrew has pointed out how in Arran and Rousay, conveniently bounded islands, the megalithic tombs have a logical relationship to the available arable resources, while Ashbee was able to divide the earthen long barrows of Dorset and Wiltshire into five distinctive regional groups reflecting strongly localized traditions. [29]

The identification of territories associated with point sites such as long barrows, known settlements and hill-forts has developed under the influence of the locational analysis school of geography and, like geography during the 1960s, archaeology is currently experiencing a quantitative revolution, indeed two, if Taylor's view is accepted. Hodder, in a concise review of recent trends, emphasizes the undoubted advantages of a more quantitative and systematic approach in providing clarity in the demonstration (one might say, description) of spatial trends, problems and relationships and the introduction of some objectivity in the analysis of spatial patterns, or at least the stimulation of specific statements concerning methods, hypotheses and assumptions. Undoubtedly this does represent a break away from conventional 'eyeball' methods of assessment, and permits the discovery of hitherto unsuspected patterns and, perhaps more importantly, often yields new questions. In all such developments, however, the new methods and approaches are an aid to study, and the advantages of computerized bulk-data handling, speeding up processes of analysis, are tremendous, permitting the testing of hypotheses, the differentiation between alternative hypotheses, and finally, prediction, indicating the possible location of undiscovered sites. Used properly these new techniques permit complex questions to be asked if sufficient data appear to be available, and by speeding up the mechanical processes, create time, a key factor in permitting the human brain to absorb and become familiar with all facets of the evidence. This circumstance leads to those conditions which encourage those vital and 'intuitive' steps into the perception of new ideas and new attitudes. Such aims can hardly be challenged: nevertheless, as Hodder makes clear, ultimately the difficulties of inferring process from form have to be faced, such as with the problem of inferring the nature and character of Neolithic 'trade' from the distribution of stone axes, and here simulation techniques may permit comparison between reality and theoretically and mathematically described processes. [30]

The identification of territories involves a classic problem of inferring the areas and possible boundaries from a known distribution of points. It must be recognized that at least three scales of enquiry are possible, the national, the regional and the local, and in practical terms these merely represent three points on a continuum. The recognition at a local scale that the economy of a given site depended directly upon the character and possibilities inherent within the terrains to which access was possible has roots in the concepts of economic prehistory enunciated by Clark in his 1952 volume Prehistoric Europe: The Economic Basis. When this is allied to the recognition that the archaeological site is a repository of matter imported from this site-catchment zone, then the possibilities for environmental archaeology become enormously enhanced and we face, once again, the problems and limitations of excavation techniques. [31] Information painstakingly and imaginatively collected at a single point in space must be interpreted logically in the context of the surrounding area, eventually permitting the identification of territories and possibly of boundaries. Of one thing alone can we be certain, reality will prove to be infinitely more complex than our models, and the territories of Iron Age hill-forts, so emphatically demarcated by Thiessen polygons, will surely be proved to have had unexpected patterns of configuration.

Before leaving this question of territories reference must be made to a corpus of work concerning the historical period: G. R. J. Jones in a long series of papers has argued that certain estates, comprising groups of hamlets and villages answering to a chief place, a lord's court, with collective rents, renders and services, and documented in twelfth and thirteenth century sources, may be of pre-Saxon origin and his general conclusion is that they could be very old indeed (see Chapter 3). He repeatedly draws attention to the fact that refuges are an integral part of their structure and that hill-forts often appear in significant association with such territories—an example being the presence of the great hill-fort of Almondbury within the multiple estate of Wakefield. In short, the presence of the antecedents of such territories during the Iron Age could, in part, account for the construction of hill-forts, whose rulers drew upon the labour services of their territories. Jones goes as far as pointing out that Stonehenge lies within the great royal estate of Amesbury and this could echo important earlier territorial situations. The case for the antiquity of these estates and their pre-Saxon origin is, subject to some qualifications concerning the processes of change which could affect them, a strong one. Projection to earlier periods is, however, a stimulating hypothesis upon which, at the moment, a verdict of 'not-proven' must be returned. Nevertheless, there is an important point here: the attraction of theoretical notions of territories must not detract from an awareness that actual territories may sometimes be detectable and that such evidence is worth seeking and considering. [32]

Vegetation Change

The question of economic prehistory and man's exploitation of the environment introduces a further theme, that of environmental change. Most obviously and closely related to man's activities is vegetation change. The millenia between the Mesolithic period and the Iron Age saw a gradual transition from ephemeral settlements of a few days or temporary settlements of a few weeks duration through to seasonal and permanent settlements taking advantage of the possibilities for rational exploitation of localized economic resources. Their surviving remains indicate a transition from an economy based entirely upon collecting, hunting and fishing to one based upon the exploitation of arable and grazing lands whose productivity was maintained by means of a scheme of manuring or management, and this is reflected in the character of the settlements found. It can be argued that a critical break was occasioned by the advent of a new food-producing economy with the arrival, during the second half of the fourth millenium B.C., of ecologically potent farming groups. Nevertheless, there is an increasing awareness of the degree to which the economy of the Mesolithic period was securely based upon a full exploitation of both the animal and the vegetational worlds; the equipment—notably the microliths, being suitable for hafting in multibladed gathering implements as well as hunting weapons. The degree to which the environment was managed may have been very much greater than previously thought, involving burning and herd manipulation. Simmons has detected temporary clearances created by these folk in North Yorkshire, and gone as far as postulating complex group territories encompassing seashore, lowlands, foothills and uplands. [33] Summer hunting grounds in the hills were exploited by small groups, which met in larger concentrations in the fat autumn (when hazelnuts may have been a key dietary item) only to disperse again for the lean months of winter and spring spent in the lowlands and strand-looping along the coasts. This hypothesis, supported by the evidence of diagrams and chipping sites, hints at well-established patterns of territoriality by the Mesolithic period and a standard of life probably more stable than the precarious farming economy which was to follow.

Fields, however, no matter how temporary, represent a more complex and potentially more potent form of land use which eventually had a permanent impact upon vegetation, initiating the processes leading to the almost wholly cleared landscapes of the present. The vegetational history of Britain has been reconstructed by counting the almost indestructible pollen grains preserved at various levels in peat deposits (which have been accumulating over thousands of years), absolute dates for which are obtained by radiocarbon methods. The interpretation of the resulting diagrams is an art rather than an exact science: the supply of pollen to a bog or lake surface involves three components, the local component from the vegetation immediately adjacent to the deposit, a regional component from the general environs, and finally pollen which has been transported long distances and is washed in by rainfall. Pollen in lake deposits also includes material transported by water from the area of the drainage basin. Obviously the proportions of these components can show entirely natural temporal variations, reflecting post-glacial vegetation successions, but clearance, local, regional or general, can cause variations in the pollen spectrum, most basically in the proportions of tree, shrub and grass pollen present, as well as in the amounts associated with each species of plant. In an effort to evaluate the real impact of man upon an area of vegetation, Turner has developed the idea of three-dimensional pollen diagrams, uniting the evidence from a series of related diagrams from a single large bog to portray a regional picture. This work leads towards questions concerning the precise character of early woodland clearances, their location, their extent, their duration and the land-use within them.[34]

Inevitably our understanding of vegetation change derived from pollen diagrams is biased by the location of work done and by constraints upon where it is possible to do such work i.e. where pollen-rich sites are available. On the chalklands of the south and east and along the coastlands of western Britain detailed counts of fossilized molluscan faunas, snail shells, provide the basis for an assessment of enviromental change, for they can be grouped into shade-loving species, open-country species and intermediate species. No brief summary can do justice to the volume of material now available, but two broad trends may be distinguished: first, the prehistoric period sees the penetration of wooded areas by what have been termed 'small temporary clearances': these occur from areas as far apart as Ayrshire, the Cumberland lowlands, Wales, Yorkshire and the Somerset Levels, and appear in Neolithic and Bronze Age contexts. During the Bronze Age, from 2000 B.C. onwards, more and more forest was being cleared, a situation which can be interpreted in terms of a gradually increasing population practising a form of shifting agriculture. During the Iron Age, in contrast, extensive disforestation frequently occurred, a process surely linked with better tools, higher populations and more developed permanent agriculture, and it appears that the relative importance of cereal production and pastoral activities can be detected in the changing proportions of certain indicator herbs. [35]

This brings the argument to the second point. It is quite clear from the material available that as early as the Neolithic period marked *regional* differences in activity were beginning to emerge: thus Evans argues that on the chalk and allied areas, on lighter well-drained soils in the Brecklands and along the costal plain of Cumberland, and probably parts of the Thames Valley around Oxford and Dorchester 'large, permanent clearances' occurred, and in this context permanent fields become a possibility. Many of the henges of Wiltshire, circular ritual enclosures of Neolithic provenance, have produced buried soils indicating that after clearance and cultivation grassland developed, grassland which may have been maintained by grazing animals for a period as long as 500 years! In contrast, in other parts of the British Isles 'small temporary clearances', short-term *landnam* phases, are more usual, linked with a type of shifting agriculture. These regional differences, at first no doubt limited in character, were the initial beginnings of the process of differentiation still continuing today. Evans makes the point that the real contrasts between the Highland and Lowland Zones (the first comprising the area of Palaeozoic rocks with limited areas of lowland, a wetter climate and impoverished soils, the second made of geologically younger rocks, gentle lowlands interspersed with low escarpments of drier and generally fertile soils), began to emerge with clarity during the first millennium B.C. Before this the contrasts between the two zones were more muted, indeed the difference between them in terms of the quality of their environment may well reflect man's impact, changes in soil type being initiated by the clearances of prehistoric man. [36] A complex of problems emerges, which Kinvig has succinctly described: 'The geographical personality of a region is, to use the words of Vidal de la Blache, "not something delivered complete from the hand of nature'' but is a quality which unfolds itself in the course of time as a result of the interaction between man and his physical and social environment.'[37]

Spatial Analysis and Hypothesis Testing

The wider spatial context of individual archaeological sites is also receiving more attention. One example has already been cited: Simmons and Spratt in their study of the Mesolithic of North Yorkshire have concentrated upon the interconnections between individual sites rather than upon their particular artifact assemblages. They make the assumption that the variations in artifacts and areal extent of sites reflect differing types of economic activity rather than distinct cultures, and that we are seeing the remains of spatially and seasonally distributed contrasts in the life-style of a single group or community. A logical extension of this basic idea, allied to increasing attention to settlement territories, also considered above, is the application of central place theory to archaeological data and the identification of settlement hierarchies. Geographers, largely concerned with the contemporary world with its demonstrable and measurable connections, do well to reflect upon the archaeologists' problems. A site cannot be considered in isolation and the excavator has to seek within it information pertinent to the relationship between it and other sites. This is rarely direct, and depends heavily upon the examination by experts from other fields of the material evidence unearthed, much of which may prove to be exotic, brought to the site as a part of normal day-to-day life. This approach is described in Hodder's work but a fascinating example is to be found in Clarke's re-analysis of the finds from the Iron Age lake-village of Glastonbury, where he demonstrates vividly the possibilities inherent in a rigorous application of this spatial thinking. A key section in the argument, which follows a lengthy examination of the possible relationships between the modular units which make up the village and Celtic social structures, concerns the link between the lake-village and Maesbury, a hill-fort, over eight miles away. The ridge upon which this fort sits apparently produced the clays which are the most likely source of the fine 'Glastonbury Group 2' pottery, and the sandstone used as querns by the fen-dwellers. He concludes, 'we may hypothesise and subsequently test by excavation that it was from this centre that Glastonbury imported much of its raw materials and to which it exported its own products . . . it was to this centre that Glastonbury owed its political allegiance and thus its customary tribute', a logical leap which is challenging, if unprovable. He continues his argument to construct a schematic model of the fully developed Celtic settlement hierarchy—essentially hut-groups, small enclosures, large enclosures (hill-forts) and very large enclosed sites (*oppida*)—suggesting the nature of its possible integration with the social hierarchy and grades on one hand and the economic hierarchy on the other. This model, emphasizing the degree to which individual settlements would 'inexorably tend to become reciprocially specialised and mutually supporting . . . provides a basis for prediction and thus for testing the degree of its reality or unreality'. It is grounded in known archaeological facts, draws upon the 'literary' evidence of Irish laws and Caesar, and incorporates concepts, questions and attitudes derived from anthropology.[38] It is an exciting and stimulating synthesis, even for those who may challenge certain of the interpretations. The parallels with some of G. R. J. Jones' arguments, based upon very different material, are obvious.

Explicit within Clarke's argument is the difficult question of hypothesis testing. It can hardly be doubted that the excavation of any site should occur within a wider context of scholarly questions, but as Barker has recently pointed out an excavation designed to answer one specific question will almost certainly run into completely unexpected evidence, quite unconnected with the original problem and hypothesis it may have generated. Many new excavators are now wholly commited to the problems of complex multi-period sites and Barker is quite explicit: 'I am becoming more and more convinced that the only valid questions to ask of a site are "What is here?" and "What is the whole sequence of events on this site from the beginnings of human activity to the present day?" Any other question must only be part of this all-embracing one.'[39]

Finally, while not denying the prerequisite of a firm foundation in systematic studies and the need for broad generalizations, it is the local region, the *pays*, which offers exciting possibilities for integrative research. Having said this it would be logical to conclude with an example of such a study: however, selection would be invidious and the literature increasingly contains examples of excellent case studies considered at more length than is possible here. The case study selected is systematic and it permits the consideration of a further category of hard archaeological fact so far not considered. It raises further questions concerning the extent to which technological processes and social and economic arrangements can be inferred from their end-products.

Neolithic Science, Technology and Social Organization: A Problem of Interpretation

One of the most remarkable applications of quantitative techniques to prehistoric archaeology has been Thom's discovery that the great circular monuments of Neolithic and Early Bronze Age provenance, known as 'henges' were carefully laid out using measuring rods of 2·72 ft (0·829 m). [40] This he inferred from the statistical study of scores of sites, and has argued that not only is the 'megalithic yard' constant in size throughout these islands, it is also found in Brittany. According to Mackie it is possibly ultimately based upon the Sumerian *shusi* of 2·75 ft (0·8382 m). The geometry of these structures is exceedingly sophisticated and Thom has suggested, one can indeed say demonstrated, that they were set up to allow the movements of the sun and other celestial bodies to be tracked with precision, and even the more complex movements of the moon to be analysed.

Work by other scholars is producing further ideas and confirming Thom's work. It is clear that Neolithic communities possessed great skill in civil engineering and organization, and the corrected radiocarbon chronology implies that these skills were developed independently from those of the Middle Eastern civilization. The idea of such intellectually sophisticated practices raises many questions and Atkinson has pointed out the contradiction between the clear evidence for mathematics and astronomy on one hand and the negative evidence for recorded numeracy on the other. Mackie, drawing upon Mayan parallels has argued a case for the presence of an élite, dwelling in or near ceremonial centres whose central focus lay in Wessex (the henges of Stonehenge, Avebury, Durrington Walls and Woodhenge cluster in this zone) but whose activities were nationwide, as suggested by the widespread distribution of a distinctive type of pottery, Rinyo-Clacton ware, and the henges themselves. Woven clothes (the evidence of the only spindle whorl so far known from Neolithic Britain, found at Durrington Walls) in contrast to the more usual skin clothes, and a differing diet (more pig bones—the result of offerings?) serve to distinguish the astronomer-priests. These monuments are clear evidence for the concentration of political and economic power, but Renfrew has argued not in terms of an élite but in terms of chiefdoms. In this case, drawing upon Polynesian and other anthropological parallels, he suggests that henges represent the periodic meeting places for a chiefdom and perhaps the permanent home of the chief, as well as the foci of ceremonial and religious activity. The chief, the recipient of gifts, was in the key position of being able to redistribute resources and concentrate wealth for public projects.

The above discussion comprises, in essence, one set of facts, two theories, and many questions, and substantiates the maxim that 'In archaeology there is no truth; only hypothesis.'[41]

References

1. K. H. Jackson, *The Oldest Irish Tradition: A Window on the Iron Age*, (Cambridge, 1964).
2. V. G. Childe, *Piecing Together the Past*, (London, 1956); S. Piggott, *Approach to Archaeology*, (London, 1959; Harmondsworth, 1966); E. W. Mackie, *Science and Society in Prehistoric Britain*, (London, 1977), pp. 1–23.
3. Mackie, *Science and Society*, p. 5.
4. G. Jobey, 'A field survey in Northumberland' in A. L. F. Rivet, *The Iron Age in Northern Britain*, (Edinburgh, 1966), pp. 89–109; Jobey, 'A Romano-British settlement at Tower Knowe, Wellhaugh, Northumberland', *Archaeologia Aeliana*, 5th ser., **I** (1973), pp. 55–79.
5. D. L. Clarke (ed.), *Models in Archaeology*, (London, 1972), pp. 804–5.
6. C. Renfrew, *Before Civilisation*, (London, 1973; Harmondsworth, 1976), Chapter 2.
7. V. G. Childe, *Prehistoric Communities of the British Isles*, (London, 1940), pp. 2–3.
8. V. G. Childe, *The Dawn of European Civilisation*, (1st edn.) (Edinburgh, 1925); *idem*, *Prehistoric Communities*, pp. 1–15 *et seq.*, 141; Renfrew, *Before Civilisation*, Chapter 2.
9. H.M.S.O. *Field Archaeology*, Ordnance Survey Professional Papers, New Series, No. 3 (London, 1951), pp. ii, 67–8.
10. S. Piggott, *The Neolithic Cultures of the British Isles*, (Cambridge, 1954), p. 381; R. J. C. Atkinson, *Stonehenge*, (London, 1956; Harmondsworth, 1960), p. 13.
11. J. Bradford, *Ancient Landscapes*, (London, 1957); L. Deuel, *Flights into Yesterday*, (Harmondsworth, 1973); J. K. S. St Joseph, *The Uses of Air Photography*, (London, 1973), pp. 112–26; D. R. Wilson (ed.), *Aerial*

Reconnaissance for Archaeology, Council for British Archaeology, Research Report No. 12 (1975).

12. D. Benson and D. Miles, *The Upper Thames Valley*, Oxfordshire Archaeological Unit Survey, No. 2, (1974), and references cited therein.

13. P. J. Fowler (ed.), *Archaeology and the Landscape*, (London, 1972), pp. 96–126; P. A. Rahtz (ed.), *Rescue Archaeology*, (Harmondsworth, 1974); in P. J. Fowler (ed.), *Rural Archaeology*, (Moonraker Press, Bradford-on-Avon, 1975), pp. 105–19.

14. E. Fowler (ed.), *Field Survey in British Archaeology*, Council for British Archaeology, (1972); C. Thomas (ed.), *Rural Settlement in Roman Britain*, Council for British Archaeology, Research Report No. 7 (1966), pp. 43–67, especially 54–5; C. P. Hall and J. R. Ravensdale, *The West Fields of Cambridge*, (Cambridge, 1976), pp. 52–4.

15. Fowler, *Rural Archaeology*, pp. 121–35.

16. C. Taylor, 'The study of settlement patterns in pre-Saxon Britain' in P. J. Ucko, R. Tringham and G. W. Dimbleby (eds.), *Man, Settlement and Urbanism*, (London, 1972), pp. 109–13.

17. R. J. C. Atkinson, in Fowler, *Field Survey*, pp. 60, 62.

18. I. Hodder and C. Orton, *Spatial Analysis in Archaeology*, (Cambridge, 1976), p. 29.

19. Fowler, *Rural Archaeology*, pp. 121–3, 136; D. A. Spratt and I. G. Simmons, 'Prehistoric activity and environment on the North York Moors' *Journal of Archaeological Science*, 3 (1976), pp. 193–210; R. Miket, in C. Burgess and R. Miket (eds.), *Settlement and Economy in the Third and Second Millenia B.C.*, British Archaeological Reports, 33, (1976), pp. 113–42.

20. Piggott, *Neolithic Cultures;* A. C. Smith, in Renfrew, *British Prehistory*, (London, 1974), pp. 100–136; E. Issac, *Geography of Domestication*, (New Jersey, 1970).

21. J. G. Evans, *The Environment of Early Man in the British Isles*, (London, 1975), p. 110.

22. Renfrew, *Before Civilisation*, pp. 53–92; *idem*, *British Prehistory*, pp. 1–40; see also Snodgrass, in J. V. S. Megaw (ed.), *To Illustrate the Monuments*, (London, 1976), pp. 58–62, and H. MacKerrell, 'On the origins of British Faience Beads and some aspects of the Wessex-Mycenae relationship', *Proceedings of the Prehistoric Society*, 38 (1972), pp. 286–301; T. Watkins (ed.), *Radio-carbon: Calibration and Prehistory*, (Edinburgh, 1975).

23. Smith, in Renfrew, *British Prehistory*, pp. 128,107.

24. Renfrew, *Before Civilisation*, pp. 93–132.

25. C. Fox, *The Personality of Britain*, (Cardiff, 1952).

26. G. Clark, 'The invasion hypothesis in British archaeology', *Antiquity*, 40 (1966), pp. 172–89; C. Musson, 'House-plans and prehistory', *Current Archaeology*, 21 (1970), pp. 267–74.

27. S. Piggott, *The West Kennet Long Barrow: Excavations 1955–6*, Ministry of Works Archaeological Report, No.14 (H.M.S.O., 1962).

28. D. D. A. Simpson, *Economy and Settlement in Neolithic and Early Bronze Age Britain and Europe*, (Leicester, 1971), pp. 40–52; Smith, in Renfrew, *British Prehistory*, p. 132; J. X. W. P. Corcoran: a report on his work in *Current Archaeology*, **34** (1972), pp. 381–7; *idem*, 'The Cotswold-Seven Group' in T. G. E. Powell (ed.), *Megalithic Enquiries in the West of Britain*, (Liverpool, 1969), pp. 13–104; *idem*, 'Multiperiod construction and the origins of the chambered long cairn in Western Britain and Ireland' in F. Lynch and C. Burgess (eds.), *Prehistoric Man in Wales and the West*, (Bath, 1972), pp. 31–63; R. J. C. Atkinson, 'Old mortatality: some aspects of burial and population in Neolithic England' in J. M. Coles and D. D. A. Simpson (eds.), *Studies in Ancient Europe*, (London, 1968), pp. 83–93.

29. Renfrew, *Before Civilisation*, pp. 146–56, 250–66; P. Ashbee, *The Earthen Long Barrow in Britain*, (Oxford, 1970).

30. I. Hodder, 'Spatial studies in Archaeology', *Progress in Human Geography* **1**, No.1 (1977), pp. 33–64.

31. J. G. D. Clark, *Prehistoric Europe: The Economic Basis*, (London, 1952); G. de G. Sieveking, I. H. Longworth and K. E. Wilson (eds.), *Problems in Economic and Social Archaeology*, (London, 1976), pp. xv–xxvi.

32. The papers by G. R. J. Jones are listed in the References, Chapter 3, of this volume.

33. D. L. Clarke, in Sieveking *et al.*, *Problems in Economic and Social Archaeology*, pp. 449–81; Spratt and Simmons, 'Prehistoric activity and environment on the North York Moors'; *The Effect of Man on the Landscape of the Highland Zone*, Council for British Archaeology, Research Report No. 11 (1975), pp. 57–63.

34. J. Turner, in D. Walker and R. G. West, *Studies in the Vegetational History of the British Isles*, (Cambridge, 1970), pp. 97–116; see also A. C. Smith, *ibid*, pp. 81–96.

35. W. Pennington, *The History of British Vegetation*, (London, 1969), pp. 62–77.

36. Evans, *The Environment of Early Man*, pp. 113–57.

37. British Association for the Advancement of Science, *Birmingham and Its Regional Setting*, (Birmingham, 1950), p. 113.

38. Clarke, *Models in Archaeology*, pp. 801–69; Hodder, *Spatial Analysis in Archaeology*, pp. 60–97.

39. P. Barker, *Techniques of Archaeological Excavation*, (London, 1977), pp. 37–67.

40. This final section is based upon Renfrew, *Before Civilisation* and Mackie, *Science and Society* and the references cited therein.

41. P. Connor, 'Britain's ancient elite' *The Sunday Times*, April 17 (1977).

2
The Human Geography of Roman Britain

I. Hodder

Study of the human geography of Roman Britain has made little use of modern geographical approaches. Even quantitative analysis is often shunned 'since it cloaks the information that we have with a spurious authenticity'.[1] This is claimed despite the large amounts of quantitative data (for example, on pottery frequencies, distributions of *mortaria* or Samian, or town size) readily obtainable in Romano-British studies, and is in direct contrast to the objective and explicit qualities usually claimed for quantitative work. As to geographical model-building, Professor Frere has recently rejected any such approach while wondering 'whether there is not . . . a close connection between the present-day ungovernability of our society—the modern rejection of authority—and the comfortable geographical approach to early settlement'.[2] It is not surprising, therefore, that two recent major volumes on Romano-British towns[3] contain no attempts to assess objectively, by artifact distribution studies, the areas served by towns, in spite of many pages devoted to town–hinterland relationships. No use is made in these volumes of models or ideas developed in the numerous other disciplines concerned with town organization, function and development.

Recently, however, more rigorous analytical methods and more explicit hypothesis formation have begun to be used in Romano-British archaeology. This is especially the case in the sphere of pottery studies, analyses of the distribution of coins, and within-site spatial patterning.[4] There will necessarily be a strong emphasis on these studies in this chapter, the basic themes of which comprise the spatial structure of late Iron Age society and its influence on Romano-British society, the growth of towns and their functional character, the pattern and nature of rural settlement and the route network of England and Wales during the Roman period.

The Late Pre-Roman Iron Age

There is some evidence that the latest Iron Age in lowland England saw at least two forms of social and political structure. In the south-east the growth of large defended areas termed *oppida* is connected with a massive increase in trade with the continent and the great wealth of a minority. Fig. 2.1 shows the distribution of Welwyn-type burials, [5] which contain large amounts of imported and locally-made valuables including wine amphorae which Peacock has shown were imported from the Mediterranean in the first centuries B.C. and A.D. [6] The material culture styles found in the same area (pottery types and burial customs, for example) also point to close contacts with the continent. In the decades immediately before the Roman conquest (43 A.D.), much of this contact was probably channelled through the main *oppida* which acted as nodes for wide areas. These 'territorial' *oppida* often contain evidence of moulds for the manufacture of coin blanks. [7] The latest Iron Age coins in England (the dynastic series) [8] carry the names of individual rulers, several of whom are mentioned by the early Roman historians.

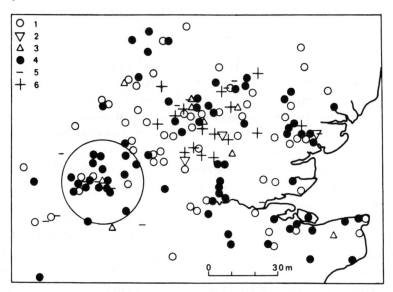

Fig. 2.1. Coins of Cunobeline and Welwyn-type burials in the late Iron Age. (1) bronze coins; (2) *oppida* with many bronze coins—major markets; (3) many bronze coins—minor market; (4) gold coins; (5) silver coins; (6) Welwyn-type burials.

It has usually been supposed that the distributions of the coins of such rulers indicate the tribal areas over which they held sway and the identification of the cantonal (tribal) areas in Roman Britain (Fig. 2.3) is based largely on the coin distributions. However, there are a number of difficulties with the equation of tribes and coin distributions. In the first place, analysis of the fall-off in coin densities away from the supposed distribution centres has indicated that few of the distributions show any deviation from normal distance-decay principles.[9] Thus, there is little evidence that coins were restricted within tribal zones, and coins from different centres overlap to a considerable degree. This apparently blurred picture may be the result of our imprecise chronologies in that tribal areas may have changed within the lifetime of one ruler. However, the second point to be made here is that most of the coin distributions show no close relationship with the distributions of other traits. An analysis of the Catuvellaunian-Trinovantian area supposedly indicated in Fig. 2.1 showed that different pottery types spread different distances outside the core area around Verulamium (St Albans) and Camulodunum (Colchester), as did different burial practices and styles of decorated bronze metalwork.[10] None of these distributions showed any close relationship with the distribution of Cunobeline coins (Fig. 2.1). Therefore, different 'tribal' areas could be defined by choosing different cultural traits. This is seen even amongst the coins and is the third problem with their use to identify tribal areas. For example, Fig. 2.2 shows the distributions of coins of two Dobunnic leaders, supposedly distributed from Bagendon in Gloucestershire. Which of these distributions indicates the Dobunnic tribe? In view of these difficulties, it is my opinion that it is not possible to use the majority of the coin distributions to define tribal areas as if these were similar to modern political groupings in which institutionalized boundaries are of importance. Most late Iron Age social groups formed open and not closed systems and the archaeological evidence, with its variety of differing distributions according to different artifact types, relates to different patterns of interaction and participation rather than to simple social or tribal groupings. The central or nodal areas containing 'territorial' *oppida* interacted socially, politically and economically with a surrounding area which varied with time and with the nature of the relationship being considered.

Loosely structured but centralized cultural patterning of the type described above seems especially characteristic of state systems of government.[11] The historical and archaeological evidence for the south-

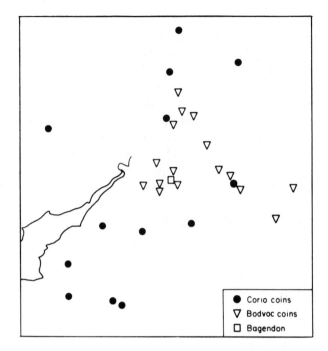

Fig. 2.2. The distribution of Corio and Bodvoc Iron Age coins.

east of England certainly suggests centralized political control organized from the 'territorial' *oppida*. Cunliffe [12] has pointed to a pattern of second-level centres around the peripheries of the areas 'served' by the main *oppida*.

However, not all the evidence of late Iron Age settlement and artifact distributions points in the direction of centralized political systems. In the south-west, for example, a rather different situation occurs. The Durotrigian coins, centred on the Dorset area, are the only ones in the late Iron Age which are not inscribed with names. Analysis of their distribution showed relatively marked fall-off near the boundaries. [13] In the case of these coins, then, there were mechanisms which retained coins within a particular area. It has long been recognized that Durotrigian coins cover an area which is distinctive in terms of a range of material culture traits. [14] For example, while some pottery types are found extending outside the main Durotrigian area, others (such as Brailsford's Class I) have more restricted distributions. [15] It appears, therefore, that in the Dorset area a number of cultural traits were retained by a territorial group such that they symbolized and identified that group. In view of the 'non-random' patterning and associations of 'Durotrigian' material culture, it is reasonable, in this case only, to identify the area of a pre-Roman 'tribe'.

Why should it be possible to identify a distinct tribal group in the south-west and not elsewhere? The answer perhaps lies in Cunliffe's[16] demonstration that the Dorset and adjoining areas retained a settlement pattern which is rather different from that described above in the south-east. In the south-west, 'territorial' *oppida* are not found and, instead, hill-forts continue to be the foci of the settlement pattern. These often developed to their fullest extent in the late Iron Age with complex multivallate defences enclosing heavily occupied acres. They appear to have been fairly regularly spaced across the countryside controlling areas of approximately 35 square miles (91 km^2).[17] This settlement pattern suggests the continuation in the south-west of a more decentralized political system. There is no evidence of the overall rulers and major controlling centres found to the east. The Durotrigian 'tribe' is made up of numerous smaller-scale centralized systems.

The effect this socio-political difference had on the patterning in material culture is that artifacts took on a greater significance in the Dorset area for the symbolizing of group identity. There is considerable ethnographic evidence that less centralized social and political groups feel a greater need to conform overtly with accepted behaviour patterns.[18] This is largely because a person's security and livelihood, especially in such a warring competitive society as that of the late Iron Age, depended not on a centralized authority, but on the group as a whole and its local interdependence. Since the artifacts that an individual uses or is associated with necessarily convey information about that individual, material culture is often part and parcel of the overt expression of group identity when such expression becomes important. It seems possible that the distinctiveness of the material culture patterning in the Durotrigian area occurs, at least partly, because social pressures placed a premium on the expression of membership of the group.

Outside the areas of the south and east of Britain where late Iron Age coins are found, there is even less evidence of fully centralized political systems. The general poverty of the surviving late Iron Age artifact evidence, especially in the Highland Zone, means that the identification of identity groups is scarcely possible. But more evidence is available from settlement patterns. In south Wales, apart from some unenclosed hut-groups and hill-forts with multiple wide-spaced ramparts, a distinctive characteristic of settlement is the small hill-fort or rath, often enclosing less than an acre. For example, excavations at Walesland Rath in Pembrokeshire revealed an oval area 64 m by 49 m enclosed by a bank and ditch with two entrances. At least six circular huts, rebuilt many times, occurred inside. Many such sites continued in use into Roman times, and some may have been constructed then. The relative lack of large hill-forts in the Iron Age in south Wales suggests an absence of strongly centralized government. In the north of Wales, large stone-walled hill-forts do occur enclosing sizable communities of perhaps 100 to 400 people living in circular stone-walled huts.[19] Whether these forts indicate a greater degree of centralization than in the south of Wales is unclear since the forts may have been used simply as summer refuges in a transhumant economy, the lowlands containing the winter farms.[20]

The Early Roman Phase of Transition

The discussion provided above is important for our understanding of many aspects of the period after the Claudian invasion of Britain in 43 A.D. In particular, the establishment of Roman control was considerably easier amongst the more centralized political groups to the south-east. Here, ultimate control passed from one authority to another under local leaders such as Cogidubnus. The Catuvellauni, Trinovantes and Cantiaci formed early cantons or *civitates*, with the Atrebates and Iceni added as client kingdoms.[21] 'Within little more than a month of landing, the south-east was firmly in Roman hands.'[22] In addition, it is precisely these areas which had previously had greatest trade contact with the romanized world in the late Iron Age so that the establishment of the new regime may have been somewhat easier.

The conquest and control of the more western areas of Britain where there were less developed centralized systems was more difficult. This is seen most clearly in the subjugation of the Durotrigian area, where the Second Legion under Vespasian found it necessary to destroy more than twenty separate fortified settlements. Archaeological evidence such as the Maiden Castle war cemetery and the finds from Hod Hill provide ample evidence of these attacks and it was necessary for the invaders to scatter forts at strategic points within the tribe as at Hod Hill and Waddon Hill.

The *civitas* of the Durotriges was set up in the Flavian period (69–96

A.D.) together with the *civitates* of the Dumnonii, Dobunni, Coritani and slightly later the Cornovii.[23] The Atrebatic area was divided into the *civitates* of the Regni, Atrebates and Belgae. In the following Hadrianic period (117–138 A.D.), the *civitates* of the Parisi, Brigantes, and the Silures and Demetae in south Wales were added. In parts of Wales and the Highland Zone of England a pattern of forts was retained throughout the Roman period. Pacification and the development of towns never took place.

The Roman use of administrative areas of *civitates* encourages the

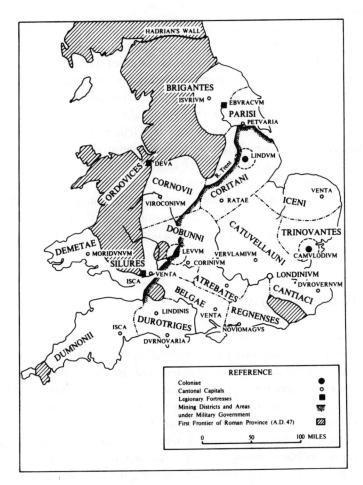

Fig. 2.3. The political map of Roman Britain as suggested by Rivet.[26]

archaeologist to draw up political maps of Roman Britain (Fig. 2.3) indicating the territories of each *civitas*. [24] But as Rivet points out, there is very little reliable evidence for the construction of such maps. [25] The attribution of a few towns to tribes by the writer Ptolemy, inscriptions and the evidence of a few milestones such as that from Kenchester, provide scanty support for Fig. 2.3. Much reliance has traditionally been placed on the pre-Roman coin distributions, although 'it is not always clear how far the prehistoric divisions were perpetuated by the Romans'. [26] In addition, there is the point made earlier that, apart from the Durotriges, it is questionable whether the pre-Roman coin distributions do indicate precise tribal areas.

Indeed many of the *civitates*, and in particular their precise territories, may have been much more artificial creations that is often supposed. The *civitas* of the Belgae at least 'appear to have been an artificial creation of the Roman government'. [27] A possibly analogous situation concerns the colonial approach to government in Africa and the problem of the concept of 'tribe'. Groups and areas without centralized political control were often artificially classified into tribes by the British authorities in order to facilitate administration. Fried has in fact suggested that tribes often did not exist prior to colonial rule. [28] In many areas in Africa the tribal concept was imposed on a less structured social pattern. Much the same may have been true of many areas in Britain in the Roman period. The neat division of the map into *civitates* may not only be difficult to achieve based on pre-Roman evidence, it may also be a false concept in terms of late Iron Age society at least in parts of the country.

The Growth of Towns

At the hub of each Roman *civitas*, a *civitas* capital developed on or near a major pre-Roman site, often a 'territorial' *oppidum*. This development is especially clear in the more centralized areas in the south-east. Another form of major centre is the *colonia*. These colonies were established for the settlement of Roman citizens—often veterans from the Roman legions— at Colchester, Lincoln, Gloucester and York.

Subsidiary to the *civitas* capitals were *vici*—small nucleated centres sometimes capable of being called towns, or villages. Some of these *vici* were walled and while there is no literary or epigraphical clue as to which sites were *vici*, archaeological research has identified a large number of walled centres.[29] These seem to have been densely packed nodes, sometimes with a regular grid of streets (as at Alchester).

While it is generally accepted that the cantonal or *civitas* capitals grew from pre-Roman sites and developed as a result of their economic and servicing functions, there has been doubt and controversy about the growth of the lesser walled centres. The following review of this problem concerns only those towns away from the military zone and to the south of Wroxeter and Leicester. The traditional view about their growth is that the towns grew from civilian settlements attracted to military forts.[30] After these forts were abandoned in the 70s A.D., the civilian settlement remained, usually to be surrounded by earthwork defences in the late second century A.D. and by stone walls in the third and fourth centuries. The earthwork defences were 'normally constructed as the result of decisions taken at provincial level and seldom reflected local events'.[31] Walling was 'based on military and administrative factors'[32] since many settlements as large or larger than those walled remained undefended.

An alternative approach examined the spatial distribution of the walled towns.[33] Figure 2.4 shows that the lesser walled towns in the southern part of Britain tend to have a peripheral location in respect to the cantonal capitals. This pattern suggested two hypotheses based on the servicing function of these towns.

The first is that the walled towns are those that grew up out of the need to supply the dispersed population with services of an economic and administrative nature. Such services would include the collection of taxes and the distribution of imported pottery and other materials. Godlund has suggested a model in which secondary centres will develop at the boundaries between existing centres because it is here that there is greatest need and least competition.[34]

A second hypothesis provides a further reason for the peripheral location of second level centres. It has been shown above that *civitas* or tribal areas became formalized in the Roman period whether they had existed in the previous phase or not. A number of anthropologists and geographers have noted that markets often grew up in the boundary zones between tribal areas. Sahlins has defined a zone of intertribal exchange on the tribal periphery where barter or haggling may occur,[35] and it is in such zones that markets may provide the necessary fora for trade.[36] Such factors would again encourage the observed peripheral pattern of second level centres in Roman Britain.

Models such as these, with their apparent emphasis on economic

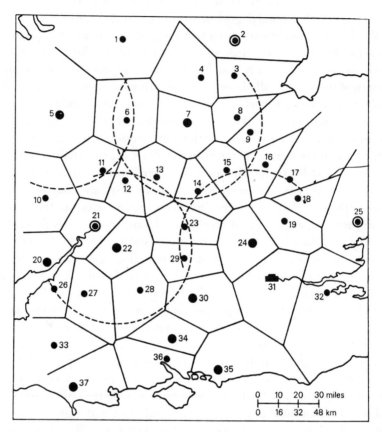

Fig. 2.4. Thiessen polygons drawn around Romano-British walled towns. Arcs of circles (dashed lines) have also been drawn around some of the major centres (cantonal capitals) to show the regular spacing of the lesser walled towns (smaller filled circles) in relation to the cantonal capitals (larger filled circles). Encircled symbols: *coloniae*. Numbers: 1 Buxton, 2 Lincoln, 3 Ancaster, 4 Castle Hill, 5 Wroxeter, 6 Wall, 7 Leicester, 8 Great Casterton, 9 Water Newton, 10 Kenchester, 11 Droitwich, 12 Alcester, 13 Chesterton, 14 Towcester, 15 Irchester, 16 Godmanchester, 17 Cambridge, 18 Great Chesterford, 19 Braughing, 20 Caerwent, 21 Gloucester, 22 Cirencester, 23 Alchester, 24 St Albans, 25 Colchester, 26 Gatcombe, 27 Bath, 28 Mildenhall, 29 Dorchester, 30 Silchester, 31 London, 32 Rochester, 33 Ilchester, 34 Winchester, 35 Chichester, 36 Bitterne, 37 Dorchester.

factors, have not been accepted in Romano-British studies. Frere's comments have already been quoted in the opening paragraph of this chapter, while the traditional historical approach, with its emphasis on military factors, has recently been restated by Rivet,[37] Wacher[38] and Webster.[39] The main reason for their rejection of alternative models, at least as far as Frere is concerned, is the undoubted relationship between early forts and walled towns. A large number of the walled towns have evidence of early military occupation and a military origin for the towns is assumed. But this argument cannot explain the growth of the towns. Even if all walled towns prove to have forts beneath them the important point is that, in the area studied, these forts were abandoned by the 70s A.D. The question to be answered is why the *vici* (settlements) around some, but not all, forts developed or retained sufficient importance over the next 200–300 years for them to be provided with stone walls. Frere himself admits that 'it is only after the troops have moved forward in the Flavian period that untrammelled economic influences become predominant'.[40] Once the position of a site had been chosen 'economic forces decided the level of prosperity which thereafter became possible'.[41]

A second reason for the rejection of the application of locational models seems to derive from a misunderstanding of what is meant by servicing factors. Second-level centres develop in peripheral areas because it is here that the services they provide are in least competition with the major centres. This applies equally to administrative, taxation, and economic services.[42] The dichotomy between economic models and administrative or imposed models for the growth of the towns is a false one.

A third reason for the unwillingness to accept the play of basic servicing factors in the growth of the lesser walled towns is the underestimation of the importance of the pre-existing Iron Age settlement pattern for the Roman distribution. The tendency towards peripheral locations of second-level centres around the 'territorial' *oppida* in the late Iron Age has been noted by Cunliffe.[43] The distinctive settlement structure of the Romano-British towns already existed in the pre-Roman phase. In addition, several of the lesser walled towns have late Iron Age occupation beneath them. Of the 19 lesser walled towns in the area of study, 11 (and possibly 13) have late Iron Age evidence beneath or in the immediate vicinity. In many cases forts may have been attracted to settlements rather than settlements to forts. In a detailed study of the Trinovantian area, Rodwell notes that 10 (perhaps 13) of the 15 small towns (mostly undefended) have late Iron Age (Belgic) occupation, whereas only 6 (perhaps 9) have early Roman military occupation.[44] 'It is perhaps noteworthy, too, that in the several towns where excavation has taken place in the Belgic levels it has been revealed that the site was a fairly affluent and probably nucleated centre in the pre-Roman period.'[45] In view of the differences between the late Iron Age in the south-east and the rest of Britain, such a close correspondence between Roman and pre-Roman settlement patterns should not necessarily be expected elsewhere.

It seems, then, that most archaeologists would accept that economic and servicing factors were important in the growth of the Romano-British lesser walled towns. It is not unreasonable, therefore, to suggest that these factors were reflected in their locational pattern. This is not to say that military and imposed decisions played no part in initial site location. They often did. Indeed, it may have been the high degree of centralized control which forced a precise structure onto the less stringent demands of economic and servicing factors.

Patterning within Towns

Study of the internal layout of Romano-British towns is hindered by the lack of total excavation of these sites. Many Roman towns lie beneath modern counterparts so that large-scale excavation is impossible. Pieces of the jigsaw are gradually being fitted together for some towns, and ultimately it is to be hoped that approaches such as that used by Raper on the site of Pompeii will be applicable in Roman Britiain.[46] The huge quantities of artifacts recovered from most Romano-British excavations may also have discouraged detailed analysis of spatial patterning.

However, a pioneering study in this sphere has been carried out by Millett in his analysis of the contents of 73 pits from the fort at Portchester Castle, Hants.[47] The pits cover a short period between about 330 and 350 A.D. and no variation in the pottery from the filling of the pits could be related to chronological change. Any differences between the pit contents therefore resulted from other factors. The pottery rims occurring in each pit were described according to 'functional categories'—dish, bowl, flagon, beaker, jar, storage jar, lid, *mortarium* (mixing bowl), fine wares. These shape characteristics were assumed to be related to the functions of the vessels.

Millett examined the question of whether pits close together on the site were more similar in terms of the functional categories than those further apart. For each pit the five most similar pits were assessed, and the spatial patterning was examined. Although standard geographical techniques, such as those for detecting spatial autocorrelation were not used, it was concluded that 'in general . . . pits closer together at Porchester castle are more similar than those further part'.[48] It was suggested that the similarity clusters correlated with the pit spatial clusters, the open areas between the pits being occupied by buildings of which the traces have been largely destroyed. 'It seems reasonable to suggest that the clusters of pits represent functional areas within the fort . . . . Although it does not seem possible to tell what these differences in function mean from the scanty remains at Portchester, they are probably indicative of organized activity.'[49]

This work raises interesting questions about the nature of spatial variation within Romano-British sites, and about the methods necessary to establish that variation. Within any site it may be assumed that there will be spatial variation in the use of different pottery shapes due to social and activity localization. But even in the unlikely event that there were no preferred localities for social groups and activities, the archaeologist actually excavates rubbish which, in a Romano-British context at least, was discarded according to local rules, not necessarily immediately adjacent to where the items had been used. Thus variation in pit content may reflect rubbish disposal habits rather than functional or activity differences.

The main problem in the analysis of within-site variation is how to determine a realistic null hypothesis. In the study described above, typological similarity between pits was assumed to be unrelated to spatial propinquity. This is certainly a valid procedure, but it may be suggested that gradual spatial variation in pit contents across a site would be expected without functional localization or variation. Consider a process in which pots are broken, are moved around and disturbed in habitation areas, and end up or are deposited in pits (from which there may then be secondary disturbance). Rim sherds from the same pot are likely to remain spatially close to each other and to end up in nearby pits. Thus a more realistic null hypothesis might be the stochastic random walk of sherds from their breaking points. The end result of such a process might be the gradual spatial variation in pit content so that nearby pits had more similar contents than distant pits. A simulation approach based on stochastic processes might provide a more informative method of analysis.

Town–Country Relationships: Regional Artifact Studies

The relatively large number of sites from which Romano-British pottery has been collected, and the ability to identify several classes as to origin (either by style, makers' stamps or petrological analysis) mean that detailed studies of Romano-British pottery distributions are feasible. Most effort in pottery studies has, however, been concerned with establishing chronologies and allocating types to kilns without the use of any explicit theoretical framework. Some initial generalizations and model-building can, however, be attempted.

The production and distribution of coarse wares was carried out at different scales, larger concerns being especially common in the later Roman period. At the most localized level, a number of coarse ware kiln centres are known which are not located near any nodal centre. For example, Hamstead Marshall is placed between Silchester and Mildenhall, while the Woodrows Farm (Compton), Bradfield and Maidenhatch Farm kilns are between Silchester and Dorchester-on-Thames. Other rural examples are the Congresbury kilns in north-west Somerset and the Hallcourt Wood kilns in south Hampshire. Although certain of these kilns have distinctive products, their distribution areas are very scanty and restricted (Congresbury and Hallcourt Wood) or without any evidence at all (Hamstead Marshall). Although the overall evidence is slight, it seems possible that there were quite a number of small-scale production concerns providing small overlapping areas of rural markets with many of the coarser wares. The distribution of pottery tiles at this localized rural level is indicated in Sussex at Itchingfield. [50]

Much coarse pottery and other goods seem to have been channelled through the towns. In many cases coarse ware kilns are located within easy reach of a town and the main area of distribution of the products appears to relate to that town's area of influence. [51] For example, Fig. 2.5 shows the distribution of Savernake ware. This pottery was made in the first and second centuries A.D. at a number of kilns in an area two miles south of Mildenhall (a town walled in the fourth century). The main distribution of the products is the localized area around Mildenhall, and this area appears to correspond with Mildenhall's probable market or service area as predicted by Reilly's breaking point formula derived from the gravity model. [52]

A further example is provided by the distribution of Malvernian

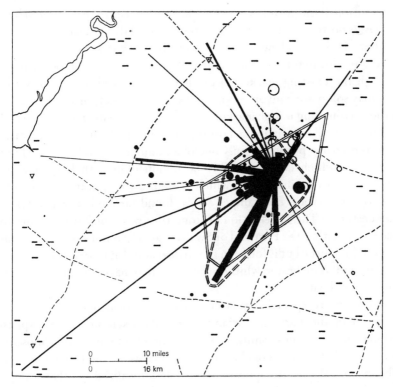

Fig. 2.5. The distribution of early Romano-British Savernake pottery. Radiating bars connect sites to the main marketing centre at Mildenhall. Their width and the size of the circles indicate the percentages of pottery found at the sites. Radiating bars: sites with more than 30 coarse ware sherds and only first and second centuries A.D. pottery. Filled circles: sites with more than 30 coarse ware sherds and more than first and second centuries A.D. pottery. Open circles: sites with less than 30 coarse ware sherds. Triangles: walled towns. Double dashed line encloses the area covered by Savernake ware lids. Continuous double line: the market area of Mildenhall predicted by the gravity model. Dashed lines: roads. Horizontal bars: contemporary sites without Savernake pottery.

pottery.[53] In the second century A.D. a centre in the Malvern area, but whose exact location is as yet unknown, was producing a number of types distinctive in shape and fabric. The area in which sites with the highest percentages of these products are found includes both the presumed kiln centre and the town at Worcester, while high percentages are also found in and near the town at Kenchester. It is also of interest that the overall distribution of the pottery covers a very similar area to that covered by late Iron Age pottery manufactured in the same Malvern district.

There is thus evidence that Romano-British coarse ware kiln centres were often located in such a way that their products could be channelled through the existing marketing mechanisms centred on a nearby town. This may solely have involved sale in the town market, or in addition, sale in the surrounding minor markets connected to the main town market by traders or pedlars moving according to some periodic cycle of market days. But coarse pottery is only one of a number of goods supplied at the local level which could probably be obtained in both large and small towns. Other distributions in which walled towns appear central include that of the types of stamped tiles found around Cirencester and Gloucester. [54] The distribution of stone tiles made of Purbeck limestone quarried in either the Portland or Swanage area [55] is not evenly distributed around the source but is found in the *civitas* capital at Dorchester and in the area around Winchester whither the stone may have been taken much of the way by boat.

Rather more specialist services, with less local demand, were only provided in the more important towns. An example is the expensive installation of mosaics. Smith's examination of fourth century mosaics in rich villas led to the conclusion that there is a 'tendency for certain subjects and themes to appear more or less localized' so that groups of related mosaics can be identified. [56] 'Each group is characterized by features which are not found, or are found significantly less often or in a significantly different form, elsewhere.' [57] Smith suggests that this indicates 'schools' of mosaicists with their workshops at, for example, the cantonal capitals of Cirencester and Dorchester (Dorset). The mosaics produced by each 'school' are, in general, confined to the service areas around these towns as predicted by the gravity model and Thiessen polygons. [58] These two mosaic distributions correspond to the pre-Roman Durotrigian area and what can be ascertained as to the Dobunnic *civitas*. Although servicing factors are adequate to explain the distributions, and although discrete distributions only occur when the two schools are contemporary, an additional factor which may be relevant is the desire for the expression of a common group identity. This will be further discussed below.

The evidence discussed above demonstrates the importance of the towns as foci for the surrounding areas. Many large-scale concerns, often producing more valuable items such as finer pottery, were located away from the towns. The goods were probably channelled through the towns, but the production was not necessarily dependent on them and the distribution was on a wide scale, well beyond the area of influence of one town. Thus the large-scale fine pottery production centre at Oxford is located midway between the towns of Alchester and Dorchester-on-Thames and the pottery made there is found widely in southern England. The fine ware products from the Nene Valley and the dispersal of coarse wares from Alice Holt (Farnham, Surrey), at least in the late third and fourth centuries A.D.,[59] reached far beyond the areas served by Water Newton and the centre at Neatham, Farnham.

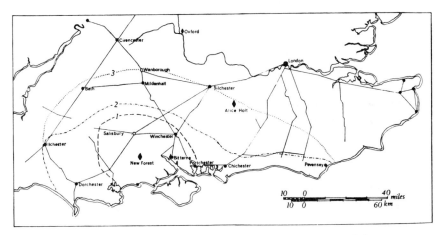

Fig. 2.6. The distribution of pottery from the New Forest kilns. Source: Fulford.[60]

A good example of this type of large-scale production is provided by the detailed studies carried out on New Forest pottery.[60] The New Forest kilns produced a wide range of pottery types in the late third and fourth centuries A.D. and Fulford has shown that the distributions of each type varied considerably. In Fig. 2.6, contour 1 shows the limit of the coarse wares made at the kilns. Contour 2 shows the area reached by colour-coated and painted wares and *mortaria*. Particular types of colour-coated wares (bottles, jugs and beakers) reach contour 3, while beyond this line occasional finds of these types occur, but probably not as regularly traded items. These differences in distributions relate to the level of demand for the different products. Coarse wares, of lower value and high demand, were produced by neighbouring centres (for example, Alice Holt) within the total area covered by the New Forest fine wares. The latter, with less local demand, were produced by more widely spaced centres, such as at Oxford. The greater distribution of New Forest beakers occurs because the nearest competitor producing this form in quantity was not Oxford, but the Nene Valley centre.

The marketing patterns so far considered have been concerned with the civilian market in lowland Britain. Another class of distributions consists of those distorted by supply to the army. The distribution of *mortaria* made in the Midlands and stamped by, for example, Sarrus, has a marked bias towards the northern frontier. [61] A similar effect is seen with Derbyshire ware which shows both a local distribution and an extension north-wards. [62] The finding of 'Severn Valley' fabrics on Hadrian's Wall, well outside their main area of distribution, is another example. [63] The distribution of *Classis Britannica* tiles shows the influence of non-civilian forces in the dispersal of another commodity. [64]

In most of the above discussion it has been assumed that straightforward market forces were the main determinants of the structure of the Romano-British economy. But the existence of identity-conscious tribes in some areas of Britain has been suggested in the immediately pre-Roman period, while the Roman *civitates* formalized less distinct groupings in other areas. It is possible that 'tribal' feelings had an effect on the distribution of goods and ideas in the Roman period. In many parts of Africa the pre-colonial groupings still affect the present-day dispersal of cultural items, while the identities imposed by outside administrations often came to take on an overtly expressed reality. [65] In this context it is of interest to examine the diffusion of religious cults in Roman Britain. 'It is possible to isolate a few local cults—a horse-cult among the Cornovii, a Mars-horse-man-cult among the Catuvellauni, . . . the "Matres" and Genii Cucullati among the Dobunni.' [66] Other deities such as Mercury, Mars and Jupiter are more widespread, but in general there are major distinctions between the Dobunnic and Catuvellaunian *civitates* in religious evidence. For example, 'the Catuvellauni may have favoured the more Roman-influenced "sky-cults" whereas the Dobunni inclined more to local nature-gods and deities connected with fertility and prosperity.' [67] The greater familiarity with and acceptance of continental traditions seen in the south-east in the late Iron Age continues in the Roman period, and differences between 'tribal' groups are perhaps detected.

Rural Settlement

Villas (farms with 'romanized' buildings) are found widely in lowland Britain and to a limited extent in south Wales (see the distribution map provided by Rivet). [68] But throughout England and Wales the majority of farmsteads and hamlets followed the form common in the pre-Roman phase, as is only now being discovered through detailed survey and the expanding cover of aerial photography. Two detailed locational studies of these rural settlements are available.

The distribution of sites in the Fenlands has been established from air photographs and field survey by Salway et al. [69] As a result of the fieldwork, an individual site was defined as 'a scatter of ploughed domestic debris, often over an area of dark occupation soil'. [70] The sizes of these sites ranged from about 50 ft (15·2 m) long to 300 ft × 400 ft (91 × 122 m). Such surface spreads in the ploughsoil may represent farms which sometimes clustered into settlements. The investigators confronted the problem common to many archaeologists of how groupings of sites can be distinguished. 'Although it is very convenient to regard the world's population as distributed in a series of discrete and isolated clusters . . . this is a somewhat artificial concept. Our definition of a cluster depends largely upon how we draw our boundaries, and how we define the term isolated.' [71] Sites were grouped into the same 'settlement' when separated by less than an arbitrary 500 ft (152 m), although support for this figure was obtained from other studies. An attempt was made at a more objective clustering of 'settlements' into 'complexes'. Histograms of the frequencies of distances between 'settlements' were examined. These frequency distributions appeared bimodal, suggesting that 'neighbouring settlements lie between 500 and 1500 ft of each other, more frequently than one would expect if they showed random scatter, giving a unimodal curve of spacing'. [72]

As a result of the analysis, the changing settlement pattern in the Fens could be demonstrated. In the first century A.D. there was a pattern of single farms and small hamlets. In the second century all the existing settlements grew bigger and 'new ones are added, often near an existing bunch'. [73] In the third and fourth centuries A.D. the percentage of people living in agglomerations increased. This trend towards larger and more agglomerations was seen as being possibly related to the changing drainage patterns and wetter conditions.

In a very different, 'un-romanized' and upland area in north-west

Fig. 2.7 Homesteads in north-west Wales. Mopphological classes Ia, Ib, Ic and Id.

Wales, Smith has examined the enclosed hut groups which he terms homesteads of the Iron Age and Romano-British periods. [74] Few of these have been excavated but many are well preserved and their stone walls can be planned by surface survey. Twenty-one attributes were used to describe these sites—for example, the area enclosed, thickness of enclosing wall, shape index (site area/area of smallest enclosing circle × 100), number of round huts. A Simple Matching Coefficient was employed in assessing the similarities between all pairs of sites and average link cluster analysis was used to group the homesteads. The Class I subdivisions resulting from this cluster analysis are shown in Fig. 2.7. But what do the differences between types mean? The houses or compartments within the homesteads appear, from what excavation has been carried out, to have been roofed. The high proportion of open to covered space in Class Ib is taken as possibly suggesting that these homesteads were mainly engaged in stock rearing. Rectangular and subrectangular buildings have been suggested by excavation to have been stalls for plough oxen or milch cattle. Therefore, 'Class Id could be interpreted as representing wealthy members of the community having small amounts of residential accommodation in relation to the other installations provided.' [75] Smith's attempt at a rigorous and explicit analysis is certainly welcome in Romano-British studies and it is hoped that further applications will ensue.

Routes and Networks

It is commonplace that the network of metalled roads in Roman Britain had a profound impact on the economic landscape. Settlements were attracted to the roads and goods reached further along these corridors of easier communication. Dicks has used a graph theoretic approach to examine the relationship between the road system and the large and undoubtedly important town of London. [76] Dicks ordered the main roads on the basis of accessibility to London. Initially 'indifference points' were identified on the network that were equidistant from London. A hierarchy of roads was then established using the path ordering method shown in Fig. 2.8, and the ordered network is shown in Fig. 2.9. This pattern supports what is already known about the road system. The three main arterial routes are identified, leading to the legionary fortresses at York, Chester and Caerleon. The *coloniae* are also linked to London by major routes. 'Of

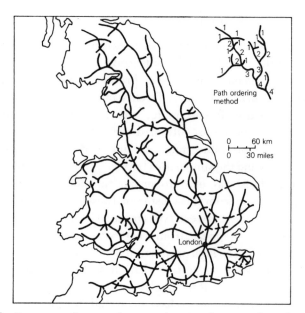

Fig. 2.8. The Roman road network centred on London. Roads are broken where alternative routes to London are estimated to be of equal length.

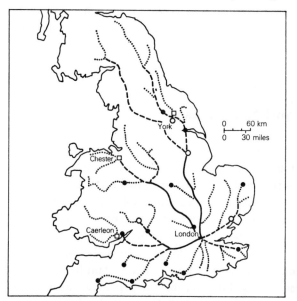

Fig. 2.9. The Roman road network ordered with reference to London, showing *coloniae* (open circles), cantonal capitals (filled circles) and fortresses (squares). Dotted lines: second order routes; dashed lines: third order routes; solid lines: fourth order routes.

the cantonal capitals, eight are . . . on fourth or third order routes and eight on second order routes. The majority of the smaller settlements, together with the forts of the highland zone are related to the first order routes which have been omitted from figure [2.9] for the sake of clarity.'[77] Problems affecting this analysis include the incomplete evidence of the road network, while there has been adequate further discussion by Hindle, Hutchinson and Langton.[78]

In some areas, the growth of the road network can be compared with that proposed by Taaffe, Morrill and Gould for developing countries,[79] with a basic skeleton network penetrating the interior and thereby allowing the establishment of political control and the exploitation of primary products, followed later by a more intricate network of feeder roads extending outwards from nodes on the main lines of penetration (see also Chapter 14). A similar sequence might be read into the pattern of road and villa development in the area to the west of the cantonal capital at Verulamium during the first and second centuries A.D. The first century villas stand close to the arterial routes connecting the major nodes. 'All the known first century villa sites were therefore able to transport surplus produce quickly to Verulamium.'[80] In the second century a new crop of villas emerged in the Chiltern valleys, possibly connected with the filling in of the road network although there is little reliable independent dating evidence for the roads. The end result was a pattern of villas spaced every $1\frac{1}{2}$ to 2 miles along the valleys.

Conclusion

There is abundant evidence that the human geography of Roman Britain depended on the geography of the pre-Roman Iron Age. But the full impact of, for example, tribal groupings on Romano-British marketing patterns, the growth of towns and the development of the road network cannot be assessed without the application of more sophisticated techniques of spatial analysis and the use of a wider range of explanatory models. It is clear from the above account that large amounts of data could be collected which would allow detailed locational analysis. Hopefully such work will be carried out in the future. It is only then that Romano-British studies can break out of a narrow historical approach and contribute to our understanding of wider problems of development, town growth, early economies and human relationships.

Acknowledgements

I am grateful to Martin Millett for allowing me to refer to unpublished work, and to Richard Reece for his comments.

References

1. J. S. Wacher, *The Towns of Roman Britain*, (London, 1974), p. 13.
2. S. S. Frere, 'The origin of small towns', in W. Rodwell and T. Rowley (eds.), *Small Towns of Roman Britain*, British Archaeological Reports, **15** (1975), p. 4.
3. Wacher, *The Towns of Roman Britain*; Rodwell and Rowley, *Small Towns of Roman Britain*.
4. M. Fulford, 'The pottery', in B. Cunliffe, *Excavations at Portchester Castle. Roman*, (London, 1975), Vol. 1, pp. 270–367; M. Fulford, *New Forest Roman Pottery: Manufacture and Distribution, with a Corpus of the Pottery Types*, British Archaeological Reports, **XVII** (1975); R. Reece, 'Roman coinage in the western Empire', *Britannia*, **IV** (1973), pp. 227–51; idem, 'Clustering of coin finds in Britain, France and Italy', in J. Casey and R. Reece (eds.), *Coins and the Archaeologist*, British Archaeological Reports, **6** (1974), pp. 64–77; M. Millett, 'Functional groupings in Romano-British pottery with special reference to Portchester Castle', in M. Millett et al. (eds.), *Pottery and the Archaeologist*, (London, in press).
5. I. Stead, 'A La Tène III burial at Welwyn Garden City', *Archaeologia*, **CI** (1967), pp. 1–62.
6. D. P. S. Peacock, 'Roman amphorae in pre-Roman Britain', in D. Hill and M. Jesson (eds.), *The Iron Age and its Hillforts*, (Southampton, 1971), pp. 161–88.
7. B. Cunliffe, in G. de G. Sieveking, I. H. Longworth and K. E. Wilson (eds.), *Problems in Economic and Social Archaeology*, (London, 1976).
8. D. F. Allen, 'The Belgic dynasties of Britain and their coins', *Archaeologia*, **XC** (1944), pp. 1–46.
9. I. Hodder, 'How are we to study distributions of Iron Age material?', in J. Collis (ed.), *The Iron Age of Britain: a Review*, (Sheffield, 1977).
10. I. Hodder, 'Some new directions in the spatial analysis of archaeological distributions at the regional scale', in D. L. Clarke (ed.), *Spatial Archaeology*, (London, 1977).
11. C. S. Lancaster, 'Ethnic identity, history and "tribe" in the middle Zambezi valley', *American Ethnologist*, **I** (1974), pp. 707–8.
12. Cunliffe, in Sieveking et al., *Problems in Economic and Social Archaeology*.

13. Hodder, 'How are we to study distributions of Iron Age material?'; A. H. A. Hogg, 'Some applications of surface fieldwork', in Hill and Jesson, *The Iron Age and its Hillforts*, pp. 105–25.
14. J. Brailsford, 'Early Iron Age "C" in Wessex', *Proceedings of the Prehistoric Society*, **XXIV** (1958), pp. 101–19; B. Cunliffe, *Iron Age Communities in Britain*, (London, 1974).
15. C. Blackmore, personal communication.
16. Cunliffe, *Iron Age Communities in Britain*, pp. 96–100.
17. B. Cunliffe, 'Some aspects of hillforts and their cultural environments', in Hill and Jesson, *The Iron Age and its Hillforts*, p. 59.
18. J. Goody, *Comparative Studies in Kinship*, (London, 1969).
19. Cunliffe, *Iron Age Communities in Britain*, p. 199.
20. D. P. Webley, 'How the west was won: prehistoric land-use in the southern Marches', in G. C. Boon and J. M. Lewis (eds.), *Welsh Antiquity, Essays Presented to H. N. Savory*, (Cardiff, 1976), pp. 19–35.
21. Wacher, *The Towns of Roman Britain*, p. 25.
22. B. Cunliffe, *The Regni*, (London, 1973), p. 20.
23. Wacher, *The Towns of Roman Britain*, p. 28.
24. A. L. F. Rivet, *Town and Country in Roman Britain* (2nd edn.) (London, 1964), Fig. 9.
25. *Ibid.*, pp. 131–4.
26. *Ibid.*, p. 133.
27. *Ibid.*, p. 140.
28. M. H. Fried, 'On the concept of "tribe"', in *Essays on the Problem of Tribe*, American Ethnological Society (1968), pp. 3–22.
29. M. Todd, 'The small towns of Britain', *Britannia*, **I** (1970), pp. 114–30.
30. Rivet, *Town and Country in Roman Britain*; Frere, 'The origin of small towns'.
31. J. S. Wacher, 'Village fortifications', in Rodwell and Rowley, *Small Towns of Roman Britain*, pp. 51–2.
32. G. Webster, 'Small towns without defences', in Rodwell and Rowley, *Small Towns of Roman Britain*, pp. 53–66.
33. I. Hodder, 'The spatial distribution of Romano-British small towns', in Rodwell and Rowley, *Small Towns of Roman Britain*, pp. 67–74.
34. S. Godlund, *The Function and Growth of Bus Traffic within the Sphere of Urban Influence*, Lund Studies in Geography, B, **XVIII** (1956).
35. M. D. Sahlins, 'On the sociology of primitive exchange', *American Society of Anthropologists Monograph*, **I** (1965), pp. 139–236.
36. F. Benet, 'Explosive markets: the Berber highlands', in K. Polanyi, C. M. Arensberg and H. W. Pearson (eds.), *Trade and Market in the Early Empires*, (Glencoe, Illinois, 1957); B. W. Hodder, 'Some comments on the origins of traditional markets in Africa south of the Sahara', *Transactions, Institute of British Geographers*, **XXXVI** (1965), pp. 97–105; J. Vansina, 'Trade and

markets among the Kuba', in P. Bohannan and G. Dalton (eds.), *Markets in Africa*, (Northwestern University, 1962), pp. 190–210.

37. A. L. F. Rivet, 'Summing up: the classification of minor towns and related settlements', in Rodwell and Rowley, *Small Towns of Roman Britain*, pp. 11–4.
38. Wacher, 'Village fortifications'.
39. Webster, 'Small towns without defences'.
40. Frere, 'The origin of small towns', p. 5.
41. Frere, 'The origin of small towns', p. 7.
42. I. Hodder, 'Locational models and the study of Romano-British settlement', in D. L. Clarke (ed.), *Models in Archaeology*, (London, 1972), p. 900; Hodder, 'The spatial distribution of Romano-British small towns', p. 68.
43. Cunliffe, in Sieveking, *et al.*, *Problems in Economic and Social Archaeology*.
44. W. Rodwell, 'Trinovantian towns and their setting', in Rodwell and Rowley, *Small Towns of Roman Britain*, pp. 85–102.
45. *Ibid.*, p. 93.
46. R. A. Raper, 'The analysis of the urban structure of Pompeii: a sociological examination of land use', in Clarke, *Spatial Archaeology*, pp. 189–222.
47. Millett, 'Functional groupings in Romano-British pottery with special reference to Portchester Castle'.
48. *Ibid.*
49. *Ibid.*
50. T. K. Green, 'Roman tileworks at Itchingfield', *Sussex Archaeological Collections*, **CVIII** (1970), pp. 23–8.
51. I. Hodder, 'Some marketing models for Romano-British coarse pottery', *Britannia*, **V** (1974), pp. 340–59.
52. W. J. Reilly, *The Law of Retail Gravitation*, (New York, 1931).
53. D. P. S. Peacock, 'Romano-British pottery production in the Malvern district of Worcestershire', *Transactions of the Worcestershire Archaeological Society*, **I** (1967), pp. 15–28.
54. Hodder, 'Locational analysis and the study of Romano-British settlement'.
55. J. H. Williams, 'Roman building materials in south-east England', *Britannia*, **II** (1971), p. 178.
56. D. J. Smith, 'The mosaic pavements', in A. L. F. Rivet (ed.), *The Roman Villa in Britain*, (London, 1969), pp. 71–126.
57. *Ibid.*, p. 95.
58. Hodder, 'The spatial distribution of Romano-British small towns', p. 68.
59. M. Millett, 'The dating and distribution of Farnham (Alice Holt) pottery', (in press).
60. M. G. Fulford, 'The distribution and dating of New Forest pottery', *Britannia*, **IV** (1973), pp. 160–78; Fulford, *New Forest Pottery: Manufacture and Distribution*.
61. For further examples see K. F. Hartley, 'The marketing and distribution of

mortaria', in *Current Research in Romano-British Coarse Pottery*, Council for British Archaeology, Research Report No. 10, (1973), pp. 39–51.

62. S. O. Kay, 'The Romano-British pottery kilns at Hazelwood and Holbrook, Derbyshire', *Derbyshire Archaeological Journal*, **LXXXII** (1962), pp. 21–42.

63. P. V. Webster, 'Severn Valley wares on Hadrian's Wall', *Archaeologia Aeliana*, **L** (1972), pp. 191–203.

64. G. Brodribb, 'Stamped tiles of the "Classis Britannica"', *Sussex Archaeological Collections*, **CVII** (1969), pp. 102–5.

65. Fried, 'On the concept of "tribe"'.

66. M. J. Green, *The Religions of Civilian Britain*, British Archaeological Reports, **24** (1976), p. 78.

67. *Ibid.*

68. Rivet, *The Roman Villa in Britain*, Fig. 5.6.

69. P. Salway, S. J. Hallam and J. l'A. Bromwich, *The Fenlands in Roman Times*, Royal Geographical Society Research Series, **V** (1970).

70. Salway *et al.*, *The Fenlands in Roman Times*, p. 49.

71. P. Haggett, *Locational Analysis in Human Geography*, (London, 1965), p. 100.

72. Salway *et al.*, *The Fenlands in Roman Times*, p. 57.

73. *Ibid.*

74. C. A. Smith, 'A morphological analysis of late prehistoric and Romano-British settlements in north-west Wales', *Proceedings of the Prehistoric Society*, **XL** (1974), pp. 157–169.

75. *Ibid.*

76. T. R. B. Dicks, 'Network analysis and historical geography', *Area*, **IV** (1972), pp. 4–9.

77. *Ibid.*, pp. 7–8.

78. B. P. Hindle, P. Hutchinson and J. Langton, 'Networks and Roman roads. Comments', *Area*, **IV** (1972), pp. 137–8, 138–9, 279–80.

79. E. J. Taaffe, R. L. Morrill and P. R. Gould, 'Transport expansion in underdeveloped countries: a comparative analysis', *Geographical Review*, **LIII** (1963), pp. 503–29.

80. K. Branigan, 'Romano-British rural settlement in the western Chilterns', *Archaeological Journal*, **CXXIV** (1967), p. 136.

3
Celts, Saxons and Scandinavians

G. R. J. Jones

The period between the departure of the Roman legions and the coming of the Normans is one of the most formative in our history, but also one of the most obscure. It witnessed the subjugation of the Celts at the hands of the incoming Saxons and later, in the north, the settlement of the Scandinavians. In the same period the territorial foundations of the economy were strengthened. All these were momentous developments but their elucidation is fraught with difficulty, depending as it must on the integration of archaeological evidence and the testimony of place-names with the sparse record of written sources.

The Phase of Transition

Between Roman Britain and Saxon England there was no complete break, for, as recent archaeological discoveries have shown, the roots of the Saxon settlements were planted while Britain was still part of the Roman Empire. Throughout the fourth century the exposed frontiers of Roman Britain were menaced by Scots from the north-west, Picts from the north and Saxons from beyond the North Sea. In the face of these threats eastern Britain was provided with improved defences and the fortifications of civilian towns from Aldborough in the north to Chichester in the south were modernized.[1] No longer were these towns mere centres of adminstration, service and civilization in a peaceful countryside; instead they became focal points in a system of military defence. Troops were required to man the town defences and for this purpose Anglo-Saxon mercenaries were employed. Their presence is attested by finds of Imperial belt-buckles and of Romano-British pottery decorated to suit barbarian

57

tastes. [2] Anglo-Saxon pottery, of surprisingly early date, occurs in pagan cemeteries in the immediate vicinity of towns like Caistor-by-Norwich, Canterbury and Winchester, but similar pottery has also been found within these towns, so that the Roman practice of stationing barbarian military detachments in re-strengthened towns was probably continued into the fifth century. Beyond the area of foreign settlement, however, native levies would have been the sole source of defence. Thus the famous rescript of 410 telling the towns of Britain to look to their own defences was less an abdication of imperial authority than a directive in the exercise of that responsibility. With the subsequent decline of the economy, as sources of capital dried up, political authority in the typical cantonal capital (*civitas*) appears to have passed from the hands of elected magistrates into those of the local tyrant who exercised military power. Thus, the eastern Romano-British towns would have become increasingly Germanic in character. Yet during the fifth century the Germanic mercenaries failed to adopt from their hosts even the simplest of technical improvements such as the potter's wheel and adhered staunchly to their own tongue and pagan religions. In the absence of effective social contacts with their employers the mercenaries probably lost interest in their role as defenders and apparently encouraged others, including humble folk, from their homelands to join them. With their hold on the rural hinterlands of the towns thus enlarged, there followed in the period 400-450 a transfer of territorial lordship from Romano-British to Saxon hands.

The Coming of the Saxons

The best narrative of the *Adventus Saxonum* is that presented by Gildas, the British monk who wrote in the mid-sixth century. [3] He reports that, even as the Romans were returning home, the Scots and Picts 'seized the whole northern part of the land', so that the Britons abandoned 'the wall' and their cities. External threat and internal strife caused the whole country to be deprived of all food save that provided by hunting. Severe famine compelled many Britons to come to terms with the conquerors but others carried on the war unceasingly until victory was achieved and the enemy withdrew. Subsequently the island grew rich but the kings then anointed became cruel tyrants and the wealth of the north was distributed by faction.

Meanwhile, in the south, a devastating plague was accompanied by the rumour of an intended conquest of Britain by the Scots and the Picts. Thus 'the proud tyrant', apparently an over-king, decided in conjunction with the assembly to invite Saxon troops into the island in order to repel the northern invaders. To this end, Gildas claims, three boat-loads of troops were settled in the eastern part of the island. But these supposed defenders regarded their allowances of provisions as inadequate and became attackers. They then ravaged all the neighbouring cities and lands as far as 'the western ocean' before returning to their bases in the east. The area thus devasted was not named by Gildas but apparently lay to the west of the Saxon bases. It was well populated and besides its fortified settlements contained at least one important ecclesiastical centre with stone-built towers. In the attacks, priests and people were mown down and there were no burials save in the ruins of houses or the entrails of beasts and birds. Yet there were survivors; of these, some, as the price of food, yielded themselves to their enemies to be slaves forever; some emigrated beyond the sea; but others remained in their native land, trusting their lives to dense forests and *fortified hills*.

There followed a rally of the British forces and then a period of indecisive warfare until a great victory was won by the Britons at *the siege of Mons Badonicus*. The scene of the encounter has been variously identified, among other sites, with a hill overlooking Bath or the hill-fort of Badbury Rings (Dorset) but, wherever it took place, the British victory served to stem further Saxon advances for some 40 years. Thus Gildas contrasts the prosperity of his own days with former calamities brought about by the wars against the foreigners, and portrays for Britain in the sixth century an ordered society. Land boundaries were recognized and cursed was he who moved them. The kings of Britain were tyrants, and her judges ungodly, but their very presence denotes the existence of more than the rudiments of administrative and fiscal organization. Unfortunately however, there were civil wars between contending kings. Thus, according to Gildas, the cities were not inhabited as formerly but lay deserted and dismantled, so that barbarism was overtaking civilization.

To the west, British kings, claiming to be the legitimate heirs of Roman authority but governing their subjects by ancestral Celtic custom, put armies into the field and even made gifts to the Church. Of five such kings castigated as sinners by Gildas, three are clearly recognizable as the rulers of Dumnonia, Dyfed, and Gwynedd (Fig. 3.1). All three ruled in the far west but this should not be taken to imply that the centre of southern Britain was then in English occupation, for there were certainly other British kings of whom Gildas takes no account.

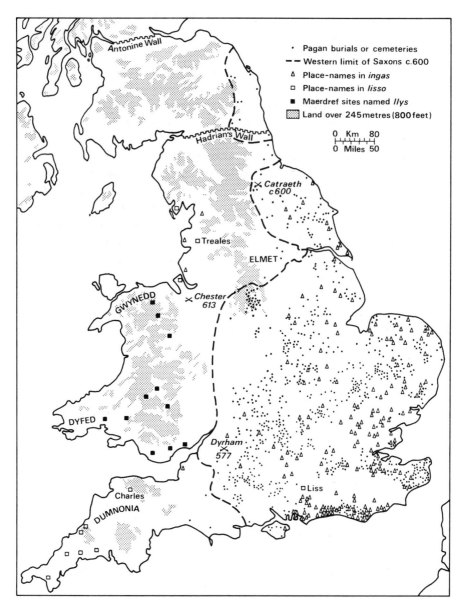

Fig. 3.1. The Saxons in southern Britain *c.* 600.
(Based on Ekwall, Jackson, Rahtz and Smith.)

Bede, who wrote *c*. 730, used the narrative of Gildas and added further details such as the date 449-56 for the *Adventus* and one 44 years later for the battle of Mount Badon. [4] He also implied that the area settled by the three boat-loads of mercenaries was in Kent but revealed that, in addition, large numbers of other newcomers settled in eastern Britain, a claim now fully substantiated by archaeological evidence.

The Emergence of the English Kingdoms

After the middle of the sixth century the advance was resumed but meanwhile the kingdoms of England had already begun to take shape. The earliest to emerge were those of the south and east, Kent, Sussex, Essex, East Anglia and Lindsey. These kingdoms however were hemmed in behind interior forest or fen. For the future, the more significant powers were those of Wessex, Mercia and Northumbria, all kingdoms with frontiers exposed to the surviving British communities of the west. These major English kingdoms battled long against each other and the Britons for supremacy, a struggle which carried Saxon colonists to the foothills of the Highland Zone by the middle years of the seventh century. Such events, and notably the expansion of Wessex, are fitfully outlined by a propagandist source of later date, the Anglo-Saxon Chronicle. [5] For a more detailed impression of the spread of the Saxons as a whole we must turn to the evidence of pagan burials (Fig. 3.1). [6] These belong to the age before the conversion of the Saxons to Christianity, a process initiated by Augustine's mission to Kent in 597 and which had led to the conversion of every English king by 670.

The extension of English authority appears to have been achieved by an incorporative process whereby pre-existing petty British kingdoms were absorbed *en bloc* into the expanding English kingdoms. Thus, as the Anglo-Saxon Chronicle records, when three British kings lost their lives at the battle of Dyrham in 577 the victorious rulers of Wessex captured the three once-important Roman cities of Bath, Cirencester and Gloucester with their dependent territories (*civitates*), apparently three petty kingdoms. Again both Deira and Bernicia in the north had been British kingdoms before they were taken over by the Anglians. Following the defeat of the Britons at Catraeth (Catterick) *c*. 600 the two kingdoms were united in a powerful Northumbria whose forces inflicted another major defeat on the Britons at Chester in 613; and shortly afterwards the once-powerful

British kingdom of Elmet was absorbed. The Britons of Wales, thus divided by the expansion of both Wessex and Northumbria from their fellow Britons in Dumnonia and the north, were marked off as a separate people in their western strongholds and, in the late eighth century, were delimited behind the Mercian dyke ascribed to Offa.

Early Social Organization

The social structure of the Welsh kingdoms which persisted behind Offa's Dyke is perhaps our surest guide to the social order which had once existed within the British petty kingdoms incorporated within the expanding English kingdoms. Within the typical early Welsh petty kingdom the old social order was essentially hierarchical with the king at the apex followed in descending order by his royal officers, then the nobles and, at the lowest levels, the bondmen and slaves who supported the higher echelons. Already by Gildas' day the larger kingdoms like Gwynedd had absorbed most of the old petty kingdoms but the latter retained their identity and emerged in later centuries as administrative hundreds. Within the typical hundred there would be two administrative neighbourhoods and in each, reflecting the social order, was a hierarchy of landed estates. The most important was that of the king, comprising a *llys* (court), lowland demesnes for its sustenance in an adjoining *maerdref* (reeve's settlement), distant royal pastures and hunting grounds, together with a network of satellite hamlets spread over wide areas of countryside. The hamlets were occupied in the main by bondmen who practised mixed farming on the lands they held from their lord, the king. In return they paid the king food rents and performed for him various services including the tasks of cultivating his demesnes, building his court and encampments for his troops, and helping with the hunt. Nobles held lesser estates but even these contained a multiplicity of satellite hamlets and thus merit the designation multiple estate. Among the most celebrated of these estates was that in the Anglesey Hundred of Aberffraw, whose court adjoining the *maerdref* at Aberffraw proper was one of the ancient capitals of Gwynedd. Located some two miles from the convenient refuge provided by a promontory fort of the Iron Age, the court of Aberffraw itself occupied the site of a Roman fort whose defences had been refurbished possibly as late as the sixth century. [7]

The *llys* (court) with its *maerdref* (reeve's settlement) and satellite hamlets was a characteristic feature of all the early Welsh kingdoms (Fig. 3.1). That similar royal estates existed within the other early British kingdoms in territories which became English is implied by settlements bearing names in *lisso*, the British word from which the Welsh *llys* was derived. [8] In Dumnonia was Charles, literally the rock court, and in the north-west Treales, whose name in British meant the settlement or township (*tref*) of the court. In south-east England, Liss refers simply to a court and indicates the survival on the western fringe of the Weald of an organized British estate; subsequently this came to form part of the Out-Hundred of Odiham, a component of a large English royal estate whose focus was at Odiham some 15 miles to the north.

Multiple estates closely resembling those of Wales were to be found throughout England. That of Selsey where the king of Sussex himself resided was granted to the Church in the 680s to be the seat of a bishopric. A further endowment of land followed, comprising at least eleven settlements on the Selsey peninsula, seven settlements around Chichester, and three more including Amberley on the flanks of the South Downs; their inhabitants numbered, among other folk, no less than 250 male and female slaves. At the north-eastern extremity of England near Bamburgh, the capital of Bernicia, was the royal estate of Islandshire which had once extended from the mainland to Holy Island; but its headquarters was still known in the late seventh century by its British name of *Broninis*, literally the breast of the island. [9]

The rents and services of these estates not only resembled those of Wales but occasionally even bore names indicative of a British origin, as for example with *metreth*, the due paid for moving cattle on the estates of Durham. Again *Welsh ale* was a normal component of the food rents imposed on the larger estates of Wessex in the late seventh century. These identities of terminology and usage as between England and Wales can hardly be ascribed either to parallel evolution or to diffusion. Instead they must be attributed to a common origin for the socio-economic system of the multiple estate in the period before the coming of the Saxons. Among them no doubt was the duty of building encampments, for a striking feature of multiple estates alike in England and in Wales is the frequency with which their focal settlements are located near hill-forts. Certainly many of the battles associated with the Saxon advance took place near hill-forts, as at Old Sarum in 552, Barbury Castle in 556, and Posbury in 661.

The chief sufferers from the Saxon conquest, as the Chronicle makes clear, were British kings and nobles. On the other hand, more lowly

Britons are likely to have survived, for without their labour the conquerors could not have exploited the estates newly acquired from the displaced British aristocracy. The decline and fall of the Roman villa was linked to a general economic and social collapse, accompanied by the removal of the villa proprietors, or possibly their reduction in status; hence, in Britain, the loss of all specific villa names save one. Nevertheless in parts of Britain like the Cotswolds some kind of rural life based on the villas could well have continued for at least two centuries after 400. There is also the possibility that barbarians either took over villa-estates after a very brief abandonment or were deliberately planted on such estates, perhaps under British direction in the fifth century and by Anglo-Saxon leaders in the sixth. [10] Moreover, abandonment of a Roman villa probably did not mean the abandonment of its arable land; instead this is likely to have remained in continued use albeit often from another centre and under new direction. Yet attached to the former villas were dependants in outlying settlements, part of a complex of socio-economic relationships increasingly seigneurial in character. Some Saxon immigrants no doubt secured for themselves substantial rural holdings. If these or their heirs prospered they would have formed an upper crust supported by their own dependants; but if these did not prosper they would lose their freedom and become the dependants of more powerful men. Indeed it is possible that, as in the Celtic west so in England, whole lineages or kindred groups could descend to servile status if all kinsmen could not be provided with a standard holding. [11] For the evidence of early laws makes it clear that the English countryside in the seventh century was largely dominated by aristocrats holding demesnes cultivated for them partly by slaves and partly by tenants with servile antecedents. Magnates like these would have owed their position to royal favour and even when succeeded by their sons the latter would have held their estates only precariously in return for service to the king. At first only the Church could acquire by charter permanent endowments carrying full possessionary rights and not until the late eighth century did kings grant lands to laymen in hereditary possession. [12] With the proliferation of such permanent endowments royal multiple estates could be so reduced that only a few satellite settlements would have remained as direct dependencies of the estate focus, the cyninges tūn (the king's settlement). The latter, managed by the royal reeve, would normally have retained its function as the administrative centre for the encompassing hundred.

    The survival on some estates of enslaved British dependants would help explain the persistence not only of names in *lisso* but also of other British names like Dover. Moreover there are some settlements, often former satellites of multiple estates, which bear names indicating that they had once been inhabited by Britons, among them Bretton (the *tūn* of the Britons) in Derbyshire, and Walton (the *tūn* of the Welsh) in Essex. A Walton of the same meaning together with Tidover (Tuda's bank), a neighbouring settlement recorded as the abode of Britons in later seventh century Yorkshire, formed part of a small multiple estate severed from the large royal estate of Burghshire so that it could be granted to Bishop Tuda *c*. 663-4. Within the limits of the former kingdom of Elmet too there were several large estates embracing numerous dependencies, some with names indicative of former British occupation. Thus among the numerous satellites of Sherburn-in-Elmet was Bretton (now Burton-in-Elmet) (Fig. 3.2). Again, among the widely scattered dependencies of Wakefield were no less than four such settlements, West Bretton, Walton, Walshaw (the copse of the Welsh) and Upper Cumberworth (Welshman's homestead), as well as Eccleshill whose name in *eclēsia* betokens the presence of a British church somewhere within the confines of this estate.[13]

The claim that the settlement of England was organized by large estates also accords well with the 'new look' in the interpretation of English place-names. At first it was argued that the oldest identifiable English place-names were those in *ingas* . When suffixed to a personal name the Old English *ingas* denotes the followers or dependants of the person named so that Reading, for example, means 'the followers or dependants of Rēada'. It was claimed that there was a close relationship between these place-names and Anglo-Saxon pagan burial sites dating from the fourth century to *c*. 700. There are, it is true, occasional coincidences between the two, as at Reading, but given that both occur in substantial numbers in the same southern and eastern districts of England, these coincidences are comparatively rare. Thus it is now argued that *ingas* names do not go back to the earliest immigration phase of the Anglo-Saxon settlements. Instead it is claimed that in general they belong to a phase of internal colonization when the Anglo-Saxons were settling lands avoided by their immigrant forebears and their burial places were no longer pagan cemeteries but Christian churchyards.[14]

The gap left by the revised dating of *ingas* names has been filled in part by the demonstration that the Old English *wīchām* was used by the earliest Germanic immigrants. This compound of *wīc*, derived from the Latin *vicus*, and *hām* (a homestead) denoted a small settlement bearing a special

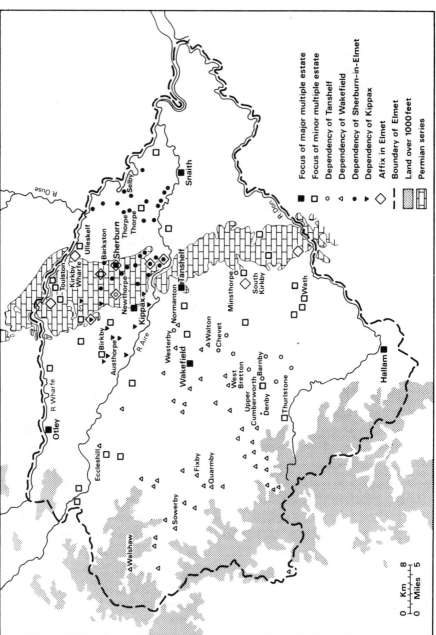

Fig. 3.2. Multiple estates, as recorded during the eleventh century, within the limits of the former British kingdom of Elmet.

relationship to a Romano-British settlement. Its presence indicates not only some direct connection between the Britons and the Saxons but also reveals the early use of *hām*.[15] It has likewise been demonstrated that place-names in *hām* also occur close to, or in association with, Roman villas,[16] as for example at Middleham in Wensleydale. Indeed it seems likely that *hām* came to be used as a generic term for the kind of estate focus which succeeded the Romano-British villa. *Ingahām* names in which *-inga-*, the genitive plural of *ingas*, is compounded with *hām* arose at a later date, whereas *ingas* names, many representing settlements shared by kinsmen, were adopted later still. These diagnostic place-names often occur in meaningful association in many multiple estates. A striking example is provided in the Hundred of Weighton to the south-east of York on the flank of the Yorkshire Wolds, the one part of Deira where pagan burials have been found in substantial numbers. Here at Goodmanham (*Godmunddingahām*) was the pagan temple where, according to Bede, the high priest Coifi abjured heathenism *c.* 626. Along with other satellites including Sancton, the site of a major pagan cemetery, Goodmanham was a dependency of the ancient royal estate of Weighton (*Wīctūn*); yet Goodmanham, together with other satellites including Londesborough, the site of yet another major pagan cemetery, was also a dependency of the ancient multiple estate of Everingham, an *ingahām* designated after an Eofor. An Eofor figures too in *Eoforwīc*, the Old English name for York, where shortly after Coifi's abjuration King Edwin of Deira was baptized a Christian. Clearly therefore habitative place-name elements like *wīc*, *hām* and *ingahām* bear a significant relationship to ancient units of lordship. But the same is also true of topographic names which are often older than habitative names. Just as the multiple estate and Hundred of Aberffraw in Anglesey bore a topographical name meaning 'the mouth of the Ffraw', so too did the large multiple estate and Hundred of Blewbury in Berkshire; and, named as it was in Old English after the hill-fort a mile to the east of Blewbury village, this large land unit had probably been in existence from the Iron Age if not earlier.[17]

Changing Rural Settlements

The existence of hill-forts and of Roman villas itself presupposes a large number of dependent settlements within their catchment areas. As the recent explosion in archaeological evidence has shown, Britain was characterized by a close network of small Romano-British settlements, particularly in the lowlands. [18] Probably many of these were dependencies of Roman villas but, despite the decline of many villas and their occasional use for burials, the once-dependent settlements could have survived. Moreover, given the likely persistence of villa-estates, it is possible that during the turmoil of the barbarian invasions some villas began to turn into hamlets or even villages by gathering around themselves the dwellings once located in the outlying dependencies; hence the not infrequent occurrence of Roman remains under churches, as for example at Rivenhall (Essex). [19] Into the interstices thus enlarged between surviving Romano-British settlements the newer establishments of Saxon soldier-settlers could have been intruded. Thus, the Saxon settlement at West Stow (Suffolk), which appears to date from before 400, was fitted into a corner of the still-flourishing domain of Icklingham, a Romano-British settlement known to have continued well into the fifth century, [20] if not, as its name suggests, even later. Again Church Down (Hampshire) was one of a number of Saxon settlements established between the sixth and seventh centuries on the tops of the chalk downs; [21] but, to judge from the very recent discovery of contemporary pottery at the church village of Chalton in an adjoining valley, these upland settlements could well have been dove-tailed into a pre-existing network of old-established valley settlements. Be that as it may, at Church Down, as at West Stow, a wide spectrum of settlers is perhaps to be inferred from the presence both of substantial framed buildings of timber and of less elaborate sunken-featured structures. [22]

Adaptation to pre-existing patterns of settlement is also evident from the fate of some Roman forts. A striking feature of early donations to the Church is the frequency with which these were made by kings and yet involved Roman forts. Thus, as Bede records, Burgh Castle, a massive Roman fort on the Suffolk coast, was granted by Sigeberht, king of East Anglia, in the 630s to an Irish monk for the foundation of a monastery; and this monastery, as excavation has shown, was sited within the Roman walls. Again, in the far west, the Roman fortlet at Caergybi was granted by Maelgwn of Gwynedd in the sixth century to St Cybi and became the site of his intra-mural church. That this kind of siting within Roman forts was a response to more than the availability for re-use of a visible and convenient, yet deserted, stone ruin is indicated at Leintwardine (Hereford), significantly enough the *caput* of Leintwardine Hundred; for here there were three successive Roman forts but the sites of the two earlier forts remained unoccupied whereas the earthern ramparts of the latest fort encompass the church and part of the village.[23] It is likely therefore that the Roman forts where early churches were sited had become the royal possessions of tyrants in the sub-Roman period. Located near Iron Age forts, as so often is the case with Roman forts, they were well placed to remain as centres of authority.

We may envisage that the largest rural settlements were those located in such centres of authority. In the west, at important centres like Aberffraw, the *maerdref* adjoining the court was but a small village, and dependencies no doubt were still smaller clusters of dwellings. The need for self-sufficiency meant that, even in the west, the cultivation of food crops played a part in the rural economy; hence the presence of arable lands, divided not so much into rectangular fields but increasingly into bundles of narrow 'open' strips. Near the settlements this arable was apparently an infield cultivated for both winter and spring cereals; but, for spring cereals, there was also temporary cultivation of outfields taken when required from the encompassing open pastures and also, as Gildas hints, from distant upland summer grazings.

Further east too the rural economy was one of mixed arable and pastoral farming but, especially on the best lands, crop cultivation was more significant. Exactly how that arable was cultivated we do not know, although a passage in the early laws of Wessex can be taken to show that a simple form of 'open-field' agriculture was permissible in the seventh century.[24] In the east, likewise, rural settlements were probably larger than in the west, if we may judge from the numerous dwellings recently excavated at Mucking (Essex), although all these need not have been of the same date, and we may err in making the early village too populous.

Life in Towns

Despite the claims of Gildas that numerous cities were destroyed a degree of continuity seems likely in almost every Romano-British town. Thus Bede could still refer to cities, bridges and roads which, even in his day, testified to the Roman occupation. Caistor-by-Norwich, Silchester and Wroxeter are notable exceptions but, even so, each of these has retained a village nucleus. Nevertheless, by the mid-fifth century, with the decline in trade, intensified perhaps by famine, most Romano-British towns were effectively non-urban, and although they survived as occupied places they supported life in towns rather than true town-life. [25] In these settlements, as Biddle has cogently argued, royal residence if only by tyrants was probably the operative factor in maintaining a thread of continuity. Thus, in Winchester there is a striking coincidence between the site of the Roman *forum* and that of the Saxon royal palace. Again at Gloucester, the siting of the Saxon rural palace at Kingsholm, in an area which witnessed an important fifth century military burial, could well have stemmed from the survival of the legionary-fortress site in official possession until it passed into Saxon royal hands. [26] Carlisle, on the other hand, was probably the seat of a surviving diocese. [27] Yet it could be granted by King Ecgfrith of Northumbria to St Cuthbert in 664; and when the latter paid his first visit in 685 he was taken on a conducted tour by the reeve, who pointed out not only the city wall, evidently still standing, but also the still-operating Roman fountain.

In London a similar survival of authority is implied by the location of the Saxon royal palace within the former Roman fort at Cripplegate. But, in addition, since London was located at the main focus of a still functioning network of Roman roads, mercantile activity may well have continued here unbroken. Certainly by the early seventh century the truly urban character of London is revealed by such functions contained within its walls as those associated with a king's hall, the cathedral church of St Paul's, and a mint.

York too, where the *principia* of the legionary fortress continued to be used (and repaired) into the late Saxon period, may not have been dissimilar. Flooding during the later fifth and sixth centuries substantially reduced the habitable area of York. Nevertheless York appears to have been subject to the authority of Britons, among them Efrawc Iarll (literally York Earl) and his son Peredur until, in the late sixth century, control was gained by Deira. Then, apparently before the conquest of Elmet *c.* 617 permitted access to the Permian limestone quarries within the northern boundary of that still-surviving British kingdom, the defences of the legionary fortress were refurbished, an act which amply testifies to the continuing importance of York. [28]

Apart from London and York no other royal centres had a claim to truly urban character in this period but from the later seventh century onward there developed new settlements for trade and industry. Thus Hamwih, Saxon Southampton, emerged as an important commercial and industrial settlement serving as an outlet for an increasingly prosperous Wessex. Functionally very different from Winchester, which remained essentially an administrative centre, Hamwih developed a close symbiotic relationship with the ancient capital of Wessex. So too Ipswich performed a similar role in relation to the kingdom of East Anglia. Indeed, each of the early Anglo-Saxon kingdoms of the south-east came to be served by one or more new places of urban character.[29] Soon, however, the economic development which had made this possible was to be interrupted by the advent of newcomers from beyond the North Sea.

The Impact of the Scandinavians

Sporadic raids on England by the Norwegians and Danes began in the last decade of the eighth century and gradually increased in intensity until 851 when the Vikings first wintered on the Isle of Thanet. In 867 the nature of the Scandinavian impact changed when Healfdene seized York and put a Saxon puppet on the Northumbrian throne. Then in 876, as the Chronicle records, 'Healfdene shared out the land of the Northumbrians and they proceeded to plough and to support themselves.' Soon part of Mercia was likewise shared out and so also was East Anglia. But, despite settlement, the invaders continued to make plundering raids in the south and west. Thus there ensued a period of confused warfare until Alfred of Wessex in a treaty, possibly of 886, placed a limit on the Danish held area. This gave formal recognition to the Danelaw where a predominantly Danish aristocracy administered Danish laws. The heart of this Danelaw lay in the east midlands where the Danes had grouped themselves around five fortified towns—Lincoln, Stamford, Nottingham, Leicester and Derby— known collectively as the Five Boroughs. Yorkshire was also well settled.

Meanwhile, Norwegians, largely drawn from the Norse Kingdom of Dublin, had colonized large areas of north-west England. From these they spread eastwards across the Pennines and founded a new kingdom of York. This continued, not without some interruptions, until 954, when it was re-absorbed into Northumbria, which in turn was incorporated within England.

The struggle to re-establish English control had been mounted from Wessex, but the process was interrupted after 980 by the renewal of Danish raids which ravaged parts of southern England. These raids culminated in 1016 with the conquest of the realm by Svein of Denmark, a victory which, ironically, finally unified the whole of England apart from the extreme north-west.

Scandinavian Settlement

The nature of Scandinavian settlement has long been the subject of debate. Apart from numerous pieces of churchyard sculpture it has left few archaeological traces; and with the possible exception of the late ninth-century farm site at Ribblehead (Yorkshire) no Scandinavian rural settlement has been positively identified, probably because the Scandinavians adopted the settlements of the indigenous people. [30] Accordingly, recourse has been made to the evidence of Scandinavian place-names of which there are large numbers in northern and eastern England (Fig. 3.3). Originally these were seen as a direct result of the settlements made by the Danish armies which wrought havoc in England from 865 onwards. It was assumed that the armies were very large and that their many soldiers took over substantial numbers of existing English villages and renamed them. [31]

Sawyer convincingly demonstrated, however, that the largest Danish army in the ninth century was to be counted in hundreds rather than thousands. [32] Other scholars, while accepting the case for the smallness of the armies, have nevertheless argued for large numbers of settlers in order to account for the numerous Scandinavian place-names and for general Scandinavian linguistic influence. In particular, Cameron has suggested that these came as secondary migrants, colonists who settled in the north-east midlands under the protection of the armies of the Five Boroughs. [33] Important centres like Cambridge, Northampton and Nottingham were taken over by the Danes and yet their names were left unchanged. Soon too they settled in many English villages without changing their names, as is shown by the presence in the churchyards of stone sculpture executed in Scandinavian taste. In addition the Scandinavians were sufficiently numerous to have changed the names of large numbers of settlements. Cameron has cogently demonstrated, on the basis of a detailed analysis of settlement sites, that the kind of place-name most likely to represent a very early take-over of an English settlement is a hybrid name of the Grimston type in which English *tūn* is added to the genitive of a Danish personal name. A slightly later stage of settlement, on sites less satisfactory than those of English-named villages, appears to be represented in the east midlands and in Yorkshire by place-names in *bȳ*, meaning a farmstead or village; and, on the basis of the personal names with which they are compounded, the place-names in *bȳ* have been taken to refer in the main to the earliest new settlements on land not colonized

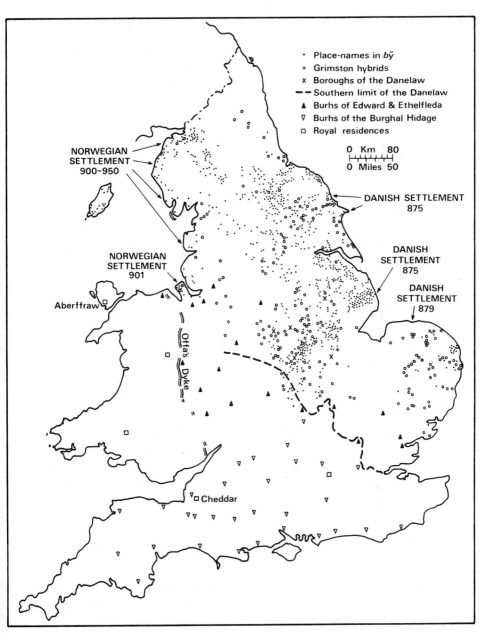

Fig. 3.3. The Scandinavians in southern Britain and the Anglo-Danish struggle. (Based on Cameron, Ekwall, Fellows Jensen and Smith.)

on a large scale by the English. Appropriately enough such names are most numerous in eastern Lincolnshire, behind the protective screen of the Five Boroughs (Fig. 3.3). A still later stage in the colonization, characterized it is claimed by the exploitation of land immediately less favourable for agriculture, has been equated with names in *thorp*, meaning a secondary or dependent settlement.

This new interpretation is presented with numerous qualifications. It has been shown that some settlements with names in *bȳ*, notably appellatives like Kirkby (a village with a church), occupy sites resembling those of English villages thus suggesting that these at least represent earlier English villages re-named by new settlers.[34] Moreover, Cameron has suggested that places with names in *bȳ* were not necessarily on virgin land but rather were sites not at that time occupied. Similarly he has stated that place-names in *thorp* need not necessarily be evidence of Danish settlement itself, but instead simply represent widespread and considerable Danish influence.[35]

Accordingly there are good reasons for viewing the Scandinavian settlement not as an occupation of virgin land but rather as an adaptation of a pre-existing, and in large measure surviving, organization of the multiple estate.[36] Thus, for example, within the limits of the former kingdom of Elmet the names of two out of every three multiple estate foci as recorded in the eleventh century were English rather than Scandinavian although all these estates were probably subject to the political mastery of the Scandinavians. The remainder bore names in whole or in part Scandinavian but, as in the cases of Thurlstone or Ulleskelf, these were usually the foci of small multiple estates (Fig. 3.2). This suggests that Scandinavian name-giving was associated with the process whereby large multiple estates were fissioned into smaller multiple estates or even unitary manors. In the Elmet area approximately half the names in *bȳ* were borne by estate dependencies and half by separate manors. Among the latter was Denby (the *bȳ* of the Danes), but this is unlikely to have been a new creation for its location in the midst of estate dependencies suggests that it too had been a dependency before being allocated to Danish settlers; even the particular form of the genitive-plural *Denabi* (Denby) suggests that it was coined by neighbouring Englishmen in an area then inhabited predominantly by the English. Again Birkby, the one name in *bȳ* borne by a multiple estate focus, probably refers to an old settlement rather than a new creation, as is also suggested by its site, its situation and the earlier form of its name, *Bretebi* (the *bȳ* of the Britons). Moreover, the names in *thorp* in the Elmet area were divided almost equally between estate dependencies and separate manors. Among the former was the Tanshelf dependency of Minsthorpe (the *thorp* belonging to the community or the *thorp* on common land), which, to judge from its site on fertile limestone soils, was not a new settlement. On the other hand, Newthorpe, one of many dependencies of Sherburn, but with soils less favourable than those of its immediate neighbours, was undoubtedly a new creation; yet this too was dovetailed into the established framework of an ancient multiple estate.

Rural Development

Scandinavian settlement, by speeding the process which brought about the fission of multiple estates, exerted a profound influence on the pattern of settlement in those parts of northern and eastern England where the old socio-economic order had persisted. On the typical lesser multiple estate which had been severed from a larger entity, the presence of a new lord, less remote than his aristocratic predecessor and more dependent on local resources, no doubt led to a more intensive agrarian effort. Such effort was probably concentrated at the settlement chosen to be the focus of the new estate, for this is likely to have occupied the most fertile land. Here therefore, rather than in the dependencies, arable land would be enlarged at the expense of surrounding common pastures and woods.

Where free and equal soldier-settlers took over unoccupied territory, or enlarged the arable of existing settlements, a standard portion of allotment, the *manslot*, was probably used to ensure that each acquired a fair share of the good land as well as the merely adequate. It is perhaps to such equitable allocations that we may best trace the origins of an open-field system more regular and efficient than hitherto used, a system possibly adopted only at a later date in favoured parts of 'English' England like the west midlands. [37]

In the Danelaw the enlargement of the arable land at the typical estate focus might well lead to the disappearance of the hamlets of outlying dependencies. Instead the dwellings of tenants could come to be concentrated at the focus which therefore would grow from a hamlet into a village. In 'English' England, on the other hand, where a more precocious development of the economy had promoted the fission of large multiple estates and enhanced the role of local lordship, there was probably a similar growth of villages at the expense of outlying hamlets. Alike in the north and the south, estates which prospered frequently became unitary manors completely severed from the multiple estates of which they had once formed part. In keeping with such changes the unitary manor would come to be less dependent on the religious provision hitherto made for the whole multiple estate by the mother-church or minster. For, with growing prosperity manorial lords or even prosperous freemen of the Danelaw were able to endow local churches; hence the appearance of the village church serving a parish often coterminous with the manor.

Urban Growth

With the coming of the Scandinavians urban life received a new stimulus. Their principal settlements, like the Five Boroughs, well-fortified and under military control for at least the first generation, developed into thriving trading towns. York, as a capital, grew quickly to become one of the principal urban centres of England, and Lincoln also thrived. Both emerged under the Anglo-Scandinavian kings of the eleventh century as the administrative centres for the two largest shires in England.

Already in the eighth century the rulers of Mercia had begun the fortification of major settlements, as at Hereford on the Welsh border, but it was the need for an integrated system of defence versus the Danes which promoted the most rapid growth of defended centres in southern England. Thus, in Wessex no less than 30 defended places were established and so spaced out that no part of the kingdom was more than 20 miles from a fortified centre of refuge and resistance. According to the Burghal Hidage, a document datable to between 914 and 918 but which probably recapitulates the practice of Alfred the Great, responsibility for fortifying and garrisoning these *burhs*, as they were known, was placed on the surrounding countryside. Ten were forts, some of them new, but others re-used old defences as at the Iron Age hill-fort of Chisbury (Wiltshire) or the Roman fort of Portchester (Hampshire). In the main, however, the *burhs* were fortified towns devised for permanent settlement so that military effectiveness was based on economic viability and a growing population.[38] Some were re-used Roman walled towns like Winchester but others were new creations like Axbridge in Somerset. Characteristically the latter was set within the framework of a large multiple estate, one recorded in King Alfred's will, and the known site of an important royal residence from at least 941. Thus placed, Axbridge was provided with a ready-made market catchment to favour its trade, for traditionally the occupants of such an estate would have repaired to the estate focus for the discharge of their customary obligations.

The reconquest of England and the eventual unification of the state was based on the gradual extension of *burh* foundation. Thus Ethelfleda adopted the burghal system for the protection of Mercia by the fortification of towns like Warwick and, significantly, the refurbishing of Eddisbury hill-fort in Cheshire. Subsequently, between 911 and 919, the system was extended over the remainder of England south of the Humber by her brother Edward the Elder of Wessex.

By contrast the towns which came into being during the last century of the Anglo-Saxon state seem to have been the result of a general expansion of economic life and to have emerged more gradually. Yet, like the majority of *burhs*, these stood in most cases on land which was royal property. By reserving their rights over the *burhs* the rulers of an increasingly unified England began a close association with their boroughs which was to be beneficial to them both. It was no accident that the towns and the power of the ruler grew together. The grafting of new on to old, evident with these towns, epitomizes much of the process whereby southern Britain came to be more closely settled during the period between the departure of the Romans and the advent of the Normans.

References

1. J. N. L. Myres, *Anglo-Saxon Pottery and the Settlement of England*, (Oxford, 1969), pp. 62-141.
2. S. C. Hawkes and G.C. Dunning, 'Soldiers and settlers in Britain, fourth to fifth century', *Medieval Archaeology*, **5** (1961), pp. 1-70.
3. H. Williams (ed.), *Gildae, De Excidio Britanniae*, (London, 1899), pp. 15-92, 261-6.
4. B. Colgrave and R. A. B. Mynors (eds.), *Bede's Ecclesiastical History of the English People*, (Oxford, 1969), pp. 48-53.
5. D. Whitelock (ed.), *The Anglo-Saxon Chronicle*, (London, 1961).
6. A. L. Meaney, *A Gazetteer of Early Anglo-Saxon Burial Sites*, (London, 1964).
7. G. R. J. Jones, 'Post-Roman Wales' in H. P. R. Finberg (ed.) *The Agrarian History of England and Wales*, **I-ii** (Cambridge, 1972), pp. 281-382; *idem*, 'Multiple estates and early settlement' in P. H. Sawyer (ed.), *Medieval Settlement: Continuity and Change*, (London, 1976), pp. 15-40.

8. K. Jackson, *Language and History in Early Britain*, (Edinburgh, 1953), pp. 285, 343; E. Ekwall, *The Oxford Dictionary of English Place-Names*, (4th edn.), (Oxford, 1960); A. H. Smith, *English Place-Name Elements* (Cambridge, 1956).

9. B. Colgrave (ed.), *The Life of Bishop Wilfrid by Eddius Stephanus*, (Cambridge, 1972), pp. 82-3; W. de G. Birch (ed.), *Cartularium Saxonicum*, **I** (London, 1885), p. 99; G. R. J. Jones, 'Settlement patterns in Anglo-Saxon England', *Antiquity*, **XXXV** (1961), pp. 224-5; *idem*, 'Historical geography and our landed heritage', *University of Leeds Review*, **XIX** (1976), pp. 64-6.

10. K. Branigan, *Latimer*, (Bristol, 1971), pp. 173, 186-9; P. J. Fowler, 'Agriculture and rural settlement' in D. M. Wilson (ed.), *The Archaeology of Anglo-Saxon England*, (London, 1976), pp. 23-48.

11. T. M. Charles-Edwards, 'Kinship, status and the origins of the hide', *Past and Present*, **56** (1972), pp. 3-33.

12. E. John, *Land Tenure in Early England*, (Leicester, 1960), pp. 24-63.

13. Jones, 'Historical geography and our landed heritage', pp. 62-74; *idem*, 'Early territorial organization in England and Wales', *Geografiska Annaler*, **XLIII** (Stockholm, 1961), pp. 174-81; *idem*, 'Early territorial organization in Gwynedd and Elmet', *Northern History*, **X** (1975), pp. 3-25.

14. J. M. Dodgson, 'The significance of the distribution of the English place-names in -ingas, -inga- in south-east England', *Medieval Archaeology*, **10** (1966), pp. 1-29.

15. M. Gelling, 'English place-names derived from the compound wīchām', *Medieval Archaeology*, **11** (1967), pp. 87-104.

16. B. Cox, 'The significance of the distribution of English place-names in hām in the Midlands and East Anglia', *Journal of the English Place-Name Society*, **V** (1973), pp. 15-73.

17. M. Gelling, *The Place-Names of Berkshire*, **III** (Cambridge, 1976), pp. 800-33; *idem*, 'The evidence of place-names' in Sawyer, *Medieval Settlement*, pp. 200–11.

18. Fowler, 'Agriculture and rural settlement', pp. 33-4.

19. J. Percival, *The Roman Villa*, (London, 1976), pp. 166-82.

20. S. E. West, 'The Anglo-Saxon village of West Stow. An interim report of the excavations 1965-8', *Medieval Archaeology*, **13** (1969), pp. 1-20; A. and W. Selkirk, 'West Stow', *Current Archaeology*, **IV** (1973), pp. 151-6.

21. B. Cunliffe, 'Saxon and medieval settlement pattern in the region of Chalton, Hampshire', *Medieval Archaeology*, **16** (1972), pp. 1-12.

22. P. V. Addyman, 'The Anglo-Saxon house: a new review', *Anglo-Saxon England*, **I** (1972), pp. 273-307; P. Rahtz, 'Buildings and rural development' in Wilson, *Archaeology of Anglo-Saxon England*, pp. 50-96.

23. M. Biddle, 'A widening horizon' in P. Addyman and R. Morris (eds.), *The Archaeological Study of Churches*, (London, 1976), pp. 65-71.

24. H. P. R. Finberg, 'Anglo-Saxon England to 1042' in Finberg, *Agrarian History of England and Wales*, **I-ii**, pp. 416-7.
25. J. Wacher, *The Towns of Roman Britain*, (London, 1975), pp. 411-22.
26. M. Biddle, 'Towns' in Wilson, *Archaeology of Anglo-Saxon England*, pp. 103-6; M. Biddle and C. Heighway, *The Future of London's Past*, (Worcester, 1973), pp. 16-25.
27. C. Thomas, *The Early Christian Archaeology of North Britain*, (Oxford, 1971), pp. 11-19; N. Chadwick, *The British Heroic Age*, (Cardiff, 1976), pp. 116-19.
28. Jones, 'Early Territorial Organization', pp. 12, 25; H. G. Ramm, 'The growth and development of the city to the Norman Conquest' in A. Stacpoole (ed.), *The Noble City of York*, (York, 1972), pp. 225-48.
29. Biddle, 'A widening horizon' pp. 112-20.
30. D. M. Wilson, 'The Scandinavians in England', in Wilson, *Archaeology of Anglo-Saxon England*, pp. 392-403.
31. F. M. Stenton, *Anglo-Saxon England*, (3rd edn.) (Oxford, 1971), pp. 520-5.
32. P. H. Sawyer, 'The density of Danish settlement in England', *University of Birmingham Historical Journal*, **VI** (1958), pp. 1-17; idem, *The Age of the Vikings*, (2nd edn.) (London, 1971), pp. 154-69.
33. K. Cameron, *Scandinavian Settlement in the Territory of the Five Boroughs: the Place-Name Evidence*, (Nottingham, 1965), pp. 1-24; idem, (ed.), *Place-Name Evidence for the Anglo-Saxon Invasion and Scandinavian Settlements*, (Nottingham, 1975); H. Loyn, *Anglo-Saxon England and the Norman Conquest*, (London, 1962), p. 52.
34. Gillian Fellows Jensen, *Scandinavian Settlement Names in Yorkshire*, (Copenhagen, 1972), pp. 5-41, 195-251; idem, 'The Vikings in England: a review', *Anglo-Saxon England*, **IV** (1975), pp. 181-206.
35. K. Cameron, 'The significance of English place-names', *Proceedings of the British Academy*, **LXII** (1976), pp. 17-21.
36. G. R. J. Jones, 'Early territorial organization in Northern England and its bearing on the Scandinavian settlement', in A. Small (ed.), *The Fourth Viking Congress (1961)*, (Edinburgh, 1965), pp. 67-84.
37. Finberg, *Agrarian History of England and Wales*, **I-ii**, pp. 487-97.
38. Biddle, 'A widening horizon', pp. 120-47.

4
The Early Middle Ages, 1066–1350

R. A. Dodgshon

Introduction

Few historical events spring more easily to mind than the Norman Conquest of 1066. Yet its significance as a break-point in the narrative of English and Welsh history has been increasingly questioned. For an earlier generation of historians, it was seen as having a profound impact on all aspects of life. Apart from the revolution in political power and in the control over land, the Normans were portrayed as innovators of feudalism and manorialism, those vital organizing forces behind society and its spatial order. Aided by them, the century or so after their arrival was instated as the most formative in the history of the rural landscape, with many new settlements founded and vast areas of waste reclaimed. Nor was their impact confined to the rural sector. They were credited with instituting a vigorous exchange economy which, in the space of barely two centuries, overspread the country with a mature urban network based on the novel concept of the borough.

Such claims on behalf of the Norman achievement have been greatly diluted by modern work. Feudalism and manorialism are now accepted as familiar concepts long before the Normans crossed the Channel. Qualifying their effect in other directions has been the realization that neither England nor Wales abounded with unlimited or unfettered opportunities for colonization in 1066. Some scholars would have us believe that England was already an old and settled country, with its pattern of village settlement complete and a level of cultivation equal to that of the nineteenth century. In Wales too, the permanent occupation of the countryside was probably more advanced than older views allowed. Even the notion of the borough has been challenged as a purely Norman

81

innovation. Admittedly, the number of boroughs increased dramatically, but the essence of their character is now seen as anticipated by the Anglo-Saxon *burh*. In fact, it has been argued that England was as urbanized in the eleventh as in the fourteenth century, and that this pre-Norman system of towns was linked to the expansion of trade no less closely than their growth after 1066.

If accepted without demur, these re-appraisals cast the period 1066–1350 in a new light. Instead of being characterized by pioneering change and innovation, its history would appear as a play on themes already established by the time it began. However, it would be premature to assert that everything about it is older than we once thought. The original contribution of the period to its own spatial order is not so easily emasculated. Rather is it a case of having to strike a more considered balance between what was genuinely new and those institutions which the Normans inherited. The geographer's contribution to this debate must be to give its spatial component more form and dimension. Medieval England and Wales were congeries of regional societies and economies that were, as yet, only weakly integrated. The fortunes of one were not necessarily those of another. If he can bring out the structure of this variation, then the geographer will have contributed usefully to a debate in which national trends are too often regional trends writ large.

Types of People: Types of Society

Medieval society comprised groups of different legal status. Its superior was the king. Beneath him were the great territorial lords, the *maiores barones*. These graded down into lesser barons, knights and an extensive category of freemen, or *liberi homines*, and the semi-free, such as sokemen. Below these were the villeins and bordars, groups tied by burdening work-service to a lord. At the base of the system were the unfree, or serfs. Any review of post-Conquest social geography must take the changing nature and distribution of these various groups as its fundamental problem.

Social Geography at the Time of the Conquest

As regards England, the patterns depicted by the analysis of Domesday Book (1086) by Darby *et al.* can be adopted as a base-line. [1] At this point, the main concentration of English population was in the east and south-east (see Fig. 4.1), particularly East Anglia and Kent, where densities exceeded 15 persons per square mile. Westwards and northwards, numbers fall away, progressively in some directions but unevenly in others. The resultant contrast between a well-settled east and south-east and a more sparsely settled north and west is clearly delineated in the Midlands. Counties like Rutland, Northhamptonshire and Gloucestershire appear well-populated, but as one moves north-westwards across Leicestershire, Warwickshire and Worcestershire into counties like Staffordshire and Shropshire, we increasingly find a thinly spread population interspersed

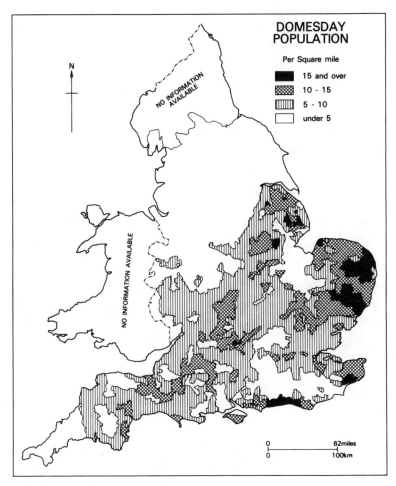

Fig. 4.1. Domesday population (after Darby).

with *terra wasta*. One cautionary note to this is that Domesday Book omits to mention groups like *censarii*, or rent-paying villeins. As a group, they are mostly found in areas like the west and north-west Midlands. If allowance is made for them, then the westward slope of population density may not have had so steep a gradient as Darby's maps suggest.

Superimposed on this westward and northward sloping surface of population is one of personal freedom tilted in a broadly similar manner (see Fig. 4.2). In 1086, the main concentration of freemen and sokemen was in eastern England, especially Lincolnshire, Norfolk and Suffolk. Here, the number of individuals so classed by Domesday Book was around 40 per cent of the total. The favoured explanation for this concentration is that it reflects the persisting impact of the Scandinavian settlement, indirectly if not directly. As with population, the proportion of freemen and sokemen falls away northwards and westwards. In the south-west and along the Welsh border, they account for barely 10 per cent of recorded

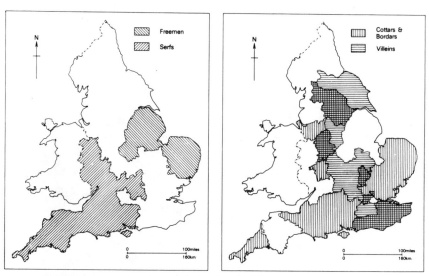

Fig. 4.2 (*left*) Types of Domesday society. Counties in which freemen and sokemen formed over 30 per cent of local population and in which serfs formed over 15 per cent.

Fig. 4.2 (*right*) Types of Domesday society. Counties in which villeins formed over 50 per cent of local population and bordars and cottars over 30 per cent. Except for Herts, Middlesex and Cambridgeshire, the distribution of the latter two groups largely reflects the distribution of bordars.

individuals in 1086. Across Offa's Dyke, older notions of a free, tribal society surviving everywhere with little alteration until the eleventh century and in areas like Merioneth until much later need to be handled cautiously. The free element is now conceded only a modest place in medieval Welsh society, more so in the eleventh than the fourteenth century.

The main concentrations of villeins and bordars were in southern England, from Kent across to Cornwall, and stretching in a broad belt up through the southern and eastern Midlands into Yorkshire. Status-wise, they had much in common with each other, but whereas villeins held standard tenement units, bordars held only a few acres or so. It has been argued that the latter represented cottagers grafted onto a settlement's older core of standard or villein tenements. If so, it would tell us a great deal about the landholding history of areas where bordars outnumbered villeins, as in Cornwall, Dorset and Hampshire, or areas where bordars but not villeins were significant, such as East Anglia. By comparison, the distribution of serfs was more confined. Only in the south-west or along the Welsh border, where they could form over 15 per cent of the local population, can they be described as an important element in society. Broadly speaking, it is a case of the further west, the more substantial were their numbers. Indeed, in Wales at this point, they were probably the majority social group.

The Changing Legal Condition of Men

The foregoing pattern was not stable. Changes in personal status, acting in conjunction with rapid population growth, conspired to transform it by the mid-fourteenth century. However, there is considerable disagreement over the precise configuration of these status changes. For Hilton, the most notable was that affecting villeins, who lost any pretensions to freedom before the law and became unfree by the thirteenth century. [2] This process of enserfment affected some areas more than others. Kent, for example, had a high villein population in 1086, with 58 per cent of those recorded falling into this category. Yet in later centuries, its peasantry was renowned for its freedom. This freedom has been interpreted by some scholars as a deeply rooted cultural trait, but Hilton prefers to see it as reflecting the success of the Kentish peasant in resisting the forces of lordship that depressed his like elsewhere during the Middle Ages. It must be stressed that not everyone subscribes to these views and their implication that the twelfth and thirteenth centuries witnessed the final descent into servility, albeit unevenly across the country, of groups that once ranked as free. Only recently, for example, Scammell has reiterated Aston's point that pre-Conquest villeins or peasants show no sign of ever having been unattached.[3] In other words, it is debatable whether they had any freedom to lose in the first place. But no matter how this debate over villein status is resolved, it does not preclude the further possibility that the number and proportion of freemen in society may have increased. Sensibly, if those villeins who failed to resist the heavy hand of lordship cannot be regarded as a loss to the ranks of freemen, then those whom Hilton believes did, such as the Kentish peasant, can be counted as a gain. Some unfree also managed to achieve or purchase freedom by legal manumission. A promising line of argument is that the nature of free communities, with their more open, self-adjusting relationship between land and people, engendered higher rates of demographic growth than elsewhere. Homans and Hallam, for instance, see this as the reason why East Anglia and Kent were more closely settled than other regions.[4] But not everyone is impressed by such reasoning. Some, like Postan, accept that the absolute number of freemen rose, but believe it to have been a purely demographic process that affected *all* social groups and *all* areas with equal weight.[5] To sum up, there is no consensus view of status-group changes over this period. Views range from those which envisage profound alterations in the nature and proportional representation of the various groups to those which admit numerical increases to their ranks but not changes of nature or importance, a case of *plus ça change* . . . .

Social change in Wales had a more easily discerned spatial component to it. Throughout the March, the *force majeure* behind this change was the Normans. Old administrative commotes, like Gower, were converted into Norman lordships. Within these lordships, their influence was more far-reaching on the fertile low ground, where regular manorial structures could be established. In the remainder, native society and institutions continued along their own path of change. This gave rise to a dichotomy that was deeply etched into the social space of communities, or that between the Englishries, where the Norman impact was social as well as political, and the Welshries, where it was only political. Characteristically, the Englishries embraced old bond settlements. Their communities of *nativi*, those bond by kin and descent, were expanded by the addition of new, English *customarii,* or those holding by custom of the manor. Overall, therefore, the Englishries moved towards a more enlarged villeinage. In the Welshries, meanwhile, and in those parts of Wales which remained under native Welsh lordship until the thirteenth century, the opposite was true. Social trends in these areas can be illustrated by the experience of north-west Wales. By the time Crown extents become available for the north-west, *c.* 1300, social change had wrought a different kind of social order to that postulated in Chapter 3, with most areas being predominantly free (as in the case of Cardiganshire and Merionethshire) or divided more equally between between bond and free groups (as in the case of Anglesey). [6] These extents afford only partial support for Jones Pierce's notion of an upland/lowland antithesis underlying the contrast between free and bond communities. As one might expect of the lord's men, bond groups do seem to have more of the fertile ground than freemen, but the association is blurred by the presence of bondmen inland on the more rugged terrain of Snowdonia and Ardudwy, and breaks down altogether if we accept G. R. J. Jones' case for interior free settlements having bond roots. [7]

Demographic Change

Another vital engine of change behind the social geography of England and Wales was rapid population growth. The earliest opportunity for assessing the population of either country is Domesday Book. Unfortunately, its use for calculating English population is fraught with difficulty. All we can be certain about is that it lists 300,000 landholders. To convert this figure into total population, a conversion factor must be devised which takes into account those areas not included in the survey, such as the four most northerly counties, and those people who lie concealed behind the stark references to landholders. There is also the thorny question of whether the *servi* or serfs which it enumerates represent all serfs or just heads of households. Depending on how writers have responded to these problems, estimates of English Domesday population vary from 1·1 million [8] to over 2 million. [9]

Inevitably, this uncertain foundation makes for an equally uncertain assessment of subsequent growth. By using fragmented sources like the Hundred Rolls (1277-9) or by extrapolating backwards from the Poll Tax of 1377, sources as problematical as Domesday Book, it has been calculated that English population rose by about 300 per cent before growth ceased. Exactly when growth ceased is another bone of contention. Postan concluded that it was around 1300, when total population stood at 7 million. It then levelled out and probably declined following the great famines of 1315–7, that is, before the Black Death ushered in a more dramatic decline in 1348-9. By contrast, Russell proposes a continuing growth up to 1348-9, at which point, he estimates total population as 3·75 million. His attempt to estimate Welsh population in 1300 as 180,000 is more ingenious than satisfactory, but the way landholding units like the *gwely* were being over-burdened by sheer numbers suggests growth had occurred.

The rapid growth of population helped re-structure the social geography of the country through the effect it had on the distribution of freemen. The connection was simple. The increase encouraged the colonization of much new land, a disproportionate amount of which was settled by freemen. Harley's comparison of the Feldon Hundred of Kineton with the Hundred of Stoneleigh in Arden (Warwickshire) over the period 1086-1277 demonstrates this connection, with the post-Conquest expansion into the more extensive waste areas of the latter spawning whole new systems of settlement and landholding, a high proportion of which were in the hands of freemen.[10] The same weighted association between post-Domesday colonization and freemen appears elsewhere in the Midlands, such as in Feckenham, Charnwood Forest, Cannock Chase and the Fen areas of Lincolnshire and Cambridgeshire, as well as throughout the broken hill country along the Welsh border, where the free element expanded dramatically after 1086. It has also been vouched for in the Weald and for parts of the south-west, notably Devon. In trying to categorize the sorts of area so affected, we cannot do better than adopt the familiar grouping of woodland-pasture and open-pasture districts: the former included the Midland forest areas and parts of East Anglia, Dorset, Wiltshire and the Weald, whilst the latter included upland areas like the Pennines, Exmoor and Dartmoor, together with parts of the Welsh border and the Fens. It was in these areas that post-Conquest colonization tended to be associated with the formation of spatially diffused systems of free communities.

Seen in its local context, two types of development can be recognized. Where old established settlements entered this period with a reservoir of untapped waste around them, such waste was colonized either by allowing customary tenements to expand into it, thus producing the characteristic tenement plus so many acres of assart, or by the settlement of rent-paying, adventitious communities of freemen on it. The older core of villeinage could thereby acquire a periphery whose social character was quite different. Alternatively, in the deeper recesses of large scale waste areas, such as those listed in the previous paragraph, colonization over the twelfth and thirteenth centuries led increasingly to the creation of more independently structured free communities.

Types of Society

The eventual outcome of the foregoing trends was that the broad contrast between areas of villeinage and areas of freedom was extended and sharpened. In recent years, a school of thought has emerged which views this contrast between two socially and spatially divorced kinds of society as prejudicial to the social and economic development of the countryside over the late medieval and early modern periods. Arguably, its significance may not have needed too long to mature. Even before 1350, their differences mattered. Indeed, for Homans, their societal differences form a *starting-point* for the understanding of such vital issues as tenure, landholding, settlement type and even the extent to which they were engaged in trade and industry, so intimately related were they to their socio-cultural context.[11] However, we still need more substantive work on what these societal differences involved along the lines of Homans' classic study of the English villager in champion areas.[12]

What is clear is that we must divest ourselves of any presumption that champion areas or areas of villeinage like the Midlands comprised stable, inward-looking, endogamous communities, in which family networks approximated to those of the community at large. In actual fact, such communities had fairly diverse social structures. As Homans put it, 'family and village tended to be two bodies different in kind'.[13] At present, there is no reason to doubt that many communities in free areas also formed open social systems constantly re-charged by inward movement and new alliances. In parts of East Anglia, Kent and Wales, though, there possibly existed scattered communities of a different kind, consisting of small groups of kinsmen or *heredes,* thrown together residentially and segregated from others by the successive partition of a family estate. Patrilocal groups bound together by ties of kin have also been identified in northern Pennine areas like Tynedale.

One of the mechanisms by which these different types of social order were mapped into the settlement pattern was through the controls exercised over land by inheritance customs. Champion areas tended to practise impartibility. Partly for this reason, Homans described their family structures as being of the stem variety. Stem families were those whose size was continually cut back as growth occurred so as to maintain a constant relationship between the family holding and those fortunate enough to occupy it. To achieve this kind of homeostasis between land and people, stem families spawned off-shoots that were forced to seek a living elsewhere. By contrast, the older free areas tended to practise partible inheritance, thereby continually adjusting the relationship between land and people. This is the reason why such areas are believed to have experienced higher rates of demographic growth than elsewhere. This facet of their distinction is highlighted by Hallam's work on Lincolnshire. The impartibility of bond communities led to 'vagabondage', whereas the partibility of free and sokemen communities made them more absorbent of any increase in their numbers. In a short, pithy phrase, he declared the sokemen 'multiplies and fills the earth'.[14]

However, if areas of villeinage had the greater need, they did not have the greater facility for spatial mobility. By their very nature, free communities could more easily export their surplus or respond to the opportunities presented by the growth of towns and trade. It was freemen, therefore, who probably predominated in the deepening flows of townward migration or adopted the itinerant life of pedlars and packmen. Likewise, it was probably they who subscribed most to the flows of seasonal migrants. A 1351 labour statute restricted the summer movement of people from the towns to the countryside, presumably an exodus prompted by the Black Death, but then conceded that 'the people of the counties of Stafford, Lancaster, and Derby, and people of Craven, and the Marches of Wales and Scotland, and other places, may come in the time of August, and labour in other counties, and safely return, as they were want to do before this time'. As this brief list of the areas involved implies, it was the open and woodland pasture districts, predominantly free areas, that not only had minimal harvest demands of their own but would have been allowed to migrate in search of harvest work.

Any differences between freemen and villeins in respect of mobility, though, were only relative. Villeins too could leave their native village. Admittedly, some of this movement was illegal. But when we read of a poor husbandman in Middleton (Northumberland) fleeing under cover of darkness with his wife, children, oxen, sheep and lambs to escape the impositions of his lord,[15] it must not be assumed that this was the only type of movement open to a villein. As Vinogradoff showed, many villeins were allowed to move under license from their lord, a fact which helps explain the significant levels of local and regional mobility evident in an early fourteenth century study of Leightonstone, Normancross and Toseland Hundreds in Huntingdonshire, a county with a fairly high villein population.[16] Quite apart from movement between rural vills, many migrating villeins (possibly the majority) gravitated to a nearby town, attracted no doubt by the prospect that 'town air makes free'. Consider, for instance, the plight of Simon de Parys, a successful London mercer and alderman, who returned to his native village of Necton (Norfolk) in 1308 only to be claimed as a villein by the lord of the manor.[17] Of course, even discharging their labour services could involve villeins in movement and therefore social interaction beyond the confines of their village: those of Buckland (Gloucestershire) were required to carry goods to Gloucester, Tewkesbury, Evesham, Chipping Camden and Worcester.[18]

Land and Society

Who Held What?

In a feudalized society, all land was held off the king. Extended beneath him was a complex hierarchy of landholders, whose apex was filled by tenants-in-chief holding their land directly off him. Foremost among them were the great territorial lords, lay and ecclesiastical. It is one of the more uneqivocal conclusions to be drawn from Domesday Book that England at least was a land of large estates. Its backward glance at conditions before 1066 allows us to say that this was truer after the Conquest than before. Strategic areas which had a fragmented estate structure beforehand, such as the lower Derwent and Dove valleys (Derbyshire) or the North Riding, were consolidated into large fiefs after the Conquest. Although such estates had a definite *locus,* around which the head manor was situated, it was common for them to have scattered outlying portions. Thus, by the early twelfth century, Ralph d'Aubigny's Honour of Mowbray, though based in Leicestershire, also had fiefs in Warwickshire, Northamptonshire, Lincolnshire, Westmorland, Lancashire, Durham and Yorkshire. For comparison, the estates which the Normans fashioned for themselves along the Welsh border and in south Wales were integral structures.

An important sub-group amongst the large estates were the monastic and episcopal estates. Although comprising only a quarter of all landholding, they have attracted a greater share of attention because of their organized, thrusting and commercial character. Those belonging to abbeys and priories divided themselves into different orders, of which the most notable were the Benedictines and Cistercians. Spatially, the two complement each other. The foundations of the former, like Winchester and Reading Abbeys, were established early and located mostly in the older settled parts of the south and east. Squeezed into a mature system of landholding and settlement, their endowments consisted of small, fragmented blocks that were bonded together to form an intricate and difficult estate structure. Cistercian estates, meanwhile, were endowed later and balanced more to the north and west. Whereas the Benedictines lived and hustled in a crowded world, the image of the Cistercians is of an order that sought seclusion. Abbeys like Bordesley and Stoneleigh, on the edges of Feckenham and Arden respectively, were consistent with this *in loca deserta* image. However, in other cases, abundant local opportunity seems a more adequate covering explanation for their location. In Yorkshire, for example, where a cluster of Cistercian abbeys like Fountains and Rievaulx were founded, they took advantage of areas devastated by William, areas which had been well-settled before the Conquest. In Wales too, it is debatable whether abbeys like Strata Florida (Cardiganshire) expressed the Cistercian search for wilderness. Part of their endowment was longstanding bond townships. A feature of Cistercian estates was that in addition to lowland arable granges, some had upland farms or vaccaries. For instance, Whalley Abbey had vaccaries in Rossendale, whilst large swaths of the Lake District fells were held as pasture runs by peripherally located abbeys and priories like Barrow, St Bees, Shap, Holme Cultram and Carlisle.[19]

The medieval countryside owed much of its variety of order to the way the great estate holders arranged their property. The most basic choice before them was whether they should farm it themselves or let others do it instead. This found its clearest expression in the line drawn between what was demesne, or in the lord's hands and farmed for his profit, and what was held by tenants in the form of customary or standard tenements. The latter were the elemental units of villeinage, held by custom of the manor in return for labour services or *ad opera*. These two, juxtaposed elements were present in most lowland vills, either as discrete or intermixed sectors.

The amount of land incorporated into the lord's demesne varied spatially and historically. Spatially, it was more extensive in areas of greatest arable potential. Thus, nationally, it was more developed in the south and east, especially on the older, larger estates, though the high proportion of land worked as demesne by the provincial Cistercians distorted this simple pattern. One can also perceive local differences. In the Chilterns, it was the better soils of the valleys rather than plateaux or ridges that carried the largest demesnes. Spatial differences of this sort could often be extreme, with some manors entirely at demesne and others leased out. Superimposed on these broad spatial variations were broad secular swings in the importance of demesne. During much of the twelfth century, the great estates found it economically more gainful to lease out their demesne. Consequently, the area under demesne contracted. However, for economic reasons, or possibly following a change in attitude, the trend was reversed from the 1180s onwards. The south and Midlands responded first, East Anglia last. This reversal initiated an age of demesne farming that lasted until around 1300, when the process was reversed yet again.

In theory, the proportion of an estate or manor given over to customary tenements was related to the labour needs of demesne. In actuality, it was more wayward. Mention has already been made of manors entirely one or the other. Their lack of direct relationship is further underlined by the way customary land was adjusted to the ebb and flow of demesne. As the latter contracted, the amount of customary land remained stable. Adjustment between the two was achieved instead by the commutation of labour services into a money rent. With the re-expansion of demesnes, a feudal reaction set in. The larger landowners, especially in the south and east, tried to re-impose labour services. They were more successful on estates that had behind them a fuller tradition of servitude. This meant that by 1300 there were pronounced spatial differences in the service character of villein tenure. The Cotswolds exemplify these differences. Old established estates on the plateau, like those of the Benedictines, still demanded a full range of services, but younger, smaller estates along the scarp had mostly commuted them by 1300.

Filling out the occupied landscape were holdings whose tenure was freehold. The character of this freehold has a strong overlay of local custom, but there were common strands. Thus, in Kent, many peasants held their sulung or soke shares by 'Kentish custom': this empowered them to alienate their land and to practise gavelkind or partible inheritance. Such processes injected a strong dynamic into the evolution of landholding. Their potential contribution is well-shown by Baker's reconstruction of how they combined to fragment landholding at Gillingham manor.[20] Similar conditions prevailed amongst freemen and sokemen in East Anglia. As Domesday Book declared, they had the 'power to sell and give their lands'. This gave rise to a type of landholding development analagous to that in Kent. In Wales, native freemen held land by *gwely* or resting-place tenure. The *gwely* was a joint proprietary unit held by kinsmen or by 'comporciones de consanguinitate' as the *Black Book of St David's* (1326) put it. It was partible in that each new generation acquired an equal *per capita* share in it, but impartible in that the *gwely* remained undivided as a tenure. It was formerly believed that it did not develop until *c.* 1100, when the nomadic, pastoral economy practised by freemen was abandoned in favour of a settled, more arable-based economy. *Gwelyau* were seen as developing after two or three generations from shares of tribal land allocated out to tribesmen at this critical juncture. Once formed, it began a career as a 'relatively fleeting phenomenon in the Welsh landscape', lasting only until around 1300.[21] By then, sheer weight of numbers caused it to break up into several tenures, 'beset by individualism from within'.[22] However, scholars now ascribe deeper roots to the *gwely* as a joint proprietary unit. Its history after 1100 being one of maturity and ultimate decay, but not origin.[23] Interestingly, joint proprietary unit shared between *heredes* also existed in Kent and East Anglia, but on a smaller scale. Adding an extra dimension to the geography of freehold were the newer freeholds established on assarted land, either as arrented appendages to customary tenements or as independent holdings occupied by freemen. It was the predominance of the latter which ensured that these newer freeholds tended to enjoin the woodland and open pasture districts to the list of free areas.

Whether a person was free or bond is no guide to how much land he held. Admittedly the colonizing activities of freemen over this period did much to enlarge the number of smallholders in woodland-pasture areas like Cannock Chase, but work on areas like Arden affirms that large freehold units were also a by-product of such activity. What can also be concluded is that average peasant holding size, whether free or otherwise, declined over the twelfth and thirteenth centuries. It did so partly because of the sheer number of smallholdings created by assarting, and partly because many standard tenements became fragmented as partible inheritance and sales re-worked them into smaller holdings. The operation of the latter has long been acknowledged for free areas, as the previous paragraph intimated. However, their association was not exact. Recent work on partible inheritance has refined our understanding of it by linking it with areas of weak manorialism and with areas 'where there was enough land for all sons, or where land was not especially significant and the distinction between land and chattels not vital to the survival of the family'.[24] Such areas were largely free but not exclusively so. Areas of villeinage could be involved too. Alienation by sales, and therefore the makings of a land market, also had some efficacy in breaking up villein tenements. Such processes probably proceeded more slowly than in free areas, and may have been halted altogether when and where the integrity of service-bearing tenements was a matter of concern to lords, but it proceeded nevertheless. Even on manors in areas of 'all-pervading lordship', such as that of Kibworth Harcourt (Leicestershire), the symmetry and order which characterized most villein tenements in 1086 could be replaced by a more rough and ready scheme of tenemental fractions. Nor was this a case of thirteenth-century land pressure fostering special circumstances. Work on the Peterborough abbey estate and a unique collection of villein charters has extended this market in villein land back to the twelfth century. The effect of such processes on both villein land and freehold is shown by Kempsey manor (Worcestershire). Between 1182–1299, the number of tenants occupying its 40 yardlands grew by 50 per cent. In addition, the number of rent-paying smallholders around the edge of these yardlands tripled.[25]

Rural Settlement

F. W. Maitland once speculated that many English villages may prove of post-Conquest origin.[26] Modern opinion has shifted to an opposite position. The pattern of village settlement is viewed as complete by 1066, later growth 'extending the frontiers of existing settlements rather than of creating new ones'.[27] For some, this accommodates the entire problem of settlement. All Englishmen lived in villages, said Lennard of Domesday conditions, villages that were within easy reach of each other, 'a world of neighbours'.[28] To declare the village pattern as complete was in effect to say that the entire settlement pattern was complete. However, there is more to the problem than villages. The essence of post-1066 colonization is that it led to new hamlets and farmsteads rather than villages. To construe the problem solely in terms of villages is to confuse rather than clarify the issue. To counter this by warning that 'we must not be too ready to fill the vacant spaces of the Domesday map with imagined woodland and marsh'[29] or point out that Domesday Book lists only the headquaters of some manors, like the Devon manor of Bowley, not their scattered berwicks, is to ignore the numerous studies of post-Conquest settlement actually in birth. For instance, in the Weald, swine pastures or denes used by low ground settlements in the Rother valley can be seen shrugging off their ties and becoming permanently inhabited sites, as with the forest villages of Kirdford and Easebourne. Likewise, in Midland forest areas like Arden, Roberts found that whilst eleventh-century colonization involved peripheral extensions to existing settlements, the process became associated with a more strident independence over the twelfth and thirteenth centuries, with separate hamlets, and then, as the interior parts were opened up, scattered farmsteads developing.[30] A multitude of studies elsewhere, involving such areas as Dartmoor, Charnwood Forest, Nidderdale, Ryedale and south Pembrokeshire, have documented how their basic pattern of hamlets and farmsteads was added to after 1066.

There is another sense in which settlement history was not played out by 1066, a sense more at the heart of Maitland's suggestion. Whether we are dealing with villages, hamlets or scattered farmsteads, it is common to find pairs or groups with a common surname, but which are distinguished from each other by prefixes like East, West or Nether, or by personal appellations like Stratfields Mortimer, Turgis and Saye (Berkshire/Hampshire). Such settlements are conventionally seen as parent-daughter groups created during an early, pre-Domesday growth phase when new filial settlements were packed around the edge of existing ones. Despite this assertion, though, the majority still appear as single settlements in 1086. Even allowing for Domesday Book's infamous shortcomings as a record of settlement, there are ample reasons for believing that the formation of this majority was still a matter of prospect not retrospect in 1086. In fact, many can be seen creeping into extents over the post-1086 period. Thus, the Boldons (Oxfordshire) appear as an integral settlement in 1086, and only as Church, Temple, Steeple and Cowley Boldon in the thirteenth century. In Essex, Domesday Book records a *Hame*, but it is not until the early thirteenth century that the more familiar *Est Ham* and *Westhamma* appear. Furthermore, their formation can be linked to the splitting of settlements into two or more parts.[31] There were various reasons why this splitting occurred. One seems to have been the growing scale of sub-divided field systems. Another was the splitting of vills into different estates. Sales, leases and family arrangements all affected the proprietary structure of vills. As Aston said, 'if the process continued long enough; they led to the sub-division of the villages themselves'.[32]

Changes in settlement morphology add a further dynamic to settlement history after 1066. Sites like Wharram Percy (Yorkshire) reveal that tofts, as well as the positioning of houses within tofts, were capable of repeated change. Particular interest has surrounded those villages in the north and in parts of the Midlands which display a measured regularity in the layout of their tofts and houses. The tofts are planned out along one, two or three row streets, with sometimes a green in between. The length of the streets, the number of tofts, their width and size, all bore a relationship to the fiscal assessment of the village, or its rated value in virgates or bovates. In some cases, this order extended to the village fields, with the sequence of toft occupation being the sequence in which the strips of the sub-divided fields were allocated, the toft being 'the mother of the acre'. Metrological analysis of those in Durham and Yorkshire has established a firm empirical basis for their classification as 'regular villages', and has dated their planned layout (but not their origin as settlements) from the eleventh to the fourteenth centuries, the Yorkshire examples dating from the earlier and the Durham examples from the latter part.[33]

The field systems developed around settlements were a vital component of the medieval spatial order. They could be arranged into subdivided fields or parcels and enclosures held in severalty. There were settlements in areas like the south and east Midlands that consisted entirely of subdivided fields, and settlements in areas like west Wales and south-west England that were wholly several. But their distinction was not always so sharp or exclusive. In the Weald, Chilterns, Midland forest areas, the south-west, and parts of East Anglia and Yorkshire, some settlements combined elements of both, usually, but not always, with a core of subdivided fields and a periphery of several parcels or enclosures. In the case of subdivided field settlements, a further distinction can be drawn between those which appear to have a planned or regular appearance and those whose layout was more evolved or irregular in character (see Fig. 4.3. I–II).

Further variety was added to the mosaic of subdivided fields by the arrangements adopted for cropping. Some subdivided field systems had no communally organized cropping scheme. Instead, cropping had a more *ad*

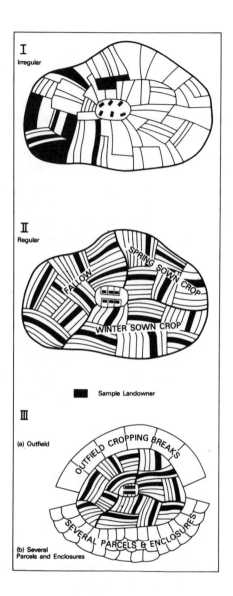

Fig. 4.3. Types of medieval field patterns showing (I) subdivided field system with both irregular landholding and irregular cropping pattern; (II) subdivided field system with regular landholding and three field cropping pattern and (III) subdivided field system with regular landholding and three field cropping pattern plus, on *non*-assessed land; (a) an outfield cropping system, or (b) a system of several parcels and enclosures.

hoc character, reflecting the decisions of individuals or small groups of landholders. Amongst those which adopted some form of communally regulated cropping, the most widespread type was the two/three field system. This came to occupy a broad belt from central-southern England northwards through the Midlands, as far as Lancashire in the north-west and Northumberland in the north-east. For reasons never adequately explained, the variant found along either side of this belt was mostly the three field system: that in the centre, the two field. The former involved the grouping of furlongs into three cropping sectors, one of which was fallow, another under a spring grain and the third under a winter grain each year. The latter simply alternated a fallow with a spring sown grain each year (see Fig 4.3.ii). In short, their differences were of degree not principle. Partly overlapping with the two/three field system, but found mostly in the extreme north, the Yorkshire Wolds, parts of East Anglia, the south-west and possibly parts of west and north Wales, was a form of cropping known as infield-outfield (see Fig 4.3.iii). It comprised an intensive cropping sector, or infield, and an extensive arable/grass sector, or outfield. [34]

Infield-outfield has been described as an archaic system that was once common throughout Britain, but which, in lowland areas, was replaced by the two/three field system from the early medieval period onwards. Without denying that subdivided fields *per se* had a longer and separate history, others prefer to see their communally organized cropping as an innovation largely of this post-Conquest period. Thirsk, for instance, tied the adoption of the two/three field system to the search for more efficient ways of using resources, especially the grazing of harvest stubble, as land became scarce over the twelfth–fourteenth centuries. [35] Another view is that the thinking out of such systems was connected with the re-organization of fields that accompanied the splitting of settlements over the same period. It then spread to other settlements once its benefits of order and increased efficiency had become apparent. [36] Infield-outfield also numbers medievalists amongst its biographers. There have been scholars who rejected its primitive tag and saw its development as contemporaneous with the two/three field system: they thought that the two systems shared the same chronology but were moulded in their differences by the contrasting demands of upland/lowland or pastoral/arable farming. Alternatively, it has been proposed that underlying infield-outfield was a distinction in the tenurial status of land, infield being the original assessed area of a settlement that was measured in virgates or bovates, and outfield a later extension into non-assessed land that was measured in acres. [37] Despite this acred fringe around it, and the break-up of tenements within it, most settlements preserved the overall identity or rating of its assessed core. As Maitland noted when discussing the assessment of Wilburton manor (Cambridgeshire), it maintained 'with wonderful conservatism what we may call its external shape'. [38] This meant a distinction took shape between the assessed core and its non-assessed periphery, a distinction which formed a fundamental territorial divide in the spatial organization of settlements, even where holdings embraced shares of both. Around it was developed a family of spatial structures involving different kinds of farming and landholding contrasts (see Fig. 4.3.III). [39] Infield-outfield was one of them. Typifying other possibilities is Wheldrake (Yorkshire). On its bovated core was a three field system. On its non-assessed land, or *forland*, were enclosures that appear later as laid down to pasture. [40]

Village and Manor

The manor was a unit of lordship whose meaning centred on the co-existence of a demesne worked by customary tenants. As stated above, the balance between these two sides of its character varied. In its wider context, the manor derived further variety from its structural relationship to settlement. Although the ideal manor equalled a single settlement, this was only one of a number of different types of relationship worked out between them. Their exact accordance was commonest in the Midlands and southern counties. Even here, though, the equation of manor with village was not universal. Hilton's study of 95 west Midland villages in the late thirteenth century found that only 45 accorded with a single manor. [41] However, we must be wary of citing his figures as representative of the entire period. Many Midland villages, and many elsewhere, became subdivided into more than one manor during the post-1066 period. For example, Clapham (Bedfordshire) was a single manor in 1086 but five by 1279. In short, the further back in time, the more likely are manor and village to coincide.

Elsewhere, they diverged to a still greater extent. In East Anglia, it was the norm and not the exception for villages to be partitioned between different manors. It was here that feudal geography lay all athwart the village geography. It was here too that peasants, as Bloch put it, belonged 'at one and the same time to two groups constantly out of step with each other; one of them composed of subjects of the same master, the other members of the same village community'.[42] In the eastern Midlands and stretching northwards into Yorkshire was another manorial subtype. The discrete manors of this region, with its scatter of sokelands and berwicks, survived from the pre-Conquest period. Since Stenton first wrote about them, we have learnt to appeciate their parallels in other areas. But whereas the discrete manor of the eastern Midlands, like Retford or Wakefield, comprised scattered settlements mixed up with the land of other manors, those in other regions formed a continuous estate. Thus, the compact manor of Wingham in Kent embraced 30 hamlets. To the west, manors like Brokenborough (Wiltshire) and Taunton (Devon) were also composite structures stretched over a number of settlements. Similar discrete manors can be found surviving into this period over large areas of the north, the shires of the north-east being simply the most clearly labelled. In Wales too, discrete manors were widespread. In the Welsheries, they appear in the guise of the old *maenor*. But even in areas of the March deeply affected by the Normans, the newly created manorial structures tended to engirdle groups of settlements or entire lordships, as with Usk and Radnor manors. Only in south Pembrokeshire did the manor equal a single settlement.

Only by grasping this diversity can we begin to understand Maitland's comment that 'we shall find nothing in common to all *maneria* save a piece of ground' and that whilst we can talk of 'an average manor . . . an average is not a type'.[43]

Assarting and the Problem of Over-population

Postan claimed that post-1066 colonization has all the hall-marks of 'a movement long past its climateric'.[44] Many of the real opportunities for expansion had been utilized. What remained was marginal. This prepares the ground for his argument that, given the restricted opportunities in 1086 and the cumulative growth of population thereafter, it is not surprising if the countryside appears acutely overcrowded by 1300. Such an argument, though, may hurry the history of colonization too quickly. During a period when rural population increased three-fold, conditions must have been radically different at the end compared with the start. It is not necessary to see England or Wales as lacking opportunity for the would-be colonizer of the eleventh century in order to arrive at a Malthusian crisis by 1300. Indeed, there are too many case studies of post-

1066 colonization for us to belittle either its scale or its returns to effort.

Looking forward from the vantage point of 1086, the north (or such of it as was covered by Domesday Book) and the south-west could still be described as wooded landscapes. In the more settled parts of the country, areas like south Essex and the Weald were equally deserving of this description. In addition, there were the legal forests that were given over to the sports of the chase and which were protected by fastidiously maintained forest laws. Their combined extent was vast, embracing as they did parts of Devon and Cornwall, New, Epping and Sherwood forests, Arden, High Peak, the Fylde and areas like Allerdale in west Cumberland. They constituted a large untapped potential, much of poor quality but some of good, that was slowly released for settlement as rising values and demand made their colonization attractive to lord and peasant alike. Taking a direct view, examples of post-1066 colonization abound. They range from inroads made into Dartmoor and Exmoor to the reclamations in the Somerset Levels and Fens, from the substantial assarting which took place in the Weald to the piecemeal efforts in dales like Bilsdale, Rosedale and Newton Dale which cut back northwards into the Yorkshire Moors. Of course, the territorial expansion of freehold mentioned earlier is also a measure of how much was achieved. Together, such evidence forces the conclusion that if land was in short supply by 1300, then it was probably a function of how much demographic growth took place over the twelfth and thirteenth centuries than of how little remained to be colonized in 1066.

The heavily over-populated conditions of the countryside by 1300 was first diagnosed by Postan. His argument was buttressed by an array of material. There was the drying up of the land supply, the cultivation of patently sterile soils, the fall in the size of peasant holdings to levels which threatened their viability and the steep rise in entry fines. There were tell-tale adjustments to peasant farming systems. In southern England, stocking levels fell as cultivation was extended into rapidly depleting pasture reserves. The reduced supply of manure, coupled with the enforced cropping of poor soils, led to a decline in yields, particularly of oats and barley. The crisis which these parameters promised became reality around 1300. By then, land was so impoverished by over-cropping, that there were signs of both demesne and villein land being abandoned. [45] Baker's study of this abandonment using the Nonarem Inquisitiones (1326) has put it in perspective by showing that only certain areas were affected: the northern home counties, Sussex, Shropshire and the North Riding. [46]

Although Postan's diagnosis has been challenged, there is too much substance in it for it not to have some validity. However, more needs to be done on delineating the regional structure of society and economy at this point. Structural elements like the medieval road network, with its strong ordering around a single node or London, may hint at a nationally integrated and responsive society, but most parameters, from livestock prices to the trading areas of medieval pottery manufacturers, suggest otherwise. The imbalance between land and people was no exception, with strong regional differences being apparent. Baker's work demonstrates this. So too does Hallam's comprehensive review of the evidence for colonization over this period. [47] It is also the central theme of Titow's comparison between the manors of Witney (Oxfordshire) and Wargrave (Berkshire) and the Devon manor of Taunton. Having more land on which to expand, conditions in the first two differed markedly from the Malthusian situation that developed at Taunton by 1300, where the land supply ran dryer sooner. [48] At the general level, it can be argued that the empirical support for Postan's thesis is biased towards estates in the south and east. Taunton apart, it is easier to find colonization ongoing into the fourteenth century in the north and west. Attention must also be given to the wider economic structure of regions. Work on the 'diversified' economy of Cornwall, for instance, has shown how its mining, fishing, shipbuilding, trading and industrial activities gave it a buoyancy which separates it from the late thirteenth century trends of Postan's England. [49] Other regions with a diversified economy, like East Anglia or the Forest of Dean, may have had a similar resilience.

The Farm Economy

The farm economy varied both spatially and socially. The main spatial differences were between the arable based systems of the south, east and Midlands and those with a prominent pastoral element in the woodland and open pasture districts. The former have long provided the stereotype models of the medieval farm economy. It was a type coincident with champion England: an area of village settlement, large open fields, strong manorialism and an over-riding concern with grain cropping. The character of the latter has only recently been defined. It was a system based as much on extensive hill pastures, woodland environments, small pasture enclosures, and holdings in severalty as on small subdivided field systems. Where situated in proximity to a town, such areas displayed a fair degree of market responsiveness. The Weald and Chilterns, for example, had specialized interests in sheep, dairy and pig farming, apple orchards and timber production.

Socially, there are also perceptible differences between the farm economy of peasants and that of their lords. The latter was represented by demesne farming. At its height in the thirteenth century, estates like the Archbishopric estates of Kent or a northern estate like that of Bolton abbey in Craven derived at least 40 per cent of their income from selling demesne produce. However, there are regional differences in how such income was earned. In arable areas, demesnes were geared to commercial grain production. They became 'federated grain factories'. In an effort to boost demesne output, some estates carried out improvements, such as introducing sheep folding systems and legumes, experimenting with sowing densities and disentangling demesne from tenant land. But despite this emphasis on grain production, stock were always present. Where resources permitted, such as on Romney Marsh, the Somerset Levels or the Fens, the numbers kept by abbeys like Ely, Crowland, Winchester or Glastonbury were substantial. However, it was the abbeys of the north and west that relied most on stock, especially sheep, for their income. Although lacking the organization of the church, lay estates in the north also kept large sheep flocks, such as those to be found in Holderness, the vale of Pickering or parts of the northern Pennines. The wool produced annually was shipped out via a network of broggers, chapmen and merchants. It says much for the intricacy of this network, and for the scale of flows involved, that Newcastle, a port which had a monopoly over the export of wool, skins and hides from the four most northerly counties, had 122 different merchants dealing in these commodities as early as 1322. [50]

The peasant economy mirrored their lords in that its mainstay was arable in the south, Midlands and east, but pasture towards the north and west. However, these differences were more polarized in respect of the peasant economy. Postan and others have stressed that as peasant holding size fell, their economy became obsessively concerned with grain by the late thirteenth century, to the total neglect of stock: their case has been built up by analyses of peasant holdings in southern-central counties and the west Midlands. It is arguable, though, whether it can be taken as a general condition. Even in the early fourteenth century, there were parts of the south and east, such as the Fens or Weald, where pasture resources were still sufficient in the early fourteenth century to allow a more balanced peasant economy. It is noteworthy too, that in his work on the

1334 lay subsidy on moveable wealth in East Anglia, Glasscock constantly explains high values by relating it to dense local sheep populations.[51] Towards the north and west, the pastoral element in the peasant economy requires no special pleading. For our model of its nature here, we can refer to Thomas' work on north-west Wales or Fox's work on Devon. In the former, the cropping of barley and oats was present but on a limited scale. Virtually all holdings sampled carried stock, with sheep being mumerically dominant but more localized in distribution than cattle.[52] In east Devon, meanwhile, Fox found that subdivided fields were being enclosed by the early fourteenth century, with stock becoming more important not less.[53]

Nor does it follow that the peasant economy had little interest in producing for the market, being too concerned with the problems of subsistence. It was not as commercialized as demesne farming, but there were still many peasants who made the seasonal trek to market. After all, most peasants, including villeins, had some financial obligations. There was also what Postan termed 'the imperfections of the household economy' which could only by rectified by market exchange.[54] However, some peasants were more involved than others. Thus, it has been argued that the areas where demesne production was strongest were the areas where villeinage was strong and labour services most exacting. Indebted with their time and service, peasants in these areas were less deeply touched by market forces, the marketing process being more sustained by demesne production. By contrast, the areas where demesne production was least developed were the areas in which the rent nexus between lord and peasant had largely been monetized. Having obligations measured entirely in cash, the peasants of such areas were drawn more wholeheartedly into a market economy.

The Medieval Town

Although the twelfth century scribe William of Malmesbury described a provincial centre like York as an *'urbs amplissima et metropolis'*, the medieval town boasted neither a large population nor an extensive built-up area. The essence of its urban status is to be understood in its functional role as a trade and market centre. Like other aspects of medieval life, this function had a feudal basis in that the right to hold a fair or market was held off the king or a lord. These rights became packaged in the form of borough status. For this reason, any discussion of medieval towns must begin with the problem of boroughs.

Domesday Book records 111 boroughs. Some were recent, post-Conquest foundations. Others, like London, Bath or York had more ancient roots. Wales on the other hand had only one urban centre, Rhuddlan, by the eleventh century. In scale and character, these early boroughs were modest affairs. The pre-eminent urban centre in 1086, or London, had barely 10,000 inhabitants. In terms of rank order, its nearest rivals, or towns like Norwich and York, had only 5000. At the base of the hierarchy were examples like Hurpston (Dorset), with only five inhabitants in 1086, 'none above the status of a coscet'.[55] It was once authoritatively reasoned that these Domesday boroughs were more rural than urban, 'walled microcosms of the world outside',[56] with a similar occupation structure to the surrounding countryside. The point is reasonable. Towns like Cambridge, Leicester and Lincoln all possessed farm land, let alone the Hurpstons. However, greater stress is now placed on the trade functions of these early centres. This conferred on them a character quite different from their surrounds and demanded a degree of personal freedom that set them apart from rural manors.

In a phase of growth that was underway by 1086, the number of boroughs underwent an impressive increase. The 111 English boroughs recorded in Domesday Book incorporate the early stages of this increase (see Fig. 4.4). By 1300, their total had risen to 480. Boroughs were also established in Wales. As the Normans secured control over the south, there followed in their wake a spate of foundations, such as Cardiff (1081–3) and Swansea (1116). Later, the Edwardian conquest of the north-west was similarly followed by a series of bastide towns replete with borough status, like Harlech (1283) and Caernarvon (1283). Complementary to their increasing number was an increase in size. By 1300, London had grown to 50,000. Ranked behind it were Bristol with 17,000 and York with 8000. A number of others had 4–6000. Naturally, part of this increase was self-generated the rest made up of inward migration. Studies of towns like Stratford, Worcester, Canterbury and York show that most of this townward migration was short-distance, or within 20 miles or less. As one might expect in a gravity formulation, Hilton discovered that in the west Midlands, the larger boroughs like Coventry and Gloucester gained more by migration than the smaller centres like Winchcombe and Dursley. London of course gained most of all.[57] In fact, according to Russell, second and lesser order towns lost ground over this period as regards their share of total population, but London managed to increase its share. [58] An analysis by Thrupp of a 1319 subsidy roll for London showed that half the personal names on it that were based on place-of-origin can be linked to settlement within the Home Counties. The rest were drawn from the eastern counties and the north. [59] By examining the changing dialects of the capital, Eckwall came to roughly the same conclusion, with elements derived from the eastern counties and the north becoming slowly more dominant over its own indigenous dialect

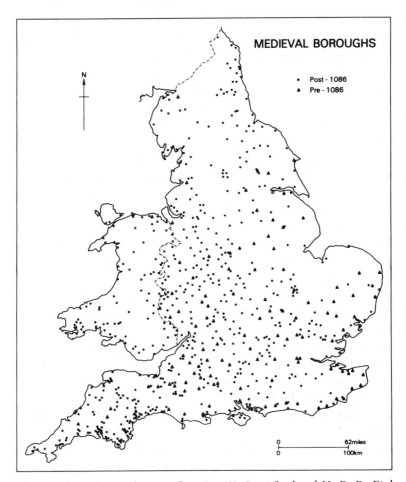

Fig. 4.4. Medieval boroughs. Based on M. W. Beresford and H. P. R. Finberg (eds.), *English Medieval Boroughs. A Hand List*, (Newton Abbott, 1973), pp. 65–193; M. W. Beresford, *New Towns of the Middle Ages*, pp. 532–4.

over the period 1250–1350. Interestingly, the most obvious dialect amongst successful Londoners was that of the east Midlands. Probing into the social background of its migrants, Eckwall emphasized the significant numbers in trade and industry, such as merchants, woolmongers, chapmen, drapers, mercers, skinners, hosiers, vintners and goldsmiths, precisely the sorts of people whose information network would have linked them closely with opportunities in London.[60] Despite the rapid growth in the number and size of boroughs, it does not automatically follow that the country was more urbanized in 1350 than 1086. Wales certainly was, but the case for England is less convincing. In Sawyer's view, the growth of the English urban system only managed to keep pace with the growth of population,[61] a conclusion which Russell's work on rank size appears to endorse.

The legal character of boroughs also developed over this period. At the heart of burghal status was the nature and function of burgesses. These held small parcels of land, or burgage plots, by a free tenure that gave them a place 'outside the feudal ranks of society, i.e. neither knights nor villeins'.[62] As a group, they had a monopoly over the practice of trade or crafts within a borough and, in some cases, for some distance outside. In addition, they were the guardians of a borough's right to hold a periodic market or fair. At first, these rights and privileges were granted out piecemeal, by the king in the case of royal boroughs and a lord in the case of seigneurial boroughs, but later they were granted out wholesale. A further development over the twelfth century was the formation of gilds, whose function was to regulate the practice, standards and entry qualifications of particular trades. Those formed by merchants and cloth weavers were the first to emerge. Such gilds helped institutionalize the borough as a centre of privilege. Their activities remind one of Pirenne's comment that 'freedom, as the middle class conceived it, was a monopoly'.[63] As the power and organization of the borough developed, it began to shake off its ties with particular lords and to establish the right to deliberate in its own affairs: the age of the *liber burgus* or free borough had dawned.

Because so much of their character hinged around certain defined privileges, boroughs continued to display a diversity of size and appearance throughout the period. Many preserved the strong rural side to their character, such as the large demesne and customary acreages recorded in late thirteenth century surveys of Tewkesbury and Fairford. As Tait remarked, the student of the medieval borough 'still has fields on his hands' after the Conquest no less than before. [64] Yet another source of diversity was that whilst some were rural manors upgraded in status, others were new town foundations laid out on a green field site. According to Beresford, 42 per cent of boroughs created in England, 1066–1300, involved some element of planning. [65] In some cases, such as Stratford and Chichester, it amounted to no more than a market place being laid out, a choice which lends credence to Lopez's view that the Commercial Revolution which swept Europe 950–1350 A.D. 'made the market, instead of the public place or cathedral square, the main focus of urban life'. [66] In other cases, like at Northallerton and Chipping Camden, it meant the planning of a single street. More ambitious still were those launched into existence with a comprehensive town plan, such as New Winchelsea or Caernarvon.

It has already been made clear that the mature borough was invested with a combination of privileges. Not all who aspired succeeded so completely. Many towns secured only the right to hold markets. These were the *villae mercatoriae* or market towns. Over 1200 were established in England and Wales, 1232–1350. However, despite their proliferation, we can still identify 'market-rich' and 'market-poor' sectors. Nationally, the market network hints at a system of redistribution rather than reciprocal trade, since the 'market-rich' sectors were not always correlated with areas of densest population. A county like Norfolk had few, but the West Country many. Attempts have been made to measure the density of the market network in a systematic way. A Staffordshire study has mapped the extent to which the different parts of the county lay within 10·6 km (or six and two-thirds miles) of a market. The choice of this distance as the critical measure of accessibility is based on the statements of a thirteenth-century lawyer called Bracton, and what he deemed was the ideal maximum distance to market for would-be buyers or sellers and what, therefore, was the ideal minimum half-distance between adjacent markets if competition was to be avoided. In Staffordshire, it was found that only a tiny pocket in the extreme north was not within 10·6 km of a market. In fact, virtually all the central areas, from the county's western border to the Trent valley, lay within this distance of at least *five* different markets. [67] In another market-dense county, Devon, a similar degree of over-provision can be discerned along the south coast and inland along the Exe valley. This high degree of market saturation reminds us that the pattern of medieval markets as it developed up to 1350 was contrived, a reflection of the eagerness with which lords siezed the opportunity of creating a new and lucrative source of income. It was only later, after 1350, that competition thinned out their ranks, and graded them into service centres of differing rank order. In a sense, the distinction between a borough and a mere market town was a form of grading. But at this stage, there were few clues as to future performance. Initially, hopes were as high for the Hurpstons and Adpars as for the Manchesters and Leeds.

The internal order of the medieval town was profoundly influenced by the fact that residential and commercial uses of land were not segregated. People lived where they worked. Moreover, persons with the same trade or occupation tended to flocculate together, either along the same street or in the same neighbourhood. At York, for example, cutlers were concentrated in St Michael-le-Belfrey parish and Bootham; pinners in St Crux's parish; lorimers and spurriers along Ousegate and Castlegate; girdlers in Girdlergate; tanners in All Saints and North Street; fullers in St Margaret and Walmgate; butchers in the Shambles; fishmongers at the markets on the Ouse and Foss Bridges; and saddlers, cordwainers and skinners on the west bank of the Ouse. This localization of trades, and the social status attached to them, was responsible for most of the socio-economic patterning evident within the medieval town. A central focus of the town's activity was the market place. However, the larger centres, like London, Ipswich or Stratford, usually had more than one, each handling a separate good, such as grain, livestock, dairy produce, poultry, fish, cloth, skins and timber. Such markets did not control trade exclusively, for as Platt observed, 'the failure to distinguish a residential from a commercial sector in the town made of each street a market of its own, the better for being more accessible'.[68]

Medieval Industry

Although we may treat him as such, the medieval craftsman did not see himself as part of an industrial system, but as a tradesman. He worked from his own domestic workshop, with the assistance of an apprentice, and traded his own products. Such trade not only poses problems of where it was located, but of how it was located for its organization as a production process often had strong spatial component to it.

As regards where industry was located, the main centres were urban, at least at the start of this period. Most towns, in fact, boasted a broad range of industries. Thirteenth-century records for Gloucester lists tradesmen as varied as ironmongers, bell foundry workers, cloth makers, leather workers, shipsmiths, parchment makers, needlemakers, hoopers, goldsmiths, glasswrights, soapmakers, girdlers, mercers and drapers. It was not untypical. Few towns, if any, had a specialized industrial economy. Over the twelfth and especially the thirteenth century, the predominantly urban location of industry was progressively broadened by the growth of new centres of production in the countryside. It has not passed unnoticed by scholars that these newer centres were in free or woodland pasture districts. In the case of the premier industry of the day, or textiles, the growth of a rural sector was facilitated by the diffusion of the fulling mill and the ability of rural areas to produce a cheap, competitive cloth in an atmosphere free from the inhibiting restrictions of the gilds. [69] In some cases, it was at the expense of a nearby urban centre: thus, its growth in rural Kent and the west Riding was at the expense of the industry in Canterbury and Beverly. In others, the two sectors continued to exist side by side. Over time, there emerged rural areas whose ties with the industry were exceptional, areas like the south Cotswolds, north Worcestershire, the Mendips and, above all, the villages of Norfolk and Suffolk.

In addition to textile production, there also developed a battery of new, rural industries that were intimately associated with woodland districts. The list included iron smelters, charcoal burners, smiths, bowyers, fletchers, carpenters, wheelwrights, tanners, hurdle-makers, basket-makers, turners, tanners and skinners, all of whom derived their material from woodland environments. Although most woodland districts shared in this growth, like the Chilterns, Cannock Chase, Tutbury Forest, Knaresborough Forest and High Furness, two areas stand out, or the Forest of Dean and the Weald. In both the latter, there developed major concentrations of charcoal burners and ironsmiths, as well as a strong representation of other woodland industries, by the thirteenth century. As in other forest areas, many of those involved were smallholders practising their craft on a part-time or seasonal basis. [70] Open pasture districts witnessed comparable developments for they contained some of the more important mining areas of the country, such as the tin mines or stannaries of Cornwall and Devon or the lead mines of the Mendips, High Peak and Hexhamshire. Iron working was less confined, with mines scattered from the North York Moors to woodland areas like the Forest of Dean. Although some mining communities comprised customary tenants compelled to mine and transport ore for their lord, they were more characteristically of free status. As Finberg said of mining in the southwest, it was a 'mainstay of freedom'.[71] Again in keeping with rural industry generally, many miners were smallholders practising a dual economy.

The problems posed by the organization of early industry are best explored in relation to textile production. The key factor was the fragmented structure of the production process. Like other major industries, cloth production was subdivided into a number of specialist sub-branches, ranging from carding and spinning to dyeing and fulling. Its main urban centres in eastern England, like Lincoln, Stamford, Northampton and Beverley, harboured groups of each. Since each artisan worked from his own dwelling, it was a case of the production line running from house to house, street to street, each stage linked with the next via face-to-face contact at the local market place. The emergent spatial structure of the rural sector was no different. Scattered operatives, engaging all the different branches except the finishing trades, were given focus and direction by the local market. Such diffused extended production systems offer problems of location which the geographer has hardly begun to grapple with, comprising as they did a minimum of fixed capital (plant and equipment) and a maximum of circulating capital (or materials), with the latter taking sometimes months to work itself along what could be a circuitous production line.

A further development of potential significance was manifest in one or two urban centres by the end of the thirteenth century. In towns like Leicester, merchants and dyers began to assert a capitalist control over the cloth industry by integrating carders, spinners, weavers and themselves into loosely bound commercial enterprises. They did so by taking over the role of the market and supervising the through-put of material at each stage of production, eventually disposing of the finished cloth at the great annual cloth fairs at Boston and Kings Lynn.[72] This backward penetration of merchant and dyer capital and expertise affected only the urban sector at this point. The urban/rural complementarity of later centuries was yet to be.

Conclusion

The foregoing review of trends, 1066–1350, or what Braudel might see as a narrative of its conjunctures, has made no attempt to disguise the constant dialectic that exists between those arguments in favour of continuity as opposed to innovation, involution as opposed to evolution, contraction as opposed to expansion, the planned as opposed to the unplanned. Rather than contribute to a synthesis of these conflicting interpretations, the geographer would be justified in seeing them as capturing regional experiences rather than competing views on a national situation. These experiences can be structured around two broad models of development, each capturing the experience of two broad types of *pays*: the strongly manorial as opposed to the weakly manorial, the mainly arable as opposed to the open and woodland pasture districts, the rivers as opposed to the wolds, the forest as opposed to Feldon. However we label them, their distinction is the same. In all facets of life, they displayed important and consistent differences in their development over this period, and beyond.

References

1. H. C. Darby *et al.*, *The Domesday Geography of England*, (Cambridge, 1952–77), Vols. I–VI.
2. R. H. Hilton, 'Freedom and villeinage in England', *Past and Present*, 31 (1965), pp. 3–19; R. H. Hilton, *The Decline of Serfdom in Medieval England*, (London, 1969), pp. 17–24.
3. J. Scammell, 'Freedom and marriage in medieval England', *Economic History Review*, 2nd ser., **XXVII** (1976), p. 524; T. H. Aston, 'The origin of the manor in England', *Transactions, Royal Historical Society*, 5th ser., **VIII** (1966), p. 73.
4. G. C. Homans, 'The rural sociology of medieval England', *Past and Present*, **4** (1953), p. 37; H. E. Hallam, 'The Postan thesis', *Historical Studies*, **15** (1972), p. 222.
5. M. M. Postan, *Essays on the Medieval Economy and Society*, (Cambridge, 1973), p. 286.
6. T. Jones Pierce, *Medieval Welsh Society*, ed. by J. B. Smith, (Cardiff, 1972), pp. 316–22; C. Thomas, 'Social organization and rural settlement in medieval North Wales', *Journal of Merioneth Historical and Record Society*, **VI** (1970), pp. 121–31; G. R. J. Jones, 'Medieval rural settlement in Anglesey', pp. 199–230 in S. R. Eyre and G. R. J. Jones (eds.), *Geography as Human Ecology*, (London, 1966).
7. Jones Pierce, *Medieval Welsh Society*, p. 2; G. R. J. Jones, 'The distribution

of bond settlements in north-west Wales', *Welsh History Review*, **II** (1964), pp. 19–36.

8. J. C. Russell, *English Medieval Population*, (Alberqueque, 1948), p. 54.

9. M. M. Postan, 'Medieval agrarian society in its prime: England', in M. M. Postan (ed.), *The Cambridge Economic History of Europe*, (Cambridge, 1966) Vol. II, pp. 548–632; *idem, The Agrarian Life of the Middle Ages* (2nd edn.) (Cambridge, 1966), p. 562.

10. J. B. Harley, 'Population trends and agricultural development from the Warwickshire Hundred Rolls of 1279', *Economic History Review*, 2nd ser., **XI** (1958–9), pp. 8–18.

11. G. C. Homans, 'The explanation of English regional differences', *Past and Present*, **42** (1969), pp. 18–34.

12. G. C. Homans, *English Villagers of the Thirteenth Century*,(New York, 1960).

13. *Ibid.*, p. 217.

14. H. E. Hallam, 'Some thirteenth-century censuses', *Economic History Review*, 2nd ser., **X** (1958), p. 368.

15. Cited in G. W. S. Barrow, 'Northern English society in the twelfth and thirteenth centuries', *Northern History*, **IV** (1969), p. 14.

16. P. Vinogradoff, *Villeinage in England*, (Oxford, 1892), pp. 158–9; For the Hunts. work cited, see J. A. Raftis, 'Geographical mobility in the Lay Subsidy Rolls', *Medieval Studies*, **XXXVIII** (1976), pp. 385–403.

17. E. Eckwall, *Studies in the Population of Medieval London*, (Stockholm, 1956), p. xli.

18. H. S. A. Fox, 'Going to town in thirteenth-century England', pp. 69–78 in A. R. H. Baker and J. B. Harley (eds.), *Man Made the Land*, (Newton Abbot, 1973), p. 73.

19. The geography of abbeys has been extensively dealt with by R. A. Donkin, See, for instance, R. A. Donkin, 'The Cistercian Order in medieval England: some conclusions', *Transactions, Institute of British Geographers*, **33** (1963), pp. 181–98.

20. A. R. H. Baker, 'Open fields and partible inheritance on a Kent manor', *Economic History Review*, 2nd ser., **XVII** (1964), pp. 1–23.

21. Jones Pierce, *Medieval Welsh Society*, p. 342.

22. W. A. Rees, *South Wales and the March, 1284–1415*, (Oxford, 1924), p. 25.

23. G. R. J. Jones, 'The tribal system in Wales: a reassessment in the light of settlement studies', *Welsh History Review*, **I** (1961), pp. 111–32.

24. C. Howell, 'Peasant inheritance customs in the Midlands, 1280–1700', pp. 112–55 in J. Goody, J. Thirsk and E. P. Thompson (eds.), *Family and Inheritance: Rural Society in Western Europe*, (Cambridge, 1976), p. 117. See also, R. J. Faith, 'Peasant families and inheritance customs in medieval England', *Agricultural History Review*, **XIV** (1966), pp. 77–95.

25. R. H. Hilton, *A Medieval Society: The West Midlands at the End of the Thirteenth*

Century, (London, 1966), p. 122.
26. F. W. Maitland, 'The surnames of English Villages', pp. 84–95 in H. A. L. Fisher (ed.), *The Collected Papers of Frederic William Maitland*, (Cambridge, 1911), p. 91.
27. J. Z. Titow, *English Rural Society, 1200–1350*, (London, 1969), p. 35.
28. R. Lennard, *Rural England, 1086–1135*, (Oxford, 1959), p. 21.
29. *Ibid.*, p. 9.
30. B. K. Roberts, 'Medieval colonization in the Forest of Arden', *Agricultural History Review*, **XVI** (1968), pp. 101–13.
31. R. A. Dodgshon, 'The origin of the two/three field system in England: A new perspective', *Geographia Polonica* **38** (1978), pp. 49–63.
32. Aston, 'The origin of the manor', p. 77.
33. J. A. Sheppard, 'Medieval village planning in Northern England: some evidence from Yorkshire', *Journal of Historical Geography*, **2** (1976), pp. 3–20; B. K. Roberts, 'Village plans in County Durham: a preliminary statement', *Medieval Archaeology*, **16** (1972), pp. 33–56.
34. The most comprehensive review of subdivided fields and their cropping systems is A. R. H. Baker and R. A. Butlin (eds.), *Studies of Field Systems in the British Isles*, (Cambridge, 1973). For subdivided fields, see also R. A. Dodgshon, 'The landholding foundations of the open field system', *Past and Present*, **67** (1975), pp. 3–29.
35. J. Thirsk, 'The common fields', *Past and Present*, **29** (1964), pp. 3–25.
36. Dodgshon, 'The origin of the two/three field system', pp. 49–63.
37. R. A. Dodgshon, 'Infield-outfield and the territorial expansion of the English township', *Journal of Historical Geography*, **1** (1975), pp. 327–31.
38. F. W. Maitland, 'The History of a Cambridgeshire manor', pp. 16–40 in Fisher, *Collected Papers*, p. 18.
39. Dodgshon, 'Infield-outfield', pp. 331–5.
40. J. A. Sheppard, 'Pre-enclosure field and settlement patterns in an English township', *Geografiska Annaler*, **48B** (1966), pp. 59–77.
41. Hilton, *A Medieval Society*, p. 125.
42. M. Bloch, *Feudal Society*, (London, 1962 edn.), Vol. 1, p. 242.
43. F. W. Maitland, *Domesday Book and Beyond*, (Cambridge, 1921), p. 111
44. Postan, 'Medieval agrarian society', pp. 550–1.
45. *Ibid.*, pp. 552–9.
46. A. R. H. Baker, 'Evidence in the "Nonarum Inquisitiones" of contracting arable lands in England during the early fourteenth century', *Economic History Review*, 2nd ser., **XIX** (1966), pp. 518–32.
47. Hallam, 'The Postan thesis', pp. 203–22.
48. J. Z. Titow, 'Some differences between manors and their effects on the condition of the peasantry in the thirteenth century', *Agricultural History Review*, **X** (1962), pp. 1–13.

49. J. Hatcher, 'A diversified economy: late medieval Cornwall', *Economic History Review*, 2nd ser., **XXII** (1969), pp. 208–27.

50. C. M. Fraser, 'The pattern of trade in the north-east of England, 1265–1350', *Northern History*, **IV** (1969), p. 56. The general importance of stock in the north is dealt with in E. Miller, 'Farming in Northern England during the twelfth and thirteenth Centuries', *Northern History*, **X** (1975), pp. 11–14.

51. R. Glasscock, 'The distribution of wealth in East Anglia in the early fourteenth century', *Transactions and Papers. Institute of British Geographers*, **32** (1963), pp. 113–23. See also, H. C. Darby, *The Medieval Fenland*, (Cambridge, 1940), Chapter IV; R. A. Pelham, 'Fourteenth-century England', pp. 230–65 in H. C. Darby (ed.), *An Historical Geography of England Before 1800*, (Cambridge, 1936), p. 241.

52. C. Thomas, 'Thirteenth century farm economies in North Wales', *Agricultural History Review*, **16** (1968), pp. 1–14; *idem*, 'Livestock numbers in medieval Gwynedd. Some Additional Evidence', *Journal of Merioneth Historical and Record Society*, **VII** (1974), pp. 113–7.

53. H. S. A. Fox, 'The chronology of enclosure and economic development in medieval Devon', *Economic History Review*, 2nd ser., **XXVIII** (1975), p. 193.

54. M. M. Postan, *The Medieval Economy and Society*, (London, 1972), p. 198.

55. R. W. Finn, *The Norman Conquest and Its Effects on the Economy 1066–86*, (London, 1971), p. 43.

56. This phrase was used by Tait of Stephenson's ideas. See J. Tait, *The Medieval English Borough*, (Manchester, 1936), p. 68. See also C. Stephenson, 'The Anglo-Saxon borough', *English Historical Review*, **XLV** (1930), pp. 177–207.

57. Hilton, *A Medieval Society*, pp. 183–4

58. J. C. Russell, *Medieval Cities and Regions*, (Newton Abbot, 1972), p. 128.

59. S. L. Thrupp, *The Merchant Class of Medieval London*, (Ann Arbor, 1962), pp. 206–22.

60. Eckwall, *Population of Medieval London*, pp. xl–lxviii.

61. P. H. Sawyer, 'The wealth of England in the eleventh century', *Transactions, Royal Historical Society*, 5th ser., **XV** (1965), p. 164.

62. Postan, *The Medieval Economy and Society*, p. 212.

63. H. Pirenne, *Medieval Cities: Their Origin and the Revival of Trade*, (Princeton, 1925), p. 221.

64. Tait, *The Medieval English Borough*, p. 68.

65. M. W. Beresford, *New Towns of the Middle Ages*, (London, 1967), pp. 271–2.

66. R. S. Lopez, *The Commercial Revolution of the Middle Ages, 950–1350*, (Cambridge, 1976), p. 86.

67. D. M. Palliser and A. C. Pinnock, 'The markets of medieval Staffordshire', *North Staffordshire Journal of Field Studies*, **II** (1971), pp. 49–63.

68. C. Platt, *The English Medieval Town*, (London, 1976), p. 45.

69. E. Miller, 'The fortunes of English textile industry during the thirteenth century', *Economic History Review*, 2nd ser., **XVIII** (1965), pp. 64–82; E. Carus-Wilson, 'An industrial revolution of the thirteenth century', *Economic History Review*, **II** (1941), pp. 41–60.

70. J. Birrell, 'Peasant craftsmen in the medieval forest', *Agricultural History Review*, **XVII** (1969), pp. 91–107.

71. H. P. R. Finberg, *Tavistock Abbey*, (Newton Abbott, 1969), pp. 71, 191.

72. E. Carus-Wilson, 'The English cloth industry in the late twelfth and early thirteenth centuries', *Economic History Review*, **XIV** (1944), pp. 44–7.

5
The Late Middle Ages, c. 1350–1500

R. A. Butlin

Both the distant and the more immediate worlds of the inhabitants of England and Wales were subject to frequent and far-reaching changes in the relatively short space of time between the Black Death and the end of the fifteenth century. These included the relative demise of the feudal power of lordship and the corresponding rise of peasant power, the incidence of the Black Death and a host of other plagues and pestilences, a decline in population size in the second half of the fourteenth century, falls in prices and rises in wages, changes in the management of demesne land and the extent of labour services, a retreat from previously established margins of cultivation, some settlement desertion, changes in the relative terms of trade as between agriculture and urban industry, and the increasing involvement of merchants and the professional classes in rural industry and land purchase.

Yet while there was change there was also continuity: there remained large numbers of settlements which were not abandoned; in many areas open fields remained unenclosed and were managed under a system which showed little or no evidence of 'improved' agricultural techniques; large areas of fen, forest and marsh retained an almost primeval character; and the communications system remained one of low density, making travel slow and difficult, and the movement of goods and produce expensive. The mental horizon and spatial consciousness of the rural inhabitant was largely restricted to the familiar territory and landscapes of village and region. But slowly the mobility of peasant labour, and the travels of soldiers, churchmen and nobles were expanding these horizons. At the same time the growth of London and its demands for people and produce began the disintegration of the existing network of regional economic systems.

Although there is some measure of agreement that changes did take

119

place in the later Middle Ages which affected society and economy, their relative significance, explanation and chronology are still much in dispute. The problem is complicated by the question of scale, for processes and structures which may account for trends at national or macro-regional scales may well differ from those which must be used to explain and identify change at the level of the village and manor. In this chapter the emphasis will be placed on the more general and larger-scale developments, but it must nevertheless be borne in mind that the aggregate society analysed, together with inextricably linked economic functions, was comprised of individuals and family units, [1] working small land units at what was frequently a precarious level of existence. An adequate explanatory framework or model for this period is needed which is capable of identifying the surface or spatial expressions of change and also the underlying and motive structures and processes.

It is possible to identify three principal types of model which have been used to explain change in this particular period, though they relate to a longer time-span. These are: the 'trade' or 'commercial' model, the demographic or population model, and the structuralist model which relates to the transition from the feudal to the capitalist mode of production. In essence the first two of these are economic models, based on the tenets of classical and neoclassical economic theory. The trade model, associated with Pirenne, [2] relates the decline of feudal society and economy in a West European context (evidenced *inter alia* by the decline of serfdom, the emergence of a free tenantry, and the beginning of capitalist agriculture) to the development of trade and the growth and force of the market. This process, mainly effected through the rise of urban centres, was constrained in the fourteenth and fifteenth centuries by the reduction of trade because of natural and political catastrophes and the development of gild restrictions. Objections to this mode of explanation have been articulated by Postan, [3] Brenner, [4] and Nell, [5] mainly in terms of what are felt to be its untenable assumptions: that trade increases the ability to produce and increases agricultural productivity, and that towns benefit more from trade than do rural areas. Little or no consideration is given to the actual terms of trade, to investment, to the possibility of the force of the market possibly intensifying rather than reducing serfdom, and to the fact that serfdom was characterized by the exaction of labour and money dues.

Partly linked to the trade model is the much-favoured demographic or population model. Identified as the 'Postan thesis' or model, [6] its basic precepts are that in the period 1100–1500 there were two major trends, divided by a watershed in the early fourteenth century. The pre-watershed trends included steady increases in trade and population size, the development of trading centres (towns) with independent legal systems, pressure of demand for food supply leading to increased use of marginal land (in both the economic and locational sense), with which were associated increases in prices. These trends slowed in the early fourteenth century and changed direction altogether with the Black Death. As a consequence of the Black Death, demand and supply were reduced. In the countryside, population decline effected the release of marginal, high-cost land from production, a fall in agricultural prices, with a resultant favouring of the terms of trade of the towns (the decline in the market having increased costs and prices in urban industries), and a reduction of the rural labour force. With the decrease of rents, empty holdings, and smaller profits from the demesne, feudal landowners became poorer and in some cases resorted to violence and extortion in an attempt to restore their income and labour services. This model is almost Malthusian in character, for it sees population movements as the main force for change. The debate on the thesis, as it applies to the events of the fourteenth and fifteenth centuries, has taken different forms and directions. It has been argued, for example, that Postan's use of wages and prices as proxy indicators of population change can be questioned, that the basis of his evidence (the estates of the see of Winchester) is regionally atypical and that his views of the course of population change in the fifteenth century and their economic and social consequences are erroneous. There are those who believe that the period of real population decline was restricted in time, perhaps to the period 1348–70, and that thereafter population ceased to decline, though it did not resume an upward climb until late in the fifteenth century. Bean has suggested, in fact, that not only had the decline of English population stopped by the end of the fourteenth century but that this was followed by an increase.[7] He and others, notably Bridbury,[8] now insist on a more optimistic view of the fifteenth century 'as an era of prosperity and enterprise'. They have, according to Hatcher 'found the hypothesis of population increase most appealing', and for them 'the fearsome spectre of recurrent plague, swingeing mortality rates, and a morbid preoccupation of death, are not readily compatible with an age of vitality'.[9] The case against this view has been well stated by Hatcher in the course of his balanced review of demographic change from 1348 to 1530, in which he argues that their reliance on the apparently negative evidence of plagues in the fifteenth century is unjustified. It has also been suggested that the declining fortunes of feudal families in that century was by no means universal. Indeed, the reverse may be true, an assumption which clearly reinforces the case of the 'optimists'. Those which did succumb are explained away as failures because of their own relative incompetence at estate and finance management rather than as part of an inescapable general trend.[10] Additional objections to the Postan thesis include disagreement with his assumption that prices will change as costs change, and the view that by attempting to invoke population change as the initiator of the transformation from feudal to capitalist institutions, 'his argument presupposes the very institutional context, free competitive factor markets, whose emergence it is ultimately supposed to explain',[11] and is therefore circular.

Perhaps the most basic of theoretical objections to the Postan model is one which applies equally to all 'economic' models of change in history, namely that it ignores the social equity side of the equation. Such an objection is most frequently found in the work of Marxist historians on the transition from the feudal to the capitalist mode of production.[12] The basis of the objection is

> that the malthusian cycle of long-term stagnation, as well as other forms of economic backwardness, can only be fully understood as the product of established structures of class relations (particularly 'surplus-extraction relations'), just as economic development can only be fully understood as the outcome of the emergence of new class relations more favourable to new organisations of production, technical innovations, and increasing levels of productive investment.[13]

The argument runs, therefore, that the change from feudalism to capitalism was only possible with a change in class relations (principally the dissolution of serfdom and the undermining of peasant property rights), seen as the outcome of a change regulated by the processes of class formation and rooted in class conflict. Hence the view that 'the rise of trade is not at the origin of a dynamic of development because trade cannot determine the transformation of class relations of production',[14] and the dismissal of the secular malthusian or demographic model, so that in consequence 'the historical problem of the origins of capitalist economic development in Europe comes down to that of the process of "self transformation" of class relations from serfdom to free wage labour—that is, of course, the class struggles by which this transformation took place'.[15] These ideas are part of a powerful body of theory which can shed much light on the social transitions of the late Middle Ages. For example, by means of a comparative study of England and France, Brenner has sought to demonstrate the unsatisfactory nature of the demographic model and, in a separate study, has attempted to demolish the general 'economic determinist framework' (market) mechanism based on the economic theory of Adam Smith and adopted even by some Marxist historians, and has asserted, *inter alia*, that the criteria traditionally employed to chart the decline of feudalism (particularly the commutation of labour dues) are invalid, arguing that 'even after commutation, the peasant-serfs remained unfree, so (were) still subject to the lord's extra-economic exactions on their freedom of movement'.[16] The debate continues, notably in relation to interpretations of the basic terms as 'feudalism', 'serfdom', and 'capitalism', and has broadened with the expanded interest in peasant studies and the formulation of models to explain the development of peasant economies and societies, including the influential Chayanovian model.[17]

It would seem that neither a simple positivist approach nor the analytical and explanatory properties of any one of the three types of model outlined above is, of itself, sufficient for the purpose of identifying the structures, processes and spatial expressions of societies in late medieval England and Wales. What is perhaps needed is a judicious combination of selected tenets of, say two of them, though it could be argued that this is logically impossible. Perhaps the nearest approximation hitherto is the 'network' model outlined by Nell,[18] who sees change being effected through 'technological' developments, including agricultural productivity and population change, which are initially exogenous or partly exogenous but subsequently take on a partly endogenous character because of interaction and feedback once the process of change and development has begun, and which, having initially changed the relations between different economic sectors ultimately 'affect the relations between economic power and military power, thus altering the relations between the classes resting respectively on the possession of the means of coercion, the various types of means of production, and the control of commerce'.[19]

The People of England and Wales in the Late Middle Ages

The evidence for population size, structure, change and mobility is indirect, and open to a variety of interpretations. The most widely used estimates of the total population of England are those of J. C. Russell, whose tentative estimates suggest that there were in 1348 about 3·75 million people in England, that this had declined to 2·2 million by 1377 and by a further small amount to 2·1 million by 1400.[20] About 1430, according to Russell, there began a slow recovery of population, and the estimates for the early part of the sixteenth century suggest figures of between 2·36 and 2·5 million. There are no equivalent estimates for Wales: in the early sixteenth century the population of Wales and Monmouthshire is thought to have been about 275,000, and it has been suggested that 'by analogy with other countries whose population history is better known, the figure was probably higher than a quarter of a million in about A.D. 1300'.[21] The figures for 1377 and 1348 given by Russell are based on the Poll Tax returns for 1377 which are difficult to convert into accurate population totals. Hatcher, by increasing the percentage which Russell allowed for omissions, evasions and exemptions from tax, has suggested a total population of England in 1377 of 2·75–3 million.[22] Allowing for demographic recovery between the major outbreaks of plague (four major epidemics) which occurred between 1348 and 1377, Hatcher has suggested a net decline of about 40–50 per cent, which indicates a population in 1348 of between 4·5 and 6 million, 'with the balance of possibilities pointing to the higher reaches of this range'.[23] His estimate of 2·25 to 2·75 million for the early sixteenth century accords with earlier estimates, and is slightly higher than the lowest point reached by the English population total which in his view occurred in the mid-fifteenth century.[24]

The most recent explanation for this population trend places very heavy emphasis on the effects of major epidemic and infectious diseases on mortality rates, with mortality rather than fertility being the principal factor in population trends. Such factors as wage-rates and the state of the harvest are seen as having a secondary role. Major variations in mortality are not regarded as invariably exogenous, and 'our understanding of the demographic experience of pre-industrial England may be advanced if we cease to regard mortality as either a Malthusian agent of an exogenous force, and instead acknowledge that these two broad categories of mortality coexisted',[25] and were obviously interrelated.

The greatest decimation in the fourteenth century was undoubtedly that wrought by the Black Death, though the nature of its impact on the rural economy is still in dispute. Death from epidemic disease was a commonplace feature of medieval experience: pulmonary disease, dysentery, famine-sickness, typhus, tuberculosis, diphtheria, measles, smallpox and a variety of fevers all took their toll in a seemingly constant procession. Plagues of the pneumonic and bubonic types were particularly virulent. The bubonic plague, whose bacillus lives in the bloodstream of a rat and which is transmitted to human beings by the flea, had been endemic in China, and had been transmitted across Central Asia to the Crimea by 1347, whence it spread across the coastlands of southern Europe.[26] By 1348 it had affected most of Western Europe, and in 1348 and 1349 it reached and spread across the British Isles. The outbreak finished in 1350, but other major plague and fever epidemics of 'national' significance followed in 1361, 1368–9, 1374, 1379–83, 1389–93, 1400, 1405–7, 1413, 1420, 1427, 1433–4, 1438–9, 1457–8, 1463–4, 1467, 1471, 1479–80 and 1485.[27] Although calculations have been made which suggest that some communities experienced population losses of between 30 and 70 per cent[28] from the plague of 1348–9, an overall figure of between 30 and 45 per cent mortality has been thought more realistic, particularly if the principal post-Black Death anomaly (rapid economic recovery and the movements of wages and prices) is to be explained.[29] The older view that the Black Death was a major and cataclysmic influence on the economy, ushering in a period of depression which did not end until the last quarter of the fifteenth century, is no longer thought to be tenable. Bridbury suggests that it is to the later plagues of the fourteenth century, both pneumonic and bubonic, the latter being increasingly confined to the towns, that we must look for the dynamic forces of fourteenth-century history.[30] The acceleration of population decline in the second half of the fourteenth century was but one of a number of interacting factors contributing to change at this time. The end product of this change was the decline of feudal society and economy and its ultimate replacement in the sixteenth century and after by a capitalist type of society and economy. How did this come about, and to what extent can it be explained by 'economic' factors, and to what extent by positive action on the part of those who consciously sought to change or maintain the social order?

The more traditional explanations for the decline of serfdom and the rise in the status, economic well-being and power of the peasantry in later medieval England rest heavily on economic and demographic causes, and are epitomized perhaps by the Postan thesis. One main tenet of this line of argument is that the decline in population, accelerated after 1348–9, produced a shortage of labour, a shortage of tenants, and therefore a decline in the revenues of estates. The labour shortage related to population decline effected a rise in wages and a general fall in prices, thus necessitating statutes restricting the movement of labour and drastic changes in rents, conditions of tenure, the use of demesne land, and the withdrawal from cultivation of marginal land. Two sets of difficulties arise from this explanation, one factual, the other interpretative. The factual difficulties arise from the now agreed facts that agricultural prices did not fall immediately after the Black Death but were maintained at a very high level until the 1370s, and beyond in some cases. [31] Equally, it has been shown that the revenues of many estate holders also continued during this time at levels not significantly below those which had obtained before 1348. There are now numerous examples investigated by medievalists which suggest that the estates of both the higher nobility and ecclesiastical estates enjoyed revenues which rarely fell by more than 10 per cent below pre-Black Death levels. The evidence cited in support derives from estates in Staffordshire, Derbyshire, East Anglia, Kent, the south-western counties, Denbighshire and Monmouthshire, and the ubiquitously scattered estates of the Duchy of Lancaster. [32] A peak of seigneurial rural prosperity has therefore been posited in the early years of the fifteenth century, though prices had begun to fall in the 1370s. The interpretative difficulties arise from attempts to link prices to population change and the need to explain the apparently delayed action of the Black Death of 1348–9. Prices, of course, reflect the behaviour of many variables, including the supply of money, the demand for it and the amount of coinage in circulation, in addition to population changes, so that the simple consideration of population movement alone is unlikely to produce an entirely credible explanation for price and wage changes, even though it may be the weightiest factor. The delayed action or relative ineffectiveness of the Black Death may either be explained in terms of an increase in the exercise of seigneurial power over peasant labour in the form of higher exactions of money and labour dues or perhaps in terms of an increasingly operative peasant opportunism, evidenced through increasing geographical mobility of labour, the speed with which vacant holdings were filled (notably on better quality land), the positive search for improved leases and rent conditions (sometimes leading to conflict and revolt), changes in inheritance systems, the vicissitudes of the land market, and capital formation. Before examining the more overtly spatial aspects of the rural economy, it would perhaps help enlighten an understanding of the processes of change by reviewing respectively the peasant economy and the seigneurial economy.

The Peasant Economy

Of the improving economic and social conditions of the present population of later medieval England and Wales there now seems to be little doubt, even though such improvement did not result in an Utopian golden age for the peasantry, some members of which continued to be poor and landless. The view is now widely held that peasants were not impotent respondents to economic change but that they exercised considerable and deliberate influence on the nature and course of that change. [33] It is possible that those peasants who were able to build up their holdings or even estates and improve their general material condition were in fact the counterparts of the opportunist seigneurs who maintained or even improved their lot, particularly in the fifteenth century, though peasant opportunism may have been more easily practised than its seigneurial equivalent. The hallmark of both was the pragmatic nature of their responses to changing circumstances, responses that were manifest in the considerable geographical variations in the nature and timing of change in both peasant and seigneurial economic conditions.

The prominent features of peasant opportunism in England and Wales in the later Middle Ages were: geographical mobility, mainly in search of better wages and conditions; expansion of land holdings, increased activity in a complex land market, and changes in tenure; an increased involvement in supplementary or alternative forms of employment; increased monetization, and perhaps capital formation; and the regional variations in all these activities.

The geographical mobility of the peasantry has been well documented, notably by Raftis, [34] and by Hilton. [35] Emigration from the 'home' manor was common before the Black Death on the Ramsey Abbey estates, and some immigration also took place, and this relative ease of movement is thought to be related to the 'flexibility' of the economy of the district, to existing marriage patterns, to seasonal labour movement, and to movement in search of additional land. In the 1390s, however, 'more Ramsey villagers began to leave their native homes with permission of the lord than over previous decades. Around 1400 on nearly all Ramsey manors, the trickle of emigration burst into a veritable tide. The exodus was largely illegal.' [36] Control by the lord of the manor over these movements was obviously inconsequential. Many of the emigrants went to other manors of the Abbey of Ramsey, to be employed in the service of other landholders. The nearest manors were those most favoured, and the motives for movement obviously economic. Male migrants included also those practising crafts and professions and their apprentices: tailors, cobblers, smiths, tanners, carpenters, and, less frequently, brewers, pewterers, and haberdashers. Women moved shorter distances from the home manors than men, and normally moved for marriage or for domestic service. Marriage migration also effected an inflow of population to manors. Though much of the movement of women was short-distance, a significant number went to London. [37]

The motivations and patterns of movement of people suggested by the Ramsey Abbey evidence can be repeated elsewhere. Rural migration for the purpose of obtaining bigger and better land holdings held by improved tenures has been identified on the estates of the Bishop of Winchester, on the Cathedral Priory estates in Durham, and the Crowland Abbey estates in Northamptonshire and Cambridgeshire in the immediate aftermath of the Black Death. As Hilton has indicated, this was a geographically widespread phenomenon, which was repeated again towards the end of the century, when evidence for manors in Essex, Berkshire, Worcester and Sussex, indicates a rate of turnover in the order of 50 to 80 per cent in the names of families occupying holdings. [38] Migration to urban centres and industrial areas was also significant, being best exemplified by the flows to industrial villages and towns in Essex, Wiltshire, and Norfolk. [39] Much of the migration was over very short distances, but migration to London and the larger towns was an important feature of the pattern of population movement. London, formerly dependent on the supply of immigrants from the Home Counties, increasingly attracted more and more migrants from farther afield, notably from the Midlands and from East Anglia. [40] The increase in various types of migration after the Black Death was an indication not only of peasant opportunism but also of the loosening of feudal ties, though opportunist migration was not ubiquitous: it was perhaps less common where the power of lordship was maintained in the late fourteenth century, and also in regions where agriculture provided only part of the peasants' livelihood.

Changes in the nature and size of holdings form an important theme in the late medieval peasant economy and perspective. The general picture is one of labour scarcity and land surplus, though in actual regional detail it varies considerably, and it must be remembered that peasant well-being need not derive solely from a holding of land. Postan has suggested that one of the distinguishing features of the late medieval rural economy, in contrast with that of the thirteenth century, for example, is the change in the respective economic fortunes of the three classes of peasant landholder. The general pattern, particularly in the fifteenth century, is seen as one wherein the average size of holding grew, so that the number of larger holdings increased, and that of the smallest holdings decreased. [41] According to Postan the numbers of smaller holdings decreased as their occupants seized the opportunity of acquiring more land during the post-plague relaxation of pressure, thereby promoting themselves into the ranks of middling landholders. The economic conditions of the larger peasant landholders also improved with the new opportunities for land acquisition, though this might be offset in part by the high wages payable for labour and the lower rents obtainable from sub-let land. [42] Because those of middle rank (in respect of the size of their holding) probably did not depend on hired labour to the same extent, most of them benefited from the changes in progress. It would be wrong to assume, however, a fixed tripartite and unchanging categorization of peasant holdings in the late Middle Ages; the situation was fluid and constantly changing, but the general trend appears to have involved an increase in the numbers of larger holdings and a decrease in smaller holdings, though the so-called 'acquisition' of land frequently comprised only short-term leasing of land between peasants. The active land market which is claimed to be such a marked feature of the peasant economy of the period is not one involving high volumes of land sales between peasants, but one where sub-letting types of transaction were more common, so that cumulative and permanent alienation did not result, [43] at least with any prominence.

The inheritance and tenurial conditions of the period are interesting and a picture emerges of 'a kind of half-way stage between the strict observance of inheritance customs and their complete abandonment. Peasants still apparently want to pass on land to their children, but it no longer matters that it should be traditionally "family land".' [44] One of the marked features of the late fourteenth and the fifteenth centuries was the turnover of family names and the prevalence of 'short-stay' surnames. It has been demonstrated by Howell, however, that this might have been only a relatively temporary phenomenon, testifying to the acquisition of land by landless men, with a return to former continuity and stability by the sixteenth century. [45] One of the important features of peasant land which came onto the market, by the extinction during the plague years of the families which held it or by appropriation of the lord, was that in some areas it retained hereditary right when changed from customary to copyhold tenure, whereas demesne land became leasehold without hereditary right.[46]

An important feature of the period was the changeover from customary tenure of holdings to leasehold tenure, which was widespread by 1500. The chronology of change varied: some estates like the Cumberland and Northumberland estates of the Percy family or the Cornish manors of the Duchy of Cornwall had already been converted largely to leasehold before 1350, and short leasehold tenures gained ground on the Prior of Durham's estate after c. 1390.[47] Much of this leasehold land was formerly peasant customary land from which customary status was withdrawn, and which was converted into leasehold. In addition, much of the new leasehold land was land to which customary rules had not applied, such as the lords' demesnes. Areas where the changeover was slow included the estates of Crowland Abbey, where leasehold tenures had not become exclusive even by the fifteenth century. A corollary of the developments in leasehold tenure was the conversion of customary tenures to copyhold tenure, which was well advanced by the mid-fifteenth century and which in some estates carried the connotation of a freedom from the servility and bondage of this type of tenure.[48]

There are clear indications that during this period the peasant economy became substantially monetized and increasingly geared to market production. Hilton has convincingly reviewed the evidence for the west Midlands, and shown that peasant rents, dues and taxes were mainly paid in money, that 'the buying and selling of commodities (of which the most important was ale) between inhabitants of the same village or groups of hamlets within the same manor was an important feature of the peasants' economy',[49] and that many of these transactions were monetary, a fact also reflected in the amount of inter-peasant indebtedness. This is not to say, however, that the 'invisible hand' of a national or international market was beginning to have an effect on the dissolution of manorial and local marketing systems, for the territorial basis of commodity marketing remained 'local', and the influence of the metropolitan market was as yet hardly felt beyond its immediately adjacent districts. Gras's study of the evolution of the English corn market indicates the existence of a multiplicity of local or territorial marketing systems, partly evidenced by his map of 'local price areas' (Fig. 5.1), which represent a stage of transition from manorial marketing systems to the wider influence, felt later in the sixteenth century, of the metropolitan market.[50] The pattern of markets that existed at the beginning of the sixteenth century indicates

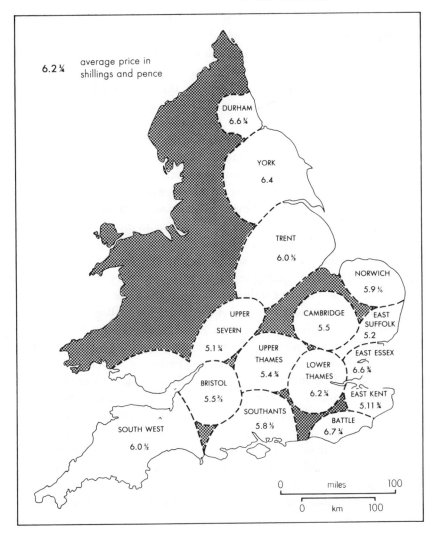

Fig. 5.1. Local price areas for corn for the period 1259–1500. Based on N. S. B. Gras, *The Evolution of the English Corn Market*, (1926), p. 47.

that there must have been a finer network of market centres than the Gras map suggests, for what that map purports to show is the market network for a single commodity, corn, whereas a much wider range of goods was marketed in the town and village markets which comprised the nodal points of the marketing system. [51] It is known that there had been a decline in the numbers of markets between the thirteenth and sixteenth centuries, possibly of the order of one-third, for 'many towns had been founded on a wave of enthusiasm like that of the Railway Age, and were left high and dry when it subsided; for neither kings nor abbots could annul the facts of geography and economics'.[52]

Capital formation by the peasantry in this period was limited, and confined principally to the buying of livestock and the building up of herds, itself a significant feature of the changing agricultural economy of the fifteenth century. The balance of the peasants' capital was used for rent.[53] It is impossible to say whether or not there was an improvement in the standard of living of the peasantry in the later Middle Ages as a result of increased wealth, for there is too little evidence and undoubtedly there were considerable variations both sectorally and spatially, though it has been suggested that there was an overall *per capita* increase in income.[54]

Did the principal trends in the peasant economy in the later Middle Ages result from economic trends alone, or was pressure by the peasantry for better conditions equally if not more important? The inevitable response is that conditions varied. Hilton has demonstrated that in the turbulent decades between 1360 and 1400, village communities demonstrated a solidarity of resistance to measures adopted by manorial lords in attempts to improve their financial position. Resistance to labour services, entry fines, control of the movement of women outside the manor, and the payment of rent arrears is well documented, and the outcome was often one of positive gain or improvement for the peasants.[55] The scale of this type of activity varied from large-scale rebellion, as in 1381, to more localized and less consequential disturbance. Their effect also varied in time and space. In the 100 years after the Black Death, however, there is indication that the balance of forces favoured the peasants, in that their collective expressions of economic and social will were implemented in the context of favourable economic conditions.

The Peasant Economy in Wales

The significant influence of its geography must be recognized in a study of later medieval Wales, but perhaps the most important feature of the period is the changing and dynamic character of economy and society.

The territorial patterns within Wales epitomize the principal political struggles which had taken place during and since the Norman conquest.

The principal distinction to be made is that between the Principality of Wales, comprising the Crown lands in Wales thus designated by the Statute of Rhuddlan (1284), and the Marcher lordships of the east and south. The Principality, together with the Welshries or Welsh areas of the marcher lordships were the regions, mainly of north and west, where Welsh customs remained, though subject to English criminal law. The marcher lordships, in contrast, were semi-independent regions with their own privileged jurisdiction, but holding of the king of England and owing homage and fealty.[56] The marcher lordships were characterized by manorial systems, castles, arable cultivation, feudal land tenures, and towns and villages. The spatial pattern of what has been called 'manorial cultivation' is interesting, the principal centres being (Fig. 5.2) along the south coast from Monmouthshire to Pembroke, in some of the inland valleys, and along the English border.[57] The actual percentage of the area of Wales characterized by Norman manorial systems was small, and in the greater part of Wales the social structures, and settlement and economic systems still derived, even as late as 1500, almost entirely from native institutions and traditions. The late Middle Ages were, in Wales as in England, times of change. The main changes have been characterized by C. Thomas as the creation of new attitudes towards traditional practices and inheritance customs as a result of uneven mortality rates and the spread of a money economy, and the increase in landed estates, initiated by the growth of a land market, augmented by purchase, lease, or illegal encroachment.[58] Detailed regional and local studies of later medieval Wales are still insufficient to test the degree of applicability of this useful general statement, but such studies as do exist enlighten the processes of change at work. Jones Pierce's study of later medieval Caernarvonshire has highlighted some of them.[59] The Black Death and subsequent pestilences, and, in 1400, the Glyndŵr rebellion, 'depopulated and impoverished the rural areas, dislocated the machinery of finance, and assisted by modifications in the law relating to real property, hastened on the transition from medieval to modern agrarian conditions'.[60] In an area where free townships (township = *tref*) were numerically dominant in almost every commote (*cwmwd*), the power of the bondmen was very much less than their English equivalents, the villeins, in a context of greater burdens and strains. Commutation of dues and services had not changed the personal status of the villein nor lessened his bond to the soil, so that depopulating plagues and revolts (though varying widely in effect) frequently increased the difficulty and strain by increasing dues payable

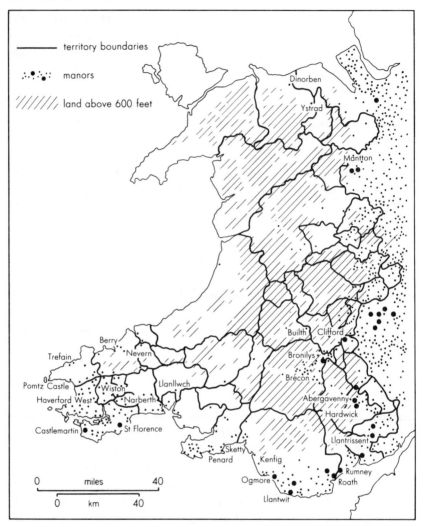

Fig. 5.2. The manors of Wales in the fourteenth century. Based on W. Rees, *An Historical Atlas of Wales*, (Faber and Faber, 1959), plate 47.

and the degree of debt. Direct action by the bondmen/villeins was impossible, and it was by means of the direct rebellion of other classes in the early years of the fifteenth century that the burden was lightened, albeit temporarily. In the longer term, the difficulty of attracting free tenants to bond land at the disposal of the Crown after the rebellion (for bond land could lead by prescription to bond status), and the illegal encroachment of such land by freeholders led to the emancipation of bondmen of the three shires of north Wales in a charter of 1507. The transformation of the agrarian structures of the free townships took a different course, involving the dissolution of both the organic territorial structure of the land of the *gwely* (see p. 94) via the concentration of holdings by purchase, mortgage and exchange, and by the dissolution of the social structures of the *gwely*, the outcome of both processes ultimately being the transformation of a hamlet into a consolidated farm.[61] Forfeiture of Welsh land to the Crown for felony and other reasons led to a new theory of tenure, the forfeited holding being granted in fee or lease in the English fashion. Parallel to the consolidation of hamlets was the rise of large freehold estates. The turbulent years of the late Middle Ages brought large quantities of both free and bond land to a land market, via the agency of the Crown, whence it could be purchased and leased, and used to build up an estate, a process which often led to consolidation of land, enclosure, and the dispersion of settlement.[62] One of the most effective factors in the building up of estates was the use of the arrangement known as *prid*, that is the mortgage or lease of native land for a short term, which was renewable. This provided 'the one loophole through which large-scale, permanent alienation of land could be brought about without trespassing unduly on native custom'.[63]

The Seigneurial Economies of England and Wales

Against the Postan thesis, a new view has been put forward that the period was not one of unremitting decline for all landowners as a result of demographic change and economic stagnation, rather that it was the competence of individuals in the management and administration of their estates that determined their well being or otherwise.[64] This argument has been supported by evidence from what have been termed 'prosperous' estates, including those of Christ Church Priory, Canterbury and other estates in Kent, the east Midland properties of the Grey family of Ruthin, and the estates of Tavistock Abbey.[65] Hatcher, however, has argued that these instances were to some extent exaggerated in respect of their degree of prosperity, and in other instances were not typical of the regions in which they were located. He suggests, for example, that the wealth of the Hungerford family who had extensive sheep farms in Wiltshire and of the Percy family (whose estates were large and widespread geographically) derived from the 'accumulation of more lands rather than the extraction of greater profits from existing lands', and from high salaries of royal office. His view of the fifteenth-century experience in England is one of a substantial and widespread agricultural depression, expressed by declining production and declining demand for land.[66] One of the obvious difficulties in any attempt to clarify this question is the problem of isolating that part of baronial incomes deriving from estates, while an additional problem is the quality of the evidence. An interesting feature of the period is the identification of regional variations in economic development including a 'highland zone' pattern characterized by decline in the early fifteenth century followed by a long depression, associated with decline in income from demesne lands, and an increase in vacant copyholdings, reflecting not just agrarian depression but also loss of income from seigneurial privilege, including the control of justice and commerce. The instability of the marcher areas of both Wales and northern England was also a potent force.[67]

One of the important conclusions to be made about the seigneurial economy in this period is that there appears to have been little scope for financial improvement. Attempts to recover a deteriorating situation include the leasing of demesnes and the abandonment of direct cultivation (which was partly responsible for the contraction in the amount of land cultivated), shifts to sheep-farming, easing of the terms of tenancy, and reductions in labour services, rents, and fines. Attempts to enforce the old order were generally unsuccessful, an indication that peasant economic opportunism was more powerful than seigneurial privilege, at least until the later fifteenth century, when the situation began to change again.

Agriculture

The complex mosaic of fields, farms, cultivation and land-use systems of this period are the surface expressions of the complex interactions between the varied physical environments and the social, tenurial and demographic systems which influenced the nature of their exploitation, and the economic context in which farming was carried out. Considerable regional variations existed in agricultural emphases, and much of the effort of recent research has been devoted to the identification and character-ization of these regional patterns and has initiated a series of debates on the origins of regional variations and associated structures. Thirsk has outlined a division of England into two principal farming types of region, divided by a line running from Tees in the north-east to Weymouth in the south-west. [68] To the north and west of this line is the 'pastoral zone', and to the east and south the 'lowland zone of mixed husbandry'. The pasture-farming regions of England were principally concentrated in the upland pastoral zone, but pasture farming was also practised in the forest and fen areas of the lowland zone. Because of low population density, the existence of large areas of pasture and waste, and topographic and climatic conditions, the characteristics of the systems which were found in this zone were an emphasis on livestock husbandry and great flexibility of land use, a fact reflected in the very wide variety of field systems. The lowland zone of mixed husbandry was characterized by a greater emphasis on arable farming and less flexible management systems. In contrast to the generally smaller settlements of the pastoral zone, the larger village settlements which were common in the lowland zone were strongly manorialized, with villagers bound by manorial obligation, though the picture, as shown above, was changing rapidly in the fifteenth century. In pastoral regions the bonds that existed were often based on kinship, and the systems of land inheritance reflected this fact. A similar two-fold classification of farming regions has been made for Wales, [69] in this case the distinction between the pastoral stock-rearing uplands of southern central and northern Wales, and the mixed farming lowlands, namely Anglesey, Llyn, the Border lowlands of Flint and Denbighshire with the Vale of Clwyd, the central Borderlands, lowland Gwent, the Vale of Glamorgan, Gower, Pembrokeshire and south-west Wales.

The complexity of agrarian systems, even within these broad farming regions, is well reflected in the almost infinite variety of field systems. [70] The broad pattern of field systems known to have existed in late medieval England and Wales does not differ substantially from the pattern outlined by Gray in 1915. [71] The outer limits of Gray's Midland zone of classic open-field systems have been extended, for example, to include the lowlands of north-east England, but the core areas of arable cultivation remains the band of country stretching south-west to north-east across the Midlands, wherein the dominant characteristics were the ubiquitous presence of large arable fields internally subdivided into unenclosed strips. The holdings of villagers comprised a series of strips variously scattered over the three or more fields, and the crop rotations employed were usually common to users of the fields, though the rotations varied from place to place. Even within the Midland zone there was, however, considerable variety in the forms and functions of the fields and field systems. For the west Midlands Roberts has made the distinction between the regular champion systems with standard tenemental units, comprising three, four or multiple fields, and irregular woodland field systems lacking standard units.[72] For the east Midlands, Thirsk has identified three types of field system: the system of the hill and vale regions, of the fen regions, and of the forest regions. The system of the hill and vale regions is that most similar to other districts of lowland England.[73] The field systems of the upland or highland regions of England and Wales differed from the lowland systems usually in respect of the amount of arable involved, for the growing of corn was not the main objective, and in the more frequent use made of the extensive pasture and waste grounds for 'intakes' of land for temporary use as arable.[74] To the east and south of the Midland belt lay a zone of differing field systems, notably those of East Anglia and Kent. The East Anglian systems were probably more complex than their classic Midland counterparts, evidenced by cropping and foldcourse shifts, the presence of infields, outfields and brecks, and the flexibility of tenurial practices.[75] The systems of Kent and neighbouring areas were different again, for in Kent the presence of subdivided fields did not necessarily indicate common cultivation and grazing practices, quite the contrary in fact.[76] The field systems of Wales bore semblance to the upland/lowland systems across the border, at least in form, though regional experience and tenurial practice varied considerably.[77]

Field systems were, of course subject to evolution and change. The Thirsk model of a gradualist evolution of the field systems of Britain,[78] related to the pressure of population on land, has now widespread acceptance, though some would place greater emphasis on the social organization of the communities which created and developed the systems.[79] The most extreme form of structural change was enclosure, and there is evidence of its progress, preceded by holding consolidation, for many areas. Fox, in an investigation of the field systems and enclosure history in medieval Devon, has demonstrated that the enclosed fields of south Devon resulted from an 'enclosure of subdivided fields which had taken place for the most part during the later middle ages as a rationalisation of farm layout in a period of slack demand for land', and that in east Devon enclosure of subdivided fields was also a significant process, though for different reasons in different areas.[80] The emergence of a pastoral farm economy in south Devon, linked to that of a rural textile industry, were perhaps the principal reasons for enclosure in that area, whereas in east Devon enclosure was both a spontaneous and deliberately rational response to agrarian depression, with decreasing demand for arable products weakening the viability of holdings and thus holding down population size and encouraging emigration, and inflexibility of the economy failing to stimulate industrial development. Both regions were able to enclose by 1500 because of the relative flexibility of their field systems, and it would appear that this was also an important permissive factor in other parts of England, such as north-west England, Northumberland, and the Welsh Borderland. Enclosure was experienced elsewhere: it appears to have been extended in the Midland open-field territory during the mid-fifteenth century, while gradual enclosure from forest and fen also took place in such regions as the Weald and the fenlands of eastern England.

The persistence of open fields needs perhaps as much explanation as their disappearance. McCloskey has suggested that they persisted because peasant farmers adopted a rational approach to survival in conditions of uncertainty. The fields and the scattered holdings are thus seen as behaviour to counteract risk. [81] This idea has some merit, but it must also be recognized that in regions where manorial control was strong and land in short supply, enclosure was difficult to achieve even by progressive rational peasants, though by the same token unilateral action to enclose by the lord of the manor was not difficult. An important question which remains unanswered and which has some bearing on the persistence of open fields is that of the exent to which open-field systems inhibited improvements in agricultural techniques and production. Assumptions have been made that late medieval agricultural practices were static and non-progressive, but interesting local evidence is coming to light that post-Black Death reductions in the area of arable cultivation may have resulted in changes in cultivation techniques and rotation practices and a closer approximation to up-and-down husbandry thereby anticipating the important changes in this respect which occurred after 1500. [82]

Rural Settlements in Late Medieval England and Wales

This broad and complex topic is difficult to condense, and only the more general trends will be considered here. Settlement desertion is one of the more important themes: sufficient detail is now known about its chronology to suggest that desertions in the immediate aftermath of the plague or during the late fourteenth century were limited, and mainly experienced in areas of marginal agriculture.[83] The major impetus towards desertion seems to have come in the second half of the fifteenth century with the beginnings of a major change in land use from arable to pasture, from crop cultivation to sheep rearing and wool production, and with the regaining by landowners of some of the power which they had lost. Studies of Midland counties well illustrate these trends: in the period c. 1350–1450, the percentages of village desertions (that is of all known deserted villages) were 17 per cent in Northamptonshire, 12 per cent in Leicestershire and 30 per cent in Oxfordshire, whereas the figures for the period 1450–1700 were 60 per cent, 60 per cent and 45 per cent respectively.[84]

The re-ordering and re-structuring of village and settlement unit morphology seems also to have been an important feature in this period. The migratory habits of the East Anglian village over a long period of time have been outlined by Wade-Martins: his study of Longham village in Norfolk indicated two major shifts of site, from the original mid-Saxon site, the first from the twelfth to the late fourteenth century, the second beginning probably in the fifteenth century. Evidence of late medieval village shrinkage is provided by Norfolk villages where gaps were left between surviving dwellings.[85] Profound changes in the settlement patterns in late medieval Wales have also been documented, with the small nucleations prevalent during the early Middle Ages giving way more and more to a dispersed pattern of single farmsteads.

Our understanding of architectural and building history of the late Middle Ages has made considerable progress in recent years. Vernacular architecture in particular has received much attention, notably in respect of building materials, methods of construction, plans, and finish, and their regional variations.[86] It has been suggested that two great 'plan families' can be identified in England and Wales: one where the dwelling and cattle byre are linked, typified by the longhouse and (to a lesser extent) the laithe house; the second comprising separate dwellings and farm buildings.[87] The longhouse, rectangular in plan, had low walls constructed of turf, stone, timber or earth, and a thatched roof. This house type was typical of the Highland Zone. The laithe house was characterized by the absence of a cross passage, so that its dwelling, barn and byre sectors had separate entrances: this plan is found in the Yorkshire Pennines. The lowland plan type in the Middle Ages 'comprised three units, the solar or private room

. . . the hall or general living space, and one or more rooms used for the storage of food and drink and usually known as service rooms'.[88] Important regional house types were the open-hall houses of the south-east, the Pennine aisled halls, and the cruck-built open hall type. It has been asserted that 'the history of late medieval vernacular housing is essentially that of medium-sized open-hall houses', many of which reflect the emergence of a new class of landowner.[89]

In Wales architectural geography evidences both north-south and east-west contrasts. The eastern borderland, characterized by storeyed houses, had very high standards of material culture on account of ease of access to the markets of the west Midlands and exposure to new ideas of construction. West Wales, in contrast, has been associated with the single-storeyed cottage, with earth or stone walls, in contrast to the timber-building of the east.[90] The contrasts between north-west and south-east are indicated by the superior carpentry of roof and partitions in the former, but its relative poverty in the latter, and also by what have been called 'features of gentry pretension', such as the aisle-truss and hammer-beam late medieval roof structures, found mainly in the north.[91]

The period 1350–1500 was also marked by the building or rebuilding of large numbers of churches and the construction of castles and bridges. The types of church constructed ranged from the numerous private oratories and chapels to the massive structures in the Perpendicular Gothic style characteristic of churches built in south-west England at this time. Church towers are common features deriving from this period, the most striking being those associated with prosperity deriving from local industrial development, notably the wool industry.[92] The construction of houses with moated sites continued to about 1500, with the style of house and form of moat being fairly clearly status-related features.[93]

Towns, Trade and Industry

The rural economy of England and Wales in the late medieval period was not a self-contained, autonomous sector, but part of an integrated and interlocking economic system which included centres of purchase, sale and redistribution, and processing. The historical geography of central places, marketing, industry and urban development in the late Middle Ages has been subject to varied interpretation on account of the contrasting views of the period as either one of growth or one of stagnation and decline. Thus, as far as urban history is concerned,

> The interpretation which has almost assumed the status of orthodoxy is one of degeneration from the churning vitality and political promise of earlier times. War and agrarian 'retreat' into peasant subsistence farming sapped at the foundations of urban economies; much urban land had fallen into the 'dead hand' of the church, whose indifference to economic considerations prevented real estate development and urban capital accumulation; urban rents collapsed; empty tenements abounded; gilds became restrictive societies for the jealous protection of dwindling markets, and oligarchies crystallised to preserve what was left for the few.[94]

This hypothesis has, in fact, been disputed, both at the level of generalized polemic[95] and at the more specific empirical level: a study of late medieval Gloucester, for example, has indicated overcrowding, new building, and lay and ecclesiastical investment in urban property.[96]

The pattern of towns, markets and fairs is of interest. The greatest number and highest density of 'central places' comprised the small market centres, with populations of between 500 and 1500. Their market function was basic to both the rural and urban economy, hence their ubiquitous distribution. This type of town formed the base of a pyramidal urban hierarchy, and it has been estimated that in 1500 there were about 500 or 600 of them in England, to which perhaps should be added 50 in Wales.[97] Such towns were far removed in character and landscape from larger provincial capitals and from London itself. They were rural in atmosphere, but differed from village market centres in the amount of industrial and commercial activity and employment. Many of them were not highly specialized in function, simply providing services and manufactured goods for the small hinterlands which they served,[98] and generally lacking the complex urban institutions of the larger towns and cities. Next up the urban hierarchy were the regional centres, with populations between 1500 and 5000 by 1500, some of which were ports, others with specialized industries, and others multifunctional county towns, such as Lincoln, Chester, Preston and Leicester.[99] At the top were the major towns and cities, and the largest of all was London, with a population of about 60,000. The others included Bristol, Norwich, York, Exeter and Newcastle, with populations in excess of 7000. These major provincial capitals served large market areas with a very wide range of goods, and also functioned as important political and ecclesiastical centres.[100] Their administration required special offices and institutions: courts, councils, gilds, mayors aldermen and recorders, and was reflected in organized ceremony. [101] London was at the apex of the urban pyramid, with a complex urban society and landscape. By the end of the fifteenth century it was beginning to erode the regional marketing system of late medieval England through its demands for foodstuffs and other goods for consumption and trading, and asserting itself as a truly national centre of influence.

The nature of industrial development at this time is fairly well known, and resulted in changes in both rural and urban economies. The best known instance of industrial growth is that of the textile industry, developing against a background of aid in export markets by export duties, giving price advantages, and of labour costs kept down by the use of fulling mills powered by water and saving on dyeing costs in the case of undyed cloths. Development occurred mainly in rural areas of pastoral economies where time was available for peasants to engage in a supplementary occupation, and where gild restrictions of the towns did not operate. Changing technology and organization also played a part. The general increase in *per capita* wealth also increased demand from the home market, which was largely supplied by native cloth after the mid-fourteenth century. The major contrasts between the English textile industry in the late Middle Ages and its continental counterparts in Flanders and Italy were the predominantly rural location in England and the later development in England of the merchant class and of inter-regional trade. [102] The major producing regions included Wiltshire and Gloucestershire, producing broad cloth for export, the West Riding of Yorkshire, producing a lower grade of cloth for the home market, the worsted region of Norwich, and the traditional cloth regions of Essex and Suffolk which gradually became more specialized in the fifteenth century, and the cloth-producing region of Devon and Somerset. [103] The extractive industries in this period are thought to have experienced a rise in *per capita* production, notably tin, coal and iron. The iron industry is a good example of technologically innovative response to labour cost pressure, resulting in improved output. The main centres of iron production were the Weald, the Forest of Dean and the Cleveland Hills. [104] Over this period the Tyne valley was the principal centre of coal production, while tin was mined in Cornwall, where the mining of tin, lead and silver competed with agriculture for labour and investment and also stimulated demand for agricultural produce. [105]

A distinguishing feature of the late Middle Ages is the increase in the value of English trade, resulting from the change from the export of raw wool to the export of more profitable finished cloth. Cloth export markets were widened, the principal markets being in the Low Countries, with smaller markets in the Baltic region and the Mediterranean. The story is not, of course, one of continuous prosperity for cloth or any other

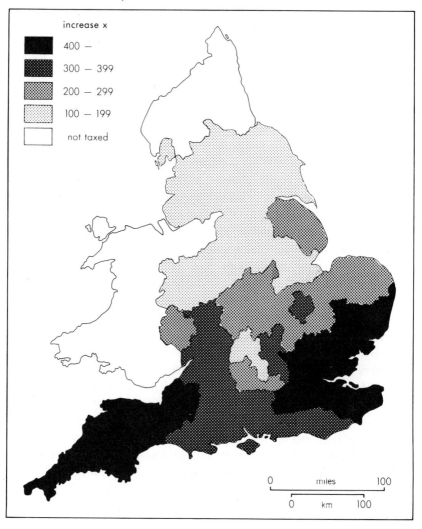

Fig. 5.3. Rates of growth of lay wealth, 1334–1515, from R. S. Schofield, 'The distribution of wealth in England, 1334–1649', *Economic History Review*, 2nd ser., **XVIII** (London, 1965). p. 99.

exported product, and the trade slump of the mid-fifteenth century badly affected places like York, and also some of the Devon cloth towns.[106] The export of cloth in the mid-fourteenth century was principally from London, Yarmouth and Bristol, but by the end of the fifteenth century London was dominant. However, export trading must not be over-emphasized, for the domestic market was very important, and most products sold on the home market. They were distributed mainly by road and to a much lesser extent by river and coastal transport, notwithstanding the limited 'main' road network, and the poor state of other roads.[107]

Conclusion

It is impossible to summarize the main aggregate effects of the change over the late Middle Ages, except perhaps through their impact on the regional distribution of wealth. No calculations have yet been made for Wales, but crude statistical assessments, based on tax records for England demonstrate apparent shifts in the regional wealth pattern, highlighting the increasing importance of the south-west and of London and the Home Counties (Fig. 5.3) and the cloth regions of East Anglia.[108] This new pattern of wealth owed a great deal to the cloth industry, but any attempt to explain the pattern must take into account the wide and complex matrix of economic and social factors which interacted, to variant geographical effect, in the late Middle Ages.

References

1. J. A. Raftis, *Tenure and Mobility. Studies in the Social History of the Medieval English Village*, (Toronto, 1964), p. 11.
2. H. Pirenne, *Economic and Social History of Medieval Europe*, (London, 1936).
3. M. M. Postan, 'The chronology of labour services', *Transactions, Royal Historical Society*, 4th ser., **XX** (1937), pp. 192–3; and, 'The rise of the money economy', *Economic History Review*, **XIV** (1944), pp. 123–34.
4. R. Brenner, 'Agrarian class structure and economic development in pre-industrial Europe', *Past and Present*, **70** (1976), pp 30–75.
5. E. J. Nell, 'Economic relationships in the decline of feudalism: an examination of economic interdependence and social change', *History and Theory*, **VI** (1967), pp. 313–50.

6. M. M. Postan, 'The fifteenth century', *Economic History Review*, **IX** (1939), pp. 160–7; *idem*, 'Some economic evidence of the declining population of the later Middle Ages', *Economic History Review*, 2nd ser., **II** (1949–50), pp. 221–46; *idem*, *The Medieval Economy and Society*, (London, 1972).

7. J. M. W. Bean, 'Plague, population and economic decline in England in the later Middle Ages', *Economic History Review*, 2nd ser., **XV** (1963), pp. 422–37.

8. A. R. Bridbury, *Economic Growth England in the Later Middle Ages,* (London, 1962); *idem*, 'The Black Death', *Economic History Review*, 2nd ser., **XXVI** (1973), pp. 557–92.

9. J. Hatcher, *Plague, Population and the English Economy 1348–1530*, (London, 1977), p. 15.

10. A. J. Pollard, 'Estate management in the later Middle Ages: the Talbots and Whitchurch, 1383–1525', *Economic History Review*, 2nd ser., **XXV** (1972), pp. 553–66.

11. Nell, 'Economic relationships in the decline of feudalism', p. 325.

12. M. Dobb, *Studies in the Development of Capitalism*, (London, 1946); E. Kamenka and R. S. Neale, *Feudalism, Capitalism and Beyond*, (London, 1975); R. H. Hilton et al., *The Transition from Feudalism to Capitalism*, (London, 1976).

13. R. Brenner, 'The origins of capitalist development: a critique of neo-Smithian Marxism,' *New Left Review*, **104** (1977), pp. 25–94.

14. *Ibid.*

15. Brenner, 'Agrarian class structure'.

16. Brenner, 'The origins of capitalist development'.

17. R. H. Hilton, *The English Peasantry in the Later Middle Ages*, (Oxford, 1975), Chapter I; J. Banaji, 'The peasantry in the feudal mode of production: towards an economic model', *Journal of Peasant Studies*, **III** (1976), pp. 299–320; A. V. Chayanov, *The Theory of Peasant Economy*, (Illinois, 1966).

18. Nell, 'Economic relationships in the decline of feudalism'.

19. *Ibid.*, p. 332.

20. J. C. Russell, *British Medieval Population*, (Albuquerque, 1948).

21. F. V. Emery, 'The farming regions of Wales', in J. Thirsk (ed.), *The Agrarian History of England and Wales, Vol. IV 1500–1640*, (Cambridge, 1967), p. 142.

22. Hatcher, *Plague, Population and the English Economy*, p. 14.

23. *Ibid.*, p. 69.

24. *Ibid.*, p. 69.

25. *Ibid.*, p. 72.

26. N. J. G. Pounds, *An Economic History of Medieval Europe*, (London, 1974), pp. 151–2.

27. Hatcher, *Plague, Population and the English Economy*, pp. 17–18.

28. Russell, *British Medieval Population*, pp. 215–18, 221–6, 232–5; A. E. Levett and A. Ballard 'The Black Death on the estates of the See of Winchester', in *Oxford Studies in Social and Legal History*, (Oxford, 1916), Vol. V; J. F. D. Shrewsbury, *The History of Bubonic Plague in England* (Cambridge, 1970).

29. Hatcher, *Plague, Population and the English Economy*, p. 25.

30. Bridbury, 'The Black Death', p. 588.

31. Hatcher, *Plague, Population and the English Economy*, p. 50; J. E. T. Rogers, *Six Centuries of Work and Wages*, (London, 1884).

32. G. A. Holmes, *The Estates of the Higher Nobility in Fourteenth-Century England*, (Cambridge, 1957); Hatcher, *Plague, Population and the English Economy*, p. 32; R. A. L. Smith, *Canterbury Cathedral Priory: A Study in Monastic Administration*, (Cambridge, 1943); R. Somerville, *The Duchy of Lancaster, 1265-1603*, (London, 1953); J. A. Raftis, *The Estates of Ramsey Abbey: A Study in Economic Growth and Organisation*, (Toronto, 1957).

33. R. H. Hilton, *The Decline of Serfdom in Medieval England*, (London, 1969), p. 57.

34. Raftis, *Tenure and Mobility*.

35. Hilton, *The Decline of Serfdom*, pp. 32–43.

36. Raftis, *Tenure and Mobility*, p. 153.

37. *Ibid.*, p. 180.

38. Hilton, *The Decline of Serfdom*, pp. 33–4; C. Howell, 'Peasant inheritance customs in the Midlands 1280–1700', in J. Goody, J. Thirsk and E. P. Thompson (eds.) *Family and Inheritance*, (Cambridge, 1977), pp. 112–55.

39. Hilton, *The Decline of Serfdom*, pp. 32–3.

40. C. Platt, *The English Medieval Town* (London, 1976), p.90.

41. Postan, *The Medieval Economy and Society*, p. 156 *et seq.*

42. *Ibid.*, p. 157.

43. Hilton, *The English Peasantry in the Later Middle Ages*, pp. 41–7.

44. R. J. Faith, 'Peasant families and inheritance customs in medieval England', *Agricultural History Review*, **XIV** (1966), p. 89.

45. Howell, 'Peasant inheritance customs' pp. 130–1.

46. *Ibid.*, p. 132.

47. R. A. Lomas, 'Developments in land tenure on the Prior of Durham's Estate in the later Middle Ages', *Northern History*, **XIII** (1977), pp. 26–43; J. Hatcher, *Rural Economy and Society in the Duchy of Cornwall 1300–1500*, (Cambridge, 1970); J. M. W. Bean, *The Estates of the Percy Family 1416–1537* (Oxford, 1958).

48. Hilton, *The Decline of Serfdom*, p. 47 *et seq.*

49. Hilton, *The English Peasantry in the Later Middle Ages*, p. 43 *et seq.*

50. N. S. B. Gras, *The Evolution of the English Corn Market* (London, 1926), p. 47.

51. A. Everitt, 'The marketing of agricultural produce', in Thirsk, *Agrarian History of England and Wales*, Vol. IV, pp. 467–88.

52. Everitt, 'The marketing of agricultural produce', p. 468.

53. R. H. Hilton, 'Rent and capital formation in feudal society', *Proceedings, Second International Conference of Economic History*, (1962), pp. 33-68.
54. S. Pollard and D. W. Crossley, *The Wealth of Britain*, (London, 1968), p. 68.
55. Hilton, *The English Peasantry in the Later Middle Ages*, p. 67.
56. F. V. Emery, *Wales* (London, 1969) pp. 35–6; W. Rees, *An Historical Atlas of Wales* (London, 1959), pp. 41–2.
57. Rees, *Historical Atlas of Wales*, p. 44.
58. C. Thomas, 'Peasant agriculture in medieval Gwynedd', *Folk Life*, (1975) pp. 34–5.
59. T. Jones Pierce, 'Some tendencies in the agrarian history of Caernarvonshire during the later Middle Ages', reprinted in J. Beverly Smith (ed.), *Medieval Welsh Society. Selected essays by T. Jones Pierce*, (Cardiff, 1972), pp. 39–60.
60. *Ibid.*, p. 40.
61. *Ibid.*, pp. 50–1.
62. Emery, *Wales*, p. 55.
63. T. Jones Pierce, 'Landlords in Wales', in Thirsk, *Agrarian History of England and Wales*, Vol. IV, p. 367.
64. Pollard, 'Estate management in the later Middle Ages', p. 554.
65. Hatcher, *Plague, Population and the English Economy*, p. 42 et seq.
66. *Ibid.*, p. 39.
67. Pollard, 'Estate management', p. 565.
68. Thirsk (ed.), *Agrarian History of England and Wales*, Vol. IV, pp. 1–112.
69. Emery, 'The farming regions of Wales', pp. 113–41.
70. J. Thirsk, 'The common fields', *Past and Present*, **29** (1964), pp. 3–25; *idem*, 'The origin of the common fields', *Past and Present*, **33** (1966), pp. 142–7; C. S. and C. S. Orwin, *The Open Fields*, (3rd edn.) (Oxford, 1967); A. R. H. Baker and R. A. Butlin (eds.), *Studies of Field Systems in the British Isles* (Cambridge, 1973).
71. H. L. Gray, *English Field Systems* (Cambridge, Mass., 1915).
72. B. K. Roberts, 'Field systems of the West Midlands', in Baker and Butlin, *Field Systems in the British Isles*, pp. 188–231.
73. J. Thirsk, 'Field systems of the East Midlands', in Baker and Butlin, *Field Systems in the British Isles*, pp. 232–80.
74. R. A. Butlin, 'Field systems of Northumberland and Durham', and G. Elliott, 'Field systems of northwest England', in Baker and Butlin, *Field Systems in the British Isles*, pp. 93–144, and pp. 42–92.
75. M. R. Postgate, 'Field systems of East Anglia', in Baker and Butlin, *Field Systems in the British Isles*, pp. 281–322.
76. A. R. H. Baker, 'Field systems of south-east England', in Baker and Butlin, *Field Systems in the British Isles*, pp. 377–429.
77. G. R. J. Jones, 'Field systems of north Wales', and M. Davies, 'Field systems

of south Wales', in Baker and Butlin, *Field Systems in the British Isles*, pp. 430–79, pp. 480–527.

78. Thirsk, 'The common fields', and 'The origin of the common fields'.
79. G. C. Homans, 'The explanation of English regional differences', *Past and Present*, **42** (1969), pp. 18–34.
80. H. S. A. Fox, 'The chronology of enclosure and economic development in medieval Devon', *Economic History Review*, 2nd ser., **XXIV** (1975), pp. 181–202.
81. D. N. McCloskey, 'The persistence of English common fields', in W. N. Parker and E. L. Jones (eds.), *European Peasants and their Markets* (Princeton, 1975), pp. 73–119.
82. R. H. Britnell, 'Agricultural technology and the margin of cultivation in the fourteenth century', *Economic History Review*, 2nd ser., **XXX** (1977), pp. 53–66.
83. M. W. Beresford, *The Lost Villages of England*, (London, 1954); M. W. Beresford and J. G. Hurst, *Deserted Medieval Villages* (London, 1971).
84. K. J. Allison, M. W. Beresford, and J. G. Hurst, *The Deserted Villages of Northamptonshire*, (Leicester, 1966), p. 15.
85. P. Wade-Martins, 'The origins of rural settlement in East Anglia', in P. J. Fowler (ed.), *Recent Work in Rural Archaeology*, (London, 1975), pp. 137–57.
86. J. A. Sheppard, 'Vernacular buildings in England and Wales', *Transactions, Institute of British Geographers*, **40** (1966), pp. 21–37; M. W. Barley, *The English Farmhouse and Cottage* (London, 1961); E. Mercer, *English Vernacular Houses*, (London, 1975).
87. Sheppard, 'Vernacular buildings', p. 28.
88. *Ibid.*, p. 29.
89. Mercer, *English Vernacular Houses*, p. 23.
90. P. Smith, *Houses of the Welsh Countryside*, (London, 1975), pp. 14–15.
91. *Ibid.*, p. 15.
92. W. G. Hoskins, *The Making of the English Landscape*, (London, 1957), pp. 99–101.
93. F. V. Emery, 'Moated settlements in England', *Geography* **XLVII** (1962), pp. 378–88; B. K. Roberts, 'Moats and Mottes', *Medieval Archaeology*, **8** (1964); pp. 219–22; *idem*, 'Moated sites in Midland England', *Transactions Birmingham Archaeological Society*, **LXXX** (1965), p. 27.
94. J. Langton, 'Late medieval Gloucester: some data from a rental of 1455', *Transactions, Institute of British Geographers*, New Series **2**, (1977), p. 259.
95. Bridbury, *Economic Growth*.
96. Langton, 'Late medieval Gloucester'.
97. P. Clark and P. Slack, *English Towns in Transition 1500–1700*, (Oxford, 1976), pp. 7–8.

98. Hilton, 'The small town as part of peasant society' in *The English Peasantry in the Later Middle Ages*, Chapter V, pp. 76–94.
99. Clark and Slack, *English Towns in Transition*, p. 9.
100. *Ibid*.
101. C. Phythian-Adams, 'Ceremony and the citizen: the communal year at Coventry 1450–1550', in P. Clark and P. Slack (eds.), *Crisis and Order in English Towns*, (London, 1972), pp. 57–85.
102. E. Power, *The Wool Trade in English Medieval History* (Oxford, 1941); E. M. Carus-Wilson and O. Coleman, *England's Export Trade 1275–1574*, (Oxford, 1963); E. M. Carus-Wilson, 'Evidences of industrial growth on some fifteenth-century manors', *Economic History Review*, 2nd ser., **XII** (1959), pp. 90–205.
103. Pollard and Crossley, *The Wealth of Britain*, p. 73.
104. Pollard and Crossley, *ibid.*, p. 75; H. R. Schubert, *History of the British Iron and Steel Industry from c. 450* B.C. *to* A.D. *1775*, (London, 1957).
105. J. Hatcher, *English Tin Production and Trade before 1550*, (Oxford, 1973); idem, *Rural Economy and Society in the Duchy of Cornwall, 1300–1500*, (Cambridge, 1970).
106. Platt, *The English Medieval Town*, p. 92.
107. J. A. Chartres, *Internal Trade in England 1500–1700*, (London, 1977); B. P. Hindle, 'The road network of medieval England and Wales', *Journal of Historical Geography*, **2** (1976), pp. 207–22.
108. R. S. Schofield, 'The geographical distribution of wealth in England', *Economic History Review*, 2nd ser., **XVIII** (1965), pp. 483–510.

6
Agriculture 1500–1730

J. A. Yelling

In the past 1500–1730 was seen as a period of preparation for great agricultural developments which were to follow. Although the degree of preparation was emphasized or belittled, it is only recently that such a viewpoint has been dropped completely, and the events of the sixteenth and seventeenth centuries given greater significance. These included technical advances, greater commercialization, and a stripping away of customs and institutions regarded as economically inefficient. Such processes of agricultural modernization necessarily involved geographical re-organization, and the study of that re-organization has an indispensable contribution to make to the general debate on the nature and extent of improvement.

Agrarian Structure and Organization

A distinctive feature of the British experience, compared with most parts of the continent, was the early and thoroughgoing nature of changes in agrarian organization. All these might once have been referred to under the title 'enclosure', but it has long been recognized that at least one of them, engrossment, requires separate treatment. The other ingredients, spatial consolidation of holdings, abolition of common rights and physical enclosure, also merit independent consideration, but they were often achieved by the one decision to 'enclose', and will be described together in this short account.

Enclosure of Common Fields [1]

Gonner wrote that enclosure
  took place first in the districts … where its advantages were greatest. The

151

factors which determined which these were are not difficult to find. Land where enclosure was profitable, owing either to change in its use or to a considerable increase in yield, came under enclosure because the profit would compensate for the loss incurred. [2]

This implies that common field still existing at the end of this period—mainly in the belt later affected by parliamentary enclosure—was that land which would have been unprofitable to enclose and, more specifically, that on which suitable land-use changes or increases in productivity would not have been possible.

Such a thesis cannot be supported, and indeed Gonner's explanation forms only one main part of the equation leading to enclosure. The other comprises those factors which made the process easier to achieve. Several of these operated at a local scale. The policies of major landlords might speed or delay enclosure in the short run. More enduring were the effects of varying landholding structures, so that the more widespread and complex the property distribution in any township then, other things being equal, the more difficult it was to enclose. Such factors help to explain contrasting patterns of development in neighbouring townships on apparently similar land.

There was, however, a further factor connected with the organization of enclosure which operated on a wider geographical basis. This lay in the presence of two distinct methods of achieving enclosure. One of these may be termed 'piecemeal'; it came about mainly through individual initiatives, and although groups of landholders often co-operated in taking land from the fields, it never involved a wholly collective action. Each holding in a township had a separate enclosure history. The only collective decision needed was one which permitted piecemeal activity to take place. This might involve some formal agreement, but more usually consent was implicit, often not clearly defined, and some enclosures were made unilaterally.

Piecemeal enclosure was not easily accomplished, even where it was most frequently found, for objections were often encountered from other landholders, or manorial lords. This must have encouraged a gradual policy, care being taken not to arouse hostility by over-ambitious assault. In any event, most enclosures were designed to modify the existing system rather than to replace it completely. The common fields therefore dwindled in size and importance over a lengthy period, sometimes many centuries. Portions of common field of varying sizes were surrounded and eaten into by small hedged closes to provide what contemporaries described as 'woodland' landscape. Holdings still often consisted of small and scattered parcels, and consolidation might continue long after final enclosure.[3]

At the national scale the incidence of piecemeal activity is known only in broad outline, although it was undoubtedly the most important method of enclosure in this period. Large parts of England including notably most of Essex and Kent, most of the south-west peninsula and most of Wales and north-west England were already enclosed by 1500. In another large part piecemeal enclosure was resisted, and had a lesser importance. This included the north-east lowlands, and those areas that formed the core of the later belt of parliamentary enclosure, such as east Yorkshire, much of Lincolnshire, a broad midland area stretching from Worcestershire to Bedfordshire, and parts of Wiltshire and Dorset. It was in the remaining districts that piecemeal enclosure was most active, especially in Norfolk, the Chiltern Hills, Somerset, the Vales of Gloucester and Glamorgan, the Welsh borderland, the north-west Midlands and west Yorkshire. In all these districts extensive amounts of common field land had been removed by 1730, and in some only small remnants survived.[4]

The other main form of enclosure I shall term 'general' enclosure. By this method the whole body of landholders came to a collective decision to enclose the whole or part of their lands. The manner in which the decision was arrived at distinguishes one form of general enclosure from another. General enclosures sometimes occurred in townships already largely enclosed by piecemeal methods, but they were particularly important where little piecemeal activity had taken place. In such cases, all the constituent holdings of a township experienced an identical enclosure history.

There is one major circumstantial feature of general enclosures which needs to be emphasized. Had they been mainly achieved in a series of partial steps, the contrast with the piecemeal form would not have been so important. But the political effort needed to arrive at a collective decision to enclose seems to have been such that compromise was rarely attractive, and usually general enclosures involved the complete removal of common field. The effect of this was that townships passed straight from common field to enclosure at one particular date, and such entirely enclosed townships might border others wholly in common field, and were destined to remain so for decades or even centuries. Such circumstances occurred in the area most resistant to piecemeal enclosure which has already been described. In many cases, however, large demesne estates had been removed from communal control, and these might be set aside in a distinct block of closes.

The abruptness with which general enclosures came about made them, potentially, the most radical form of enclosure, but they were correspondingly difficult to achieve. If there were no strong economic pressures many landholders would not wish to risk such a venture; whilst if strong pressures did exist, an enclosure might involve consequences, such as depopulation, which some landholders would wish to resist. The existence of various interest groups, which might be differentially affected by enclosure, could be masked in a piecemeal scheme, but was brought sharply to the fore in any general project. To many scholars these enclosures have provided a typical example of one of the main problems of the developing modern economy: how to promote economic progress whilst ensuring a fair divison of the spoils.

Before 1500 general enclosures were normally achieved by unity of control, the manorial lord having come into the possession of all the property in a township either by forceful acquisition or sometimes by default. Such enclosures continued into the first quarter of the sixteenth century, and later in the north-east,[5] but will not be discussed here. Afterwards, general enclosure came about mainly through some form of agreement between various parties. It is thought that the revival of economic growth in the sixteenth century, and the return to more intensive methods of farming, made such agreements more likely, whilst changed political and economic circumstances made it more difficult to acquire unity of control of entire townships.

As a rough generalization the period begins with very limited agreements, and these widen in scope towards the end. The enclosure of Cotesbach in Leicesterhire constitutes the model case of a limited agreement.[6] Here the demesne had already been enclosed in 1501, and the manorial lord had already acquired the bulk of the land. He negotiated from a position of strength with only four other landowners to achieve the complete enclosure of the township in 1603. It was followed by a partial depopulation. However, if economic circumstances were favourable, engrossment or depopulation could be avoided in a properly managed enclosure, and this encouraged agreements amongst larger bodies of landowners. The period contains many examples of such 'regulated' enclosures, especially in its last century. The enclosure of Clifton upon Dunsmore (Warwickshire) carried out in 1650 is an example.[7]

Although enclosures by agreement have attracted less attention than earlier general enclosures, they occurred on a more extensive scale. However, few areas became enclosed solely by this means, the remainder having a sporadic appearance of closes in a mainly champion landscape. Enclosure had more impact where pressures on common field farming were severe. Parts of the midland clays which had already been affected by earlier enclosures, saw a further and greater spread of closes in our period, as in east Leicestershire. Here arable farming continued to give way to a mainly pastoral economy. By contrast, the other main territory of deserted villages, the light soil uplands and heathlands, are much less affected by enclosure at this time. A further major district of general enclosure developed in the eastern lowlands of Northumberland and Durham, where a series of enclosures by agreement in the seventeenth century saw the rapid removal of common field in an area where the growth of coal mining, greater profitability of pasture farming and weak landholding arrangements told against it.

Where genuine agreement was involved, a general enclosure scheme often called for the land to be re-allotted by commissioners. This was a most important development, which clearly presaged the methods later adopted under parliamentary enclosure. Earlier general enclosures had resulted in large compact fields and farms, but there was no element of planned division or geometrical arrangement. In both these respects many enclosures by agreement show a closer resemblance to the parliamentary awards. Some of the large enclosures of earlier periods also underwent a new division as more intensive farming methods were adopted.

Much of the political and socio-economic significance of enclosure derives from the existence of the general form. It might be thought that general enclosure was simply a more radical type which supervened in areas not yet affected by piecemeal activity but, except perhaps in the north-east, this was only true when the more powerful parliamentary procedures were adopted. Before that the difficulties of arranging general enclosures meant that even in the districts where this procedure was adopted early on, many common fields survived. Yet these surviving common fields remained equally untouched by piecemeal action. Indeed, the peculiar resistance offered to piecemeal enclosure in certain districts of England would seem to be the key factor in making general enclosure necessary.

It is probable that had the piecemeal method been everywhere the main form of enclosure, the amount of common field surviving at the end of our period would have been less, and its geography would have been rather different. The causes of resistance to piecemeal activity are not entirely clear but they certainly go beyond questions of land use, and link with the nature of common field organization. Where common field farmers took their decisions on a highly communal basis, they tended to develop their agriculture, and eventually to proceed to enclosure, in a similar manner. The mode of origin of such highly communal systems is, of course, itself a very contentious issue. Here it is possible only to recognize their distinctive geography (yet to be precisely defined) and the influence that this had on enclosure.

Enclosure of Common Waste

Although it has long been realized that a considerable amount of enclosure of waste took place in our period, it has been subject to no general survey, and our knowledge is dependent on a number of important regional studies. These show immediately that action took place in very varying circumstances, by different methods, and made varying rates of progress. As with the common fields, the problem is to generalize from these experiences without losing their essential distinctiveness.

In a study of Devon, Hoskins claims that the reclamation of waste in this period was rather more extensive than that which took place by parliamentary award, and equivalent to that of the early Middle Ages. Some entirely new farms were founded, and there was some encroachment by cottagers, but 'most important was the comparatively large-scale reclamation ... which added ten, twenty or even fifty acres at a time to an adjacent farm'.[8] Such enclosures took place quietly, and there was no problem of common rights, for in the uplands 'a farmer who could take in a piece of land ... was welcome to do so'.[9] In Merioneth, too, enclosure in the sixteenth century took place from existing farms 'whose limits were extended in an irregular manner on to the commons',[10] and proceeded relatively unhindered.

In other cases enclosure of waste led to great popular resistance, ranging from small affrays to large-scale rioting, as in the fenlands. In the most serious cases such events, or the threat of them, were a key factor in preventing enclosure. Even where they proved of temporary importance, they demonstrate the value which much 'waste' had acquired. The renewed growth of population in the sixteenth century was the most decisive factor in the revaluation. Added to this there was, especially in the early seventeenth century a 'spirit of improvement': its most important feature was the drainage of fenland, but there were also attempts to improve upland soils through denshiring, or greater application of natural fertilizers.

Such pressures prohibited any free process of colonization or enclosure on most of the more accessible and improvable wastes. They did not work entirely against enclosure even there, for more intensive usage created a need for more controlled management, and disputes over inter-commoning, stinting and overstocking were not infrequent. Against this, however, any development of waste, like that of the common fields, was always confronted by the problem of the differential advantage which various parties might draw from the projected change.

The potential advantage to manorial lords was recognized by the Crown, whose need to raise revenue, particularly under the early Stuarts, acted as an important spur to the improvement and enclosure of waste. Under the Statute of Merton manorial lords were entitled to authorize enclosure, provided sufficient land be left for the tenants, a rule obviously difficult to interpret. In well-populated areas large piecemeal projects would almost certainly be opposed by tenants, and this restricted their occurrence. However, many enclosures involved only small encroachments, and whether licensed or not, villagers did not usually object to them. Their main importance lay in their contribution to the growth of population, and the form and character of waste-edge settlement.

In certain cases tenants joined with the manorial lord to agree a complete or partial general enclosure of the wastes. At Heckington in Lincolnshire, 1733 areas of fen were enclosed by this means in 1635 despite the opposition of forty of the lesser commoners.[11] Such enclosures play a particularly important part in the studies of Rossendale and Bowland carried out by Tupling and Porter.[12] They occurred at various dates in the late sixteenth century, and extensively c. 1620 when the Duchy of Lancaster agreed to enclosure as part of a deal involving copy-hold enfranchisement. Porter estimates that 14 square miles of Bowland moorland were taken in by such enclosures.[13] Evidently, the enclosure history of this district is rather different from that of Devon, although it appears to have parallels in Durham.

In the fenlands, opportunities for drainage were the main catalyst of change, and the requirements of drainage schemes largely determined the character of enclosure. The main potential lay in tackling the extensive peat fens, but for this large schemes requiring considerable finance were necessary. The General Drainage Act of 1600 authorized the alienation of land to those who undertook or ventured capital in drainage operations. With this the history of fenland drainage and enclosure passes from small partial schemes to large speculative ventures. The amount of alienated land was substantial, and to it was added land allotted to the manorial lord for his right of soil. In Alder Moor (Somerset) drained c. 1630, 300 acres were allotted to the Crown, and 140 acres to the agents, leaving the commoners with 560 acres 'in the most frequently flooded portions of the moor'.[14] These alienations were a major factor in the popular protest which was to prevent the enclosure of Kings Sedgemoor (Somerset), and destroy many Lincolnshire enclosures during the Civil War.

The most important single scheme was the drainage of the Bedford Level, which has been described by Darby.[15] This was carried out by Vermuyden and financed by a group of adventurers led by the Earl of Bedford. Under the terms of the 'Lynn Law' (1630)

> 95,000 acres of reclaimed land allotted from every quality of soil were to be handed over to the undertakers upon completion of the contract, 12,000 acres of land were to go to the king, and 40,000 were permanently charged with the maintenance of the drainage works.[16]

After a chequered history, the essentials of the scheme were completed in 1651, and the large scattered blocks of adventurers' land lay enclosed surrounded by the common fens of the villages. Despite the difficulties it was later to encounter, the Bedford Level scheme may be adjudged a qualified success. But the technical and political difficulties that had been exposed, brought large-scale schemes to a close, until they could be re-awakened under the new conditions of the late eighteenth century.

Our period also saw an important extension of enclosure in the woodlands, where special interest attaches to the Royal Forests and deer parks. It is believed that in many cases 'the large reserves of land, particularly the ample commons in areas of Royal Forest were due to obstacles placed in the way of settlement and colonization in the Middle Ages'.[17] The policy of disafforestation and disparking pursued by Tudor and Stuart monarchs resulted in considerable enclosure from the early sixteenth century, as at Leicester, through to the late seventeenth century, as at Ashdown Forest in the Weald (1693).[18] Among other categories of wasteland not yet mentioned, there were extensive enclosures of coastal marshlands and some enclosure of heathland.

However, although some heathland was becoming increasingly valuable for crop production at this time, cultivation was often extended by means of outfield brakes.

As already mentioned, much enclosure continued to take place in a relatively unplanned manner by farms extending their perimeter, or acquiring new detached portions. But this was also a major period in the development of new ideas and practices concerning the spatial arrangement of farms and fields, and in this movement the wasteland enclosures played the leading role. The main developments lay in the allotments for enclosure made by commissions. These invariably took the form of a geometrical arrangement, although especially in the earlier part of the period it might not be sharply drawn. Later, in the Bowland moorlands[19] as well as in the fenlands the pattern of allotments bears a close resemblance to that resulting from parliamentary enclosure.

Landholding

Although changes in landholding are crucial to the agrarian developments of our period, they have so far been accorded little systematic study by geographers. The main interest stems from Johnson's discovery in 1909 that the modern English landholding structure was already substantially developed by the time of the first detailed Land Tax Returns *c.* 1780. It could not therefore be associated with parliamentary enclosure, or other events of the late eighteenth century. Instead Johnson believed that 'by far the most serious period for the small owner was at the close of the seventeenth century and during the first half of the eighteenth; in short the period of final transition from medieval to modern agricultural conditions'.[20]

Subsequent research has indeed confirmed that this was a difficult time for the small farmer, and saw considerable engrossment.[21] However, it would be a mistake to think in terms of a modern pattern arriving decisively in any one period. Engrossment may have gathered pace at the end of the seventeenth century, but it was already a major issue in the sixteenth,[22] and examples can also be found at other times. At Chippenham, Cambridgeshire 'the period in which the small farmer disappeared was a very brief one, a mere thirty years at the beginning of the seventeenth century'.[23] There may have been periods in which engrossment was checked in some places, or even reversed, but the main impression is one of continuous change. This took place gradually and untidily as the growing economic advantages of large-scale farming were refracted through a mass of political, social and personal concerns.

The geographical variations in the pace of change also have something of a haphazard appearance. In one village small farms might disappear in a swift decisive period of development, while in another adjacent they retreated grudgingly if at all. At the larger scale, however, we can presume that a distinct sharpening in regional differentiation of farm structures was taking place. The greater suitability of small farms for one type of enterprise rather than another was the main factor at work. It brought about a widening contrast in landholding between, for example, the arable sheep-farming of chalkland Wiltshire and the dairying district of the north-west of that 'county'. By the end of the period under consideration, the principal features of the geography of farm size depicted by Grigg for mid-nineteenth century Britain[24] would certainly have been recognizable.

The former belief that landholding structures were decisively changed only after 1750 helped bolster the view that the agriculture of the two and a half preceding centuries was conducted along traditional lines. The common fields, in particular, were seen as the preserve of an antiquated order. Exceptions were allowed only for certain enclosed parts of southern and midland England. Early general enclosures were, indeed, often associated with marked consolidation; for example at Cotesbach 16 farms were 'decayed' in the enclosure of 1603.[25] But a few villages, like Chippenham, saw marked engrossment, yet remained in common field. Moreover, in a less spectacular fashion the loss of small farms was much more widely spread. An important conclusion to emerge from the Land Tax studies was that the common fields had been by no means sheltered from engrossment. They could thus no longer be seen as self-contained worlds opened up to agricultural development only through enclosure.

Agricultural Production

Three chief factors determined the nature of agricultural output and shaped the agricultural geography of the country: the market, productive techniques, and various obstacles to land-use change. Of the two motors of development, the main emphasis has been given in recent years to productive techniques. In Kerridge's *Agricultural Revolution* there is little mention of market forces, although their implied effects form a backcloth to the entire action. [26] We must not seek to put these factors into a false battle for supremacy, because each is required to complement the other. However, there are advantages in beginning our account with a study of markets.

Markets and Commercialization

Over the years economic historians have talked less and less about subsistence farming in referring to this period. Holderness (1976) says that 'by 1700 English agriculture was already fully in a market economy'. [27] Clarkson (1971), referring to the period as a whole, says that 'few producers were completely isolated from the market, and for a growing majority market prices were the first factors to be considered when organizing production'. However, there were also 'large pockets of subsistence production'. [28] Such caution is entirely proper. The extent to which farmers entered into trade is one of the most difficult agricultural parameters to assess, and the evidence allows only very general conclusions.

These conclusions, however fragile, affect our whole way of thinking about the agriculture of the period. Growing commercialization has a general significance in promoting new attitudes to organizational change and technical advance. It might encourage a gradual improvement in productivity even without radical change in productive systems. But there is also a more specifically geographical role; for increasing areas of the country are brought into a connecting system in which the various parts relate through competition and co-operative linkages. Developments in one part of a market area affect, to varying degrees, all other parts; whilst the nature of production in any one part is shaped by the comparative advantages that area possesses *vis-à-vis* other regions.

With such forces at work growing commercialization might be confidently expected to produce increasing regional specialization. However, there were other factors, to be considered later, which largely nullified this tendency. Even so, this effect might have been produced had the entire process been concentrated in our period, but it neither began nor ended within it. Exceptionally strong regional contrasts already existed in 1500, for example, between the champion and woodland parts of East Anglia or the West Midlands, and between the downland and dairying districts of Gloucestershire or Wiltshire. [29] Although the uniformity of subsistence agriculture may be exaggerated, these distinctions certainly highlight the extent to which regional exchange had already developed.

What occurred in the period 1500–1730 was a further economic concentration and a corresponding widening of market areas. More sophisticated methods of trade favoured the larger centres, and their consequent growth in turn fostered a greater concentration of demand. The process led to renewed growth in traditional regional centres, and these were joined by newly developing industrial districts. By the 1720s, Defoe could note of the West Riding that 'their corn comes up in great quantities out of Lincoln, Nottingham and the East Riding, their sheep and mutton from the adjacent counties every way; their butter from the East and North Riding, their cheese out of Cheshire and Warwickshire, their black cattle also out of Lancashire'. [30]

Economic concentration was most spectacularly exhibited in the growth of London, and the impact of London's demands on agricultural production has been a central theme. Gras attempted to recognize the various market areas for grain from a study of prices. He included some discussion of Von Thunen but noted that his work involved 'little or no appreciation of the historical development from the local to the metropolitan market'. [31] Gras believed that at the end of the Middle Ages the 'London area was not . . . the arbiter of prices for a district wider than its immediate vicinity'. [32] The importance of our period was that it saw the rise of the metropolitan grain market. This began to develop in the sixteenth century, and by c. 1700 covered most of England south of a line from the Wash to the Severn. Within this region 'prices diminish as the distance from the centre is increased'. [33]

Gras' statistical methods were crude by modern standards, and his data stand in great need of reworking. Until then the extent of the metropolitan grain market must remain uncertain, and in any event it would not be marked by any clear-cut boundary. Even within the area, the proportion of produce destined for London, and the proportion of farmers catering for that market would vary, and need not be high. None the less, the evidence suggests that it was within the extended area of the London market that grain prices were most radically transformed, and agricultural studies in Oxfordshire and the Chilterns emphasize this as a key developmental factor. [34]

The geography of water communications was important in controlling access to major grain markets. London received supplies by ship from Kent, and later East Anglia and much of the east and south coasts. Inland, river navigation along the Thames was a key factor. But although water transport was first choice, there was also considerable overland movement of grain. Defoe mentions Cambridgeshire, Bedfordshire, Northampton-shire and Hampshire as counties which supplied barley and wheat to a string of marketing towns around London. In these centres, such as Royston, Ware, Marlow and Guildford, the grain was usually processed into meal or malt.[35]

In contrast to the grain market, there was no regional autonomy in livestock products and 'prices everywhere were closely tied to those obtaining in the capital'.[36] Although study of the livestock industries has been relatively neglected, the overall impression is that considerable development took place. It affected all parts of the country, for even in arable areas farming methods required the close support of the livestock sector. This was further emphasized by the advent of turnip feeding in East Anglia. None the less, the western parts of Britain were particularly dependent on livestock products, and they were stimulated both by direct access to urban markets, and by regional linkages within the livestock industry.

A large tract of western England from South Lancashire to Somerset was primarily associated with the dairying industry, mainly for cheese. This was marketed over considerable distances by water and land carriage, allowing Defoe to maintain that Cheshire 'however remote from London is one of those [counties] which contributes most to its support'.[37] Further west the repercussions of the wool trade had reached into the Welsh uplands before the sixteenth century. Such areas also, strengthened their traditional breeding and rearing industries, supplying sheep and cattle to the surrounding lowlands. The driving of stock from the uplands for fattening in the midlands, East Anglia and close to London was a particularly striking part of this trade.

Despite these developments, the lack of any really radical innovation in transport necessarily restricted the extent of geographical reorganiza-tion. Overland movement of grain was still difficult, and not until the railway 'did the business of fattening move back into the lowland fringes of the great rearing areas'.[38] The growth of dairying in the west did not dislodge the large dairying district in Essex and Suffolk. The scope for striking developments in regional specialization was also reduced by the growing emphasis on convertible husbandry and mixed farming. This tended to produce a greater uniformity in land use and, with certain exceptions such as the growth of market gardens and orchards near urban centres, regional distinctions became less apparent. However, we have as yet only a little knowledge of the more subtle aspects of farm economics, of market outlets, or the detailed purposes of production. If more information were available specializations not yet apparent would surely come to light.

Productive Techniques

Ernle said that,

> the Tudor husbandman might devote himself exclusively to one or the other of the two main branches of farming, but he had not mastered the secret of their union. If he changed from tillage to pasture he did so completely. He could not, like his successor, combine the two and by the introduction of new crops at once grow more corn and carry more stock.[39]

This draws immediate attention to the fundamental character of technical advance in our period. In the main it did not consist of direct improvements in consumer products, but rather of change at the base of production, seeking a more profitable integration of crops and livestock, tillage and grass.

However, traditional husbandry had not neglected this principle. On the contrary, livestock had always formed an essential adjunct of crop husbandry, particularly necessary for the maintenance of fertility through manuring. Purely arable farms could not exist, and purely pastoral farms, outside the uplands, were mainly the product of recent enclosures. At the beginning of the period low demand for grain crops had made unusually large pasture resources available to most arable farmers, so that the maintenance of fertility posed little problem. The test was to come with renewed population growth, for there was a danger that an increase in the crop area at the expense of pasture would reduce output of livestock and manure, and so throttle expansion.

Fortunately, there were already encouraging signs that the problem could at least be mitigated. One of these, still underestimated, was the use of beans and peas as fodder crops. Hoskins found that these accounted for 43 per cent of the total cropped acreage recorded in Leicestershire probate inventories between 1500 and 1531.[40] This was an exceptionally high figure, but they were extensively grown elsewhere, except on lighter soils where their use began mainly in the seventeenth century.

Even more important results were to follow from treating grass as a fodder crop rather than a permanent land-use. Tillage and grass had, of course, often been substituted for one another in the past, but the difficulty of establishing a satisfactory grass sward had limited the use of the practice as a systematic means of improvement. By the beginning of our period this difficulty had been at least partially overcome, and systems of convertible husbandry were in use in Flanders. Ashley, writing in 1893 made convertible husbandry a central feature of his 'agrarian revolution' in Tudor England.[41] It was, however, virtually ignored by Ernle and perhaps because of this its connection with later agricultural improvement tended to be omitted despite emphasis in important regional studies.[42]

Convertible husbandry re-entered the debate on improvement more forcibly with Kerridge's *The Agricultural Revolution* (1967). He regarded it as the backbone of this revolution, and its importance is his principal justification for dating the change to the sixteenth and seventeenth centuries rather than later. He recognized that practices involving temporary grass tend to be concealed in records which (as in later periods) insist on referring either to arable or pasture. None the less he believed that in the early sixteenth century convertible husbandry 'was confined to the north-west and a few farms elsewhere. It expanded and spread rapidly after 1560, and fastest between 1590 and 1660, by which time it had conquered production and ousted the system of permanency from half the farm land.'[43] In the circumstances this must be regarded as a tentative assessment, but it has not yet been seriously challenged.

In England the system is best known from its practice on enclosed farms in the Midlands. Many of these had previously been put to permanent pasture, but the revival of demand in the late sixteenth century encouraged a more intensive husbandry. Alongside the permanent pasture, closes began to be broken up for short tillage intervals followed by long leys of six to twenty years duration. Under such a system 'three quarters of the farms was grass, and the main object was animal produce'.[44] Kerridge made very large claims for the productivity of this convertible husbandry. The quality of pasture was improved by the tillage interval and re-seeding so that 'substituted for mere grazing . . . [it] doubled, and replacing common fields quadrupled rates of stocking'.[45] And although the tillage area was restricted, the concentration of manure on this land, and improved soil texture, gave double the yields in the common fields. He believed that, allowing for a reduction in fallow and other changes, an enclosure which involved the adoption of convertible husbandry need not result in any lessening of crop production.

Without admitting these claims, most of which have yet to be properly tested, it must be allowed that such convertible husbandry systems, in their most intensive form, were far from negligible as crop producers. This opens up a potential for more widespread use than the obviously specialized system described above might suggest. Kerridge showed that there is evidence of convertible husbandry of some kind from many widely scattered parts of the country. Detailed studies are now necessary to increase our knowledge of the extent to which it entered the farming practice of different localities, and the various forms of output with which it was associated. However, by the nature of things, this geography will be extremely difficult to establish.

Developments in the middle of the seventeenth century finally made convertible husbandry practicable through the whole range of arable farming. Of particular importance was the introduction of clover, for this could be sown for a single year or, mixed with selected grass seeds, could provide leys of varying duration. The old problem of establishing productive leys speedily was greatly reduced. Unfortunately, clover was not a crop systematically recorded in probate inventories, and this makes its usage difficult to monitor. It was, however, an adaptable crop, and spread rapidly from several centres in which it had become established in the 1660s, so that its majority adoption phase can probably be assigned to our period, with the possible exception of Wales and northern England.

The turnip was the other famous new field crop of the mid-seventeenth century. Together with clover it formed part of the well-known 'Norfolk' rotation of turnips-barley-clover-wheat. Although this course was usually extended by additional years of grass ley, it illustrates very well the advantages an intensive convertible system could bring. The new fodder supplies allowed livestock carrying capacity to be maintained or increased, whilst at the same time expanding the production of grain crops. This was done partly by increased manuring, but mainly by an extension of the cropped area at the expense of fallow and permanent grass. The fallow had previously served to provide a rest interval, during which folding could take place and weeds and pests could be reduced. Clover and turnips acted together to replace these functions; they broke the cycle of grain pests, clover contributed nitrogen to the soil, and weeds could be dealt with by hoeing while turnips were on the ground.

Defoe in 1724 described east Suffolk as the place 'Where the feeding and fattening of cattle . . . with turnips was first practised in England . . . from whence this practice is spread over most of the east and south parts.'[46] This assessment appears essentially correct, large-scale use of the crop beginning in Suffolk in the 1660s. Its subsequent diffusion was, however, certainly more difficult than that of clover, and it is unfortunate that Defoe's description is vague. Kerridge provided evidence of its cultivation in many districts by 1730, but inventory collections fail to show any extensive use in counties such as Worcestershire, Oxfordshire and Yorkshire.[47]

The turnip was widely grown only on light and medium soils, and this enhanced their comparative advantage as arable producers. Improvement of the lighter soils had, however, already begun.[48] In a more commercial environment the ease of working light soils gave them an important cost advantage over their heavier competitors, forcing some of the latter out of arable altogether. Several innovations, such as the use of sainfoin, and the floating of water meadows improved the productivity of the chalk downlands. Progress was particularly spectacular on poor light soils, where restrictive outputs of rye and oats or barley were replaced by a greater range of crops headed by wheat. From the middle of the seventeenth century rye was also in retreat in many of the more difficult arable areas of the north and west, part of the improvement being due to increased use of marl, lime and other fertilizers.

It seems certain that a feature of agricultural development in our period was that poorer districts were brought closer to the standards of the naturally rich. The general level of improvement can as yet be assessed only within very wide limits, and it would be unwise to come to any fixed conclusions. There is an almost complete absence of information on yields, and only scattered accounts of livestock numbers. Despite the difficulties, progress can be made through comparative work, and the isolation of factors involved in the geography of old and new systems constitutes a major basis for such studies.

Obstacles to Land-use Change

Agricultural production is never entirely shaped by the market requirements and productive capacities of the moment, there are always historical inheritances. One group of these has a certain economic rationale: the accumulation of capital and skills of the kind that preserves Sheffield steel, and that is certainly a factor underestimated in agricultural geography, particularly in the livestock industries. The principal concern here, however, is with the cultural and institutional factors that created obstacles to land-use change. It was part of the process of modernization under review to strip these obstacles away, and progress made in this respect is central to our theme.

Cultural factors are the most difficult to deal with, but their geographical relevance is clear in at least two cases. One of these is the establishment and maintenance of 'traditional' practices and types of production widely spread through the local community. The other and related issue concerns the diffusion of innovations. So far little progress has been made in these fields, since cultural factors have to be taken as a residual when economic explanations have been exhausted, and the evidence for this is difficult to obtain. Amongst institutional factors the size of farm is obviously related to the problem of diffusion, and then there is the question of common field and waste. The significance of communal organization as an obstacle to land-use change depends on two factors. If it allowed a flexibility comparable to that on enclosed land there is obviously no problem. Failing that, the obstacle would be equally minimal if common fields and waste yielded readily to enclosure wherever faced with economic pressures.

In the past common field farming has often been portrayed as totally inflexible, and indeed as lying outside the market economy altogether. This was certainly not the case: common field townships contained large commercially orientated farms as well as many small ones, and common fields in Oxfordshire and elswhere were important suppliers to the London grain market. Before our period began it had been found possible to put varying proportions of the arable fields to grass. Clover, turnips and other innovations were introduced into the common fields more readily than was once thought, and ways were found of varying the fallow area and crop mix.[49] In some cases this was done mainly by communal arrangements, but more usually considerable individual initiatives were allowed, within regular as well as irregular field systems.

In this way the problem of flexibility in the common fields, particularly for arable farming, is reduced to smaller proportions. However, doubts remain about the speed of adoption of innovations, about flexible use of short grass leys, and about the general efficiency of management compared with enclosures. The problem is more serious in respect of the pastoral industries. It appears that common field communities could not survive with an economy based mainly on permanent grass, and the extent to which they could adapt to a convertible system with long grass leys is open to serious doubt. Hoskins and Thirsk, recognizing the presence of a substantial amount of grass in common arable fields believed it to represent such a convertible system but this has been strongly contested by Kerridge.[50]

We come then to the readiness with which common land succumbed to enclosure. Particularly where general enclosure was necessary, there must always have been some delay in the response to economic pressures, and the existence of common field townships devoted largely to grain alongside enclosed pastoral systems provides *prima facie* evidence of longer-term delay. In areas such as south Warwickshire, east Leicestershire and the Vale of Aylesbury land newly enclosed in our period passed invariably to a mainly pastoral usage, yet much common field arable survived. On common wastes, too, there were certainly limits to land-use change without enclosure, and there is good evidence that non-economic pressures delayed many enclosure schemes.

To conclude, in our period there was some lessening of resistance to enclosure which favoured piecemeal activity, and allowed the development of general enclosures by agreement. In that way a contribution was made to land use flexibility. But in the areas least susceptible to piecemeal methods, a speedy removal of common field had to await the development of the Parliamentary Acts. A substantial amount of common land thus remained that would not have been put to the same use under enclosure, and this inevitably affected land use in other places. Without this factor the geography of production might have been considerably altered.

References

1. I have treated this issue at length in my book *Common Field and Enclosure in England 1450–1850*, (London, 1977).
2. E. C. K. Gonner, *Common Land and Inclosure*, (London, 1912, 1966), p. 199.
3. D. Roden, 'Enclosure in the Chiltern Hills' *Geografiska Annaler*, **51 B** (1969), pp. 115–24.
4. A. R. H. Baker and R. A. Butlin (eds.), *Studies of Field Systems in the British Isles*, (Cambridge, 1973).
5. M. W. Beresford, *The Lost Villages of England* (London, 1954).
6. L. A. Parker, 'The agrarian revolution in Cotesbach 1501–1612' in W. G. Hoskins (ed.), *Studies in Leicestershire Agrarian History*, (Leicester, 1949), pp. 41–76.

7. A. Gooder, *Plague and Enclosure: A Warwickshire Village in the Seventeenth Century*, Coventry and North Warwickshire History Pamphlets, No. 2, 1965.
8. W. G. Hoskins. 'The reclamation of the waste in Devon 1550–1800', *Economic History Review*, 1st ser., **13** (1943), p. 85.
9. *Ibid.*, p. 87.
10. C. Thomas, 'Enclosure and the rural landscape of Merioneth in the sixteenth century', *Transactions, Institute of British Geographers*, **42** (1967), p. 159.
11. J. Thirsk, *English Peasant Farming*, (London, 1957), pp. 115–16.
12. G. H. Tupling, *Economic History of Rossendale* (Manchester, 1927), p. 54; J. Porter, 'The reclamation and settlement of Bowland with special reference to the period 1500–1650', Ph.D. Thesis, University of London (1973), p. 91 *et seq.*
13. *Ibid.*, p. 112.
14. M. Williams, *The Draining of the Somerset Levels*, (Cambridge, 1970), p. 103.
15. H. C. Darby, *The Draining of the Fens* (Cambridge, 1940, 1956).
16. H. C. Darby and P. M. Ramsden, 'The Middle Level of the Fens and its reclamation', *Victoria County History of Huntingdonshire*, **III** (1936), p. 271.
17. J. Thirsk, 'The farming regions of England', in J. Thirsk (ed.), *The Agrarian History of England and Wales*, (Cambridge, 1967), Vol. IV, p. 98.
18. P. F. Brandon, 'The common lands and wastes of Sussex', Ph.D. Thesis, University of London (1963).
19. Porter, 'Reclamation and settlement of Bowland', p. 115.
20. A. H. Johnson, *The Disappearance of the Small Landowner*, (London, 1909, 1963), p. 147.
21. G. E. Mingay, 'The size of farms in the eighteenth century', *Economic History Review*, 2nd ser., **14** (1961–2), pp. 469–88.
22. R. H. Tawney, *The Agrarian Problem in the Sixteenth Century*, (London, 1912).
23. M. Spufford, *Contrasting Communities: English Villages in the Sixteenth and Seventeenth Centuries*, (Cambridge, 1974), p. 91.
24. D. B. Grigg, 'Small and large farms in England and Wales: their size and distribution', *Geography*, **48** (1963), pp. 268–79.
25. Parker, 'The agrarian revolution in Cotesbach', p. 66.
26. E. Kerridge, *The Agricultural Revolution*, (London, 1967).
27. B. A. Holderness, *Pre-Industrial England*, (London, 1976).
28. L. A. Clarkson, *The Pre-Industrial Economy in England 1500–1750*, (London, 1971), p. 19.
29. Thirsk, 'Farming regions of England', pp. 1–160.
30. D. Defoe, *A Tour Through the Whole Island of Great Britain 1724–6*, (Dent, London, 1974), Vol. II, p. 199.
31. N. S. B. Gras, *The Evolution of the English Corn Market*, (Cambridge, Mass., 1915), p. 97.

32. *Ibid.*, p. 43.
33. *Ibid.*, p. 95.
34. M. A. Havinden, 'Agricultural progress in open field Oxfordshire', *Agricultural History Review*, **9** (1961), pp. 73–88; Roden, 'Enclosure in the Chiltern Hills', pp. 118–9.
35. F. J. Fisher, 'The development of the London food market, 1540–1640', *Economic History Review*, 1st ser., **5** (1935), pp. 46–64, reprinted in E. M. Carus-Wilson (ed.), *Essays in Economic History*, (London, 1954), Vol. I, pp. 135–151.
36. A. H. John, 'The course of agricultural change 1680–1760' in L. S. Pressnell (ed.), *Studies in the Industrial Revolution*, (London, 1960), p. 128.
37. Defoe, *A tour Through the Whole Island of Great Britain*, Vol. II, p. 72.
38. R. Trow-Smith, *A History of British Livestock Husbandry 1700–1900*, (London, 1959), p. 12. See also his *A History of British Livestock Husbandry to 1700*, (London, 1957).
39. (Lord) Ernle, *English Farming Past and Present*, (London, 1912, 1961), p. 57.
40. W. G. Hoskins 'The Leicestershire farmer in the sixteenth century' in Hoskins (ed.), *Essays in Leicestershire History*, (Liverpool, 1950), p. 167.
41. W. J. Ashley, *Introduction to English Economic History*, (London, 1893).
42. Hoskins, 'The Leicestershire farmer in the sixteenth century'; *idem*, 'The Leicestershire farmer in the seventeenth century', *Agricultural History*, **25** (1951), reprinted in *Provincial England*, (London, 1963), pp. 149–70; *idem*, *The Midland Peasant*, (London, 1957); Thirsk, *English Peasant Farming*.
43. Kerridge, *The Agricultural Revolution*, p. 194.
44. *Ibid.*, p. 202.
45. *Ibid.*, p. 211.
46. Defoe, *A Tour Through the Whole Island of Great Britain*, Vol. I, p. 59.
47. J. A. Yelling, 'Changes in crop production in east Worcestershire, 1540–1867', *Agricultural History Review*, **XXII** (1973), pp. 18–34; Havinden, 'Agricultural progress in open-field Oxfordshire', p. 77; A. Harris, 'The agriculture of the East Riding of Yorkshire before the parliamentary enclosures', *Yorkshire Archaeological Journal*, **40** (1959), p. 126.
48. E. L. Jones, 'Agriculture and economic growth in England 1660–1750', in E. L. Jones (ed.), *Agriculture and Economic Growth in England 1650–1815: Agricultural Change*, (London, 1967), pp. 152–71.
49. Havinden, 'Agricultural progress in open-field Oxfordshire'; Hoskins, 'The Leicestershire farmer, in the sixteenth century'; *idem*, 'The Leicestershire farmer in the seventeenth century'; Yelling, 'Changes in crop production'; *idem*, *Common Field and Enclosure*; Baker and Butlin, *Studies of Field Systems in the British Isles*.

50. Hoskins, 'The Leicestershire farmer in the sixteenth century'; *idem*, 'The Leicestershire farmer in the seventeenth century'; Thirsk, *English Peasant Farming*; Kerridge, *The Agricultural Revolution*.

7
Industry and Towns 1500–1730

J. Langton

An economic treatise of 1549 begins by 'considering the manifold complaints of men touching this Commonweal that we be in, moved more at this present than of long time past has been heard'. [1] The early sixteenth century was a time of unease, hardship, pessimism and dissatisfaction. Inflation of unprecedented severity seemed endemic; there was 'dearth of all things though there be scarcity of nothing'. Some historians consider that the country was returning towards the Malthusian ceiling from which retreat had been so savage in the fourteenth century. [2] Certainly England's economy was still undeveloped. The vast majority worked in agriculture and although more cloth was now exported than raw wool, most of it was unfinished and the bulk of its eventual value was added by continental craftsmen. Other exports were mainly raw materials: England was peripheral to the world economic system, an off-shore island on the edge of the known world supplying the more developed heartland with resources. 'They come for their wools, for their clothes, kerseys, corn, tin, lead, yea, their gold and silver . . . theirs be to us more to serve pleasure than necessity as tables, cards, perfumed gloves, glasses, gallypots. dials, oranges, pippins and cherries.'

Daniel Defoe described in the 1720s 'the most flourishing and opulent country in the world'. [3] Much of the transformation had been worked by improvements in agriculture and control of overseas resources, funnelled through an island which was now at the hub of the international economy. England still exported raw materials such as metals, hides, corn, salt and coal. Its economy was still pre-industrial in the generally accepted sense of the term. [4] Most of the population lived in rural areas, much of the industrial labour force was unseparated from agriculture, there was little accumulated fixed industrial capital and national well-being still rose and fell in unison with the harvest. But this does not mean that industry was of inconsiderable importance. By 1730 about one quarter of the net national product was due to manufacturing, mining and building—more than half as much as was due to agriculture. [5] At the close of the period the woollen manufacture was still the biggest industry by far but it probably accounted for less than one third of the net national product due to manufacturing, mining and building. Processed sugar and tobacco, paper, glass, chemicals, ale, beer and spirits, ferrous and non-ferrous metals, ships and machinery of all sorts, from steam pumping engines to the finest clocks and watches, added considerable diversity to English manufactures. The export industries were leading the national economy, growing by 42 per cent between 1700 and 1730 compared with the 5 per cent of industries which exclusively served the home market. In 1730 woollens and worsteds still accounted for about 80 per cent of exports by value, but 'the process of industrialisation was to an important extent a response to colonial demands for nails, axes, firearms, buckets, coaches, clocks, saddles, handkerchiefs, buttons, cordage and a thousand other things'. [6]

The Textile Industries

The importance of the cloth industry was one of the irrefragable constants of the pre-industrial English economy and increased national prosperity between 1500 and 1730 was in no small measure due to a 15-fold growth in the value of cloth exports. The expansion was neither smooth nor monolithic. Throughout the country the industry changed its nature as demand and wool supplies changed, as new fibres were introduced and as new techniques were innovated. [7]

The West Country was the centre of woollen broadcloth production and this made it the most important industrial region in sixteenth-century England. Its white undyed cloths were of high quality, made from fine short staple wool, but exports fell from about 60,000 to 30,000 pieces between 1600 and 1640. The introduction of coloured 'medley' cloths made from Spanish wool, given impetus by the depression of the 1620s, created a new industry centred in the area between Frome and Bradford-upon-Avon. The produce of this district was again the most sought after English export by the middle of the seventeenth century. Other parts of the region innovated worsted cloths in response to the crisis in broadcloth production and so did west Somerset, Devon and Cornwall, where they replaced coarse woollens. [8] There was almost wholesale change in East Anglia, too. The Essex woollen industry, amongst the most important in

England in the early sixteenth century, had dwindled away by the early eighteenth. Suffolk changed from woollens to worsteds and the ancient worsted industry of Norfolk was revivified and boosted to international prominence by the introduction of the new draperies by refugees from the Low Countries. [9] Like that of Essex, the once important industries of other south-eastern counties decayed almost completely, although worsteds were introduced in a few places and the old woollen manufacture survived in a few others such as Witney. The north repeated the pattern of wholesale change. The coarse woollens of Lancashire and Yorkshire were improved and supplemented by worsteds, fustians, cottons and linens. [10] In the East Midlands framework knitting developed rapidly in the late seventeenth and early eighteenth centuries, moving from London where it had earlier flourished at the expense of the Norfolk hand-knitters. [11]

Where it existed, the textile industry employed high proportions of relatively dense populations. In the middle of the sixteenth century 8000 people were dependent upon the woollen manufacture of Worcester, which in the early seventeenth century was said to employ 6000 in the town and as many again in carding and spinning in the surrounding villages. Fifty-four per cent of Worcester inventories related to the goods of textile workers between 1590 and 1620. [12] In 1608 five hundreds clustered on the Cotswold scarp had more than 25 per cent of their inhabitants in textiles, one of them 45 per cent. [13] Even higher proportions occurred in some northern parishes in the early eighteenth century (see Table 7.1). [14] Particular small areas within the textile regions were usually highly specialized in distinct types of cloth. In the West Country some of the towns, for example Devizes, specialized in the production of serge cloths of the worsted type, quite different from the medleys of Frome and Bradford-upon-Avon, and the Wylye valley in Wiltshire concentrated on coarse woollens known as kerseys. In Cornwall and Devon different types of worsteds were produced in different towns and in Lancashire the textile workers did not simply designate themselves as weavers in the parish registers, but as linen weavers in Up Holland, fustian weavers in Hindley and plod weavers in Great Harwood. Indeed, there were quite sharp divisions in the north between the coloured woollen producing area to the west of Leeds, the plain woollen area further west stretching between Bradford and Huddersfield and the worsted area westward again around and to the north of Halifax. This area gave way to the coarse woollen producing area of east Lancashire, which was in turn succeeded by an area specializing in fustians and then, on the extremity of the northern textiles

Table 7.1: Occupations in some Lancashire and Yorkshire parish registers in the early eighteenth century.

PARISH		No. of entries	Per cent in textiles	Per cent in other industries	Per cent in labouring etc.	Per cent in agriculture	Per cent in other and unstated designations
Up Holland	1700–30	676	23·8	8·1	17·6	14·4	35·9
Walton-le-Dale 1704–08 and	1724–28	285	46·0	0	10·5	13·0	30·5
Penwortham	1725–28	204	18·1	0	13·7	41·7	26·5
Denton	1723–26	88	38·6	14·7	4·5	9·0	32·9
Middleton	1730–34	384	59·9	0	0·5	15·4	24·2
Oldham	1725–27	568	53·3	5·6	10·4	7·4	23·2
Great Harwood	1725–35[a]	376	38·6	4·3	0·8	20·2	36·1
Saddleworth	1722–26[a]	369	75·6	—	—	11·4	13·0
TOTAL		2950	44·7	3·9	8·3	15·2	27·9

[a] Indicates entries in baptism, marriage and burial registers, the remainder baptisms only.

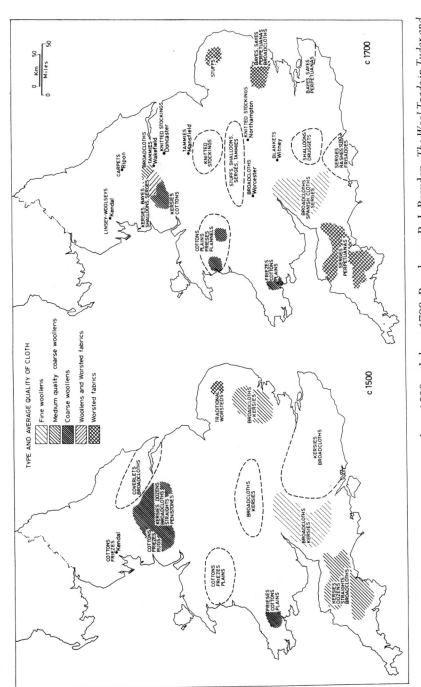

Fig. 7.1. The textile manufacturing regions in about 1500 and about 1700. Based upon P. J. Bowden, *The Wool Trade in Tudor and Stuart England*, (London, 1962), p. 49.

region, came the linen producing areas to the west of Wigan and to the south of Manchester. These textile regions, comprising spatial amalgams of distinctive cells, were widespread over the country (see Fig. 7.1). As time progressed those of the north, west and East Anglia came to contain greater proportions of the increased numbers of cloth workers whilst those of the south-east declined.

The Development of the Coalfields

Many of the other industries which grew at accelerating rates after the middle of the seventeenth century were also in the north and west. They were on the coalfields. Given the huge dominance of textiles in the value of national exports in the early eighteenth century the implication of Rees, whose book *Industry before the Industrial Revolution* deals exclusively with the coal and coal using metal industries, and the claims of Nef, who recognized an early Industrial Revolution on the coalfields in the sixteenth and seventeenth centuries, may seem difficult to justify. [15] But it must be remembered that textiles had a smaller predominance in the manufacturing economy as a whole than amongst exports alone and that the relative importance of textiles when measured in terms of value of output was much greater than when measured by weight of product or numbers employed.

In stark contrast to the lineage of the woollen industry, coal output was negligible in 1500. Even in Northumberland and Durham, the most precocious coalfield, only when coalbearing lands came into private and willingly speculative hands after the dissolution of the monasteries did production begin to grow continuously and rapidly. In 1550 output on the lower Tyne was about 40,000 tons a year; by the early seventeenth century it was about 800,000 tons a year, three-quarters bound outwards from the river, mainly to London. Although the dissolution of the monasteries gave a filip to production everywhere and references to mining are quite common by the late sixteenth century, knowledge of reserves was thin and patchy in 1600 on all other coalfields. Most exploitation was through the outcrops where coal was thought to grow. In many inland areas the lord dug coal for his own use and often allowed his tenants to get their own or to collect supplies from his workmen, just as they could get brushwood or turves within the manor. Commercial mining was generally effected through collieries with one small pit employing two or three getters who cut less than two tons each per day, under 2000 tons a year altogether.[16]

During the seventeenth century mining expanded considerably, grow-ing quickest and furthest on the coastal coalfields and those, like Nottinghamshire and Warwickshire, near navigable rivers or large towns. In the north-east the introduction of the waggonway and expansion to Wearside and the Northumbrian coast pushed output up to about one and a quarter million tons a year by 1700, a quantity worth nearly £2 millions at London wholesale prices, two-thirds the value of woollen exports at the time. Welsh coal shipments increased from about 6000 tons a year to about 90,000 tons a year during the course of the seventeenth century, mainly after the Civil War, and those of Whitehaven in Cumberland from nearly nothing to about 40,000 tons a year between the Civil War and 1707/8.[17] In south-west Lancashire output increased between two and four-fold to somewhere between 20,000 and 30,000 tons a year during the seventeenth century, probably a low rate of growth and a low level of development even for a landlocked coalfield.

Development quickened considerably during the early eighteenth century, even away from navigable water. By 1715 there were collieries in south-west Lancashire four times as large as the biggest of the seventeenth century; by 1735 the output of this coalfield was about 80,000 tons a year and one single colliery raised as much as the whole coalfield had 50 years earlier. The fact that every coalfield of any size was already mined through collieries using steam engines for drainage by 1730 is symbolic of the development achieved in the closing decades of the period.[18]

There was an acute timber shortage in the sixteenth and seventeenth centuries. The price of firewood rose much faster than prices in general and coal became, as a result, an essential item of household consumption despite considerable initial revulsion from 'that noxious mineral'. Hauled over land and water, it became the principal domestic fuel in all major towns and cities as well as large tracts of land adjacent to the coast and navigable rivers. In addition, coal was substituted for wood and charcoal in almost every significant industrial process between 1500 and 1730. Half the coal imported into London was consumed by craftsmen in 1699 and 'since the [Civil] War there is a vast Increase of Manufactures made with Coal in the North'.[19] Saltboiling, brewing, limeburning, brickmaking, potting, soapboiling, glass smelting, dyeing, alum, copperas and starch making were all converted to coal consumption during this period. Iron, tin, lead, zinc, copper, and the alloys of brass and pewter could be worked with coal from the early seventeenth century. The smelting of tin and iron ore still required charcoal until the early eighteenth century, but the vast majority of the fuel requirements of metal manufacture came after smelting, in the continual heating and reheating necessary to produce finished articles. Much has been made of the influence of charcoal supplies on the distribution of iron smelting, but this was relatively insignificant compared with the influence of coal on all other branches of the industry. [20] Indeed, the shift of charcoal smelting to the west, Yorkshire and Wales was probably as much an orientation towards the smelters' markets on the coalfields as it was towards charcoal supplies.

All the coalfields had manufacturing industries based upon their fuel by the early eighteenth century. Where navigable water allowed the combination of coal with large quantities of other raw materials, some of the industrial plants were already of an impressive size. The glass, iron and salt works of the Tyne were of international importance; so were the salt works of the Mersey and the copper and lead works of Wales and Bristol. Like mining itself had come to be, these industries were carried out in highly capitalized plants by proleterianized workers. It is their existence which has led to claims that there was already an industrial revolution before the end of this period. [21]

Far more typical and in sum more important were the small workshops thickly scattered over the Coal Measures. As early as about 1540 Leland saw smiths in Birmingham 'that use to make knives and all maner of cuttynge tools, and many lorimars that make byts, and a great many naylors. So that a greate parte of the towne is mayntayned by smiths.' [22] According to Dud Dudley there were 20,000 smiths within ten miles of Dudley castle in the mid-seventeenth century. [23] Thirty-four per cent of the 1691 people in the area between Wolverhampton and Birmingham whose goods were appraised in probate inventories between 1660 and 1710 were metalworkers. In four townships metalworkers were in a majority and in the area as a whole they were more numerous than specialist agriculturalists. [24] It was the same in the Hallamshire district of South Yorkshire. In 1772 there were nearly 600 smithies within ten miles of Sheffield; [25] metalworkers comprised 43 per cent of the occupations in a sample of 243 probate inventories taken between 1695 and 1729 and 55 per cent of the 2681 occupations in Sheffield parish registers between 1700 and 1729. [26] As in the textile regions, local specialization was pronounced. Different places specialized in the manufacture of different kinds of nail in the West Midlands, besides others in brassware, saddlery

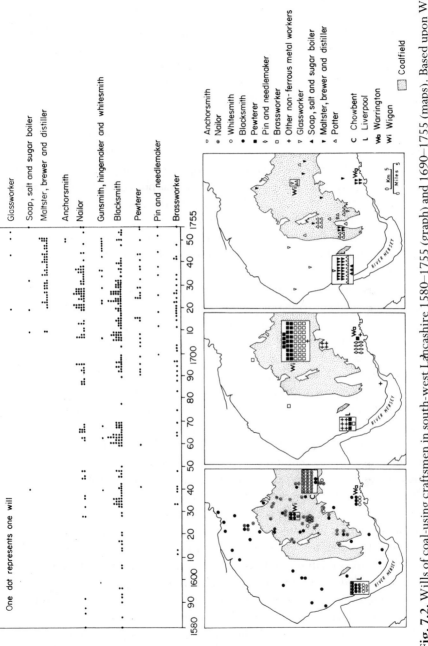

Fig. 7.2. Wills of coal-using craftsmen in south-west Lancashire 1580–1755 (graph) and 1690–1755 (maps). Based upon Wills at Chester, 1545–1620, 1621–50, 1660–80, 1681–1700, 1701–20, 1721–40 and 1741–60, *Record Society of Lancashire and Cheshire* 2 (1879), 4 (1881), 15 (1887), **18** (1888), **20** (1889), **22** (1890), and **25** (1892).

iron, locks, scythes, needles and chains. [27] Even on coalfields which were not renowned for their industries in this period the coal-based crafts showed the same patterns of growth and spatial differentiation (see Fig. 7.2).

Rural and Urban Industries

A thinly spread and widely scattered location pattern, with the most important industries penetrating remote rural settlements, was a pronounced feature of the economic geography of England between 1500 and 1730. The process of industrial growth was not generally one of urban industrialization and, so the orthodoxy goes, the rise of rural industry put urban economies under considerable stress.

The model of rural industrialization is clear and convincing in outline. [28] It applies mainly to the major growth industries of textiles and iron production. They exported a large proportion of their output, mainly through London factors, and London itself was overwhelmingly dominant in the home market. A major part of their production was thus bound for a single destination, either directly or through fairs. At the same time, raw materials provision was becoming more difficult and complex as industries originally based upon local resources grew beyond the capacity of local supplies. It was conspicuous by the seventeenth century that the textile areas were, presumably through the operation of comparative advantages, geographically distinct from the most important wool growing areas. In the iron industry smelting was forced apart from forging and finishing by competition for increasingly scarce charcoal and water power. Some manufactures were completely dependent on imported raw materials, like the ironworkers of Durham on Swedish metal and the clothworkers of the West Country on Spanish wool. The individual producer of cloth or iron was unable to collect his raw materials from their source and sell his goods in their markets because both were widely separated from him.

The role of the middleman was given greater prominence as products became more valuable in a handicraft technology. Increased value could only be added to materials by handworkers spending more time in processing them, usually by different specialists transferring them from one to the other: 'production becomes more roundabout in proportion as it becomes more efficient'. [29] The time lapse between the purchase of raw materials and the sale of finished goods thus increased progressively as industry developed and this delay was lengthened further by the common practice of London factors of only paying for goods when they had themselves sold them. Moreover although the capital equipment of production was small, easily fitting into a garret, bedroom or cellar, it could be quite expensive: a stocking frame, for example, cost £65 in 1658. Although production could be carried out in a worker's home, the worker could neither organize nor finance it.

Perhaps early on it was general practice for the craftsman to buy raw materials from and sell produce to the middleman. But as time passed it became more and more common for the dealer to retain ownership of the materials and pay the craftsman wages. The ironmonger smelted metal and sold finished ironware in London after passing it through numerous hands and processes; the clothier bought wool from London dealers and sold cloth back to them after passing it to spinners, carders or combers, weavers, fullers, shearers and dyers. Everywhere, it seems, the grip of the middleman strengthened as production became more complex. Their control was nowhere absolutely complete. In the north especially independent, smallholder craftsmen remained common, styling themselves as 'clothiers' in the Pennine parishes of Rochdale and Saddleworth. But even in the north, and particularly in the less remote parts of it, landless wage-earning craftsmen were also common by the early eighteenth century and probably in a majority in some branches of the textile industry there. In the West Country land was scarcer and more expensive, the raw materials were more precious, the two-man broadcloth looms were bigger and more costly and the grip of the Blackwell Hall cloth factors was more complete. There were few independent craftsmen there and many clothiers employed hundreds, some over a thousand, wage-earners. Control by large-scale dealers was conducive to the narrow local specialization of production. It made their business easier, cheaper and less time-consuming if their materials flowed between concentrations of specialized workers.

A shift of industry from towns to rural locations is often associated with the growth in the power of middlemen. Of course it was not the only reason. Carus-Wilson has argued that the search for water power with the diffusion of the fulling mill, which pulled out other craftsmen to rural locations, was the decisive influence. [30] But it is likely that labour supplies were the most important rural location factor. From the point of view of the clothier or ironmonger, the labour necessary for expansion was abundant in the countryside, untrammelled by gild restrictions and, at least initially, less fractious and more easily expanded or contracted as the state of trade dictated because of its only partial dependence on industrial employment. Most rural industry was in once and sometimes still heavily-wooded, rolling or upland country in the Midlands, west and north:[31] areas which were predominantly pastoral with weak manorial control, where there was abundant common or sparsely colonized land. In such areas there was usually free time from the chores of farming every day throughout the year for some members of the family and the independence to use it as they wished. It was therefore possible to supplement the generally low incomes from agriculture with industrial by-employment, and this became more necessary as competition in pastoral markets increased with the innovation of mixed farming systems on previously arable or barren land in the south and east.[32] In these areas, too, patches of land coupled with access to large areas of common grazing were available to immigrants, tempted by the opportunities offered by a dual economic system, or for the relatively abundant children which it allowed and even encouraged. Local specialization was almost inevitable when large progenies trained in industry by their fathers stayed near home after setting up their own families. So was the exhaustion of land supplies. When this occurred, the individual worker became both more dependent upon his industrial employment and less able to acquire the credit necessary to finance his own production. It was thus that dependence on the employment provided by dealers progressively increased.

Arable areas with communal social structures or strong manorial control and areas where the innovation of mixed farming techniques was making agriculture a more lucrative, complex and full-time business seem to have been much less susceptible to the development of rural industry. High rural wages and incomes generally, resulting from proximity to London and agrarian improvement, were probably responsible for the progressive decline of the textile industry of the south-east. It is quite striking, too, that industry remained largely urban in other areas where arable or improved mixed farming were predominant, as in Worcester, Norwich, Witney, Tewkesbury and the numerous small towns of Wiltshire and Somerset. Or it declined altogether, as in the Vale of Severn. Where there were no pools of cheap or common land on which they could establish a toe-hold, those who were surplus to the opportunities of established agriculture thronged the towns in search of employment. Destitute urban labour cannot have been much less attractive to clothiers and ironmongers than rural labour. Both town authorities and central government were assiduous in promoting the textile industry as a salve for urban poverty. Defoe's celebrated description of the rural industrial landscape of Halifax is often quoted, but Halifax was no more typical of industrial England at the time than towns such as Frome, which Defoe likened to Manchester, with narrow muddy streets of mean cottages, eerily silent in the daytime when the majority of their denizens were indoors earning low wages for long hours of work, as dependent upon the capitalists who employed them as any nineteenth-century factory hand.

Even in areas characterized by rural industry, manufacturing towns were common. Nottingham and Leicester contained over one-fifth of all the stocking frames in the East Midlands in 1727 and Nottingham had two-thirds of all those in Nottinghamshire in 1739. In south-west Lancashire, Wigan and Liverpool were clearly as important as industrial locations as the rural areas around them (see Fig. 7.2). Wigan illustrates what seems to have been a general trend in metalworking districts: the more complex processes were located in the towns and the cheaper simpler lines were made in the countryside.

In fact, most towns were heavily dependent upon manufactures. Only three of the towns on Table 7.2 had less than half of their freemen or apprentices in manufacturing trades. [33] These were the small ports where merchants of one kind or another were numerically predominant. The structure of the large manufacturing component of urban economies varied somewhat from town to town (see Table 7.3). York had the most evenly balanced set of manufactures, as perhaps befits the capital of the North, with a relatively small proportion in textiles. This proportion was also small in the ports generally, whilst in Norwich and Dorchester it was very large. Clearly some towns had industrial specialisms which served, like the rural industrial areas, international markets. [34]

It is also clear that urban manufacturing economies were much more varied than those of rural areas (compare Tables 7.1 and 7.3). This was, of course, because they were central places. Many of their craftsmen were artisan-retailers, selling what they made through their own shops and market stalls to the countryfolk from an area of about 10 to 15 miles around. [35] 'Daily shops and weekly markets, consumer goods and services . . . are no doubt all very dull to contemplate, but they are nearer to the truth of past urban economies than thoughtless clichés about cloth, wool, and sheep.' [36] It may well be that the more specialized manufacturing sectors of the towns came under increased and successful competition

Table 7.2: Occupations of freemen or apprentices in some English towns in the early seventeenth century. [33]

TOWN		Rank in 1662	No. of entries	Per cent in agriculture	Per cent in building	Per cent in manufacturing	Per cent in transport	Per cent in dealing	Per cent in public and professional services	Per cent in menial and domestic occupations	Per cent of independent means	Per cent with no occupation entered
Norwich	1621–39	2	1312	0·1	6·7	72·0	0·8	17·8	3·3	0	0	0
York	1621–39	3	1845	0·1	5·0	57·5	1·6	25·5	3·0	0·7	0·5	5·0
Newcastle	1621–39	5	611	0·1	9·4	52·1	9·1	25·3	3·5	0	0·2	0
Exeter	1621–39	6	483	0·8	6·0	54·5	0·4	32·3	2·5	0·4	2·7	0·4
Yarmouth	1599–1612	8	246	0	1·2	23·9	13·0	41·0	2·4	0	5·7	12·6
Chester	1614–16, 1619–29 and 1634–43	20	706	1·4	4·8	77·0	0·6	10·8	1·7	0·3	3·5	0·1
Lynn	1614–33	23	300	0·7	3·0	41·7	5·3	44·3	2·0	0·3	2·7	0
Southampton	1621–39	40	217	0		45·0	2·0	52·0	0	0	0	0
Dorchester	1621–35	>40	292	0	7·0	63·0	0	24·0	2·0	0·3	0·6	4·1
TOTAL			6012	0·3	5·7	60·9	2·6	23·9	2·8	0·3	1·2	2·3

Table 7.3: Manufacturing occupations of freemen and apprentices in some English towns in the early seventeenth century.[33]

TOWN		No. of manufacturers	Per cent in tools and instruments	Per cent in ship-building	Per cent in clothing	Per cent in victualling	Per cent in iron	Per cent in non-ferrous metals	Per cent in earthen ware	Per cent in furs and leather	Per cent in glue tallow horn etc.	Per cent in wood	Per cent in textiles
Norwich	1621–39	939	6·0	0	29·1	10·4	0·2	1·5	1·0	4·9	0·3	1·6	44·4
York	1621–39	1070	6·9	0·6	34·8	17·2	3·6	5·3	0	12·3	1·4	5·6	12·3
Newcastle	1621–39	373	0·8	21·3	7·8	19·4	11·1	0	0	12·4	0	11·3	16·4
Exeter	1621–39	264	6·5	0·0	23·6	19·4	6·5	4·2	0	7·2	2·3	7·2	23·2
Yarmouth	1599–1612	59	0	5·0	27·0	25·4	0	3·4	0	3·4	3·4	32·2	0
Chester 1614–16	1619–29 and 1634–43	532	2·7	0	28·8	19·2	9·6	1·5	0	8·7	2·2	5·2	20·3
Lynn	1614–33	125	1·6	1·6	36·0	19·2	0·8	6·4	0·8	4·8	8·0	13·6	7·2
Southampton	1621–39	98	4·0	3·0	51·0	6·0	2·0	3·0	0	0	5·0	10·0	15·0
Dorchester	1621–35	183	7·0	0	19·6	15·8	2·7	1·6	0	4·3	2·2	4·3	42·0
TOTAL		3643	5·1	2·6	28·6	16·0	4·3	2·9	0·3	8·4	1·6	6·0	24·3

from the industries of the countryside. But these very competitors provided a market for the artisan-retailer sector. Generally, the countryside became wealthier and more populous when agriculture became more productive and industries took root there, injecting a potent stimulus into urban economies. This may well have been partly responsible for the decline of specialist manufactures in some towns: they generally paid low wages and had no social prestige, so that if alternatives were available it was difficult to recruit labour into them, forcing the dealers to look for it in the countryside around. [37]

Urban craftsmen served narrowly local and international markets; they also served market areas in bands of the spectrum in between. By the seventeenth century the home market had developed sufficiently to accommodate the existence of congeries of craftsmen serving with specialist lines regions much larger than the normal market areas of the towns in which they lived. The leather trades were probably the prime example of urban crafts of this kind, with important sixteenth century centres in Chester, which served a national market for gloves, partly through the agency of London dealers, Leicester and Northampton. [38] The ironworkers of Newcastle and Chester in the seventeenth century and the woodworkers using Baltic timber imported through the east-coast ports probably served similarly large markets, otherwise they could not have existed in such relatively large numbers there (see Table 7.3). The large areas over which bells were marketed from various manufacturing centres in the west of England are shown on Fig. 7.3. Walsall supplied a similar area with pewter, bigger than those served by the less numerous pewterers in the towns of south-central England. [39] Large proportions of the craftsmen in particular towns could be involved in production for regional markets of this kind. For example, over 30 per cent of the occupations recorded in the borough court records of Wigan in the late seventeenth century concerned the making and working of pewter, copper and brass, trades which were usually only negligibly represented (see Table 7.3).

Other Urban Functions

Non-manufacturing activities added further to the growing diversity of urban economies in the sixteenth and seventeenth centuries. Amongst

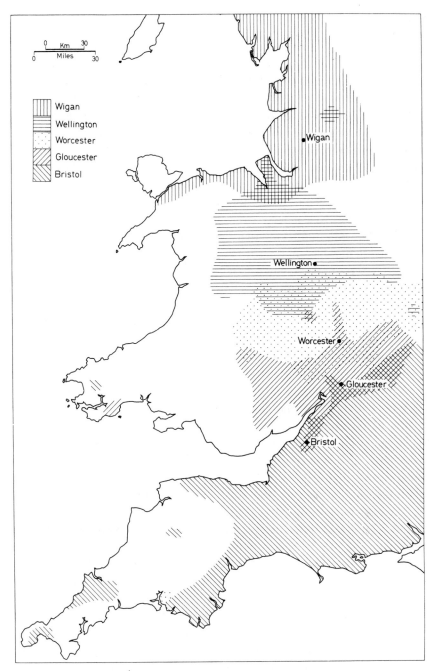

Fig. 7.3. Market areas of bell manufacturers in some west of England towns *c.* 1550 1700. Based on maps of the location of thousands of bells, plotted from local history, archaeology and campanology journals.

them dealing was paramount, but professional services such as the law, medicine and education were more important than Table 7.2 suggests because their practitioners did not handle goods and did not, therefore, usually require town freedom to practice or apprenticeship to train. As wealth increased in the countryside and as farming, land holding and rural industry became more complicated, a wide array of services as well as goods came into demand. Schools for the heirs of estates, farmers, managers, agents and dealers as their activities became more businesslike and literate; lawyers to work out contracts and entails, mortgages and other debt and credit transactions and to service the increasingly busy courts; doctors to pander to the ailments of people who required an increase in solicitude commensurate with that of their wealth—all increased in numbers in the towns. [40] On top of these functions were the various entertainments which an increasingly wealthy gentry could afford locally, if not in London. Race meetings, carnivals, processions and social seasons aping that of the capital became common in the provinces. Increased urban concourse provided increased business for townsmen, especially for the innkeepers who provided assembly rooms, rooms in which dealers could do business, bowling greens and so on as well as accommodation, stabling and victuals. [41] Most towns benifited from these activities—even Wigan had its fashionable spa. But many of them were services with high thresholds and long ranges, serving a thin smattering of gentry. They came to be concentrated in a few towns, eventually picking them out as high order service centres in an increasingly integrated urban hierarchy. The county towns, where the gentry assembled for periodic meetings of higher provincial courts, usually achieved this status: the seventeenth century was 'the Golden Age of the county town'.

The growing dealing element in the urban economy included those who pumped out goods into an increasingly wealthy countryside and those who sucked in the produce on which the receptivity was based. Among the former, mercers and grocers were prominent, purveying almost anything of high value from distant origins which retailed in small quantities. As agricultural surpluses grew, their collection and distribution became more concentrated and specialized. Many of the small market centres around which the local flows of medieval times had been articulated declined. [42] Others provided bases for the dealers despite continual attempts by town authorities to prevent the usurpation by dealers of foodstuffs and other raw materials from town markets. It was only in the towns that the institutions, communications, contacts and information that they required were all available together. Thus, marketing became concentrated in fewer but individually much more active towns which were often associated with specialized marketing or the processing of particular kinds of produce.[43] This urban preference was also usually true of dealers in rural-industrial products. Even in the Cotswolds, least urbanized of any of the rural industrial areas, the clothiers lived in little towns such as Painswick 'for they delight to live like the merry rooks and daws chattering and prating together'.[44] The dealers' contacts extended out from these places like webs into the remotest corners of the countryside in one direction, often through partners or agents in smaller settlements, and almost inevitably to London in the other.

Indeed London absorbed a huge proportion of the energizing effect of increased national production, the dealing, administration and new demands it spawned. The capital was more dominant in national life than ever before or since. Its two basic functions of government and trade both increased rapidly and became more centralized. The royal court, law courts and Parliament drew in the wealthy from the whole country for periodic or semi-permanent residence as representatives, litigants or socialites. They sustained luxury tradesmen such as silkweavers, watchmakers and jewellers in abundance as well as a whole army of servants, labourers and the poor who are always attracted by the prospect of crumbs.[45] The City of London proper, as distinct from Westminster, was a place of business and exchange. The sixteenth and seventeenth centuries witnessed the abstraction of a greater and greater proportion of national trade by London dealers. Goods of all kinds were sucked into the halls of its companies and the warehouses of their members before redistribution or export. Imports almost invariably began their circulation in the national economy in the same venues.[46] Most of the provincial ports declined as London merchants took over their trade. In 1700 80 per cent of England's imports, 69 per cent of its exports and 86 per cent of its re-exports went through London. This was the ultimate expression of the increased centralization of trade that was occurring at all scales in the economy. Under the stimulus of national government and trade, London's population increased from 200,000 in 1600 to 400,000 in 1650 to 575,000 in 1700, when it was bigger than Paris. Seven per cent of England's population lived in the capital in 1650 and 11 per cent by 1750, when London was more than ten times bigger than the next largest city in the country.

Intra-urban Geographical Patterns

The vast majority of English towns had less than 5000 inhabitants even in 1730, with not many more than half a dozen streets and perhaps as many lanes and alleys. Strongly marked zones of wealth and occupations are not to be expected in such small places. However, it is evident when information is available in sufficient detail that there could be reasonably firm patterns along the streets as they radiated from the town centre. In Gloucester in 1455 specialist dealers and victuallers preponderated in the very centre, with artisan-retailers further out and craftsmen who sold mainly to dealers further out again. Rents were highest near the centre and fell towards the gates and in the side streets, a clear reflection of the value of central sites in towns where central place functions employed a large proportion of the inhabitants. [47] Where dealers and others were engaged in trades which allowed them to accumulate far greater wealth than the craftsmen and where they were in sufficient numbers, as in even small ports, a distinct higher status zone might exist, too, even in small towns. [48]

The larger provincial capitals such as York, Norwich, Exeter, Bristol and Newcastle had between 8000 and 12,000 inhabitants in the 1520s and perhaps twice as many by 1730. In these towns configurations more closely approximating the archetypes of the pre-industrial city were evident. It is clear from the Hearth Tax Assessments that the rich lived near the centre and that wealth declined towards the periphery. The wealthy central area was occupied by merchants of one kind or another, the foremost in Newcastle being those engaged in the coal trade. In most towns the merchants had a far greater opportunity to amass wealth than the artisans because their businesses could be expanded at will and to the limit of their acumen, whereas the craftsmen were hedged about with restrictions about the quantity and type of material they could buy and sell, where they could do it, how many apprentices they could employ and what hours they could work. [49] The wealthy group in the centre was more than an amalgam of persons of equivalent riches. It often formed an oligarchy which ran the town through the institutions of town and gild halls and law courts, shot through with ties of kinship, friendship and partnership. [50] The merchant gild or company was often more or less the same thing as the town council. Outwards from the centre came the quarters of the artisan-retailers who, if their numbers were sufficient, might have their own companies and tight residential groupings of like with like to facilitate the derivation of external economies of buying and selling and the company functions of inspection, social welfare and entertainment. Beyond them again came the least wealthy and prestigious crafts and the poor.

London completely dwarfed the provincial capitals, but the basic lineaments of its social and economic geography were similar.[51] It was functionally and geographically really two cities in the seventeenth century, that of government and the royal court at Westminster and that of commerce and trade in the City of London itself. In the latter there was a rich mercantile centre right through this period, with quite distinct occupational quarters and poor districts on the outskirts. This typical pre-industrial pattern only began to disintegrate when the power of the gilds and companies as agents of social and economic cohesion began to wane in the eighteenth century: it was only destroyed when commuting between separate homes and workplaces became common in the nineteenth century.

Spatial Integration and Economic Development

Between 1500 and 1730 England became economically developed. The expansion of agriculture and industry in the provincial countryside comprised an important part of the process. Yet London grew as never before to achieve immense primacy and other towns and cities increased in size, generally though not invariably faster than in previous centuries. This association of an increasingly rural generation of wealth with urbanization is only a paradox (or unrecognizable) if urban and rural, London and the provinces are treated as separable systems. They were not. The symbiosis of town with countryside and of London with the whole of England grew closer and stronger between 1500 and 1730 than ever before or since. Modern development economists stress the importance in economic growth of spatial integration, of bringing together diverse and distant places and resources into reciprocation.[52] The agents of this process in pre-industrial England were the dealers, and they were urbanites. In Marxist terminology, it was the function of towns to redistribute surplus value.[53]

Through the activities of the middlemen, England became an integrated economic system. London, 'the great wen' in Westminster, was an integrating 'engine of economic growth' in the City of London itself.[54] The demands of London largely stimulated the massive re-organization of agricultural marketing, transforming an amalgam of separate, cellular market areas into a cumulating cascade of flows towards the capital. The north-eastern coal trade and the industries that depended upon and emanated from it were ultimately based upon London's demands. London dealers introduced the exotic goods, London's populace the social fashions and aspirations, whose provision and satisfaction stimulated the development of the county towns. London dealers channelled raw materials into and finished goods out of England. They gathered and disseminated the information, contacts and finance which energized provincial industry.

Below the national nexus of flows there was a substratum of daily and weekly contacts around the central places of the provinces, just as there had been in medieval times. These nodes became more thinly spread as dealers usurped an increasing proportion of the flows and hierarchical steps were developing as the county towns began to provide higher order services and other hinterlands became sorted beneath them. [55] But England's economic landscape was more like that portrayed by Lösch than that of Christaller. Side-by-side and interleaved with the incipient hierarchy of central places were towns with specialist manufactures which served regional markets. In addition, and largely outside the nested hierarchical system, were the industrial regions where manufacturing for international markets spread through town and countryside alike in intricate sprawling kaleidoscopes of local specialization.

It was as if the spatial system of medieval times, one of almost discrete local economies loosely linked through London, was transformed by the greater cohesion imposed by London's growth and by the interposition of hierarchical steps and whole regional economies between the two old levels. The growth process was one of regional and national integration. As yet the regional economies were umbilically tied to London. They only developed autonomous links with international economic systems in the Industrial Revolution.

References

1. The quotations in this paragraph are taken from M. Dewar (ed.), *A Discourse of the Commonweal of England, attributed to Sir Thomas Smith,* (Charlottesville, 1969), pp.11, 37, 68–9.
2. R. G. Wilkinson, *Poverty and Progress,* (London, 1973), pp.70–76.

3. D. Defoe, *A Tour Through the Whole Island of Great Britain*, (Harmondsworth, 1971), p.43.
4. D. C. Coleman, *Industry in Tudor and Stuart England*, (London, 1975), pp.11–14.
5. The economic statistics in this paragraph are taken from Phyllis Deane and W. A. Cole, *British Economic Growth 1688–1959*, (Cambridge, 1964), pp.78, 155–8.
6. R. Davis, 'English foreign trade 1700–1774', *Economic History Review*, 2nd ser., **XV** (1962), p.290.
7. E. Lipson, *The History of the Woollen and Worsted Industries*, (London, 1921); P. J. Bowden, *The Wool Trade in Tudor and Stuart England*, (London, 1962).
8. J. de L. Mann, *The Cloth Industry in the West of England from 1640–1880*, (London, 1971); K. J. Ponting, *The Woollen Industry of South-west England*, (Bath, 1971); G. D. Ramsey, *The Wiltshire Woollen Industry in the Sixteenth and Seventeenth Centuries*, (Oxford, 1943). Strictly speaking 'cloth' was woollen, made of carded short staple wool, matted by fulling and with a raised sheared nap. Worsted was made from combed long staple wool, and was unfulled, with a distinguishable warp and weft.
9. K. J. Allison, 'The Norfolk worsted industry in the sixteenth and seventeenth centuries', *Yorkshire Bulletin of Social and Economic Reasearch*, **12** and **13** (1960 and 1961), pp.73–83 and 61–77; and D. C. Coleman, 'An innovation and its diffusion: the new draperies', *Economic History Review*, 2nd ser., **XXII** (1969), pp. 417–29. New draperies were varied. They are usually described as worsteds but many had a woollen weft and some were finished by fulling and shearing like woollens.
10. H. Heaton, *The Yorkshire Woollen and Worsted Industries*, (Oxford, 1920); N. Lowe, *The Lancashire Textile Industry in the Sixteenth Century*, (Manchester, 1972); A. P. Wadsworth and J. de L. Mann, *The Cotton Trade and Industrial Lancashire 1600–1780* (Manchester, 1931).
11. J. D. Chambers, *Nottinghamshire in the Eighteenth Century*, (2nd edn.) (London, 1966); S. D. Chapman, 'The genesis of the British hosiery industry 1600–1750', *Textile History*, 3 (1972), pp.7–50.
12. Lipson, *Woollen and Worsted Industries*, p. 24; L. A. Clarkson, *The Pre-industrial Economy in England 1500–1750*, (London, 1971), pp.88–9.
13. A. J. and R. H. Tawney, 'An occupational census of the seventeenth century', *Economic History Review*, **V** (1934–5), pp. 25–64.
14. The statistics in Table 7.1 are taken from Wadsworth and Mann, *The Cotton Trade*, pp.314–5, T. Wild, 'The Saddleworth parish registers', *Textile History*, 1 (1968–70), pp.214–32 and 'The parish register of Great Harwood 1547–1812', *Lancashire Parish Register Society*, **75** (1937).
15. W. Rees, *Industry before the Industrial Revolution*, 2 Vols, (Cardiff, 1968); J. U. Nef, *The Rise of the British Coal Industry*, 2 Vols, (London, 1932). Where not otherwise referenced, material on mining is from these sources and J.

Langton, 'Coal output in south-west Lancashire 1590–1799', *Economic History Review*, 2nd ser., **XXV** (1972), pp. 28–54.

16. L. Stone, 'An Elizabethan coalmine', *Economic History Review*, 2nd ser., **III** (1950–51), pp.97–106.

17. J. E. Williams, 'Whitehaven in the eighteenth century', *Economic History Review*, 2nd ser., **XIII** (1955–6), pp. 393–404.

18. J. S. Allen, 'The introduction of the Newcomen engine 1710–33', *Transactions of the Newcomen Society*, **42** (1969–70), pp.169–90.

19. A. W. A. Moller, 'The history of English coalmining 1500–1750', D. Phil. Thesis, University of Oxford, 1933, pp.25–7.

20. T. S. Ashton, *Iron and Steel in the Industrial Revolution*, (1924); H. Roepke, *Movements of the British Iron and Steel Industry 1720–1951*, (Urbana, 1965); G. Hammersley, 'The charcoal iron industry and its fuel 1540–1760', *Economic History Review*, 2nd ser., **XXVI** (1973), pp.593–613.

21. J. U. Nef, 'The progress of technology and the growth of large-scale industry in Great Britain 1540–1640', *Economic History Review*, **V** (1934–35), pp. 3–24; S. M. Jack, *Trade and Industry in Tudor and Stuart England*, (London, 1977).

22. R. A. Pelham, 'The migration of the iron industry to Birmingham during the sixteenth century', *Transactions and Proceedings of the Birmingham Archaeological Society*, **LXVI** (1950), pp. 142–9.

23. *Metallum Martis* (1666), repr. in J. Thirsk and J. P. Cooper, *Seventeenth Century Economic Documents*, (Oxford, 1972), pp.277–84.

24. M. B. Rowlands, *Masters and Men in the West Midlands Metalware Trades before the Industrial Revolution*, (Manchester, 1975), pp.20–25.

25. D. Hey, *The Rural Metalworkers of the Sheffield Region*, (Leicester, 1972), pp.10–13.

26. Rowlands, *Masters and Men*, p.21; Clarkson, *The Pre-industrial Economy*, pp.88–9.

27. Rowlands, *Masters and Men*, pp. 22–5; W. H. B. Court, *The Rise of the Midland Industries*, (London, 1938); *idem*, 'Industrial organisation and economic progress in the eighteenth century Midlands', repr. in Court, *Scarcity and Choice in History*, (London, 1970), pp.235–49.

28. The following description is based upon works already cited plus J. D. Chambers, 'The rural domestic industries during the period of transition to the factory system', *Proceedings, 2nd International Conference of Economic History*, **II** (Aix-en-Provence, 1962), pp. 429–55 unless otherwise referenced.

29. Court, 'Industrial organisation', p. 241.

30. E. M. Carus-Wilson, 'Evidence of industrial growth on some fifteenth century manors', *Economic History Review*, 2nd ser., **XI** (1951), pp.190–205.

31. J. Thirsk, 'Industries in the countryside', in F. J. Fisher (ed.), *Essays in the Economic and Social History of Tudor and Stuart England*, (Cambridge, 1961), pp. 70–88.

32. E. L. Jones, 'Agriculture and economic growth in England, 1650–1815' and 'Agricultural origins of industry', repr. in Jones, *Agriculture and the Industrial Revolution*, (Oxford, 1974), pp.85–127, 128–42.

33. Tables 7.2 and 7.3 were drawn up from P. Millican, *The Register of the Freemen of Norwich, 1548–1713*, (Norwich, 1934); 'Register of the freemen of the city of York', Vol. II, 1559–1759, *Surtees Society*, **CII** (1899); 'The register of the freemen of Newcastle-upon-Tyne', *Newcastle-upon-Tyne Record Series*, **III** (1923); 'Exeter Freemen 1266–1967', *Devon and Cornwall Record Society, Exeter Series*, **I** (1973); 'The rolls of the freemen of the city of Chester', Pt. I, 1392–1700, *Record Society of Lancashire and Cheshire*, **LI** (1906); 'A calender of the freemen of Lynn, 1282–1836', (Norwich 1913); 'A calender of Southampton apprenticeship registers, 1609–1740', *Southampton Record Series*, **XII** (1968); C. H. Mayo and A. W. Gould (eds.), *The Municipal Records of the Borough of Dorchester, Dorset*, (Exeter, 1908), pp. 384–438. The urban rankings are based on the hearth tax figures given in W. G. Hoskins, *Local History in England*, (2nd edn.), (London, 1972), p.239.

34. See also J. F. Pound, 'The social and trade structure of Norwich 1525–75', *Past and Present*, **34** (1966), pp.49–69; D. M. Palliser, 'York under the Tudors', in A. Everitt (ed.), *Perspectives in English Urban History*, (London, 1973), pp.39–59; A. D. Dyer, *The City of Worcester in the Sixteenth Century*, (Leicester, 1973); W. G. Hoskins, *Industry Trade and People in Exeter 1688–1850*, (Manchester, 1935); *idem*, 'English provincial towns in the early sixteenth century', repr. in Hoskins, *Provincial England*, (London, 1965); P. Clark and P. Slack (eds.), *Crisis and Order in English Towns*, (London, 1972) and *English Towns in Transition*, (London, 1976); P. Lorfield, 'Urban development in England and Wales in the sixteenth and seventeenth centuries', in D. C. Coleman and A. H. John (eds.), *Trade, Government and Economy in Pre-industrial England*, (London, 1976), pp. 214–47.

35. Dyer, *City of Worcester*, pp.66–80; B. Rodgers, 'The market area of Preston in the sixteenth and seventeenth centuries', *Geographical Studies*, **3** (1950), pp.45–55; A. Everitt, 'The marketing of agricultural produce' in J. Thirsk, *The Agrarian History of England and Wales*, (Cambridge, 1967), Vol. 4, 1500–1640, pp.466–592.

36. Hoskins, 'English provincial towns', p.83.

37. Hoskins, *Industry, Trade and People*.

38. L. A. Clarkson, 'The leather crafts in Tudor and Stuart England', *Agricultural History Review*, **14** (1966), pp.25–39; Hoskins, 'English provincial towns', pp.66–80.

39. J. Hatcher and T. C. Barker, *A History of English Pewter*, (London, 1974), pp.259–61.

40. A. Everitt, *Perspectives in English Urban History*, pp.1–15; *idem, Change in the Provinces: the Seventeenth Century*, (Leicester, 1967).

41. A. Everitt, 'The English urban inn 1560–1760', in Everitt, *Perspectives in English Urban History*, pp.91–138.

42. B. E. Coates, 'The origin and distribution of markets and fairs in medieval Derbyshire', *Derbyshire Archaeological Journal,* **LXXXV** (1966), pp.92–111; H. Otsuka, 'The market structure of rural industry in the early stages of the development of modern capitalism', *Proceedings 2nd International Conference of Economic History,* **II** (Aix-en-Provence, 1962), pp. 457–72.

43. A. Everitt, 'Marketing of agricultural produce'; F. J. Fisher, 'The development of the London food market 1540–1640', *Economic History Review,* **V** (1935), pp.46–64.

44. Mann, *Cloth Industry in the West of England,* p.95.

45. F. Braudel, *Capitalism and Material Life 1400–1800,* (London, 1973), p.415; A. H. Dodd, 'Elizabethan towns and cities ', *History Today,* **11** (1961), pp.136–46.

46. Clark and Slack, *English Towns in Transition,* pp.62–81.

47. J. Langton, 'Late medieval Gloucester: some evidence from a rental of 1455', *Transactions, Institute British Geographers,* New Series, **2** (1977), pp. 259–77.

48. C. Platt, 'Southampton, 1000–1600 A.D.', *Hansische Geschischsblätter,* **91** (1973), pp.12–23.

49. J. Langton, 'Residential patterns in pre-industrial cities: some case studies from seventeenth century Britain', *Transactions, Institute of British Geographers,* **65** (1975), pp.1–28

50. C. W. Colby, 'The growth of oligarchy in English towns', *English Historical Reviews,* **V** (1890), pp.633–53.

51. R. A. P. Finlay, 'The population of London 1580–1650', Ph.D. thesis, University of Cambridge, 1977; D. V. Glass, 'London's inhabitants within the walls', *London Record Society Publs.,* **2** (1966); *idem,* 'Notes on the demography of London at the end of the seventeenth century', *Daedalus,* **97** (1968), pp.581–92; *idem,* 'Socio-economic status and occupations in the city of London at the end of the seventeenth century', in A. E. J. Hollaender and W. Kellaway, *Studies in London History Presented to P. E. H. Jones,* (London, 1969), pp.373–92.

52. H. Brookfield, *Independent Development,* (London, 1975).

53. D. Harvey, *Social Justice and the City,* (London, 1973), pp.216–61.

54. F. J. Fisher, 'London as an engine of economic growth', in J. S. Bromley and E. H. Kossman (eds.), *Britain and the Netherlands,* Vol. IV (The Hague, 1971), pp. 3–16; E. A. Wrigley, 'A simple model of London's importance in changing English society and economy 1650–1750', *Past and Present,* **37** (1967), pp.44–70.

55. J. H. Patten, 'Village and town: an occupational study ', *Agricultural History Review* **20** (1972), pp.1–16.

8
Population and its Geography in England 1500–1730

R. M. Smith

The description and interpretation of population change both at a national and a regional level in England between 1500 and 1730 is a complicated and controversial subject on which a considerable quantity of literature exists. Disagreements concern what happened, where it happened, why it happened, why it happened where it did and its consequences. The principal difficulties confronting this discussion stem from the uncertainties surrounding the available evidence so this chapter begins with a review of the sources and their interpretation.

Some Attempts at Estimating the Population Totals of England 1500–1730

For England and Wales there is no comprehensive information on population size before 1801 when the first British census was taken. As a consequence details on population totals, the 'lure of aggregates' as Postan has termed this highly seductive quest,[1] have to be sought from data sets whose prime purpose was to provide information of interest to fiscal and ecclesiastical authorities. Accordingly, a variety of sources have been used to learn indirectly of the course of population change between widely scattered points in time.[2]

However, the estimation of population totals from any one of these sources is a hazardous affair, the end-product being dependent upon assumptions about their spatial coverage, the level of under-enumeration, the sex ratio in the case of those sources that list men only, and the age structure of the population wherever coverage is confined to those above a particular age. For sources such as the Hearth Taxes that list household

Table 8.1: Some English population estimates, 1520–1695.

Source	Coverage	Assumptions		Total (millions)
1522 Muster and 1524/25 Lay Subsidies	Partial: able bodied men over 16 years of age and taxpayers listed in 1524 and 1525	(A)	All names in 1522, 1524 and 1525 lists are counted and it is hoped that omissions will balance migration. It is assumed all names listed relate to males over 16 and that the sex ratio is 100 (names × 10/3 (i.e. 3 males: 3 females: 4 children) = total population) and that counties for which the exercise can be done are in the same ratio to the total population in the 1520s as in 1377 (i.e. 11·3 per cent). (After J. Cornwall.)[a]	2·3
		(B)	Same assumptions as in (A) except a more youthful population in 1520s, i.e. 47 per cent under 16.	2·6
1545 Chantry Certificates	Partial: 'Houslyng' people assumed to be communicants	(A)	Interpolation from an estimate of the population in 1377 to a total for 1690. The total for 1545 is then read off. (After J. C. Russell.)[b]	3·1
		(B)	Use only parishes where a useful comparison can be made with taxpayer totals for 1377. Median growth 1377–1545 = 1·7 × 2·1 million (i.e. population total of 1377 based on the assumption that under 14s = 33 per cent of the total).	3·4
		(C)	Assumes that age of communion not 14 but 8 in 1545, therefore the 'houslyng' people were the over 8s. Median growth 1377–1545 = 1·24. Assumes also that under 14s in 1377 = 44 per cent of the population. Population total in 1545 = 2·4	3·0

million × 1.24. ((B) and (C) after unpublished calculations of R. S. Schofield.)

Source	Total	Notes	
		(D) Assumes parity between 1377 taxpayers and 'houslyng' people in the counties of Gloucestershire, Hereford, Middlesex, Oxford, Northampton and Somerset. Accepts population of 2·1 million in 1377 and estimates 25 per cent growth by 1545. (After J. Cornwall.)[a]	2·8
1603 Communicants Lists	Total: all communicants	(A) Assumes age of communion to be 14 and the over 14s to account for 33 per cent of total population.	3·1
		(B) Assumes age of communion to be 16 and the over 16s to account for 44 per cent of total population.	3·4
1676 Communicants Lists (Compton Census)	Total: all males and females over 16	(A) Assumes the age structure of Lichfield in 1695 to apply to the whole country. Therefore the under 16s = 40 per cent of total population.	4·5
		(B) Assumes the under 16s = 33 per cent of total population.	3·8
Gregory King 'Census', 1695	Total/partial: Based on a combination of Hearth Taxes and taxes on births, deaths and marriages	(A) Gregory Kings's own calculations and assumptions. (See D. V. Glass.)[c]	5·2
		(B) D. V. Glass's compromise total. (See D. V. Glass.)[c]	4·9
		(C) D. V. Glass corrected total. (See D. V. Glass.)[c]	4·6

[a] J. Cornwall, 'English population in the early sixteenth century', *Economic History Review*, 2nd ser., **23** (1970).

[b] J. C. Russell, *British Medieval Population*, (Albuquerque, 1948).

[c] D. V. Glass, 'Two papers of Gregory King', in D. V. Glass and D. E. C. Eversley (eds.), *Population in History*, (London, 1965).

heads only, a knowledge of the mean size of the household will be required. Table 8.1 and Fig. 8.1 indicate the discrepancies between estimates from particular sources that are possible depending upon the assumptions made by those undertaking the calculations. It is clear that population grew over the course of the sixteenth and seventeenth centuries but by what amount and during which period the growth was most concentrated is difficult to establish. A tentative conclusion derived from this evidence would be that the population grew from 2 to 2·5 million in the early sixteenth century to around 5 million by 1700 but whether growth was greater in the sixteenth than the seventeenth century would depend on whether a high or low estimate for the population in 1603 is accepted.

Historians have also made use of estimates of population totals derived from the baptisms, burials and marriages entered into parish registers. Discussions to date have been conducted with reference to data collected

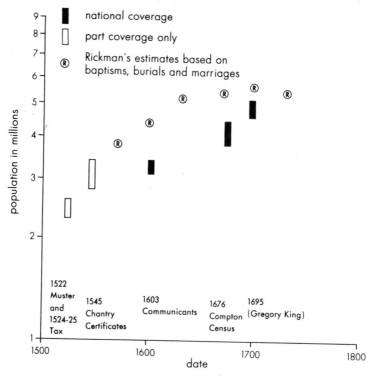

Fig. 8.1. Aggregate estimates of the population of England, 1520–1730.

in the early nineteenth century by John Rickman, the first director of the British census. Rickman initially obtained from parish incumbents totals of baptisms and burials for every tenth year from 1700 to 1780, and every year thereafter, and for marriages annually from 1754. Subsequently, he obtained counts of baptisms, burials and marriages for the years 1569–71, 1599–1601, 1629–31, 1669–71, 1699–1701, 1749–51 and 1800. From these totals Rickman estimated the population at particular dates (see Fig. 8.1 and Table 8.2). He calculated national and county birth rates for 1800 and, assuming that the same rate prevailed throughout the preceding 230 years, he was able to turn a knowledge of baptism totals into an estimate of population totals in 1570, 1600, 1630, 1670, 1700 and 1750. Similar calculations were performed with burials and marriages and a mean of the population totals so produced was accepted as the most likely figure to have been correct. Of course, these assumptions were cavalier; for instance, a constant relationship between births and population totals was most unlikely; it is also assumed that registration quality did not vary over time and that the years chosen by Rickman for analysis were 'typical' and indeed, that the incumbents and clerks who collected and totalled the data did so correctly.

Table 8.2: Population estimates for England in millions (excluding Monmouth).[a]

	Rickman (a)	Rickman (b)	Farr[b]	Finlaison[b]	Brownlee[b]	Griffith[b]	Lee[c]
1570		3·885					
1600		4·493					
1630		5·230	5·105				
1670		5·393	4·756				
1695							4·838
1700	5·114	5·646	5·718	4·796	5·441	5·449	4·941
1710	4·894		5·839	4·732	5·586	5·616	5·146
1720	5·198		5·840	4·992	5·605	5·648	5·286
1730	5·413		5·775	5·313	5·554	5·611	5·221

[a] All totals of the English population have been derived by assuming that Wales and Monmouth accounted for 6·6 per cent of the total population at each date (cf. 1801).
[b] See D. V. Glass, 'Population and population movements in England and Wales, 1700–1850', in D. V. Glass and D. E. C. Eversley (eds.), Population in History, (London, 1965).
[c] See R. Lee and R. S. Schofield, 'British population in the eighteenth century' (in preparation).

These data have, none the less, been used by historians and demographers to obtain population totals for the eighteenth century but they have shown an increasing tendency to regard the original figures and estimates subsequently derived from them very sceptically. [3]

Recent Work on the Aggregative Analysis of Parish Registers

Over the course of the last dozen or so years a good deal of new data have been collected by a large number of local volunteers and assembled by the SSRC Cambridge Group for the History of Population and Social Structure. By the middle of 1974 aggregative counts, i.e. monthly and annual totals of baptisms, burials and marriages of some 530 registers had been received in Cambridge. Of these, 404 were of sufficient quality to constitute the sample for more detailed analysis. A relatively small number of these registers span the entire period from 1538, when Thomas Cromwell instigated a system of parochial registration, to 1837 when a civil registration system began. A clear majority of the 404 parishes begin registration by 1560 and 90 per cent by 1610. Any short-term gaps in registration were then filled in by interpolation. Two periods were particularly prone to registration shortcomings: Mary's short reign in the 1550s and a period from the early stage of the Civil War, lasting until the early 1660s. As the data had not been solicited in a systematic fashion the registers did not constitute a random sample and it was therefore necessary to establish whether they were reasonably similar to a random sample drawn from the 10,000 ancient English parishes. In only one major respect did the 404 set differ from the random sample; there were too many parishes with large populations and too few with small ones and as a consequence the sample aggregate figures were reweighted to remove this bias. As the birth–baptism interval increased over time there was an increasing risk that a number of baptisms were omitted because babies were dying before they had been baptised, a tendency which also caused burial registration to become increasingly incomplete. [4] Estimates of the true number of births in the early part of the first year of life were made through biometric analysis of infant mortality. [5] To correct for the effects of nonconformity on the totals of vital events estimates of under-registration derived from the early nineteenth century were projected back through the eighteenth century following the curve describing the number of events recorded in nonconformist registers during this period.

A final inflation was needed to turn the 404 set into a 'true' national set along with an addition of totals of events in London, which were not included in the original set.

These data are still very much estimates but they have been established by employing a set of systematically performed procedures and allow us to extend our knowledge of English population back into the first half of the sixteenth century—a full 250 years before the first census.

The gross trend of English population from the second third of the sixteenth to the middle of the eighteenth century shows through in the graph in Fig. 8.2. Recordings from the earliest registers in the 404 set make it clear that births were well in excess of deaths, indicative of growth. Net increase was none the less uncertain and was clearly punctuated by furious, if only short-term, increases in deaths in the 1550s.

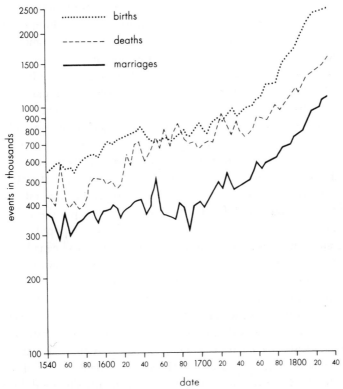

Fig. 8.2. Five year totals of births, marriages and deaths in England (based on aggregative analysis of 404 English parish registers).

Expansion of population, however, was resumed vigorously in the 1560s to be depressed only temporarily in the 1590s and 1620s. This growth phase (that may have lasted close to a century) came to a close with gradually diminishing momentum around 1640–50. It was to be followed by nearly a half-century of stagnation when the death and birth curves moved close to each other; indeed, the deaths often exceeded births. In the 1690s there is once again and for a couple of decades thereafter, a suggestion of change as the births pulled away from the deaths. But this was a slow, plodding kind of growth curtailed again in the 1710s, the 1720s and the 1740s by periods of exceptionally high mortality. Growth between 1690 and 1750 definitely was accomplished but only on a modest scale.

New Methods of Using Aggregative Data

One noteworthy attempt to overcome the limitations of simple aggregative methods has been that by Lee who, using a technique known as 'inverse projection', has been able to estimate age structure and vital rates from series of births and deaths. [6] By taking a starting population of known age structure and a series of death totals obtained from mortality schedules associated with an 'appropriate' model life table, a comparison can be made with observed death totals. Each age group is then reduced and births from the parish register based count are injected into the base of the age pyramid to produce a known age structure at time $t + 1$. By making reasonable assumptions about the age patterns of fertility, births can be allocated to the female population and data on age structure, life expectancy, total fertility rates and gross reproduction rates can be obtained at regular intervals of time. Lee's technique does, however, suffer from certain disadvantages; it assumes a 'closed population' and it requires an estimate for population size and structure to be made for a date much earlier than the first census, precisely where uncertainty is greatest. Both these unfortunately are serious weaknesses.

At Cambridge an attempt has recently been made to overcome the problems that diminish the reliability of these estimates. It works on the bases of moving backwards in time from the earliest census in which reasonably accurate age data is available. As a system, it also attempts to derive estimates of net migration. In the space available in this chapter it is not possible to describe the technique in any detail. The model uses data from the 404 parish set and it begins by 'projecting backwards' from the 1841 census. It has been tested against perhaps the best available data set, that of Sweden which permits a run from the mid-eighteenth century to the mid-twentieth century and proves able to predict mortality and fertility, net migration and the size of the cohorts of the elderly sufficiently well to match the known history from the Swedish censuses. Unfortunately projecting backwards from 1841 to 1551 there is no English evidence that can provide an independent means of validation.

The figures of population totals derived from this exercise only relate to England (excluding Monmouth). It is therefore necessary to exclude the Welsh and the Monmouth population from estimates made by other scholars before a comparison is made (see Fig. 8.3). The figures suggest a period of substantial growth in population from a total of a little over 3 million in 1550 to one of close to 5·5 million in 1650. This, however, was followed by almost half a century when a noticeable sag occurred in the total population to a low point in the 1680s before a slow growth was resumed in the 1690s. These calculations would appear to confirm Lee's claim that Rickman's figures from the Parish Register Abstracts tend to over-exaggerate the degree of population decline that took place in the

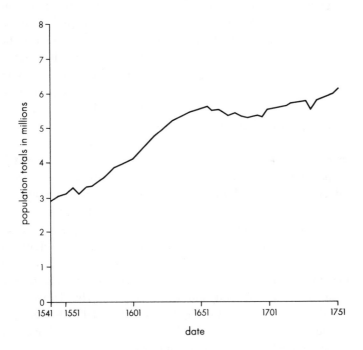

Fig. 8.3. Population of England (excluding Monmouth), 1541–1751.

early eighteenth century. Furthermore, the figures suggest that growth of roughly the same order of magnitude as that calculated by Lee took place between 1690 and 1750. The major difference between these two series is that the Cambridge Group's calculations suggest that growth occurred from a level of 5·3 million in 1690 to around 6 million in 1750 rather than from around 4·8 million to 5·7 million as calculated by Lee.[7] A striking feature of this growth pattern is that crude rates of natural increase although quite high by pre-industrial standards at 1 per cent per annum during periods of the late sixteenth century were by comparison with many population growth rates in developing countries of the present day very modest. Indeed, when population began to grow again in the very late seventeenth century it rarely exceeded rates of 0·5 per cent per annum before 1750.

Changes in the Structure of Mortality 1500–1730

Dr Wrigley has warned us that it is erroneous to assume that mortality rates in early modern England were invariably high.[8] None the less, historians frequently portray the lives of individuals in this period as 'nasty, brutish and short'.[9] Certainly, by comparison with contemporary standards of life expectancy, those of Tudor, Stuart and early Georgian England were much shorter but perhaps the correct comparison should be with other pre- or non-industrial societies which in general fared much worse than England before the industrial revolution.

As Flinn has remarked, one outstanding feature of mortality behaviour in western Europe before the twentieth century was its instability.[10] English parish registers of the sixteenth and seventeenth centuries confirm this pattern with unusually large numbers of burials occurring over short periods of time but this is less marked in the eighteenth century. On the basis of an admittedly limited sample of parishes, Schofield concluded that 'it would seem the most significant reduction in crisis mortality occurred during the second half of the seventeenth century'.[11] In this sample of parishes 1558 is by far the most common year for 'crisis' mortality and 1557 and 1559 are second and third respectively. However, certain years in the 1640s and 1650s, the late 1720s and 1740s were periods in which burials surged for a short period well above baptisms. Demographers debate the relative importance of *crises de mortalité* caused by harvest failure and famine on the one hand and those caused by epidemic disease whose pattern of occurrence or recurrence is not necessarily connected to the level of food supply on the other. A consensus of opinion suggests that England, unlike France and probably Scotland, was not subjected to crises that were strongly correlated with harvest failures. [12] Chambers, who has been the most vociferous advocate of this position, admittedly did the bulk of his research on the high mortality years of the late seventeenth and early eighteenth century when grain prices do not show much relation to mortality trends. [13] For the late sixteenth and early seventeenth centuries the evidence is more equivocal. The bad mortality years of the 1540s and the 1550s seem to have been seasons of good harvest, but those of 1597, 1598 and 1638–9 show a close association between mortality and grain prices. Some writers have argued that the harvest difficulties of the 1590s were, among other things, responsible for the demise of the East Anglian smallholder, [14] an increase in petty crime [15] and even a surge in the number of bastards. [16]

Of the epidemics, perhaps undue attention has been focused upon plague which, throughout the period before its departure in 1671, was primarily an urban-based disease. It has been noted that very few of the bad years most prone to crisis over a wide geographical area were coincidental with years of London plague (i.e. 1563, 1592–3, 1603, 1625, 1636 and 1665–6). None the less, it would be wrong to underestimate the massive increase in death that the infrequent explosions of plague brought about. The mortality peaks of 1603, 1625 and 1665 in the national series of burials are primarily the result of the incorporation into that series of London deaths.

However much effort is expended in the analysis of short-term oscillations in burials it is of little help in acquiring evidence on background mortality. To obtain, for instance, measurements of expectation of life at birth, age specific mortality rates, and the creation of life tables, requires the use of different techniques. One such technique is family reconstitution, [17] which by linking entries about individuals within the same family (i.e. the births, marriages and burials) for a sufficiently large number of families can produce incisive demographic measures that in a contemporary population would be obtained by combining information on vital events with a census. Studies such as these unfortunately are time-consuming to perform and are restricted by the limited availability of registers of sufficient quality. Yet with even a small number of such studies patterns have emerged which are common to places with varying social and economic characteristics.

Table 8.3: Infant and child mortality rates (1000_qx), 1550–1749.

	MALE				FEMALE			
	1550–99	1600–49	1650–99	1700–49	1550–99	1600–49	1650–99	1700–49
Infants:								
Alcester	175	152	205	241	155	113	171	201
Aldenham	130	119	112	153	125	112	97	137
Banbury	172	165	171	250	137	149	139	225
Colyton	140	91	104	110	118	89	100	106
Gainsborough	175	243	255	284	157	204	221	245
Gedling	90	101	101	105	78	90	103	104
Hartland	89	100	96	85	95	70	66	75
Terling	134	113	135	139	118	110	145	170
Mean	138	136	147	170	123	117	133	151
Children 1–4:								
Alcester	89	93	109	123	90	123	127	98
Aldenham	73	74	56	60	72	58	71	64
Banbury	77	115	121	133	85	95	121	111
Colyton	82	78	110	67	63	91	113	77
Gainsborough	95	117	178	197	109	150	170	163
Gedling	53	92	37	75	38	45	73	65
Hartland	39	42	43	72	37	56	56	116
Terling	65	122	103	68	51	77	105	88
Mean	72	92	95	99	68	87	105	94

Children 5–9:

Alcester	35	51	61	47	37	27	60	57
Aldenham	22	29	30	57	24	34	21	37
Banbury	46	46	36	33	66	49	33	24
Colyton	33	26	54	23	16	52	75	41
Gainsborough	31	62	61	82	25	68	62	56
Gedling	12	49	35	29	21	17	38	51
Hartland	30	21	29	22	13	39	31	40
Terling	48	50	25	39	25	37	35	36
Mean	32	42	41	41	28	40	44	43

Location of parishes by counties: Alcester (Warwickshire), Aldenham (Hertfordshire), Banbury (Oxfordshire), Colyton (Devon), Gainsborough (Lincolnshire), Gedling (Nottinghamshire), Hartland (Devon), Terling (Essex).

Source: reconstitution tabulations at SSRC Cambridge Group for the History of Population and Social Structure.

For instance based on the evidence of eight family reconstitution studies, the expectation of life at birth (e_0) appears to have worsened over the course of the seventeenth century. In fact, although infant mortality rates deteriorated, child mortality rates rose even more (see Table 8.3). This has been confirmed by work on 16 additional registers which suggest a rise of infant mortality from rates of 149 per 1000 in the 1580s to a high of 204 per 1000 in the 1680s. [18] There is some reason to suppose that this was associated with the drawing of Europe into closer contact with extra-European areas thereby exposing a population without immunity to new kinds of infectious diseases. These conditions may have affected children above the age of weaning relatively more severely than those still fed at the breast. [19]

The calculation of adult mortality by means of family reconstitution is complicated by the existence of migration which requires the making of two estimates; one an optimistic assumption about those who pass out of observation and whose burial date is unknown and the other, a much more pessimistic assumption. [20] When viewed against model life tables constructed on the basis of data from nineteenth and twentieth century European populations it is clear that early modern adult mortality was radically worse than that of the younger age groups. The decline in life expectancy, so clearly marked amongst the infants and children is detectable, but only marginally among adults. What stands out so markedly from these figures is the relatively favourable mortality circumstances of the English population in the late sixteenth and through most of the seventeenth and early eighteenth centuries, with life expectations at birth fluctuating between 35 and 40 years, considerably higher than those calculated for continental European populations of the same period (see Fig. 8.4). It is reassuring that mortality levels derived from rather localized studies would appear to be confirmed by estimates calculated by the technique of 'backward projection'. These suggest a clear tendency for life expectancy to fall after 1630 with something of a recovery in the 1690s and early 1700s before the bad years of the 1720s and 1740s brought a low point on the curve, after which some recovery occurred by the middle of the eighteenth century, although still not to levels present in the late sixteenth century. [21]

Geographical Aspects of Crisis Mortality 1500–1730

As *crises de mortalité* tended to be sharper the more local the area studied it

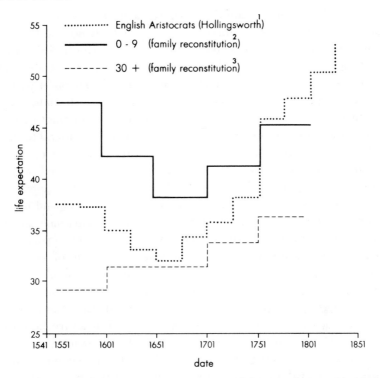

Fig. 8.4. Some characteristics of early modern English mortality, 1550–1800. 1, Based on T. H. Hollingsworth, 'The demography of the English peerage', *Population Studies,* **18** (suppl. 1964). 2, Based on average of life expectations of 8 family reconstitution studies (relating to the age group 0–9). 3, Based on average of life expectations of 8 family reconstitution studies (relating to expectation of life at 30).

is most difficult to evaluate systematic differences in this aspect of the geography of pre-industrial mortality. For the moment, the dearth of regional mortality series, compared with the comparative plenty of parochial series, means that generalizations about the spatial dimensions of the short-run fluctuations must be rather inadequately based.

The years 1595–7 were marked by starvation over a great deal of northern Europe and, it has been argued, north and north-west England were much affected by mortality coming in the wake of harvest failures. Scattered references such as those to starvation in Newcastle and Berwick and cases of terminal dysentery in Staffordshire along with a decline in conceptions possibly linked to famine amenorrhoea would seem to confirm this claim.[22] Unlike the north and north-west, where parish burial totals rise to two, three or four times their normal figure, in the country as a whole burials less than doubled. Again in 1623 a regional pattern is detectable in the burial evidence. In a model study relating to that year it was discovered that in Lancashire 51 out of 54 parishes had greater than normal mortality and of these, 41 had burials twice their normal level.[23] Furthermore, within the county a distinct geographical pattern was discernible. The badly affected areas were found to the east of a line running roughly from Manchester in the south-east to the Furness peninsular in the north-west, a line approximately followed by the 600 ft contour and enclosed by the 40 inch rainfall isohyet. Appleby's wider review of this crisis over the whole of the north of England finds excess mortality to have been much more patchy in its occurrence than was the case in the north-west corner. In Durham, only 8 out of 27 parishes, in the West, East and North Ridings of Yorkshire only 12 out of 59, 8 out of 31 and 4 out of 20 parishes respectively, showed a doubling of their mortality.[24] Appleby suggests that this pattern was not random but related quite closely to the character of local economies. In the fell parishes of Cumberland and in Rossendale in Lancashire he shows that there had been a large-scale encroachment of landless individuals who had carved out tiny holdings that were ecologically and economically highly marginal. Indeed, he argues convincingly that it was perhaps the extent to which this squatting had occurred in northern upland and frequently 'open' parishes, that accounted for the difference between the experiences of that area and the rest of the country during these difficult years. It may also have been exacerbated by the strong commitment to pastoral farming in these areas on the part of farmers who were adversely affected both by their isolation from grain supplies and by the lowering of demand for pastoral products as the terms of trade moved in favour of grain and the arable sector of English agriculture. A recent areal study of population crises in the 1730s and 1740s in Scandinavia found two distinctly different patterns of mortality.[25] Epidemic disease moved in a wave motion, spreading slowly as the infection diffused from one community to another. The famine mortality, on the other hand, was observable over very large rural areas at the same time. In this respect it is interesting that in 1623 all across the north the most severe mortality occurred in the last months of 1623 and the first months of 1624 suggesting the presence of starvation as a killer. The Scandinavian study also showed that epidemic diseases originated in the towns and then spread into their rural hinterlands; a pattern perhaps observable in Exeter and its environs in the years 1727–32 when burials rose to over one and a half times their normal level in 75 per cent of the city parishes and 57 per cent of the surrounding country parishes. Here epidemics would appear to have been the likely killers. [26]

Micro-geographical studies of mortality are giving us a clearer idea of the causes of death which were only rarely entered into parish registers. For instance, a disease such as bubonic plague is likely to have been associated with geographically clustered patterns of death, because of the very restricted range of movement of *Rattus Rattus* and its fleas. This was the pattern of death by household discovered in a recent study of Colyton's mortality peak of 1646, suggesting that the killer was bubonic plague associated with the rat flea. [27] If there had been strong clustering of deaths by household size, plague associated with the human flea, or perhaps pneumonic plague or influenza were more likely to have been responsible.

An interesting argument concerning the relation of plague to the social geography of towns had been advanced by Slack. [28] He considers that when the plague hit the richer quarters in the centre of the town, most of the casualties came not from the houses of the merchants on the main thoroughfares but the overcrowded alleys inhabited by labourers and paupers behind them. Over the course of the seventeenth century he considers urban plague outbreaks to have diminished in their virulence and to have affected poorer surburban parishes much more severely than the richer ones. He can find this pattern in London, Bristol, Exeter and Norwich and speculates that it may reflect an increasing social polarization of rich and poor in the growing seventeenth century towns or considerable rebuilding within the high status parishes. Indeed in the case of London, it may have been produced by the activities of the city authorities in attempting to shut up the poor with their plague in their own houses, thereby stopping them congregating in alehouse or the streets.

Spatial Variation in 'Background' Mortality 1500–1730

Superimposed upon these patterns reflecting the more volatile demographic happenings of the period were the broader differences between 'healthy' and 'unhealthy' areas. Both small market towns and somewhat larger provincial centres and, of course, London, were among the most unhealthy communities in the early modern period. For example, both in terms of child and adult mortality it appears that small market towns such as Gainsborough in Lincolnshire and Banbury in Oxfordshire with populations of around 2500 in 1600 were environments of considerably higher mortality than most rural parishes (see Table 8.2). At the other extreme it is clear that locally very low levels of mortality can be detected; Hartland and Gedling were particularly well favoured with infant mortality levels of 100 or less per thousand over long periods of time, a very low figure by pre-industrial standards. Rural communities, however, were not always healthy. The undrained fen-edge community of Wrangle[29] in Lincolnshire or Willingham in Cambridgeshire had infant mortality rates of over 200 per thousand—levels such as were encountered in the most crowded and insanitary areas of the great nineteenth century towns.

Although urban infant mortality levels were considerably higher than those encountered in rural areas, even within the town there was considerable variation from parish to parish. Finlay, for instance, has discovered marked differences between wealthy London parishes near the centre of the city, with expectations of life at birth of 35 years, and poor peripheral or waterside parishes with life expectancies some ten years lower.[30] St Mary Somerset on the riverside in London was particularly unhealthy and this may well be accounted for by the quality of the parishes' water supply.

Changes in the Structure of Fertility 1500–1730

It is once again to family reconstitution that we must initially turn to obtain reliable indications of fertility over the period. Since in England, as in western European societies generally, the level of extramarital fertility was usually low, it is to births produced in marriage that we should direct our attention.[31] Changes in the age at marriage could effect fertility levels considerably. Table 8.4, based on family reconstitution studies of ten parishes shows a rise in female age during the course of the seventeenth century reaching a peak towards its end or early in the eighteenth century, thereafter falling to low levels by the early nineteenth century.[32] Movements in male marriage age were much less marked. It is noteworthy that the higher ages for female marriage age occurred either in the period 1650–99 or 1700–49 in all but two of the parishes. Because the trend of change in the individual parishes was so uniform, even though they were widely scattered geographically and of markedly different socio-economic

Table 8.4: Ages at marriage in England, 1550–1749.[a]

	1550–99	1600–49	1650–99	1700–49
		Male		
Alcester[b]	24·5	29·1	27·8	27·4
Aldenham	28·6	29·1	29·7	29·2
Banbury	26·0	27·2	27·4	26·6
Bottesford	30·3	29·2	27·6	28·7
Colyton	27·8	27·4	26·4	26·6
Gainsborough	24·0	27·0	27·0	27·5
Hartland	27·9	28·8	30·7	29·6
Hawkshead		27·8	31·0	31·9
Shepshed	29·7	29·9	29·2	28·5
Terling	26·0	25·1	25·5	24·7
Mean (un-weighted)	27·2	28·1	28·2	28·1
		Female		
Alcester	22·4	25·0	27·2	28·2
Aldenham	22·0	25·3	26·2	25·8
Banbury	24·9	25·4	25·8	26·7
Bottesford	26·8	25·9	26·7	27·4
Colyton	26·9	27·3	29·4	28·6
Gainsborough	22·1	25·0	25·3	25·5
Hartland	25·7	27·8	28·4	28·2
Hawkshead		24·8	27·1	27·4
Shepshed	27·5	28·8	27·1	27·4
Terling	24·5	24·6	23·2	24·4
Mean (un-weighted)	24·8	26·0	26·6	27·0

[a] E. A. Wrigley, 'Age at marriage in early modern England', paper delivered to the XIIIth Congress of Genealogical and Heraldic Sciences, September 1976.
[b] Location of parishes by counties: Alcester (Warwickshire), Aldenham (Hertfordshire), Banbury (Oxfordshire), Bottesford (Leicestershire), Colyton (Devon), Gainsborough (Lincolnshire), Hartland (Devon), Hawkshead (Lancashire), Shepshed (Leicestershire), Terling (Essex).

types, it is likely that if similar information were available for a large and more representative sample of all English parishes, the same pattern would be visible. At the levels of marital fertility prevalent in early modern England it can be shown that a fall in the age at marriage of 2·5 years may well have been responsible for an increase of 0·75 to 1 birth per family.

Apart from information on marriage age we need to know something of the overall level of nuptiality, i.e. the age distribution of marriage and the proportions remaining unmarried. The proportion single at specified ages in six pre-industrial communities that allow us to consider this problem are highly informative. Less than a fifth of the women in the sample were married in the age group 20–24. [33] In contemporary African and Asian societies, in marked contrast to pre-industrial England, there are very few women remaining unmarried after 18 or 20 (see Table 8.5). [34] Recently a technique has been developed which permits us to obtain estimates of the proportion remaining unmarried from series of marriages and baptisms which, when applied to the English evidence, suggests a low point in the late sixteenth century and a high point in the late seventeenth and early eighteenth centuries. [35]

Data generated by the 'backward projection' method allow us to view the findings of the family reconstitution studies with greater reassurance. From a high point in the middle of the sixteenth century the gross reproduction rate (the average number of female births per woman in the child bearing years) fell by nearly a third to a low point in the late seventeenth century before beginning a steady rise through the eighteenth century. This trend is perfectly compatible with the decline in fertility that the change in marriage age and proportions marrying could have brought about if we assume mortality, marital fertility and extramarital fertility to have remained constant. [36]

Geographical Aspects of Fertility 1500–1730

It has been shown that fertility was not fixed at a constant level over time and there would appear to be no logical reason for it to have remained constant over space. With the limited data at our disposal all that can be done is to point to the variations that have so far been unearthed by localized research. The German demographer Mackenroth has emphasized that in pre-industrial European societies, the variability in nuptiality was the critical mechanism linking those societies with their environments, a feature clearly suggested by the early modern English

Table 8.5 Marital status of English women by age based on six communities, 1599–1796.[a]

Marital status	15–19	20–24	25–29	30–34	35–39	40–44	45–49	50–59	60–69	70+
Single	98·5	81·0	48·1	26·6	16·6	7·1	8·6	4·9	6·2	5·3
Married	1·5	17·9	49·8	70·9	75·7	72·0	76·2	67·4	48·2	60·5
Widowed	0·0	1·0	2·1	2·4	7·7	20·9	15·2	27·7	45·5	34·1
Total	100	99·9	100	99·9	100	100	100	100	99·9	99·9

[a] See P. Laslett, *Family Life and Illicit Love*, (Cambridge, 1977), p. 27.

evidence. [37] In communities where the number of 'niches', be they in the form of holdings, workshops or labouring jobs, remained constant, marriage age and the proportions marrying would probably have stood at higher and lower levels respectively than in communities where domestic industry or growing demand for agricultural labouring jobs was occurring. It has, for instance, been suggested that areas practising partible inheritance were likely to have higher proportions marrying and generally faster growth rates as a high proportion of all male siblings would gain access to land. [38] Similarly, in areas in which 'new' land could be acquired by squatting on commons or by grubbing up fell land, marriage may have been both earlier and involved a greater proportion of the population than in 'closed' agricultural villages. Relatively little detailed demographic analysis of these sorts of questions has been completed to date.

We are becoming better informed on the fertility behaviour of proto-industrial communities. Wage earners in such areas are distinguished by the fact that the traditional link between the local demand for labour and the real wage is broken and the demand for labour is exogenously determined. As Schofield notes the proto-industrial worker finds that 'the demand for his labour is determined in distant markets to which he is linked by the exchange network of international merchant capital'. [39] As long as these markets remain buoyant the proto-industrial worker can prosper, marry and multiply in comparative freedom from the endogenous controls applying to other sectors of the local population. This seems to be what happened in the Leicestershire framework knitting village of Shepshed with increasing intensity from the late seventeenth into the second half of the eighteenth century. [40] Employment opportunities in capitalist farming could produce the same sort of results; the Essex village of Terling with a precocious development of agricultural wage labour and integration into the London food market by the end of the seventeenth century, displays over the period a female age at marriage of a level more generally associated with the late eighteenth and early nineteenth century. [41] Terling, after 1620, did not show any noticeable growth and it is argued that the operation of the Poor Law system forced surviving children to find their 'niches' elsewhere. The proximity of London was obviously an important influence in sustaining this pattern.

Recent work by historical demographers, however, has not yet detected clear cut differences between urban and rural fertility. The classical demographers, Graunt, King and Short all argued that the towns were more infertile than the surrounding countryside. Our ignorance of these matters may solely reflect the situation caused by the difficulty of carrying out effective family reconstitutions on highly mobile urban populations. None the less, if the experience of market towns such as Gainsborough and Banbury prove typical, marital fertility and marriage age in town and countryside seem to show no marked differences. However, Wall has recently shown that in urban households of the late seventeenth century fewer children were resident than was the case in rural households. This may, though, have been the product of an earlier age of leaving home, or a higher level in infant mortality and child mortality in the towns than in the country.[42]

Notwithstanding these remarks, recent research suggests some interesting fertility features in Tudor and Stuart London where, it would seem, the classical demographers may have overstated their case. Finlay has discovered that women in certain parishes with high status residents had mean birth intervals of the order of 23 months, similar in fact to those encountered in populations with very high fertility.[43] In contrast, the mothers in poorer London parishes had longer birth intervals and consequently lower fertility. It would seem that the short birth intervals of the wealthier women could be explained by the practice among these groups of employing wetnurses, helping thereby to reduce the period of post-partum amenorrhea. A further feature of considerable interest in this study is the evidence from burial registers suggesting that the sex ratio of the London population moved from one in which there was a surplus of males to a surplus of females over the course of the seventeenth century. Finlay suggests that this may reflect a change in the economic structure of the capital city with a decline in craft industries relative to trade and commerce and an increase in the employment of female domestic servants in the households of the families involved in such activities. Finlay believes that this may have brought about an increase in marriage age as the shortage of women in the sixteenth century could have been responsible for female marriage in London taking place at ages considerably below that of the English population at large.

Migration

Migration and Turnover of the Rural Population

The population of Tudor and Stuart England was highly mobile—a condition stemming from the interplay of certain basic characteristics of that society: rarely were the basic units of production and consumption composed of extended families or kin groups; the institution of service provided a mechanism whereby adolescents left the parental household to work in the households of others; production was primarily for exchange rather than for use; individual rather than kin or family group inheritance of property was the norm; a good deal of individual choice in the selection of marriage partners was permitted and neolocal residence by the newly formed conjugal unit took place after marriage. Furthermore, England was composed of relatively small settlements so that the sphere of individual lifetime activity was often wider than the community of birth.

Establishing indices of population turnover in early modern England is a complex task. It is dependent upon sources such as listings of inhabitants surviving for years relatively close together in time. Unlike many European countries the English evidence in this respect is very poor. Our earliest evidence in the sixteenth century comes from the chance survival of two tax lists for Towcester Hundred in 1524 and 1525, where it appears that no less than 15 per cent of the tax payers had migrated in the course of a single year. [44] The Nottinghamshire village of Clayworth and the Northamptonshire village of Cogenhoe made famous by Peter Laslett indicate that over periods of roughly a decade in the later seventeenth century between 50 and 60 per cent of the population had changed (although a third of this was the consequence of deaths rather than movement). [45] Generally students of population turnover are forced to use much cruder data; for instance, Macfarlane has recently shown that in the Essex village of Earls Colne out of the 274 pieces of land listed in a rental in 1677, only 23 had been held by the same family some two generations earlier. [46] Obviously, this sort of evidence is difficult to evaluate as changes may solely reflect the strength of the local property market or the degree of social rather than geographical mobility. Rather stronger evidence comes from work on parish registers; for example, in the Leicestershire agricultural village of Bottesford a recent family reconstitution study indicates that between 1600 and 1679 only 6·3 per cent of marriages were between couples both of whom were born in the village and a further 26·4 per cent involving individuals, one of whom was a village native. [47] Even in Hartland, a large and remote Devon parish square in shape with the sea on two sides, where migratory movements were less intense than in most parishes, 60 per cent of brides' ages at marriage could not be established because they had been baptised outside of the parish over the period 1600–1850. In considering these data, however, it should be remembered that the technique of reconstitution may cause the percentage of natives marrying in a parish to be underestimated since in cases of ambiguity links are not made. The high levels of geographical mobility were therefore consistently reflected in high levels of geographical marital exogamy. Pre-industrial communities of this period were therefore not 'stable' from the point of view of the long-term permanency of families.

Social Differences and Mobility

The propensity to migrate varied considerably with social status and age. Laslett's calculations on a large number of English pre-industrial listings suggests that close to 13 per cent of the total population were servants and that they constituted the most mobile group in the population, usually in the age group of 15–25. [48] For example, at Clayworth of the 67 servants in the village in 1688 only one had been a servant there in 1676. [49] Cooper, in her detailed analysis of this aspect of servants' behaviour has shown that in the seventeenth and eighteenth centuries persistence rates of servants were usually below 0·5 per cent (i.e. proportions of names appearing in one year's list that would appear again in the next years' successive lists). [50] Evidence from the Towcester Hundred tax lists of the early sixteenth century would seem to indicate that wage earners too, were a mobile group in the population; of 91 persons taxed on wages only one had died but no less than 31 had migrated in the course of a single year, a rate of migration some seven times higher than those taxed on goods or land. [51]

The relative immobility of yeoman farmers in the pre-industrial village has been clearly established in other work. In Bottesford Levine shows a core of yeomen and husbandmen persisting over time and this leads him to argue that this geographical stability was an important means by which the village élite stamped their control as economic and social superiors over a peripatetic proletariat—a feature confirmed in the seventeenth century Essex village of Terling. [52]

The Distances Moved

While mobility in pre-industrial England was high it rarely involved long distances. P. Spufford, using the exceptionally rich late seventeenth century survey of Eccleshall in Staffordshire, discovered that of the 68 stated immigrants to the parish 53 came from places no further away than 20 miles and of the remaining 13, 10 references are to London, far more numerous than the neighbouring market town of Stone, only 6 miles away.[53] Similar biases towards short distance movement have been confirmed by historians using the evidence of the depositions of witnesses in ecclesiastical courts and the settlement certificates and removal orders that derive from the workings of the 1662 Law of Settlement.

Urban Population Growth and Immigration to the Towns

Recent work suggests that the population of greater London mushroomed from about 50,000 to 60,000 persons in the 1520s to some 200,000 by 1600, some 400,000 by 1650 and perhaps 575,000 by 1700.[54] If these figures are considered in the context of the population trend in the country at large it can be seen that London grew much more rapidly than the rest of the nation. Using the recent estimates of the English population (excluding Monmouth) it would seem that London's share of the population increased from around 3 per cent in 1550 to around 5 per cent in 1600. By 1650 London's population stood at 7 per cent of that of the English total and by 1700 during a phase when the English total had probably fallen slightly London's population accounted for 10 or 11 per cent of the total. Throughout this period London's growth continued in spite of some catastrophically high mortality peaks and a generally high background mortality especially among infants and children. Rapid growth, then, was entirely dependent upon an enormous excess of immigrants to London over emigrants from it. Wrigley estimates that on average about 8000 more people moved to London every year than left it in the period 1650–1700;[55] indeed, it may have absorbed up to half the natural increase of the total population, recruiting its migrants from considerable distances. This latter assertion still awaits systematic testing but there are some indications of the scale of distance moved in recent publications. In an analysis of 104 working men living in Stepney and Whitechapel between 1580 and 1639, well over two-thirds came from more than 50 miles away, from an area spread fairly evenly over the country while reference has already been made to the extremes of movement displayed by the people of Eccleshall in Staffordshire.[56]

In the sixteenth century it would seem that very few provincial towns experienced growth rates that were significantly higher than that of the population of the country as a whole. Indeed, a recent study argues that the larger towns did not show any signs of growth in the first two-thirds of the sixteenth century and in many centres absolute decline in numbers seems to have occurred.[57] It is worth speculating that the urban proportion of the population actually fell. Whether this was because of the persistence of recurrent epidemics in the town or, as Phythian-Adams suggests, through erosion of urban economic viability by the protracted continuance of costly civic ritual and displays remains to be thoroughly investigated.

This relative decline was reversed in the late sixteenth and early seventeenth centuries so that whereas in 1500 only six or seven towns had populations of over 5000, by 1700 there were over 30 such towns. The town was outstripping the countryside. In Norfolk and Suffolk between 1603 and 1670 the urban population increased by 50 per cent whereas rural growth was a mere 11 per cent.[58] In peripheral Cumberland and Westmorland total population probably fell but towns such as Carlisle and Kendall increased their populations by well over a third.[59] Furthermore, by the late seventeenth century it is possible to see this growth biased towards the north-west and the Midlands in settlements such as Birmingham, Coventry, Liverpool and Manchester.[60]

Like London the provincial centres needed immigrants to grow, indeed even to maintain stationary populations. Migration to these centres was over a generally short distance. Clark's work on deponents in cases dealt with by ecclesiastical courts in Canterbury in the period 1580–1640, indicates that 70 per cent were migrants although only 13 per cent had moved more than 20 miles.[61] This same pattern is observable in the movement of apprentices to Norwich in the sixteenth and seventeenth centuries;[62] in this region migration seems to have been heaviest from the immediate surroundings of the town, followed by other smaller towns in the region; and then by areas which had a special link, such as similar manufacturing areas. It was also marked from areas of high population and low agricultural opportunities such as the quite densely populated areas of central High Suffolk and from areas of declining industry in the broad cloth communities of the Essex and Suffolk borders.

Trends in Migration 1500–1730

We are as yet ill-informed on gross trends in migration over this period; we cannot be certain whether there were tendencies for more or fewer people to become mobile or whether the distances moved increased or decreased over time. There are possibly some indications that mobility was at its greatest at the end of the sixteenth century and the early part of the seventeenth century, subsequently slowing down as the Settlement Laws were more effectively enforced and population growth fell away. It is argued by some that the fall in the number of husbandmen who were tenant farmers in the late sixteenth and early seventeenth centuries meant that only the yeomanry and the gentry were kept in place by their land. In this respect Clark has distinguished 'betterment' from 'subsistence' migration; 'betterment' migration, it is claimed, was associated with the socially respectable, bound up with tight, established local networks of kin and social and business relations.[63] Clark showed that 60 per cent of the migrants in the poorer leather trades in the town of Faversham had come from outside Kent and that they came more frequently from an urban than a rural environment. He argues that subsistence migration of this sort was especially important in the late sixteenth century provoking the vagrancy fears of the 1590s and 1620s and the 1630s. Some areas seem to have been more prone to exporting their poor than others. Lancashire and Yorkshire appear during this phase as counties which contributed disproportionately to the flow of long-distance migrants reflecting their sorry state in the late Tudor and early Stuart period. They are detectable in the towns of Kent and figure prominently among the poor families in the 1570 census of Norwich.[64] Whether the stagnation of population numbers and the improvement in real wages in the second half of the seventeenth century acted to reduce the quantity of 'subsistence' migration is impossible to say until more research has been completed. Clearly, the expansion of the urban component of the population should have increased the volume of rural-urban movement. However, this may have become primarily of a short-distance sort. For instance, there is some evidence that London's migration field contracted in the late seventeenth and early eighteenth centuries.

None the less, some would argue that the institutional control of migration was increased over the course of the seventeenth century. Levine suggests that an increasing proportion of men entering observation in the family reconstitution of Terling after 1625 were natives of the village suggesting that the increasingly tighter social control of the village élite limited the amount of immigration.[65] In addition, structural changes in the economy may have increased the stability of local populations. P. Spufford argues that in Burslem,[66] home of the nascent pottery industry, the population was immobile in the late seventeenth and early eighteenth centuries and Levine has indentified a similar development in the

Leicestershire stocking-frame knitting village of Shepshed which was industrializing rapidly. In pre-industrial Shepshed just 46 per cent of the families entering observation on the family reconstitution forms had been married in the parish whereas during proto-industrialization the proportion rose to 63 per cent, subsequently rising to over 70 per cent by the end of the eighteenth century.[67] Furthermore, the number of families whose children remained in the village as married adults increased from 37·2 per cent to 57·4 per cent. There are indications from other family reconstitution studies that patterns such as those encountered in these two parishes were more widely prevalent in the later seventeenth century.[68]

Broad Spatial Patterns of Population Change 1500–1730

In the absence of censuses giving population numbers, historians and geographers working in the early sixteenth century have used the distribution of tax payers as surrogate data for the distribution of population. In this respect the lay subsidies of 1524–5 remain the most comprehensive source.[69] They suggest that the counties of East Anglia, together with parts of the West Country, possess some of the highest densities of population. If anything, the south-eastern corner had increased its importance from the late Middle Ages. The striking increase in the importance of the south-west has been noted by many commentators on these patterns. Equally pronounced is the low density of rural population at this date, a feature that did not fail to impress contemporaries. Historians are fond, in this context, of referring to the *Dialogue* between Cardinal Pole and Thomas Lupset as composed by Thomas Starkey which reflects on 'the grete lake of pepul and skarseness of men' in the England of the 1530s.[70]

Although population growth, particularly after the 1550s, was general over England, not all areas expanded at the same rate. We are still very uncertain about the spatial variations in this pattern but some features are clearly observable from regional studies. The greatest relative growth of population took place in those areas that were economically the most marginal and very lightly populated at the beginning of the sixteenth century. Surplus populations which could not be absorbed in crowded fielden parishes were channeled towards those rural areas which retained some capacity to support greater numbers. M. Spufford's work on the population of Cambridgeshire identifies these points admirably.[71] Over the sixteenth century the fens of Cambridgeshire became the most densely peopled part of the county, since their extensive pastures and opportunities for fishing and wild fowling provided a living for families whose tiny holdings of land would have been inadequate for their support in the corn-growing uplands. Indeed, numbers in the densely populated areas of south Cambridgeshire actually fell by 6 per cent between 1524 and 1563. In contrast a county such as Leicestershire with its population at a very low ebb at the end of the fifteenth century may have increased in size by up to 31 per cent between 1524 and 1563, and a further 58 per cent between 1563 and 1603.[72] Norfolk and Suffolk appear to have grown in total by only 24 per cent from 1524–5 to 1603, mirroring, it would seem, the adjacent upland area of south Cambridgeshire.[73] The highly marginal environments in the uplands of the north-west were increasingly populated; in the diocese of Carlisle the population probably expanded by some 43 per cent in the 40 years between 1563 and 1603, a development confirmed by the evidence on the number of tenants in manorial surveys.[74] For instance, in the Cumbrian forest of Inglewood numerous encroachments on the waste produced a multiplicity of marginal agricultural holdings.[75] In many respects it could be argued that this pattern of growth was similar to that which occurred in England at the end of the thirteenth century when a phase of rapid demographic growth produced a movement to the margins of cultivation.[76] These structural similarities suggest that English agriculture, since its response to population growth was still constrained within a highly inefficient technological straight-jacket, illustrates Le Roy Ladurie's characterization of this phase of western European economic change as a further example of 'histoire immobile'.[77]

In the seventeenth century national population totals continued to grow but at a progressively slower and slower rate until mid-century, but at the regional level this trend was highly variable. In Norfolk and Suffolk the rural population grew by only 11 per cent between 1603 and 1670;[78] in Hertfordshire the growth was of a similar level[79] and in Leicestershire numbers expanded by only 5 per cent.[80] Since growth often peaked about the mid-century, a comparison of totals for 1603 and the 1670s may well fail to uncover demographic decline between 1640 and 1676, or conversely the amount of growth taking place before 1640. Recent work on the counties of Sussex and Nottinghamshire argues for a decline of population between 1642 and 1676 in the order of 20 per cent.[81] We have already noted how urban populations expanded very generally over the country during this period; the net effect of a rise in mortality and a fall in fertility may have been exacerbated in the countryside by a 'flight to the towns'. We are, however, a long way from confirmation of these patterns and Palliser has recently argued that they would not be applicable in the case of Staffordshire. [82] He writes, 'almost all the parish registers of the county which have been analysed in full reveal a baptism surplus during most decades of the seventeenth century no less than the sixteenth'. Arguing that this is linked with the growth of rural and semi-rural industry he cites Thirsk who has demonstrated that in most of Staffordshire pastoral farming was combined with other occupations, especially small-scale industry. [83]

Complexity in the spatial pattern of change between the 1680s and the middle of the eighteenth century persists. Growth, but only of a modest kind, does take place at national levels over these years. A leading economic historian of this period has drawn the following picture of population change; when referring to the north, north-west and the West Midlands he writes:

> it was here that the population was probably growing at its fastest in the early eighteenth century, it was from the countryside in those areas that people were moving, not now so much to London, but rather to Bristol, Birmingham, Coventry, Leeds, Liverpool, Manchester, Newcastle, Sheffield or Whitehaven. . . . They came from the woodlands, from the forest villages, already growing faster than others in the sixteenth and seventeenth centuries i.e. those of Northamptonshire (on the very edge of the Severn Wash line) from Sherwood forest and the Pennines; from the Lake District and Lancashire; from the North and West Ridings of Yorkshire. Despite the increased mortality of the 1720s and 1730s the north and northwest counties showed a consistently higher ratio of baptisms to burials. [84]

This view does not go without challenge. Krause considered the baptism/burial ratio of some 200 parishes, which had been divided into two roughly equal groups, the dividing line between them linking the Humber and the Severn. [85] Unfortunately we do not know the size composition or the exact spatial distribution of the parishes—in other words whether they are a representative sample of all parishes in the north-west and the south-eastern sectors of the country. A cursory reading of the figures in Table 8.6 would suggest that the baptism/burial ratio in the set of north-western parishes was greater than that in the southern parishes. However, Krause argues that the real rate of growth in the south-east in the first half of the century was probably equal to that of

Table 8.6: Quinquennial baptism, burial, and marital totals together with vital indices.[a]

Years	NORTH				SOUTH			
	Baptisms	Burials	Marriages	Vital index	Baptisms	Burials	Marriages	Vital index
1690–4	6490	5527	1399	1·17	9107	8514	1729	1·07
1695–1700	6858	6097	1629	1·12	9557	7911	2214	1·21
1700–4	7460	5423	1865	1·38	10,126	8250	2403	1·23
1705–9	6890	5529	1555	1·25	9567	8640	2296	1·11
1710–14	6559	5499	1691	1·19	8834	8834	2363	1·04
1715–19	7402	5662	1987	1·31	9710	8104	2557	1·20
1720–4	7353	6373	2160	1·15	10,044	9017	2670	1·11
1725–9	6924	8162	1848	0·85	9955	10,333	2465	0·99
1730–4	7712	6317	2167	1·22	10,486	10,221	3079	1·03

[a] Based upon J. T. Krause, 'Some aspects of population change, 1690–1790', in E. L. Jones and G. E. Mingay (eds.), Land, Labour and Population in the Industrial Revolution (London, 1967), p. 195.

the north, since registration of baptisms was '*undoubtedly* more defective in the south than in the north during that time' (my italics). This claim is disputable as there is no obvious evidence in print to support it. Indeed, since nonconformity was probably more prevalent in the emerging industrial areas in the north and west than in the south, it might seem more plausible to suppose that the baptism surplus in the northern parishes was understated. However, if rural migration to emerging urban centres was relatively greater in the north-west than the south-east it could have acted to depress the burial relative to baptismal totals and create a spuriously high ratio in the non-urban parishes in the area.

Deane and Cole have also done extensive work on this matter and reached some interesting although tentative conclusions.[86] They note that in the first part of the eighteenth century population growth was more rapid in industrial and commercial counties than in agricultural ones, and more rapid in the north-west than in the south-east. In their view the industrial and commercial areas grew more rapidly not because of immigration but because they possessed a higher rate of natural increase due to high fertility rather than low mortality. Their work provides support for those who argue for the existence of a strong relationship between fertility levels and the availability of economic opportunities.

Unfortunately, despite their impressive clarity, these figures must be treated very cautiously until they can be compared with studies based on more complete and carefully collected data. A principal shortcoming of this work is that it is based upon the Rickman data series and depends upon estimates derived from these figures by Brownlee.[87] As has been suggested nonconformity, and hence poorer registration, may have been more prominent in the industrializing areas and it has been noted by critics that migration itself effects the age structure of sending and receiving areas in highly complex ways.[88] It is therefore not at all clear how these figures will stand up to more detailed research.

We may conclude by referring to a few regional studies where some confirmation of relatively high rates of population growth in manufacturing areas during the early eighteenth century has been established. In 12 parishes around Bromsgrove in Worcestershire where industrialization was rapid in the course of the eighteenth and early nineteenth centuries, estimated population rose from 7167 in 1700 to 9018 in 1750, an increase of approximately 25 per cent.[89] In seventeen parishes centring on the Shropshire village of Coalbrookdale the population leapt from 11,500 in 1711 to 17,326 in 1750, an average annual growth rate of 1·3 per cent.[90] Recent research suggests that the very rapid growth of Birmingham between the Restoration and 1730 coincided with exceptionally large surpluses of baptisms over burials in many rural parishes, especially in the Forest of Arden.[91] Chambers argued that the last decade of the seventeenth century and the early decades of the eighteenth were marked by substantial natural increase in Nottinghamshire so that by 1725 the population may have been 30 to 40 per cent higher than in 1670.[92] We can perhaps see in these studies evidence of a change in the spatial balance of the English population that was to become more fully apparent in the second half of the eighteenth century.

References

1. M. M. Postan (ed.), *Cambridge Economic History of Europe*, (Cambridge, 1966), Vol. 1, p.561.
2. A useful discussion of these sources is J. Thirsk, 'Sources of information on population', *Amateur Historian*, (1959), iv, pp. 129–33, 182–5; see also T. H. Hollingsworth, *Historical Demography*, (London, 1969), pp. 78–88, 111–26.
3. A useful summary of the literature on this issue which is highly critical of the reliability of the Parish Register Abstracts is to be found in M. W. Flinn, *British Population Growth, 1700–1850*, (London, 1969). Geographers have produced maps based on the data derived by Rickman from the Parish Register Abstracts; see for example, H. C. Darby (ed.), *A New Historical Geography of England after 1600*, (Cambridge, 1976), pp. 6–7. These maps can prove highly misleading.
4. R. S. Schofield and B. Midi Berry, 'Age at baptism in pre-industrial England', *Population Studies*, **25**, 3 (1971), pp. 453–63.
5. E. A. Wrigley, 'Births and baptisms: The use of Anglican baptism registers as a source of information about the numbers of births in England before the beginnings of civil registration', *Population Studies*, **31**, 2 (1977), pp. 281-312.
6. R. Lee, 'Estimating series of vital rates and age structures from baptisms and burials: a new technique, with applications to pre-industrial England', *Population Studies*, **28**, 3 (1974), pp. 495–512.
7. R. Lee and R. S. Schofield, 'British population in the eighteenth century' (in preparation).
8. E. A. Wrigley, 'Mortality in pre-industrial England: the example of

Colyton, Devon over three centuries', in D. V. Glass and R. Revelle (eds.) *Population and Social Change*, (London, 1972), pp. 243–73.

9. See, for example, L. Stone, *The Family, Sex and Marriage in England 1500–1800*, (London, 1977) especially Chapter 2, 'The demographic facts', and L. Clarkson, *Death, Disease and Famine in Pre-industrial England*, (Dublin, 1975).

10. M. W. Flinn, 'The stablization of mortality in pre-industrial western Europe', *Journal of European Economic History*, **III** (1974), pp. 285–318.

11. R. S. Schofield, '"Crisis"mortality', *Local Population Studies*, **9** (1972), p. 20.

12. For France see, P. Goubert, *Beauvais et le Beauvaisis de 1600 à 1730*, (Paris, 1960) 2 Vols, and the same author's 'The French peasantry of the seventeenth century', *Past and Present*, **10** (1956). For Scotland see M. W. Flinn (ed.), *Scottish Population History from the Seventeenth Century to the 1930s*, (London, 1978), pp. 116–32.

13. J. D. Chambers, *Population, Economy and Society in Pre-industrial England*, (London, 1972), pp. 77–106.

14. M. Spufford, *Contrasting Communities: English villagers in the Sixteenth and Seventeenth Centuries*, (Cambridge, 1974), pp. 46–57.

15. J. Samaha, *Law and Order in Historical Perspective. The Case of Elizabethan Essex*, (London, 1974).

16. D. Levine and K. Wrightson, 'The social context of illegitimacy in early modern England', in P. Laslett, K. Oosterveen and R. M. Smith (eds.), *Bastardy and its Comparative History*, (in press, 1978).

17. E. A. Wrigley (ed.), *An Introduction to English Historical Demography*, (London, 1966), pp. 96–159.

18. R. S. Schofield and E. A. Wrigley 'Infant and child mortality in late Tudor and early Stuart England', in C. Webster (ed.), *Sixteenth Century Medicine*, (in press); Wrigley, 'Births and baptisms', p. 293.

19. J. D. Durand, 'The modern expansion of world population', *American Philosophical Society Proceedings*, **11** (1967), pp. 136–59; W. H. McNeill, *Plagues and Peoples*, (Oxford, 1976), especially Chapter V.

20. Wrigley, in Glass and Revelle, *Population and Social Change*, pp. 247–53.

21. This information will be presented in much greater detail in R. S. Schofield and E. A. Wrigley, *Population Trends in Early Modern England*, (in press).

22. A. B. Appleby, 'Disease or famine? Mortality in Cumberland and Westmorland 1580–1640', *Economic History Review*, **XXVI** (1973), pp. 419–20; D. M. Palliser 'Dearth and disease in Staffordshire', in C. W. Chalklin and M. A. Havinden (eds.), *Rural Change and Urban Growth 1500–1800; Essays in English Regional History in Honour of W. G. Hoskins*, (London, 1974).

23. C. D. Rodgers, *The Lancashire Population Crisis of 1623*, (Manchester, 1975).

24. I am very grateful to Professor Appleby for allowing me to read the proofs of his forthcoming book on *Famine in Tudor and Stuart England*.

25. A. E. Imhof and B. J. Lindskog, 'Les causes de mortalité en Suède et en Finlande entre 1749 et 1773', *Annales Économies, Sociétés, Civilisations*, **4** (1974).

26. R. S. Schofield, 'An anatomy of an epidemic: Colyton, November 1645 to November 1646' in *The Plague Reconsidered*, A Local Population Studies Supplement, (Matlock, 1977), p. 123, note 21.

27. *Ibid*.

28. P. Slack, 'The local incidence of epidemic disease: the case of Bristol 1540–1650', in *The Plague Reconsidered*, A Local Population Studies Supplement, (Matlock 1977), pp. 49–62 and in his forthcoming book on *The Impact of Plague in Tudor and Stuart England*.

29. F. West, 'Infant mortality in the East Fen parishes of Leake and Wrangle', *Local Population Studies*, **13** (1974), pp. 41–4.

30. R. A. P. Finlay, 'The population of London, 1580–1640', Ph.D. Thesis, University of Cambridge (1976), Chapter 5.

31. For a review of the evidence on English illegitimacy see P. Laslett, *Family Life and Illicit Love in Earlier Generations*, (Cambridge, 1977), Chapter 3.

32. E. A. Wrigley, 'Age at marriage in early modern England', paper delivered to the XIIIth Congress of Genealogical and Heraldic Sciences, September 1976.

33. Laslett, *Family Life and Illicit Love*, pp. 26–7.

34. G. Hawthorn, *The Sociology of Fertility*, (London 1970), p. 20.

35. M. Livi Bacci, 'Can anything be said about the demographic trends when only aggregative vital statistics are available?', in R. Lee (ed.), *Population Patterns in the Past*, (London, 1977). A technique outlined in this paper has been developed by Schofield to estimate proportions of the population never marrying and the results will appear in Schofield and Wrigley, *Population Trends in Early Modern England*, (in press).

36. See Schofield and Wrigley, *Population Trends*, where this is discussed in greater detail

37. G. Mackenroth, *Bevölkeringslechre*, (Berlin, 1953).

38. J. Thirsk, 'Industries in the countryside', in F. J. Fisher (ed.), *Essays in the Economic and Social History of Tudor and Stuart England*, (Cambridge, 1961).

39. R. S. Schofield, 'The relationship between demographic structure and environment in pre-industrial western Europe', in Werner Conze (ed.) *Sozialgeschichte der Familie in der Neuzeit Europas*, (Stuttgart, 1976), pp. 156–7.

40. D. Levine, *Family Formation in an Age of Nascent Capitalism*, (London, 1977), pp. 58–87.

41. *Ibid*., pp. 116–26.

42. R. Wall, 'Changes in English household structure, 1650–1971', A paper

presented to the Joint Meetings of the British Society for Population Studies and the Population Geography Study Group (Institute of British Geographers) at the University of Liverpool in September 1977.

43. Finlay, 'Population of London', Chapter 6.
44. J. Sheail, 'The distribution of taxable population and wealth in England during the early sixteenth century', *Transactions, Institute of British Geographers*, **55** (1972), p. 123.
45. Laslett, *Family Life*, Chapter 2.
46. A. D. J. Macfarlane, 'A mythical model of the peasantry in England before the industrial revolution' in D. Green *et. al.* (eds.), *Social Organization and Settlement*, (in press).
47. Levine, *Family Formation*, pp. 37–41.
48. Laslett, *Family Life*, pp. 34–5. See also R. S. Schofield, 'Age-specific mobility in an eighteenth century rural English parish', *Annales de Démographic Historique*, (1972) pp. 261–74.
49. Laslett, *Family Life* pp. 73–4.
50. Information presented by Ann K. Cooper in a paper delivered to the Kings College seminar in Social History (March 1975) entitled 'The mobility of farm servants in the seventeenth and eighteenth centuries'.
51. Sheail, 'The distribution of taxable population', p. 123.
52. Levine, *Family Formation*, pp. 122–5.
53. P. Spufford, 'Population mobility in pre-industrial England', *Genealogists' Magazine*, **17**, Nos 8–10, (1974).
54. E. A. Wrigley, 'A simple model of London's importance in changing English society and economy 1650–1750', in P. Abrams and E. A. Wrigley (eds.), *Towns in Societies*, (Cambridge, 1978), p. 215.
55. *Ibid.*, pp. 220–1.
56. D. Cressy, 'Occupations, migration and literacy in East London 1580–1640', *Local Population Studies*, (1970), pp. 53–60.
57. C. Phythian Adams, 'Urban decay in late medieval England', in Abrams and Wrigley, *Towns in Societies*, pp. 159–85.
58. J. H. C. Patten, 'Population distribution in Norfolk and Suffolk during the sixteenth and seventeenth centuries', *Transactions, Institute of British Geographers*, **65** (1975), p. 62
59. Appleby, *Famine in Tudor and Stuart England*.
60. P. Corfield, 'Urban development in England and Wales in the sixteenth and seventeenth centuries', in D. C. Coleman and A. H. John (eds.), *Trade, Government and Economy in Pre-industrial England*, (London, 1976), pp. 214–7.
61. P. Clark, 'The migrant in Kentish towns 1580–1640', pp. 117–68 of P. Clark and P. Slack (eds.) *Crisis and Order in English Towns 1500–1700*, (London, 1972).
62. J. H. C. Patten, 'Patterns of migration and movement of labour to three pre-

industrial East Anglian towns', *Journal of Historical Geography*, 2 (1976), pp. 111–29.

63. Clark, 'The migrant in Kentish towns', pp. 135–49; *idem*, 'Eighteenth century migration: some problems of quantitative analysis', *Poverty and Social Policy 1750–1870*,(Milton Keynes, 1974), p. 17.

64. Clark, 'The migrant in Kentish towns'; J. F. Pound, *Poverty and Vagrancy in Tudor England*, (London, 1971), p. 28.

65. Levine, *Family Formation*, p. 122.

66. P. Spufford, 'Population mobility', p. 539

67. Levine, *Family Formation*, p. 40.

68. Information from Mr David Souden of Fitzwilliam College, Cambridge who is researching into this matter.

69. Sheail, 'The distribution of taxable population'.

70. S. J. Herrtage (ed.), *England in the Reign of King Henry the Eighth*, Early English Text Society, extra ser., **XXXII** (1878), p. 72.

71. M. Spufford, *Contrasting Communities*, pp. 10–18.

72. C. T. Smith, in *V.C.H. Leicestershire*, **III**, pp. 137–45.

73. Patten, 'Patterns of migration' p. 56.

74. Appleby, *Famine in Tudor and Stuart England*.

75. A. B. Appleby, 'Agrarian capitalism or seigneurial reaction? The northwest of England, 1500–1700', *American Historical Review*, **80** (1975).

76. Postan describes this process most eloquently when he refers to the colonization of 'superannuated' acres in the late thirteenth and early fourteenth centuries. See Postan, *Cambridge Economic History of Europe*, **I**, p. 560.

77. E. Le Roy Ladurie, 'L'histoire immobile', *Annales Économies, Sociétés, Civilizations*, (1974).

78. Patten, 'Patterns of migration' (1975), p. 62

79. L. M. Munby, *Hertfordshire Population Statistics*, 1563–1801, (Hitchin, 1964), p. 21.

80. C. T. Smith, *V.C.H. Leicestershire*.

81. D. Turner, 'A lost seventeenth century crisis? The evidence of two counties', *Local Population Studies* (in preparation). Dr Anne Whiteman, who is working on a detailed study and edition of the Compton Census of 1676 and comparing the population of that date with those of the 1603 Communicants suggests that parishes with market towns grew far faster than rural parishes between 1603 and 1676.

82. Palliser, 'Dearth and disease in Staffordshire', p. 72

83. J. Thirsk, 'Horn and thorn in Staffordshire: the economy of a pastoral county', *North Staffs. Journal of Field Studies*, **ix** (1969), pp. 1–16.

84. D. C. Coleman, *The Economy of England 1450–1750*, (Oxford, 1977), pp. 98–9.

85. J. T. Krause, 'Some aspects of population change, 1690–1790', in E. L.

Jones and G. E. Mingay (eds.), *Land, Labour and Population in the Industrial Revolution*, (London, 1967), p. 194.

86. P. Deane and W. A. Cole, *British Economic Growth, 1688–1919*, (2nd edn.) (Cambridge, 1967).

87. J. Brownlee, 'The history of the birth and death rates in England and Wales', *Public Health*, **XXIX** (1916), pp. 211–22, 228–38.

88. L. Neal, 'Deane and Cole on industrialization and population change in the eighteenth century', *Economic History Review*, **XXIV** (1971), pp. 643–652.

89. D. E. C. Eversley, 'A survey of population in an area of Worcestshire from 1660–1850', *Population Studies*, **X** (1957).

90. S. Sogner, 'Aspects of the demographic situation in seventeen parishes in Shropshire, 1711–1760', *Population Studies*, **XVIII** (1963).

91. J. M. Martin, 'The rise in population in eighteenth century Warwickshire', *Dugdale Society Occasional Paper No. 23*, (Stratford-upon-Avon, 1976), p. 15.

92. J. D. Chambers, *Nottinghamshire in the Eighteenth Century*, (2nd edn.) (London, 1964), p. ix.

9
Agriculture 1730–1900

J. R. Walton

The role of agriculture in an industrializing economy is both complex and diverse. On the one hand, agriculture's importance gradually declines as growth in the industrial sector gathers momentum: between 1730 and 1900 agriculture's contribution to British national income diminished from an estimated 40 or 45 per cent to just over 6 per cent. [1] On the other, the transition to an industrialized economy is rarely attained without radical change within the agricultural sector. Improvements in technique and increases in output were the outstanding characteristics of British agriculture during the Industrial Revolution.

The history of eighteenth and nineteenth century agriculture therefore offers something of a paradox. Growth rates were much less impressive than those in industry: agricultural output increased by no more than 43 per cent during the eighteenth century compared with 187 per cent in industry and commerce as a whole. [2] Nor need we find this surprising. Agriculture was, by its very nature, too established and too sedate to experience rates of growth comparable with those occurring in new and emergent industries. But, at the same time, it was neither inflexible nor stagnant. A responsive agricultural sector was beneficial to the whole process of industrialization, for it provided capital, entrepreneurship, labour, markets and raw materials in varying but significant quantities. [3] And, within the limitations imposed by its size and its history, agriculture witnessed truly radical improvements in technique during the eighteenth and nineteenth centuries, these being reflected in a substantial increase in output.

Many of the subtleties of agriculture's position were not appreciated by contemporary observers. Although agricultural writers were always keen to identify and praise progress, it was the less dynamic aspects of rural life which appealed to others. Often, contemporary comment did not acknowledge that agriculture was experiencing change. For example, the country dweller was rarely regarded as a progressive. Even if country cousins had previously been treated with a certain amount of sympathetic disdain, it is to this period (and, in particular, to the endeavours of *Punch*) that we owe the traditional stereotype of the country bumpkin. It is during this period, too, that we see the countryside increasingly revered as a retreat from the uncomfortable realities of urban and industrial living; as the last refuge of the values, attitudes and customs of the true, non-industrialized England; as a place where time stands still and nothing changes. 'When I am in the country', wrote Hazlitt, 'I wish to vegetate like the country.'

These states of mind had important consequences: an underlying belief in the implicit desirability of an agricultural way of life was reflected in, and, in its turn, was fostered by the disproportionate political influence of the landed interest which prevailed well into the nineteenth century. Nor were all their assumptions necessarily misguided. The implacability of rural labour manifested itself in the pronounced reluctance of labour to leave the land in quite the numbers that the contrasting opportunities of agricultural and non-agricultural employment might have warranted. Throughout much of the period 1730–1900, labour abundance posed a much greater problem to farmers than dearth. [4]

Nevertheless, resistance to change was not the universal condition of the agricultural sector, even though it may have appeared so to some at the time. Agriculture formed an integral part of an economic system undergoing massive change, and as such it also changed, although not in quite the same way as industry. It is with the configurations of this change, with the events which have come subsequently to be referred to as the 'agricultural revolution' that this chapter is concerned.

An Agricultural Revolution

Given the relative novelty of agricultural history as a field of academic enquiry, the term 'agricultural revolution' may be considered old-established. In its conventional form it is most commonly associated with Lord Ernle's volume *English Farming Past and Present*, first published in 1912. But during the intervening years the concept has undergone a transformation almost as radical as the changes to which it alluded.

To Ernle, whose statement differs from many others made at about the same time only by virtue of its considerable length and the cogency with which it was expressed, the events which were crucial in transforming agriculture from its state of medieval torpor occurred during the second half of the eighteenth century, and were the result of the benign influence of a limited number of landowners and innovators:

> The great changes which English agriculture witnessed as the eighteenth century advanced, and particularly after the accession of George III are, broadly speaking, identified with Jethro Tull, Lord Townsend, Bakewell of Dishley, Arthur Young and Coke of Norfolk. With their names are associated the chief characteristics in the farming progress of the period, which may be summed up in the adoption of improved methods of cultivation, the introduction of new crops, the reduction of stock breeding to a science, the provision of increased facility of communication and transport, and the enterprise of capitalist landlords and tenant farmers. . . . Without the substitution of separate occupation for the ancient system of common cultivation, this agricultural progress was impossible. But in carrying out the necessary changes, rural society was convulsed, and its general conditions revolutionised. [5]

Some of the shortcomings of this view stem from the way in which it is expressed. It seems to have mattered more that a statement should be striking than necessarily true. But Ernle's distortions all had the same stamp: a tendency to exaggerate the novelty of many eighteenth-century changes and the influence of a small number of major landlords in promoting them. In advocating this hectic and heroic view of agricultural progress Ernle was undoubtedly guided by his own professed sympathy with the landowning classes, for his work was consciously intended to advance their interests at a time of external criticism and self-doubt. But Ernle did not need to be a particularly selective reader of the most readily available source—the published opinions of the late eighteenth and early nineteenth-century agricultural writers—to find enough evidence in support of his views.

Most criticism of Ernle has arisen from the detailed analysis of sources other than those which he consulted. Estate and private papers have revealed that the contributions of many of the supposed innovators were either impractical in relation to the demands of the time and therefore not widely adopted (as in the case of Tull's seed drill) or much less far-reaching and less novel than either the innovators or their publicists claimed. [6] For example, Parker has shown how Thomas Coke's image as a progressive was deliberately fostered in the interests of social prestige and political advancement when his achievements at Holkham were really relatively limited.[7] Land tax assessments have indicated that parliamentary enclosure had a much less devastating effect upon the status of the small owner-occupier than Ernle and his contemporaries imagined.[8] And, perhaps most important of all, the analysis of seventeenth-century sources, notably probate inventories, has uncovered ample evidence of progress well before the mid-eighteenth century, often in open-field areas (see Chapter 6).[9]

For all this, the prevalent image of the agricultural revolution still remains much closer to Ernle's view than to any other. To some extent this reflects the inherent attractions of a simple statement which elevates a few individuals almost to the status of gods. But Ernle's thesis has more to sustain it than this, for the evidence for the eighteenth and nineteenth centuries does indicate that change was fundamental. Whether it amounted to a 'revolution' in the strictest sense need not concern us here, although Mingay has asked whether agriculture's capacity to feed an increasing population can really be construed in any other way. Between 1700 and 1870 population increased five-fold yet the domestic agricultural sector still managed to provide 80 per cent of the nation's food requirements.[10] What is clear is that although many of Ernle's interpretations are insupportable, recent research indicates that not all his presumptions are quite as false as once supposed.

Parliamentary enclosure may be taken as a case in point. The agricultural revolution of the eighteenth and nineteenth centuries consisted, essentially, of three categories of change: much larger amounts than hitherto were committed to various forms of fixed capital expenditure; innovations in both products and techniques gained widespread acceptance; and all this was made possible by changes in attitude among the farming population. Expenditure on enclosure was one item of fixed capital investment. Substantial amounts were also committed to underdraining and arterial drainage schemes, and, especially, to farm buildings. Indeed, the latter are thought at present to consume about 60 per cent of the long-term capital invested in British agriculture.[11] Available estimates for the eighteenth and nineteenth centuries suggest that the sums committed to buildings were substantial; a large proportion of today's farm buildings date from the eighteenth and nineteenth centuries.[12]

Parliamentary enclosure was therefore by no means the only manifestation of long-term capital expenditure during the agricultural revolution. Nevertheless, the acreages involved testify to its importance. During the eighteenth and nineteenth centuries, some 5300 enclosures were enacted in England, involving some 6,817,000 acres altogether, of which 4,492,000 were predominantly open-field arable and 2,325,000 common and waste.[13] The years 1760–80 and 1793–1815 witnessed the heaviest concentrations of acts involving open field, and the counties of Yorkshire, Lincolnshire and Nottinghamshire, the south-east Midlands and central-southern England their greatest impact. Some 47 per cent of Leicestershire, 53 per cent of Oxfordshire, 30 per cent of Warwickshire and 49 per cent of Bedfordshire were affected.[14]

Somewhat different was the enclosure by Parliamentary Act of commons and waste, which occurred principally after 1800 and continued well into the second half of the nineteenth century. This resulted in the reclamation of substantial areas of upland waste in the northern and western counties of England and in Wales. An estimated 32 per cent of the total land area of Northumberland, 46 per cent of Westmorland, 47 per cent of Caernarvon and 32 per cent of Cardigan were enclosed or reclaimed between 1800 and 1873.[15] Wasteland reclamation represented a clear addition to the fixed capital stock of agriculture. It did not impose the strains of re-organization upon established farming communities nor could it do other than make a net contribution to agricultural output. For these reasons, it need not concern us further.

The enclosure of open field was different. We now accept that enclosure did not, as once supposed, dispossess the small occupier, pauperize the rural labour force, and depopulate the countryside, forcing its unwilling inhabitants to take up residence in the industrial towns. We also accept the validity of sixteenth and seventeenth-century evidence which clearly indicates that innovations could be adopted in open fields. Nevertheless, parliamentary enclosure of open field did have the capacity to make substantial changes and recent work suggests that it was not wholly neutral in its effects. Local studies in Buckinghamshire and Oxfordshire have drawn attention to extraordinarily high rates of turnover of landowners and tenants.[16] Indeed, Oxfordshire tenancies advertised as vacant in the local press were on average about three times more likely to be located in parishes recently enclosed or about to enclose than would have been expected.[17] Similar local evidence also suggests a relatively muted response to many agricultural innovations in parishes which retained substantial areas of open field. As Table 9.1 shows, turnips were very rarely mentioned in farm-sales advertisements relating to such parishes, while similar responses were also observed in the case of most

Table 9.1: References to turnips in farm-sales advertisments for Oxfordshire, 1785 1836.

	Sales notices which mention turnips	Sales notices which do not mention turnips	Total
Parishes of which more than one half of the total acreage was unenclosed	6 (1·8 per cent)	273 (97·9 per cent)	279
Other parishes	85 (6·4 per cent)	1243 (93·6 per cent)	1328

innovations in sheep and cattle breeds. [18] Furthermore, the parliamentary enclosure movement probably did much to advance the early growth of the agricultural professions (notably surveying, auctioneering and land agency) and the rural capital market and country banking system. These, in their turn, provided facilities invaluable for further growth. [19] These facts are not intended to suggest that the evidence for the eighteenth and nineteenth centuries invariably discloses a tardier response to innovation in open field areas. Clover, for example, showed (in Oxfordshire at least) little discernible preference for wholly enclosed parishes. [20] Nevertheless, the effects of enclosure were evidently considerable.

The function of the landowner is another influence which Ernle did not entirely misconstrue. The significance of the Norfolk improvers lies not so much in the great value or the extraordinary novelty of their activities as in the fact that these activities exemplify a commitment to improvement which became widespread during the eighteenth and nineteenth centuries amongst landowners both large and small. A conspicuous interest in agricultural advance reinforced the considerable social prestige of landed proprietorship and consequently among those who sought it most assiduously were many who had gained admission to the ranks of the landed via the profits of industrial or commercial investment. [21]

However, it was not only these *parvenus* who carried experiment to unprofitable extremes. Many established landlords were content to write off part of their total investment in agriculture, along with amounts spent in building country houses and landscaping their grounds, as a necessary capital-consuming requirement of enlightened landed proprietorship. Richard Jefferies' Cecil was not alone in believing that massive investment in novelty was a panacea for the worst ills of agricultural depression, nor George Eliot's Sir James Chettam unique in finding unattractive the unsolicited advice that 'fancy farming' was the 'most expensive sort of whistle you can buy; you may as well keep a pack of hounds'.[22] Indeed, Lord Althorp, Third Earl Spencer, one of the first large-scale breeders of pedigree Improved Shorthorns, only secured sufficient capital to become a pedigree breeder when he renounced hunting; despite their tremendous success his Shorthorns never represented anything other than a severe financial liability.[23] Time and again the accounts of home farms bear testimony to the unprofitable character of excessive experiment.[24]

The principal beneficiaries of all this activity were the tenants. Although not incapable of independent initiative, they were in the advantageous position of not having to risk all on untried experiments. Instead, they could exercise their own more considered judgement in selecting from the wide range of novelties their experimenting superiors offered. For example, it was said of Philip Pusey, founder member of the Royal Agricultural Society and owner of an estate near Faringdon in Berkshire, that 'the benefit which [he] does to the district round him by introducing new agricultural implements is widely recognized by the farmers, who profit by adopting those which he finds successful, while they avoid his failures.'[25]

However, it should not be imagined that the relationships between landlords and tenants were perfect, for it was the frequent complaint of contemporary writers that they were not. In some cases, lease agreements offered insufficient security of tenure; indeed, a great many tenants farmed without the security of any lease agreements at all. It was said of Staffordshire in 1869 that no leases were granted over the greater part of the county.[26] Other leases were criticized as too rigid, imposing conditions which prevented the tenant responding to changing circumstances or certain innovations. Evidently, there was scope for reform; but although reforms (especially the increasing recognition that out-going tenants had a right to compensation for unexhausted improvements) did occur, many deficiencies remained.[27] Nevertheless, leases which may have appeared unsatisfactory from the tenant's standpoint were often so interpreted as to cause little real inconvenience or hardship to him. Generally speaking, the landlord and tenant system, for all its intrinsic injustices, encouraged progress. Mill repeated approvingly the opinion of a German economist that great proprietors were necessary 'to lead the way in new improvements'. [28] Even if, as some recent evidence suggests, it was not the greatest of proprietors who were the most innovatory or the tenantry who were always least so, we can consider this assessment broadly correct. [29]

The evidence relating to parliamentary enclosure and the landed proprietor draws attention to the essential validity of some of Ernle's presumptions. But perhaps the most compelling reason for continuing to regard an approximation to Ernle's thesis as valid lies in the evidence for agricultural innovation during the eighteenth and nineteenth centuries. To argue this is not to deny that some innovations were introduced at an earlier date: Ernle was certainly mistaken in saying that they were not. Nevertheless, the eighteenth and nineteenth centuries still saw both the wider adoption of techniques known already but only to a restricted circle, and the introduction and dissemination of complete novelties. In the first category fall a great many innovations in fodder cropping. Improvements in this sector provided a basis for many other innovations. In the second may be placed a wide range of innovations in sheep and cattle breeds, agricultural implements and farm machinery.

Figure 9.1 derived from local newspaper advertisements for farm sales, shows suggested adoption curves for three major improved sheep breeds in Oxfordshire: the Cotswold (or New Cotswold)—a longwoolled cross of local stocks with Bakewell's Improved Leicester; the improved shortwoolled Southdown and its local Hampshire Down variant; and the Oxford Down—a cross between the two main families of improved longwoolled and improved shortwoolled strains. Figure 9.2 shows similar adoption curves for various innovations in agricultural implements and machinery, with the addition of information for the Welsh Borderland. Clearly, many innovations in both sectors came into widespread use only during the period which concerns us.

In fact, no one sector was entirely free from innovation of some sort. Even in the case of fodder supply, where improvements can be detected as early as the sixteenth century, change was not only a question of the widespread imitation of established antecedents. More resistant and higher yielding strains of many artificial grasses were either developed within the country or imported from overseas during the eighteenth and nineteenth centuries, the more successful becoming widely adopted. For example, new varieties of clover were introduced from continental Europe in 1752, 1777 and 1789, and from Egypt in 1798. [30] During the nineteenth century, Italian rye-grass supplemented and to some considerable extent supplanted the various indigenous strains.[31] Nor were these changes confined to the grasses. The swede (introduced during the 1760s) and the mangold-wurzel (introduced some 20 years later) offered attractive alternatives to established varieties of turnip, gaining widespread support during the following century and a half.[32] The former was not only hardier than the common turnip, but provided fodder further into the spring, while the mangold was peculiarly well adapted to those heavier soil areas which were unsuitable both for turnip husbandry and the swede.

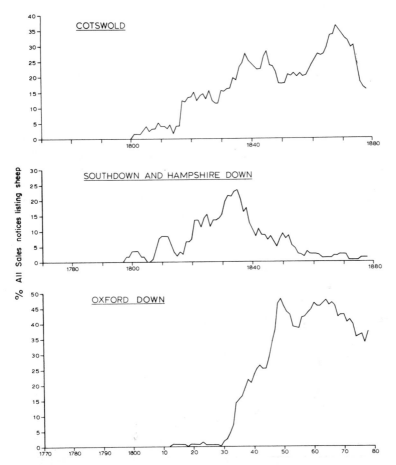

Fig. 9.1. Adoption curves for major improved sheep breeds in Oxfordshire (five year moving means).

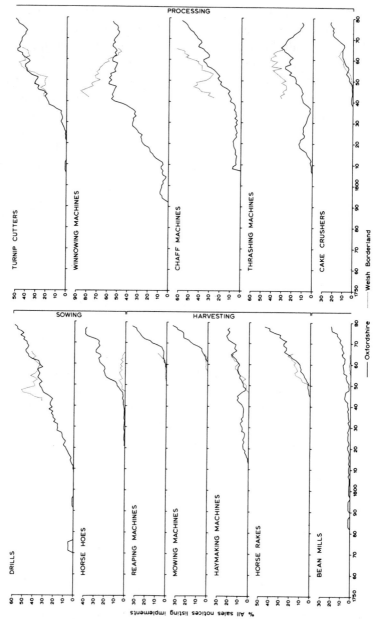

Fig. 9.2. Adoption curves for implements and machinery (five year moving means).

SOWING

DRILLS

HORSE HOES

HARVESTING

REAPING MACHINES

MOWING MACHINES

HAYMAKING MACHINES

HORSE RAKES

BEAN MILLS

PROCESSING

TURNIP CUTTERS

WINNOWING MACHINES

CHAFF MACHINES

THRASHING MACHINES

CAKE CRUSHERS

% All sales notices listing implements

——— Oxfordshire   ········· Welsh Borderland

The methods of cultivation of fodder crops also changed. The adoption of the Norfolk four-course system, involving the alternation of two fodder crops, clover and turnips, with equal acreages of wheat and barley, has often been represented as the culmination of all progress in this sector. In fact, this was far from being the case. As the Norfolk four-course became more widely adopted during the eighteenth century, so it came to be appreciated that the cultivation of clover and turnips in frequent succession was not beneficial in the long term, the increasing incidence of the 'finger and toe' disease in turnips and 'clover sickness' being two important causes of diminishing returns, particularly in areas climatically less suited to a rigid four-course rotation than was Norfolk itself. The agricultural writings of the period bear witness to increasing dis-satisfaction with the Norfolk system and the increasing popularity of modifications. For example, in 1809 it was said of the Henley district of Oxfordshire that 'clover dies from repetition, so that [the farmers] omit their courses alternatively'.[33] In some other areas, this was not appreciated so readily. As late as 1845, the Norfolk four-course system was described as the 'usual course' of south Wiltshire, although a rotation involving the cultivation of clover only once in eight years 'had been adopted by many' to avoid problems of 'clover sickness' which were by then becoming evident.[34]

Change, it seems, fostered more change. Indeed, the very wealth and complexity of agricultural change during the eighteenth and nineteenth centuries calls into question the whole notion of a single, unitary agricultural revolution. As the nineteenth century progressed so changes were made which bore less and less resemblance to eighteenth-century or earlier antecedents. Thompson has argued that these events represent an agricultural revolution different in principle from that which had occurred earlier, and coined the term 'second agricultural revolution' to describe them.[35]

The underlying causes of the second agricultural revolution were manifold. The loss of protection resulting from the repeal of the Corn Laws in 1846 exposed the cereals producer to the threat (initially more imagined than real) of foreign competition. This provided a sufficient inducement to increase output and shift production towards the less threatened livestock sector. The result was the widespread dissemination of so-called 'high farming' systems in which substantial inputs of fertilizers and artificial feedstuffs were directed towards producing ever higher outputs of cereals and fatstock, the former being sold as a cash crop if cereals prices were favourable, but otherwise consumed on the farm as an animal feedstuff. [36]

The movement towards high farming was assisted by a number of developments. In the first place, Peel's repeal legislation also contained provisions designed to mollify the landed interest by offering long-term loans for capital improvements, particularly the drainage of heavy soils. In fact, agricultural advance generally was sustained by technical developments reflecting the achievements of the age. The developing railway network, in 'annihilating distance', contributed to a pronounced widening of markets. An expanding world economy brought imported materials in hitherto unimagined quantities, these being particularly significant in providing processed fertilizers and feedstuffs. And scientific, technical and industrial advances at home were the basis of striking changes in the fields of agricultural chemistry and agricultural engineering. Mechanical innovation received a further filip as the countryside began to shed labour in quantities sufficient to make the adoption of labour-saving devices attractive.

Marked improvements in the availability of information about innovations further contributed to their more rapid rate of adoption. These took a variety of forms. In the first place, the railway network reduced the isolation of rural communities and improved the availability of many agricultural innovations, offering for the first time conditions appropriate to national networks of distribution and supply. As a consequence, farmers began to enjoy the regular experience of examining innovations produced by distant manufacturers and suppliers at their local market towns. Second, the volume of printed information concerned with agriculture increased substantially. Particularly important in this respect was the very marked expansion in provincial newspaper publishing during the 1840s and 1850s in response to rising standards of literacy within the rural community at large, the repeal of the advertisement duty in 1853 and of the stamp duty in 1855. Agricultural matters, whether represented by advertisements or news items, received greater exposure in this expanded provincial press. Third, the mid-nineteenth century also witnessed a marked increase in the number and activities of agricultural societies. Although some of these had been founded during the late eighteenth and early nineteenth centuries, it was only after the mid-nineteenth century that the number of societies expanded to a point where they made any significant impact upon the rural scene. The foundation in 1839 of the first truly national society, the Royal Agricultural Society, was especially important, for besides its own considerable activities in organizing meetings and publishing, this society served as a model for a great many local societies established during the 1840s and 1850s. [37] Membership of agricultural societies rarely appears to have encouraged farmers to adopt agricultural innovations earlier than they might otherwise have done. [38] But the societies did offer agriculturalists additional opportunities to see and hear about the latest developments at shows and meetings.

Of course, progress in these various respects was not everywhere as rapid as it might have been. Many concerned parents must, like Mr Tulliver, have been frustrated in their half-articulated desires for some sort of practical training for their sons by the reluctance of clergymen schoolmasters to recognize that anything other than Latin, Greek and Euclid had a place in the curriculum. [39] Agricultural societies and farmers clubs attracted seekers after political prestige who generally contributed little to the cause of agricultural advance. Richard Jefferies' Marthorne, who took up speaking at agricultural society meetings for exactly this reason, adopted the rule 'never to say anything original', and the newly founded Oxford Farmers' Club was warned of the dangers of 'windy orations by professed speech-makers'. [40] However, these deficiencies amounted to no more than a superficial inconvenience in the history of agricultural progress. The later part of the nineteenth century was a period of remarkable and rapid change.

Patterns of Agricultural Change

To speak of the chronology of agricultural change without reference to its geography makes little sense in relation to the practical nature of agricultural history, for improvements were neither equally acceptable nor equally well accepted everywhere. But the task of identifying geographical variations in patterns of change is no easy one. Unlike large-scale industry, agriculture was not by its very nature confined to a few relatively small areas. Even though certain regional variations can be recognized readily, the greater part of England and Wales still awaits the detailed research which should establish exact patterns of local response to the various changes already described.

One contrast so fundamental as to have been acknowledged often is the distinction between clayland and lightland agriculture. Obviously, this simple two-fold division could not be considered an acceptable solution to the taxonomic problems posed by England's immensely varied soils and farming systems, nor is it offered as such. Rather it represents a recognition that most innovations were best suited to light and least suited to heavy soils. In the south and east this meant a virtual reversal of previous regional relationships. Whereas the clay vales had formerly been major grain-producing regions and the scarplands in many cases little used except as inferior sheepwalk or rabbit warrens, the moisture retentive soils of the vales proved ill-suited to the fodder courses and folded sheep of the Norfolk four-course system and its subsequent 'high farming' variants. While the vales suffered the scarps benefited, their technically advanced state standing in sharp contrast to their previous condition (which, in the case of west Norfolk, was evocatively described as 'two rabbits struggling for every blade of grass'). Yields per acre and stocking densities were still low—lower in most cases than clayland equivalents. But rental and other production costs were also low and the financial prospects in this sector therefore generally good. [41]

However, to represent the agricultural history of the years 1730–1900 as a simple matter of lightland advance and clayland retardation undervalues both the variety of regional experience and the changing circumstances of the time. By the early 1840s, various technological developments had made available a cheap and effective drainage pipe, and this, it has been argued, together with the provisions of Peel's drainage loans, provided conditions conducive to widespread investment in underdraining, and the consequent adoption on the clays of systems of production formerly confined to the more progressive lightlands. [42]

Although attractive in many ways, not least in equating progress in clayland agriculture with the events of the 'second agricultural revolution', this thesis has not gone uncriticized. In a denial of the whole notion of clayland advance, Collins and Jones argue that the amount underdrained was inadequate, the claylands continuing to suffer competitive disadvantage. [43] To say with certainty which of these contradictory assessments is correct depends upon knowing exactly how much was invested in underdrainage from all sources, both public and private, a figure which even a massive survey of all the available evidence could not supply. But it can be no coincidence that a rough survey of the surviving official records discloses a greater readiness to take up government loans in the northern and western parts of the country, while instances of progress appearing in other contemporary evidence most commonly relate to the north and west and counter-instances of retardation to the south and east. [44] For example, as early as 1852 as much as 120,000 acres of Cumberland was thought to be in a 'properly drained state'. In 1869, it was said of Staffordshire that 'a large area in this county recently required draining; a large extent has been done, and that which remains is chiefly on the smaller and less important properties. Like other great improvements, it has been principally effected in the last thirty years.'[45] It seems that the revolution on the clays may well have been a regional rather than a national phenomenon.

Be this as it may, the question which still remains to be answered is whether the whole concept of a clayland/lightland dichotomy of some sort is strictly compatible with the regional structure of eighteenth and nineteenth-century agriculture. Were the lightland/clayland distinction to serve as an acceptable model of regional change, not only would all the farming systems of the country have clearly to belong to one group or the other (which they do not), but it would also have to be demonstrated that soil quality was the dominant cause of regional variation, when in fact it was only one of several influences embracing the facts of physical geography as a whole and the nature of market demand.

The influence of market demand, especially, must not be under-estimated. By the early eighteenth century, very few farmers still produced solely for personal subsistence, and urban markets were sufficiently well developed for agriculture no longer to be concerned simply with supplying the immediate locality. The provisioning of London was especially important. Defoe in particular has shown how the complementary specialisms of the different parts of Great Britain were redistributed via the mechanisms of internal trade to meet the demands of the capital.[46] These demands were considerable and could be far-reaching. For example, even at this early date, store cattle reared in the remote uplands of Scotland and Wales found their way to the fattening pastures of the East Midlands and East Anglia and thence to metropolitan markets.

Nevertheless, the magnitude and influence of urban demand can be over emphasized. It was, after all, still only the privileged metropolitan few who derived a large proportion of their food from distant sources, and, even in their case, the effects were most keenly felt in the south-east within relatively close proximity of the capital. Defoe has been accused of exaggerating the importance of distant supply patterns. [47] Indeed, it may be that high levels of metropolitan demand together with expanding continental markets for grain, especially in Holland, served as a stimulus to the agriculture of south-east England during the early eighteenth century, promoting and consolidating its status as the major area of innovation and change. [48]

Elsewhere, the influences of the metropolitan market or export trade were less important. Agriculture instead responded more to local markets. Within these locally articulated systems of supply and demand, dietary habits were usually adjusted to the varying agricultural potential of the region, the continuing preference for non-wheaten flours outside the south-east being, to some extent, an example of such adjustment. [49] But the overall result was much less regional specialization than the physical geography of the country might lead one to expect, and especially the growth of substantial grain crops in the wetter north and west. The derelict water corn mills still to be seen in these areas as much as elsewhere bear testimony to the sometime influence of a balanced local demand which the freer flow of national and international trade gradually undermined, clearing the way for patterns of production more fully attuned to the potential of each region.

However, it need hardly be said that this was not the only cause of change. As the urban market expanded so did its basic geography alter. Whereas in the early eighteenth century long-distance supply patterns had been more or less dictated by the requirements of London, the rising urban and industrial centres of the Midlands and north gradually imposed both a much higher level and an entirely different pattern of demand. This increase was particularly pronounced in the livestock sector, for not only did dietary changes consequent upon improved standards of living favour that sector, but the cereals producer was increasingly exposed to the competitive effects of cheap foreign importations.

In geographical terms, the effects were most evident within relatively close proximity of the consuming centres, although, thanks to the developing railway system, demand increasingly permeated more distant areas of supply. [50] The nature of these new influences may be appreciated from prize reports published in the *Journal of the Royal Agricultural Society* during the mid-nineteenth century. The reporter for the West Riding wrote as follows:

> When it is remembered that within the limits of the coal formation are situated all the populous manufacturing towns of the county, it will not be thought singular that little or no general system of cultivation should be pursued beyond that which may be deemed the best for securing the greatest amount of marketable produce in the shortest time. [51]

But the result, in this as in other areas, was not short-term gain and long-term ruin. The fertility of the soil under such conditions of intensive production was maintained by the reciprocal movement of manures from the towns into the neighbouring countryside:

> The ready markets and comparatively higher value of produce in these districts, coupled with the greater facility of procuring manure, not only stimulate the smaller occupiers within easy reach of the towns to what might otherwise prove an impoverishing course of cropping, but they also conduce to some of the larger and more enterprising farmers adopting a system which, a few years ago, would certainly have brought down upon them the displeasure and apprehension of the owners of the soil, and probably the ridicule or contempt of their neighbouring occupiers. [52]

Patterns of land use around many major centres consequently developed in a fashion reminiscent of the von Thünen model, the intensity of production declining as distance from the market increased. This had, of course, long been a characteristic of the area around London and so it remained. The 'great object' of Middlesex farming was 'to supply the London market with hay' (for which an ever increasing urban horse population created an ever increasing demand) [53] 'and [to] maintain the productive power of the soil by the application of London dung'. [54] In north Cheshire, intensive market garden crops were grown along the banks of the Bridgewater canal and conveyed thereby to Manchester markets, while further south in the county, in the Hundred of Nantwich, the only green crop grown was potatoes 'for which there has been a good market in the [nearby] Potteries'. [55] In Lancashire, it was said that 'around the large towns the grass-land is mostly preserved undisturbed, and the produce in milk and butter daily conveyed to supply their never-failing wants'. [56] Even a town as small as Northampton imposed certain regularities upon the farming of the immediate area: 'Potatoes are grown extensively around Northampton for the supply of the town, but are not much cultivated in other parts of the county, being considered great exhausters of the soil.' [57]

At greater distances from the major centres of consumption the effects of enhanced demand were less pronounced but still noticeable, many being directly related to the changes just described. For example, when surveying north Lancashire, Garnett wrote, 'In many parts of Cheshire, where formerly cheese was made, the milk is now taken at once by the railways to Manchester and Liverpool, and the effect of this is that the cheese-merchants come down into the north to look for that supply which formerly they obtained from the neighbouring county. This has given a new stimulus to the dairy farmers.'[58] Blackman has shown how, further afield, the growing market for fatstock in the north of England resulted in shortages of locally reared cattle and a consequent increase in the exportation of Scottish stores, while the continued expansion of southern demand had a similar effect upon the Welsh cattle trade.[59]

Clearly, the gradual shift in the centre of gravity of the urban market favoured producers (especially of livestock) in the north and west who enjoyed free access to the developing industrial centres. It would be an exaggeration to say that the result was a complete reversal of established regional patterns of agricultural prosperity. But areas outside the south-east did prosper to a degree hitherto unknown. The so-called 'Great Depression' of the 1880s and 1890s appears to have left more or less unscathed those substantial areas of the north and west which enjoyed expanding urban markets for livestock and dairy products. It is simply a reflection of the considerable political influence of the large southern grain-producing landlords, who *were* badly affected by the collapse of cereals prices in 1879, that the depression should ever have been considered universal.[60] Northern farmers were also obliged to hire labour at rates competitive with those being offered in industry. The result was not only a labour force that was better paid, better educated and, according to some authorities, more diligent than their southern counterparts, but also, a growing enthusiasm among northern farmers for ways of increasing labour productivity. By the mid-nineteenth century, it was Northumberland not Norfolk that offered the best examples of progressive farming.

Finally, it may be noted that the increasing prosperity of the north-west casts a certain amount of light upon some of the unresolved issues of the lightland/clayland controversy. It has been suggested, tentatively, that the clayland areas of the north and west progressed while those of the south-east stagnated. The favourable position of the northern and western producers in relation to their markets goes some way towards explaining why this divergence may have occurred.

The Mechanisms of Change

Thus far, regional patterns of agricultural change have been treated as a direct function of physical and economic determinants. In fact, any fundamental adjustment in regional farming systems represented the combined effects of a whole variety of minor changes made as a consequence of the separate decisions of countless individuals. To understand the agricultural revolution better it is necessary to explore this process in greater depth.

In geographical studies of innovation, it has often been shown that diffusion patterns display a degree of regularity which reflects the strength of contacts and flows of information between adopters and potential adopters; generally, a new adopter will live close to someone who has already adopted. However, there are many reasons why we would not expect all patterns of agricultural change to conform precisely to the conventional spatial diffusion model. Theoretically, patterns displaying a high degree of regularity would only be expected where all that distinguishes one potential adopter from another is the probability of his hearing about an innovation from someone who has already adopted it. A perfect world, as far as agricultural innovations are concerned, would therefore be one where all farms are identical in respect of size, land-use and product-mix, where all farmers are equally well- or equally ill-informed about a given innovation and share similar levels of personal mobility, and where the innovation itself diffuses from one original point of introduction rather than from several without making use of any intermediate centralized distribution or publicity facilities such as town-based agencies or farmers' clubs.

Needless to say, this is not a description of rural England in the eighteenth and nineteenth centuries or at any other time. Innovations associated with arable agriculture would have little immediate appeal in pastoral areas; farms and estates varied considerably in size, as did the general levels of education and amount of information available to those who ran them; and innovations (particularly in cropping) appeared simultaneously in different areas, while others made use of urban facilities, thereby giving an advantage to those who enjoyed superior accessibility to towns. In Wales, linguistic patterns were also of importance. 'It is curious', wrote C. S. Read in 1849, 'that wherever English is spoken the farming is very superior, and has much progressed of late, whereas in the Welsh parts little improvement can be traced.' Of course, the English-speaking areas were, as Read himself readily admitted, also the most fertile. 'But', he continued, 'few of the Welsh have the chance of witnessing and seeing the effects of good farming, and the language forbids them to wander out of their district in search of practical information, and the Englishman who would introduce improvements finds the strange tongue presents an insurmountable obstacle to his laudable effort.'[61]

Clearly, there are many reasons why we would not expect regular patterns of adoption to be a characteristic of eighteenth and nineteenth-century innovations. Nevertheless, the comments of contemporary observers often suggest that personal contacts were important, and that these were reflected in resultant adoption patterns. For example, Arthur Young's *General View of the Agriculture of Norfolk* speaks of Southdown and Leicester sheep 'creeping in' to Loddon and Clavering Hundreds.[62] Tuke's report on the North Riding stresses the importance of hierarchical as well as contagious factors: 'gentlemen of property' who 'reside constantly on their estates' serve as pioneers of new techniques, being 'attentive to introducing the improved practices of other counties, and liberal in communicating of the knowledge of them.'[63] In Oxfordshire, Young speaks of the possibility that one farmer breeding New Leicester sheep would soon have requests for the loan of rams from his neighbours. He also considered it likely that the practice of horse hoeing would soon spread into the county from the neighbourhood of Henley.[64] In Cumberland, Bailey and Culley identify Collins of Wetherall as the first farmer to grow turnips. 'From this source may be traced the various patches of turnips we observed at Netherby, Burgh, Dalston, and a few other places.'[65]

Furthermore, where statistical evidence is sufficiently detailed to provide a precise insight into adoption patterns (which is rarely the case) then it, too, suggests that personal contacts and the flow of information were important controls. One example, derived from the pedigrees of Improved Shorthorn cattle recorded in successive volumes of *Coates's Herd Book* will suffice. Although the breeders entered in these volumes represent only a very small proportion of those who were actually breeders of the strain, the source does have the advantage, first, of relating to a breed which almost displaced all others in Britain during the nineteenth century, and second, of identifying all of those who were pedigree breeders.   \

Figures 9.3 and 9.4 show the distribution of recorded pedigree breeders during the two decades 1800–9 and 1810–19. In the first we see evidence of concentration in the region of origin of the breed, the northern part of Yorkshire and the southern part of County Durham, with evidence of southward movement along the Great North Road, a major droving route. In the second, there is further evidence of outward

movement into a number of Midland and western counties and also into
Fife. But more interesting are the clusters appearing around previously
isolated individuals, particularly in north Northumberland, in the lower
Aire valley of Yorkshire, on the Howardian Hills and, especially in south
Yorkshire and north Nottinghamshire in an area roughly defined by the
towns of Bawtry, Worksop and East Retford. This is highly suggestive of
an interlinked hierarchical and contagious diffusion process, one or two
precocious or innovative individuals seizing upon an innovation available
at a distance and then serving as both the inspiration and in this case often,
also, the source of supply for the further adoption of the innovation within

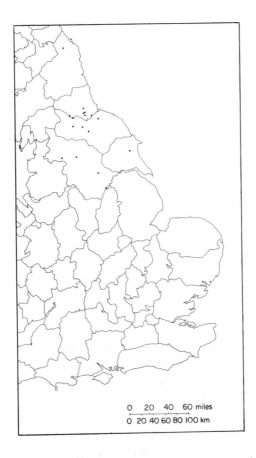

Fig. 9.3. Pedigree Improved Shorthorns: recorded breeders, 1800–9.

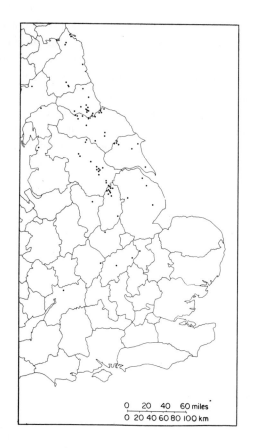

Fig. 9.4. Pedigree Improved Shorthorns: recorded breeders, 1810–19.

their immediate neighbourhoods.

It may be said that if coherent spatial diffusion patterns should be evident in the case of an activity as specialist and as aristocratic in appeal as pedigree Shorthorn breeding, then it may reasonably be supposed that the same would apply to the vast majority of innovations which enjoyed a much larger potential demand. Change should not be seen as an instant response to economic necessity but as something which occurred gradually as information about alternative possibilities penetrated the remoter reaches of the farming community.

Conclusion

Thanks to our ignorance of the precise adoption patterns of almost all the innovations mentioned in this chapter, generalization can only be hazardous. Nevertheless, the salient characteristics of eighteenth and nineteenth-century agriculture are clear, and two points made during the foregoing discussion are worth reiterating in conclusion. In the first place, it is evident that whatever the inadequacies of orthodox views on the nature of the agricultural revolution, agricultural change during the eighteenth and nineteenth centuries cannot be regarded as anything other than fundamental. Some, at least, of the presumptions of the orthodox view are valid. Second, the changing geography of the English urban market appears to hold the key to an understanding of changing patterns of agricultural prosperity. Clearly, the state and structure of the market are variables which have a direct bearing upon the historical geography of agriculture, and their importance in this respect deserves to be more widely recognized.

References

1. Phyllis Deane and W. A. Cole, British Economic Growth, 1688–1959, (2nd edn.) (Cambridge, 1969), pp. 157, 166.
2. Ibid., p. 78.
3. See, for example, S. Kuznets, 'Economic growth and the contribution of agriculture: notes on measurement', in C. Eicher and L. Witt (eds.), Agriculture in Economic Development, (New York, 1964), pp. 102–19; E. L. Jones (ed.), Agriculture and Economic Growth in England, 1650–1815, (London, 1967), pp. 17–46; P. Mathias, The First Industrial Nation, (London, 1969), p. 64.
4. E. L. Jones, 'The agricultural labour market in England', Economic History Review, 2nd ser., XVII (1964), pp. 322–38.
5. Lord Ernle, English Farming Past and Present, (6th edn.), (London, 1961), p. 149.
6. T. H. Marshall, 'Jethro Tull and the "new husbandry" ', Economic History Review, II (1929), pp. 41–60; see D. Woodward, 'Agricultural revolution in England 1500–1900: a survey', The Local Historian, IX (1971), pp. 323–33 for a review of this research.
7. R. A. C. Parker, Coke of Norfolk. A Financial and Agricultural Study 1707–1842, (Oxford, 1975).

8. G. E. Mingay, *Enclosure and the Small Farmer in the Age of the Industrial Revolution*, (London, 1968).

9. M. A. Havinden, 'Agricultural progress in open-field Oxfordshire', *Agricultural History Review*, **IX** (1961), pp. 73–83; E. Kerridge, *The Agricultural Revolution*, (London, 1967).

10. G. E. Mingay, 'The agricultural revolution in English history: a reconsideration', *Agricultural History*, **XXVI** (1963), p. 132.

11. N. Harvey, *A History of Farm Buildings in England and Wales*, (Newton Abbot, 1970), p. 15.

12. B. A. Holderness, 'Capital formation in agriculture', in J. P. P. Higgins and S. Pollard (eds.), *Aspects of Capital Investment in Great Britain 1750–1850. A Preliminary Survey*, (London, 1971), pp. 159–95.

13. Michael Turner, 'Parliamentary enclosure and population change in England, 1750–1830', *Explorations in Economic History*, **XIII** (1976), p. 465.

14. G. E. Mingay, *The Agricultural Revolution 1750–1880*, (London 1966), p. 77; Turner, 'Parliamentary enclosure', p. 464.

15. M. Williams, 'The enclosure and reclamation of waste land in England and Wales in the eighteenth and nineteenth centuries', *Transactions, Institute of British Geographers*, **LI** (1970), p. 61.

16. M. E. Turner, 'Parliamentary enclosure and landownership change in Buckinghamshire', *Economic History Review*, 2nd ser., **XXVIII** (1975), pp. 565–81; J. R. Walton, 'The residential mobility of farmers and its relationship to the parliamentary enclosure movement in Oxfordshire', in A. D. M. Phillips and B. J. Turton (eds.), *Environment, Man and Economic Change*, (London, 1975), pp. 238–52.

17. J. R. Walton, 'Aspects of agrarian change in Oxfordshire, 1750–1880', D. Phil Thesis, University of Oxford (1976), p. 158.

18. *Ibid.*, pp. 312, 342.

19. F. M. L. Thompson, *Chartered Surveyors. The Growth of a Profession*, (London, 1968), pp. 32–8; L. S. Pressnell, *Country Banking in the Industrial Revolution*, (Oxford, 1956).

20. Walton, 'Aspects of agrarian change', p. 269.

21. E. L. Jones, 'Industrial capital and landed investment: the Arkwrights in Herefordshire, 1809–43', in E. L. Jones and G. E. Mingay (eds.), *Land, Labour and Population in the Industrial Revolution*, (London, 1967), pp. 69–71.

22. Richard Jefferies, *Hodge and his Masters*, (Fitzroy edn.), (London, 1966), Vol. I, pp. 19–27; George Eliot, *Middlemarch*, (Penguin English Library edn.) (Harmondsworth, 1965), pp. 38–9.

23. Humphrey Wyndham, 'The farming activities of the Third Earl Spencer', *Northamptonshire Past and Present*, **III** (1961), pp. 40–8.

24. See, for example, R. J. Colyer, 'The Hafod estate under Thomas Johnes and Henry Pelham, Fourth Duke of Newcastle', *Welsh History Review*, **VIII**

(1977), pp. 257–84; also 'The Gogerddan Demesne Farm 1818–22', *Ceredigion*, (1973), pp. 170–88.

25. Quoted in C. S. Orwin and E. H. Whetham, *History of British Agriculture 1846–1914*, (2nd edn.) (Newton Abbot, 1971), p. 51.

26. H. Evershed, 'The agriculture of Staffordshire', *Journal of the Royal Agricultural Society of England*, 2nd ser., **V** (1869), p. 302.

27. J. R. McQuiston, 'Tenant right: farmer against landlord in Victorian England, 1847–1883', *Agricultural History*, **XLVII** (1973), pp. 95–113; Joan Thirsk, *English Peasant Farming*, (London, 1957), pp. 266–7.

28. J. S. Mill, *Principles of Political Economy*, (New edn., W. J. Ashley ed.), (London, 1909), p. 152.

29. G. E. Mingay, *The Gentry. The Rise and Fall of a Ruling Class*, (London, 1976), pp. 94–7.

30. J. M. Wilson, *The Farmer's Dictionary*, (Edinburgh, 1850–2), Vol. I, pp. 345–7.

31. *Ibid.*, Vol. II, p. 499.

32. *Ibid.*, Vol. II, pp. 129, 651.

33. Arthur Young, *General View of the Agriculture of Oxfordshire*, (2nd edn.) (London, 1813).

34. Edward Little, 'Farming of Wiltshire', *Journal of the Royal Agricultural Society of England*, **V** (1845), pp. 162–3.

35. F. M. L. Thompson, 'The second agricultural revolution, 1815–1880', *Economic History Review*, 2nd ser., **XXI** (1968), pp. 62–77.

36. D. C. Moore, 'The Corn Laws and high farming', *Economic History Review*, 2nd ser., **XVIII** (1965), pp. 545–61; Susan Fairlie, 'The Corn Laws and British wheat production', *Economic History Review*, 2nd ser., **XXII** (1969), pp. 88–116.

37. For example, the Essex Agricultural Association was founded in 1858 on the basis of the profits made at the annual show of the R.A.S., held at Colchester two years previously. (J. Oxley Parker, *The Oxley Parker Papers*, (Colchester, 1964), p. 143.)

38. Walton, 'Aspects of agrarian change', pp. 317, 381.

39. George Eliot, *The Mill on the Floss*, (Edinburgh, 1860), Book II, Chapter I.

40. Richard Jefferies, *Hodge*, p. 143; Bodleian Library, G. A. Oxon 8° 1055.

41. E. L. Jones, 'The changing basis of English agricultural prosperity, 1853–73', *Agricultural History Review*, **X** (1962), pp. 102–19.

42. R. W. Sturgess, 'The agricultural revolution on the English clays', *Agricultural History Review*, **XIV** (1966), pp. 104–21.

43. E. J. T. Collins and E. L. Jones, 'Sectoral advance in English agriculture', *Agricultural History Review*, **XV** (1967), pp. 65–81.

44. P.R.O. IR/3 and MAF/66 *passim*.

45. Evershed, 'Staffordshire', p. 306; W. Dickinson, 'On the farming of

Cumberland', *Journal of the Royal Agricultural Society of England*, **XIII** (1852), p. 289.

46. Daniel Defoe, *A Tour through the Whole Island of Great Britain*, (Everyman edn.) (London, 1962), 2 Vols.

47. J. H. Andrews, 'Some statistical maps of Defoe's England', *Geographical Studies*, **III** (1956), p. 43.

48. A. H. John, 'English agricultural improvement and grain exports, 1660–1765', in D. C. Coleman and A. H. John (eds.), *Trade, Government and Economy in Pre-Industrial England*, (London, 1976), pp. 60–1.

49. A liking for the more expensive wheaten loaf has also to be seen as a fashion which developed in the south-east and spread to other areas as they became more prosperous. See E. J. T. Collins, 'Dietary change and cereal consumption in Britain in the nineteenth century', *Agricultural History Review*, **XXIII** (1975), pp. 97–115.

50. See, for example, D. W. Howell, 'The impact of railways on agricultural development in nineteenth-century Wales', *Welsh History Review*, **VII** (1974), pp. 40–62.

51. J. H. Charnock, 'On the farming of the West Riding of Yorkshire', *Journal of the Royal Agricultural Society of England*, **IX** (1848), p. 293.

52. *Ibid.*, pp. 294–5.

53. F. M. L. Thompson, 'Nineteenth-century horse sense', *Economic History Review*, 2nd ser., **XXIX** (1976), pp. 60–81.

54. J. C. Clutterbuck, 'The farming of Middlesex', *Journal of the Royal Agricultural Society of England*, 2nd ser., **V** (1869), p. 9.

55. W. Palin, 'The farming of Cheshire', *Journal of the Royal Agricultural Society of England*, **V** (1845), p. 68.

56. W. J. Garnett, 'Farming of Lancashire', *Journal of the Royal Agricultural Society of England*, **X** (1849), p. 8.

57. W. Bearn, 'On the farming of Northamptonshire', *Journal of the Royal Agricultural Society of England*, **XIII** (1852), p. 60.

58. Garnett, 'Farming of Lancashire', p. 47.

59. Janet Blackman, 'The cattle trade and agrarian change on the eve of the railway age', *Agricultural History Review*, **XXIII** (1975), pp. 48–62; R. J. Colyer, *The Welsh Cattle Drovers*, (Cardiff, 1976), pp. 52–90.

60. T. W. Fletcher, 'Lancashire livestock farming during the Great Depression', *Agricultural History Review*, **IX** (1961), pp. 17–42; also 'The Great Depression of English agriculture, 1873–1896', *Economic History Review*, 2nd ser., **XIII** (1960–1), pp. 417–32.

61. C. S. Read, 'On the farming of South Wales', *Journal of the Royal Agricultural Society of England*, **X** (1849), p. 164.

62. A. Young, *General View of the Agriculture of the County of Norfolk*, (London, 1804), p. 461.

63. J. Tuke, *General View of the Agriculture of the North Riding of Yorkshire*, (London, 1800), p. 28.
64. Young, *Oxfordshire*, pp. 75, 304.
65. J. Bailey and G. Culley, *General View of the Agriculture of Northumberland, Cumberland and Westmorland*, (3rd edn.) (London, 1805), p. 222.

10
The Framework of Industrial Change 1730–1900

E. Pawson

Characteristics of Change

In the early eighteenth century, England was already considered a rich country: rich, that is, by the standards of the time. In terms of average annual income per head both Gregory King, in 1688, and Adam Smith, in 1776, placed her second only to Europe's greatest trading nation, the Dutch. English agriculture was quite well developed, with a high degree of regional specialization. Her overseas trade had been growing steadily for most of the previous hundred years, she had a number of basic industries and, in London, the biggest city in Europe. And, significantly, a high proportion of Englishmen participated in the market economy. This early degree of advancement is important, because it helps to explain why England (or, more correctly, Britain) became the first industrial nation, and how in the nineteenth century she came to dominate the international economy as 'the workshop of the world'.[1] The England of Daniel Defoe was certainly not an 'underdeveloped' country in the modern sense of the term.[2]

And yet, early eighteenth century England still had many of the classical characteristics of a pre-industrial society. Her economy was relatively unspecialized, with two-thirds, maybe four-fifths of the population engaged wholly or partly in agriculture, and with just under half the national income deriving from this sector. Industry was dominated by wool textiles, to Arthur Young in 1767, 'the sacred staple and foundation of all our wealth'. Wool alone accounted for about one-third of industrial production and as much as two-thirds of the total value of exports (but significantly, the trade was in manufactured textiles, not in raw wool). The linkages between agriculture and industry were very strong. Industry

267

was often a secondary employment for the agricultural community, and agriculture supplied the major industrial raw materials—apart from wool, also leather (the second biggest industry overall), flax, food products and the essential fuel of the transport services—horse fodder. Correspondingly, most units of industrial production were small, and many were located in the countryside away from the towns. The overall degree of urbanization was low. Only a quarter of the population lived in towns of more than 2500 people and a very large proportion of those lived in London.

The Industrial Revolution of the eighteenth and nineteenth centuries changed all this. By 1800 many of these pre-industrial characteristics were being steadily dissolved and by 1900, Britain had been transformed into a heavily industrialized state, exporting manufactured goods, capital and services (e.g. shipping) to a world that was rapidly altering around her. The major internal changes that occurred over these two centuries can be sorted into four groups.

(1) There was *expansion*, in absolute and *per capita* terms, in all the sectors of the economy, particularly in industry, but also in the services (trade, transport and the professions), and in agriculture. After 1800, the economy as a whole maintained a growth rate in excess of 2 per cent a year, reaching a maximum of over 3 per cent after 1850. Industrial production was growing at about 3·5 per cent a year for most of the first

Table 10.1: The changing structure of the British national product.

	Agriculture, forestry, fishing (per cent)	Mining, manufactures, building (per cent)	Trade, transport (per cent)
1700	c. 40–45	c. 20	12
1801	33	23	17
1851	20	34	19
1901	6	40	24

Note: the table excludes government, defence, domestic service, the professions, etc. The 1700 figures are rough estimates for England and Wales, the remainder refer to Britain as a whole. See Phyllis Deane and W. A. Cole, *British Economic Growth 1688–1959* (1969), Chapter V.

half of the nineteenth century, but slowed down to around 2 per cent from the 1870s with the rise of foreign competition—particularly from America and Germany. (These rates, impressive of course by contemporary standards, are however nothing exceptional for modern economies).

(2) Economic expansion was accompanied by, and was largely due to, *structural change*—the shift of resources away from primary activities into the more productive industrial and service sectors. Table 10.1 gives the general outline of this process. Industry, including mining and building, grew in relative terms to contribute two-fifths of the GNP and occupy a similar proportion of the workforce by 1901. The service activities, many of which are vital complements of industry, also underwent marked expansion, particularly after 1851 with the building of the railways and the growth of British shipping interests. Both sectors developed at the expense of agriculture, whose relative decline in the nineteenth century was steady and very pronounced. [3]

(3) As Chapter 13 demonstrates *Urbanization* took place on a massive scale, largely as a result of the congregation of industrial firms in existing towns and rapid urban growth in successful, formerly rural industrial areas—areas such as the mining and metal working districts of South Wales and the West Midlands, and the textile valleys of south Lancashire and the West Riding. [4]

(4) Industrialization and urbanization brought about a fundamental alteration in the *social structure* of society, away from an order based on land to one determined by the occupational hierarchies of industrial and service activities. With this came changing life-styles. The casual, seemingly disorganized worker-oriented routines of the domestic craftsman and the farm labourer were replaced by the extreme order of the machine, a time-discipline that precluded daily and seasonal variety. [5]

Industrial change was therefore central to both the economic and social re-organization of England and Wales in the eighteenth and nineteenth centuries. The industrial sector, however, not only grew as a whole, generating changes beyond itself, it also underwent continuous and very considerable internal changes. One of the most significant of these internal changes was the declining role of agriculture in industrial production. Adam Smith constantly propounded the view that the productivity of the land controlled the growth of industry; but when he published *The Wealth of Nations* in 1776, the economic transformation that proved him quite wrong was just beginning. The great staple industries of the nineteenth century had few forward linkages from agriculture: cotton, iron, the non-ferrous metal trades and then, steel, machinery, shipbuilding, mining and chemicals were not dependent on domestic agricultural raw materials. Amongst the major industries, only wool textiles, which remained a staple, albeit far less important than formerly, and the food-processing trades maintained such links. Neither did industry retain a secondary employment relationship with agriculture. The predominance of

Table 10.2: The structure of industry in 1907.

Output by value of the principal industries as a proportion of total industrial output.

	per cent	per cent
Mining		15·5
Coal	14·9	
Iron and steel		14·6
Metals	4·2	
Goods, machinery, tools	10·4	
Non-ferrous metals and goods		1·2
Vehicles		4·6
Ships	2·6	
Timber products		3·1
Textiles		12·2
Cotton yarn, cloth	7·5	
Wool and hosiery yarn, cloth	2·8	
Linen yarn, cloth	1·0	
Food		9·8
Flour and bread	2·5	
Beer	3·7	
Tobacco	0·8	
Paper		0·7
Leather		2·6
Chemicals		0·6
Gas and electricity		2·4
Building		5·7
		73·0

Source: W. G. Hoffmann, *British Industry, 1700–1950,* (Oxford, 1955), Table 2.

mechanical power, large-scale machinery, and centralized factory production in nearly all the quantitatively important branches of late nineteenth century industry spelt the end of such functional associations. Industry in the Industrial Revolution displaced its agricultural origins.

By the time of the first census of production in 1907 England and Wales had come a long way from the relatively unspecialized, agriculture-dominated economy of 200 years before (Table 10.2).

Causes of Change

Describing the general currents of industrial change is relatively straightforward, although throughout this period detailed and accurate description is complicated by the inadequacies of the statistical base. Accounting for change is, however, altogether more difficult. As a first step, it is necessary to establish a general framework, which can then be used to pursue a more detailed analysis. The central constructs of this framework are the economic forces of demand and supply. Industry could not have expanded without an increasing demand for its products. Demand could be for consumer goods or for capital goods, and could be generated both at home and overseas. Conversely, rising demand could not be met without an increase in the output, or supply, of industrial goods. This could be achieved in two ways: by an increase in the resources available for production, or by the more efficient use of those resources.

Rising Demand

Between 1700 and 1801, the population of England and Wales rose from about 5 million to just over 9·1 million. In the nineteenth century, it increased more rapidly to reach 32·5 million by 1901 (see pp. 314–22). But to assume that this population growth must necessarily have generated increasing demand is fallacious. For this to happen, a significant proportion of the population had to be participant in the market economy, and the demand for labour had at least to keep pace with labour supply.

There can be no doubt that England fulfilled the first condition in this period. Self-sufficient subsistence farming with little or no interest in producing for the market was unusual even in 1700. Admittedly, it was more common in Wales, but nearly all Englishmen either produced a marketable surplus or, if they were not self-employed, sold their labour for a wage. A basic pool of purchasing power therefore existed. And as the level of urbanization increased, the range of requisites that had to be bought on the open market increased as well. Urban families had far fewer opportunities than their rural counterparts to grow their own food, make their own clothes and furnishings or gather their own fuel.

The fulfilment of the second condition is a more difficult problem. It relates directly to one of the most intractable debates in recent British economic history—the progress of the standard of living in the Industrial Revolution. [6] Over the entire span of the two centuries, the demand for labour certainly more than matched the increasing supply, and this was reflected in levels of real wages and earnings that were substantially higher in 1900 than in 1700. Between 1800 and 1900, real national income *per capita*—the best overall measure—rose four-fold. In very general terms, therefore, rising demand for industrial consumer goods came from a population that was both growing in numbers and growing in wealth. However, the rise was far from even, either over time, or between different occupational groups, or across regions.

In the eighteenth century, a slow rise in living standards seems to have been fairly general. Arthur Young remarked that 'the people [were] consuming more food, and of a better sort: eating wheat instead of barley, oats and rye—and drinking a prodigiously greater quantity of beer' (the latter, a product of an important contemporary industry). [7] Such literary evidence is abundant, and the statistical material, although limited, is in general accord. Demand extended to other basic industrial products: soap, candles, cheap metal goods and increasingly, textiles. In the nineteenth century, however, the picture is rather more complex. The rapid rise in population growth does seem to have generated excessive labour supplies in three broad and large, essentially 'residual' occupational groups: the agricultural labourers, the domestic industrial workers and the general labourers. Their real earnings consequently remained static or even fell over long periods. However, those whose labour was in high demand to man the new industrial order gained more consistently: the skilled workers (in new crafts such as the iron puddlers and fine spinners and in other, non-mechanized crafts, such as the joiners and blacksmiths), the factory operatives, and those in commerce and the professions. A qualification that must be made here, however, is that in times of industrial recession, in the trough of the trade-cycle (as in the late 1820s and 1838–43) all groups tended to lose out with high levels of short-time working and unemployment.

The rise of industry in northern England, the Midlands and South Wales generated a growing demand for labour, and with it, rising wages. By 1800, money wages of Lancashire labourers and craftsmen, which in 1700 had been only half those of equivalent workers in London, Kent and Oxfordshire, had increased proportionately more to very similar levels. [8] After 1800, the wage levels of the industrial north continued to rise, pulling ahead of the agricultural south, the divergence between the two increasing. Structural change was not sufficiently rapid to prevent considerable under-employment in agriculture, with the absolute numbers of farm workers actually growing until the 1850s. The plight of the agricultural labourer was very real, particularly in those regions well removed from the industrial districts (where agricultural wages tended to be higher). [9] It was exacerbated by the decline of supplementary earnings from domestic manufacture as markets were lost to the new mass-produced goods. Furthermore the introduction of machinery brought great hardship to those domestic workers who were primarily reliant on manufactures. The handloom weavers were in very high demand for several decades after the introduction of mechanized spinning in the textile industries and prospered accordingly. But with the slow diffusion of machine looms from the 1810s they became gradually redundant; by 1831 their wages were a quarter of the peak figure of 23 shillings per week of 1805, and over a quarter of a million families were caught. [10] The woolcombers and framework knitters suffered equally but more sharply with the introduction of machinery in their trades in the 1850s and 1860s. Those in the third occupational group to lose out—the general labourers, who had no particular skill in country or town—were especially vulnerable to under-employment and unemployment. Many could get only casual work. Even in a rapidly industrializing area like the Black Country, in which more than half the workforce fell in this group, they lived continuously between the margins of subsistence and the lowest levels of human comfort, [11] with temporary relief coming only in boom years. Right at the end of the century, Charles Booth's survey of *Life and Labour in London* (1889) and Seebohm Rowntree's investigations in York (1899) revealed excessive poverty in this group: between a quarter and a third of the families in both places (and there is no reason for them to have been atypical) lived at or just above the margins of subsistence. The proportion, however, would undoubtedly have been very much higher without industrial growth.

It is necessary to stress the diversity of occupational and regional experiences in order to show the uneven effects of the spread of industrialization and, following on from this, the uneven nature of the rise in domestic demand. Nevertheless, the willingness and ability of manufacturers to produce cheap, mass market goods did mean that the growth in demand from domestic consumers was very broadly based. Obviously, the propensity to consume industrial goods was highest amongst the better paid in the middle and upper working-classes, but when employment was full, it extended right down to the poorer groups in society. In 1786, Sir Robert Peel, a famous cotton manufacturer, estimated that '3 parts out of 4 of printed goods are consumed by the lower class of people'. A few years earlier, the London Magazine had reported that 'every servant girl now has her cotton gown and her cotton stockings'. This was not surprising. Cotton prices were tumbling in real terms with the immense increase in the output of the industry. By the early nineteenth century, plain cotton cloth was selling for $2\frac{1}{2}d$ a yard, and colourful printed designs for as little as 4d. At these sorts of prices, despite the high cost of food in the Napoleonic Wars, even the farm and town labourers on 8 to 10 shillings a week could make occasional purchases of cottons; the factory workers, paid anything between 25 and 40 shillings, could be more regular consumers. A similar concern with the mass end of the market characterizes the other growth industries of the period. The basis of the West Riding's textiles success was the production of cheap, durable worsteds and coarse cloths such as blankets. The Birmingham tradesmen produced all manner of metal goods, boxes, buttons, knives, locks and toys. The up-and-coming potters of Stoke-on-Trent (with the exception of Wedgewood) made their money not from expensive china but from very common wares indeed.

It was the English manufacturers' concentration on the mass market rather than the luxury market—although a lot of firms catered for both—that also won them many overseas customers. To quote the historian David Landes: 'in the long run, this was Britain's forte: the ability to manufacture precisely those articles for which foreign demand was most elastic'[12] (and it is the Japanese and South Korean forte today). The great bulk of Britain's domestic export trade was in industrial goods—over 90 per cent for most of the century. By 1830, very nearly three-quarters of all domestic exports were provided by the textiles industries—half by cotton alone. The overall textiles figure still stood at over 30 per cent at the end of the nineteenth century (Table 10.3). Or, to look at the figures from the other end: over 50 per cent of the cotton industry's output was being exported in the 1820s, over three-quarters by the 1890s; a consistent quarter to one-third of the woollen and worsted industries output was sent overseas throughout the nineteenth century.

Table 10.3: The changing pattern of British domestic exports, 1700–1900.

	1700	1800	1830	1870	1900
Cotton yarn and manufactures	0·8	24·1	50·8	35·8	24
Wool yarn and manufactures	64·7	28·4	12·7	13·4	6·9
Linen yarn and manufactures	0·2	3·3	5·4	4·8	2·1
Iron and steel and manufactures	2·3	6·6	10·2	14·2	12·1
Machinery	—	—	0·5	1·5	6·7
Non-ferrous metals and manufactures	7·0	5·8			
Coal and coke	1·7	2·0	0·5	2·8	13·3
Vehicles (ships, carriages, etc.)				1·1	3·1
Chemicals				0·6	1·1

Table shows principal exports as a percentage of total domestic exports (for England and Wales in 1700, Britain in 1800 and the United Kingdom for the remaining dates.)
Source: Deane and Cole, British Economic Growth, 1688–1959 (1969), and An Abstract of British Historical Statistics, compiled by B. R. Mitchell and Phyllis Deane (Cambridge, 1962).

Consumer demand was not, however, the complete story. In the nineteenth century, two industries in particular—iron and steel, and coal—became mainly concerned with the producer goods markets. This had not always been so, for most of the eighteenth-century ironmasters had been primarily interested in ordnance contracts and a limited range of consumer goods; as a result, despite the frequent wars of the period, the industry remained small. From the late 1780s, however, with the considerable growth in demand for infrastructure (beams and bars for bridges and factory frames, pipes, and of course, rails) and machinery (steam engines, spinning mules, power looms, blast furnaces themselves) iron industry output expanded rapidly: actually at a sufficient rate to haul alongside the cotton industry by the 1870s. With the beginnings of modern steel production in this decade, and the rise of an important shipbuilding industry, this group of manufactures then swept ahead to form the largest component of total industrial production by 1907 (Table 10.2). They were closely followed by coal, an industry which provided Britain's only significant primary export—some 10 per cent of total production was sent overseas in the 1870s, but almost one-third in the peak year of 1913. Of the domestic total, only one-eighth was then for household use—the rest being consumed by the iron industry, railways, steamships, utility companies and other manufacturers.

The growth of the key industries in response to the massive home and overseas demands for consumer and capital goods is summarized in Table 10.4. It reveals the immensely impressive record of British industry in this period, and particularly in the nineteenth century. By the time of the international Great Exhibition held in 1851 in Crystal Palace (itself a monument to Victorian progress), Britain was producing over 40 per cent of the entire world output of traded manufactured goods. In 1880, the British share of the world export trade in manufactures still stood at 38 per cent. By 1900, however, her dominant position had been eroded away. Others were catching up. Competition from the newly emerging industrial machines of Germany and America inevitably slowed the rate of expansion of British manufacturers. And on the eve of the First World War, Britain's share of international industrial output had slipped back to one-eighth. [13] This was no absolute decline, but rather a reflection of the changing realities of a rapidly developing world. But it was still a very large proportion for a very small island.

Some space has been devoted to the nature and growth in demand for industrial products because it is an essential part of the framework of industrial change. The role of demand in the historical experience of industrialization must be underlined because so often it has been forgotten in the ambitious industrial expansion plans produced by politicians and development economists for today's poorer countries.

Supply Factors

These massive increases in industrial output required very extensive changes in production processes. Production itself is the end result of the combination of four factors, or resources: raw materials, capital, labour

Table 10.4: The growth of industrial output.

	Raw cotton consumption (million lb)	Wool consumption (million lb)	Coal output[c] (million tons)	Pig iron production (000 tons)	Steel production (000 tons)	Ships built (000 tons)
1720	1·8(GB)			25		
1788	19·6(GB)			68		
1800	52	c. 100	11	244[b]		
1820–4[a]	142·6	140	17·4	428		66
1850–4[a]	704·8	241	49·4	2757		170·2
1870–4[a]	1197·6	435·5	110·4	6378	486	396·4
1900–4[a]	1608·4	655·6	225·2	8639	4955	735·5

[a] Annual averages.

[b] Figure for 1806.

[c] Figures refer to first year of each period only.

Source: as for Table 10.3. All figures are for the United Kingdom (which included Ireland), except where indicated.

and entrepreneurship. As output rose, the nature of these four factors changed significantly: the supply of each increased and the efficiency with which each was deployed improved continuously.

Raw Materials

Raw materials are important as sources of production material and motive power. The supply of raw materials expanded enormously (Table 10.4), with a very large proportion of those used for the former purpose being imported: they accounted for over half of total imports in the mid-nineteenth century. For example all raw cotton was bought overseas, and an increasing amount of wool (rising from 30 to 80 per cent of the total used over the nineteenth century). The tremendous growth of English textiles was largely due to the extent and productivity of the new lands of America, and later, Australasia.

Aside from the provision of textile materials there was, however, a basic change in the character of raw materials: the substitution of inorganic for organic, of mineral (most notably iron and coal) for vegetable, animal, wind and water.[14] Not only did this permit much higher levels of efficiency, it also greatly increased elasticities of supply. Timber usage for example was inherently limited; the annual cut could only be exceeded by jeopardizing future production. Suitable waterpower sites were not infinite in number and windmill sails did not turn in all weathers. No such restrictions accompanied the use of iron and coal. 'We cannot, it is true, boast of mines of gold or silver', wrote J. R. McCulloch in 1837, 'but we possess what is of still more importance for a manufacturing nation, an all but inexhaustible supply of the most excellent coal.' Inexhaustible, easily worked and very responsive to industry's needs (Table 10.4).

The changing raw material function is best illustrated by examining selectively several key areas.

(1) The transition in industrial *power* supplies was gradual, and very much later than convention has admitted.[15] The real growth in the use of steampower came after 1870 rather than in the heroic age of Boulton and Watt in the years after 1770. In 1800 there were fewer than 1200 steam engines in England and Wales, with a combined horsepower of less than 20,000. Steam made its greatest impact initially in mining, being used for pumping purposes at coalpits and Cornish tinworks, and in cotton spinning, the first heavily mechanized factory industry. Even so, the

improved overshot waterwheel powered most of the early mills of the 1770s and 1780s, and as late as 1838, when there were 3000 steam engines in British textile factories (cotton, plus wool, worsted, linen and silk), there were still more than 2200 waterwheels in use, providing one-quarter of the total power capacity. But in textile weaving, the handicraft method survived throughout these years: steam-driven cotton looms did not finally triumph until the 1830s, mechanical knitting frames and silklooms till the 1850s and 1860s. In other industries, the transfer to steampower was delayed for equally long. The Birmingham and Sheffield trades relied on waterwheels until well into the nineteenth century. High pressure steam did not effectively take over from the horse in long-distance transport until the 1840s. The first tinplate rolling mill in South Wales to install an engine did so in 1851. However, by 1870, the total UK steampower capacity was nearly 1 million hp; waterwheels, with only 55,000 hp had been eclipsed. Yet the tremendous surge in steam capacity came in the next forty years, providing nearly 10 million hp by 1907: a reflection, not only of industrial growth, but of the number of industries that did not mechanize until the last few decades of the nineteenth century.

(2) The general introduction of *coal* in place of timber as a smelting or refining material came very much earlier. It was being used in tin, copper, glass and saltworks in the seventeenth century, and by 1800 coke furnaces and forges had completely taken over in the iron industry.

Abraham Darby achieved the initial success in iron coke-smelting at Coalbrookdale (Shropshire) in 1709, but it was 50 years before the process began to spread. Charcoal pig-iron long remained cheaper than coke pig-iron and did not lose this advantage until the demand for iron, and with it the need for timber, began to climb in the 1760s. England was by then one of the least wooded countries of Europe and rising levels of charcoal iron production could not be sustained without marked increases in costs. By 1790, 81 coke furnaces produced 90 per cent of the country's pig-iron. They were overwhelmingly concentrated on four coalfields: South Wales, which had risen to prominence in the 1760s, and Shropshire, Staffordshire and Yorkshire, each formerly important charcoal iron producers. The remaining charcoal iron areas—the Weald, Dean, Furness—had sunk into insignificance. [16]

(3) The substitution of coal for timber in iron production was directly related to the growing substitution of iron for timber in a wide range of *construction* activities. The early steam engines and spinning frames were

wooden structures; unsuited to high levels of operating efficiency. Watt achieved considerable improvements in fuel consumption and reliability with his steam engine, partly by using an accurately bored iron cylinder. Yet one of the reasons for the relatively slow diffusion of steam was the advances in waterwheel design achieved by Smeaton and a host of Lancashire millwrights, including ironplating for durability and iron gear and axlework for efficiency. The use of iron permitted considerable economies of scale in building, most fundamentally in factories, warehouses and bridges, but more flamboyantly in railway architecture and the great Crystal Palace. The use of the steel industry in the 1870s further underlined this trend. Steel, according to Bessemer standing 'to the engineer . . . in much the same relation as granite to the builder', rapidly achieved huge substitution markets in rail production and one of the great late nineteenth-century industries—shipbuilding.

(4) The *chemical* industry was small, but important out of all relation to its size.[17] Until the rapid take-off of textiles production, it relied predominantly on vegetable materials. Potash and soda—necessary ingredients of glass and soapmaking—were obtained from wood ash and kelp respectively. Soda was also made from barilla, the ashes of a comparatively rare plant imported from the Canaries. The potential bottleneck in soda production was removed by the adoption from France in the 1820s of the Leblanc process—based on the use of mineral salt and sulphuric acid. A similar advance in the making of bleaching powder—by absorbing chlorine in slaked lime (patented 1797), was equally vital: the age-old method of slow sun bleaching with the aid of sour milk could never have coped with the rocketing output of the cotton industry. The shortage of potash, however, was not overcome until the Germans began to mine their rich mineral deposits around Stassfurt in the 1860s.

(5) The introduction of *gaslighting* serves as a final example.[18] The vast majority of homes and workplaces long made do with daylight and candles (made from animal tallow). Oil lamps were used in the streets, if they were lit at all. Significantly, gaslighting was first introduced in cotton mills (1805), many of which worked in two 12-hour shifts, consequently needing constant, reliable and reasonably bright light. By the mid 1820s, most big towns also had coal gasworks and by the 1850s, when household use of gaslighting became common, they were to be found in nearly all towns. But the gas companies did not actively expand into heating and cooking until the 1880s, when competition from electric lighting developed.

As early as 1791, Arthur Young remarked that 'all the activity and industry of this kingdom is fast concentrating where there are coalpits'. He might have added that where there was coal in England and Wales, there was usually iron as well. The obvious long-term effect of the changing raw material function was the spatial concentration of industry, the antithesis of the pre-industrial pattern. Organic raw materials were ubiquitous, inorganic ones were not.

Capital

Closely tied in with the changing raw material function was a gradual shift in the nature of capital investment. The direct relationship between capital and industrial output worked along two routes: output could be raised by expanding the number of simple hand tools or machines (capital widening), or by building more complex, larger-scale, power-driven machinery and more functional premises (capital deepening). There was also an indirect relationship, via the greater efficiency introduced into industry as a whole by the growth of social overhead capital, e.g. transport infrastructure.

The annual rate of capital investment in England and Wales rose from a long-term mean of less than 5 per cent of national income before 1750, to 6 or 7 per cent by 1800 and then more quickly to reach 10 per cent in the 1830s and 1940s. Thereafter it remained at 10–13 per cent until the First World War. Not all of this long-term rise was due to industrial capital accumulation alone: the initial reason for the jump to 10 per cent was the railway construction boom, whilst it was extensive British investment overseas after 1870 that helped maintain this level.[19]

The process of capital deepening can be recognized in the most rapidly expanding industries from the late eighteenth century. The adoption of capital intensive methods in cotton spinning was the reason for its great operating efficiency. The same pair of hands that drove a simple spinning wheel could operate a cast iron mule with as many as 200 spindles. Further gains were made with the introduction of machinery for the preparatory processes (e.g. carding engines) and steampower. A similar process took place in coal mining: a 16 horsepower steam engine enabled deeper pits to be operated than the single horse-gin, whilst the increasing amount of coal raised necessitated the construction of horse waggonways, then—as in South Wales—canals, and later railways. A third example is the development of integrated ironworks from the 1780s and 1790s, complete with engines to drive the bellows and hammers, blast furnaces and reverberatory furnaces to produce and refine the pig, with moulds, rolling mills and slitting mills for shaping the final product.

Nevertheless, these examples must be kept in perspective. The investment ratio did not rise greatly before the building of the railways because capital deepening was the exception rather than the rule. In most other branches of industry, increasing output was achieved by capital widening: in textile weaving until about 1830, and in the small metal trades, tool making, precision engineering, pottery, furniture manufacture and food processing until very much later (hence the corresponding lateness of the general adoption of steampower). It has been suggested that the popularity of capital widening was due to the relative cheapness of labour—relative, that is, to America, where the widespread use of capital deepening technology came considerably sooner, giving American industry the means to outpace British industry so decisively from the 1870s onwards. [20]

In most early nineteenth-century industries, even those with large amounts of fixed capital, the highest proportion of capital assets was in stocks and outstanding balances (i.e. circulating capital). The fixed capital worth of Truman's London brewery in 1760 was £30,000, but the firm's total capital was £100,000 more than this. The corresponding figures from the first big integrated woollen mill, Benjamin Gott's in Leeds, were £28,000 and £65,400 in 1801. The ratios were less in the iron industry, but even the great Cyfarthfa ironworks in South Wales had £95,00 worth of stocks to £69,000 fixed capital in 1812. Industry in general had to keep high stocks in an age before the railway and clipper enabled closer and speedier contact to be kept with suppliers and markets. [21]

Industrial capital needs at this time were therefore predominantly short-term and could be partly satisfied from within the existing structure of business by the provision of credit from well-established mercantile firms, i.e. the importers and exporters. It was usual, for instance, for Liverpool cotton merchants and their factors to give three or four months credit to the spinners, and for Hull merchants and Sheffield steel factors to accommodate the cutlers of Yorkshire and metal workers of south Lancashire in the same way. Otherwise credit could be obtained from the banking system that developed throughout the country in the second half of the eighteenth century. The country bankers and their London Clearing House (1773) efficiently mobilized national savings by channelling funds from the south and east, where farmers' surpluses were high with the continuous rise of agricultural prices from the 1750s to 1815, to the industrializing parts of the north, Midlands and Wales. [22]

Fixed capital needs came generally from ploughback of retained earnings, although initial capital was provided by the proprietors of the firm. Right through the nineteenth century, the fundamental business unit was the individual or family proprietorship, or the partnership. Before 1825, joint stock enterprises could only be established by Act of Parliament (and only the canal companies, several insurance companies and very few industrial concerns received Acts), but this does not seem to have acted as a brake to industrial development. Limited liability was not introduced until 1856 yet there was no rush to take advantage of it. Not for a long time did the marketable share become a common means of raising capital. 'By 1885, limited companies accounted for only between 5 and 10 per cent of the total number of important business organisations.' [23]

Labour

The two most characteristic forms of industry in the early eighteenth century were the small independent workshop, run by a master employing several men (e.g. the Sheffield cutlery and Halifax woollen trades) and the outworking networks of domestic craftsmen, controlled and financed by urban merchants. Outworking survived long into the nineteenth century (particularly in weaving, nail and tool making, leather work, hosiery and clothing), whilst the small workshop remained very common. However, they were joined by a new form, the factory, something which involved locational concentrations of workers virtually unknown in pre-industrial England, except in the naval dockyards.

The factory had obvious advantages. For firms such as those cotton spinners who adopted Arkwright's vast water-frame machinery, it was necessary for mechanical reasons to house equipment. But the basic gain it offered was organizational productivity. It was ideal for the practice of Adam Smith's principle of the division of labour and it enabled industrialists (to quote one of them, Matthew Boulton, who ran the Soho Manufactory outside Birmingham in partnership with James Watt) to keep the workers 'under our eyes and immediate management . . . every day and almost every hour'. Soho, like Wedgwood's Etruria pottery, housed very traditional tools and machines and did not need to be a factory for mechanical reasons, it was the organizational efficiency that was important. Likewise the spinners' mulè—a competitor of, but a much more compact and capable machine than the waterframe—could be housed in a domestic workroom, but most were to be found in big urban workshops and factories. And for the same reason, the domestic weaving systems of Lancashire were gradually re-organized into a series of large weavers' sheds, each with a supervisor and anything from 20 to 200 looms.

But if centralized, controlled production had advantages for management, it had few for workers. It meant a radical change from the freedom of domestic work habits to a rigid routine determined by the need to keep machinery working continuously. Except in trade depressions, this meant all night as well as all day. John Byng, visiting Arkwright's mills at Cromford (Derbyshire) in 1790 'saw the workers issue forth at 7 o'clock . . . a new set then goes in for the night, for the mills never leave off working'. It took a long time to inculcate the new work discipline. Wedgwood was plagued with stoppages during the annual wakes and the new mills of Lancashire and Yorkshire were often forced to close for two or three weeks during harvest time as the workers returned to help in their home villages. As late as the 1840s, there was only a two-thirds turnout in the South Wales ironworks after the monthly pay day—a mirror of the domestic workers weekly routine (play on Monday and most of Tuesday, work on Wednesday, very late Thursday and frequently all night Friday).

A variety of incentives had to be offered to induce workers to accept the factories' regimes. Wages were high relative to those in agriculture and the superseded domestic trades. Housing was often provided. Arkwright built a model village at Cromford, and most of the textile firms at least provided rows of cottages. Some of the nineteenth-century schemes were rather more ambitious, following Robert Owen's New Lanark (1800–24): Titus Salt's model woollen mills and towns at Saltaire, near Bradford (begun 1851), Cadbury's Bournville (started 1879), and Lever's Port Sunlight—started in 1888 for his expanding soapworks. Their basic aims were all similar, however—to provide a stable and reasonably contented workforce. This was of particular importance in respect of the highly skilled workers. They were industry's most valuable assets and they got the best housing and the highest wages. Most firms trained their own skilled workers, and had to take care not to lose them to competitors (an engineer's apprenticeship with Boulton and Watt, for instance, was considered a passport to a job anywhere in Britain). This investment in 'human capital' was very expensive and just as important as more conspicuous investment in machinery and buildings. [24]

Entrepreneurship

It was the entrepreneurs—the leaders, organizers, managers of industry—who were the lynchpin of the whole process of industrial growth. It was they who directed and controlled the other factors of production and coordinated the forces of supply and demand. The entrepreneur has been described as fulfilling 'in one person the functions of capitalist, financier, works manager, merchant and salesman'. [25] Entrepreneurship involved all these things, and often one other—the application of innovatory techniques (and sometimes their development as well). But even in the small firms it is more realistic to view these entreprenurial functions as split between the leading members of the partnership, and—in the latter part of the nineteenth century—devolving partly onto paid managerial staff. To take just two famous examples—Wedgwood supplied the flair for innovation and marketing, whilst his partner Bentley marshalled the finance; Watt was the technical genius, the engineer in the Soho steam-engine business, but it was Boulton who organized production and sold the goods.

Selling was certainly a critical facet of the entrepreneurs' role. It brought the whole equation of demand and supply into focus. The fastest growing firms were those led by men who deliberately sought out, cultivated and extended their market: either by attention to fashion and patronage (the secret of Boulton's greatly successful button and buckle-making business at Soho long before Watt's arrival, and equally the key to Wedgwood's fame), or, rather more commonly, by selling mass market goods at mass market prices. These were the firms that broke out of their local spheres to become national and international leaders. The Great Exhibition of 1851 introduced the names of many of them to these wider audiences: so too did newspaper advertising, railway hoardings and commercial travellers. And in the last decade or two of the nineteenth century, with the rising tide of working-class prosperity, came the emergence of the 'national firm', covering the market in branded consumer products throughout the country: Imperial Tobacco (over half the the tobacco sales in Britain in 1901), Lever Bros (over half the soap sales), Bass, Guinness, Jesse Boot the chemist, Cadbury's chocolate.

The years after 1870, however, also saw a decline in the national rate of industrial growth. The country was particularly slow to move into many of the new fields that were to become important twentieth-century industries: electrical engineering, whole branches of precision engineering and chemicals, vehicles. And there was a marked rise in the value of manufactures imported, from less than 5 per cent of the import total before 1860, to 25 per cent by 1900. A general failure of entrepreneurship has often been identified as the major reason, but the situation was far from simple.[26] It reflected the impact of the rise of international competition on the peculiar structure of British industry. Despite the conspicuousness of the big firms, the majority remained small: small in turnover, capital and labour. Diversity was a hallmark of their products. Competition was as much between British firms as it was between British and foreign ones. Most were not big enough to maintain their own overseas sales organizations. They relied on agencies that inevitably were not as pushing as the new American and German salesmen. It seems it was not a failure of entrepreneurship—most of the traditional British industries have a good record in innovation in this period (e.g. the general adoption of steampower)—but rather a problem of too many entrepreneurs. This was a luxury that could not be sustained in the changing economic circumstances in which late Victorian Britain found herself.

Conclusion

Patterns of Growth

Industrial growth, but for the interruptions of trade depressions, was continuous from at least the 1740s, and did not begin to slow until overseas competition developed in the 1870s. But whether or not this growth was 'balanced' across the whole range of industry, or 'unbalanced' in the sense of being concentrated in certain leading sectors, is an interesting question. In the decades after 1780, when the rate of industrial advance began to rise sharply, certain industries—notably cotton and iron—were very apparent leaders, outstripping all others in production, innovation and capital accumulation. Yet nearly all industries were then sharing in a general expansion: tin and copperworks, brewing, glass making, leather, pottery, and the old staple wool: in 1806 a parliamentary committee had occasion to report that industry 'has been gradually increasing in almost all of the various parts of the Kingdom in which it is carried on, in some of them very rapidly'. This was balanced growth. Spatially, however, the opposite was true. The evolving distribution of Victorian industry was obviously very 'unbalanced'. The great concentrations of urban-industrial power in the north, Midlands and South Wales became the most characteristic features of the geography of nineteenth-century Britain.

It was certainly the nineteenth century that witnessed the most rapid and extensive changes in industry, indeed in economic and social change as a whole. The eighteenth century was essentially a transitional period between pre-industrial and industrial, a century that saw the beginnings of growth, the introduction of many innovations that were to pay their real dividends after 1800. Adam Smith himself was representative of the ambiguity of his times: he appreciated the importance of industry, yet considered it was limited by the growth of agriculture; he advocated the division of labour, yet did not really understand the significance of machinery. Overall, the eighteenth century is best characterized as one of 'change'; it is the nineteenth that is the century of 'transformation'.

Lessons from History

The outstanding lesson is that industrial growth is a very complex process, one in which all sorts of factors are involved. The experience of the first industrial nation fully stresses the importance of demand as well as the whole range of supply variables. But for a very real reason, there are few other lessons. Britain's industrialization was unique. Until the third quarter of the nineteenth century she was virtually unchallenged as an industrial power: for both markets and raw materials the rest of the world was there for the taking. Her developments thus took place in exceptionally favourable conditions, and—by today's standards—quite slowly, and from a relatively advanced start. There is little of comfort here for today's Third World nations, trying so hard to make a far larger transformation in a very much shorter time.

References

1. The two books of these titles *The First Industrial Nation* by Peter Mathias (London, 1969) and *The Workshop of the World* by J. D. Chambers (London, 1961) are valuable economic histories of this period. For more geographical

accounts see Eric Pawson, *The Early industrial Revolution: Britain in the Eighteenth Century*, (London, 1978), and P. J. Perry, *A Geography of Nineteenth Century Britain*, (London, 1975).

2. Daniel Defoe's *Tour through the Whole Island of Great Britain*, although mentioned in the texts with monotonous regularity, is well worth reading in the original. It is actually reports of several journeys undertaken in the early 1720s (Everyman's Library, London, 1962).

3. More detailed statistics of economic change can be found in *British Economic Growth, 1688–1959*, by Phyllis Deane and W. A. Cole (2nd edn.) (Cambridge, 1969), in particular Chapters IV, V and VI. They emphasize the problems of statistical reconstruction, these being greater than is apparent from the brief presentation here.

4. See Chapter 13.

5. See for example Harold Perkin; *The Origins of Modern British Society, 1780–1880*, (London, 1969), and E. P. Thompson; 'Time, work-discipline and industial capitalism', *Past and Present*, **37** (1967).

6. The debate is lucidly surveyed by A. J. Taylor in his editorial introduction to *The Standard of Living in Britain in the Industrial Revolution*, (London, 1975) in which he has also assembled the key articles. See also the summary in Perkin, *Origins of Modern British Society*, pp. 134–49.

7. P. Mathias, *The Brewing Industry in England, 1700–1830*, (Cambridge, 1959).

8. E. W. Gilboy, 'The cost of living and real wages in eighteenth-century England', reprinted in Taylor, *The Standard of Living in Britain*.

9. E. H. Hunt, 'Labour productivity in English agriculture, 1850–1914', *Economic History Review*, 2nd ser., **XX** (1967), pp. 280–92.

10. D. Bythell, *The Handloom Weavers* (Cambridge, 1969).

11. G. J. Barnsby, 'The standard of living in the Black Country during the nineteenth century', *Economic History Review*, 2nd ser., **XXIV** (1971), pp. 220–39.

12. David S. Landes, *The Unbound Prometheus* (Cambridge, 1969): an excellent comparative history of Britain and Western Europe from 1750 to the present.

13. On the readjustments of the late nineteenth century, see S. B. Saul, *The Myth of the Great Depression, 1873–1896*, (London, 1969).

14. E. A. Wrigley' 'The supply of raw materials in the industrial revolution', *Economic History Review*, 2nd ser., **XV** (1962), pp. 1–16.

15. A. E. Musson, 'Industrial motive power in the United Kingdom, 1800–70', *Economic History Review*, 2nd ser., **XXIX** (1976), pp. 415–39.

16. C. K. Hyde, 'The adoption of coke smelting by the British iron industry, 1709–1790', *Explorations in Economic History*, **10** (1973), pp. 397–418.

17. See Landes, *Unbound Prometheus*, pp. 108–14.

18. M. E. Falkus, 'The British gas industry before 1850', *Economic History*

Review, 2nd ser., **XX** (1967), pp. 494–508. Robson discusses the spatial diffusion of gasworks in *Urban Growth: An Approach*, (London, 1973), pp. 178–84.

19. Deane and Cole, *British Economic Growth*, Chapter VIII.

20. This is the thesis advanced by H. J. Habbakuk in *British and American Technology in the Nineteenth Century*, (Cambridge, 1962).

21. S. Pollard, 'Fixed capital in the industrial revolution in Britain', *Journal of Economic History*, **XXIV** (1964), pp. 299–314.

22. For a more detailed discussion of long distance credit transfer by the banks, see Eric Pawson, *The Early Industrial Revolution*.

23. There is a useful and brief summary of 'The structure of the firm in the nineteenth century' in P. L. Payne, *British Entrepreneurship in the Nineteenth Century*, (London, 1974).

24. Chapter 5 of Pollard's book *The Genesis of Modern Management*, (London, 1965) admirably covers the themes in this section.

25. C. H. Wilson, 'The entrepreneur in the industrial revolution in Britain', *History*, **XLII** (1957), pp. 101–17.

26. See balanced assessment of Payne, *British Entrepreneurship*.

11
The Process of Industrial Change 1730–1900

Derek Gregory

If today we find it hard to understand the process of industrialization, how much harder it must have been for those who had to live through it. Few of us would deny that, as one commentator puts it, 'to free men from the dread of periodic cold, privation, famine and disease, and from the hardship of long bouts of heavy labour in the fields or at the loom by creating the means to meet men's main wants and many of their fancies' is an attractive proposition; but, equally obviously, it implies 'a vast change from the pre-individual past'. [1] It is easy to exaggerate the dichotomy, of course, and to forget that the changes which were involved—and not all of them were benign—occurred unevenly in both space and time: that the structure of the space-economy was not transformed over night and that its rhythms of production did not accelerate in anything like a continuous way. Qualifications like this are important because they draw out the subtle textures of the past as well as its more dramatic patterns and, in particular, because they remind us of the diversity of regional experience during this period. In doing so, too, they emphasize the difficulties contemporaries had to face in formulating a coherent image of their shifting world.

This was true in intellectual terms, as the heated debates among economists testified, but it was also true on a much more immediate level. To the labourer trudging across the fields on a winter morning, or the clothier leading his pack-horse along the lanes to Leeds, discussion about concepts of utility or value had precious little relevance; in making sense of themselves, their communities and their relationships with the outside world they drew on a set of usages which, for all their differences, were enshrined in common rather than academic arguement, and which were embedded in the day-to-day practice of what Thompson has called a 'moral economy' rather than in the more abstract promise of a political economy. The culture to which they subscribed reached back to—and was in large measure an affirmation of—a parochialism and a paternalism: a vision of the world in which men were bound to the earth on which (and through which) they lived, and a model of society in which men were bound to one another by a mutually reinforcing set of social obligations. [2] These twin imperatives constituted a mental landscape which was framed in peculiarly regional terms and which served to order and legitimize the conduct of practical life. But its cultural traditions could only be sustained as part of a continous translation into and out of the labour process. They depended for their very existence on an engagement with the efforts of men and women to secure a livelihood. Once that basis began to be undermined and new forms of work organization and labour discipline started to emerge, then the whole pattern of community life was called into question. The time-honoured usages were no longer adequate to the task of explaining what was happening.

This, then, was the problem in the past, and it continues to be the problem in the present. In fact there are still very few theoretical accounts of the process of industrialization on which we can rely once the issue is phrased in this way—cultural as well as economic—so that what follows is inevitably closer to caricature than characterization. [3] Even so, it seems reasonably clear that an appropriate starting-point is the labour process itself.

Regional Transformations of the Labour Process

In tracing through the evolution of the labour process a useful distinction can be drawn between three critical phases: paternalism and proto-industrialization; alienation and technological innovation; restabilization and technological differentiation. In using this typology, it is important to realize that the equivalences set out there are by no means exact and that the simple sequence which it describes was complicated by different production systems being transformed at different times.

Paternalism and Proto-industrialization [4]

Subsistence crises had racked most parts of the country at one time or another, but the spectre of dearth was most terrible in the pastoral communities, and it was often these areas which had the first families turn away from the land towards the loom and the lathe. The subsequent pace and pattern of proto-industrialization was determined at the *micro-level* by the shifting balance between production and consumption inside the household, and at the *macro-level* by changes in the co-ordinating structures of merchant capitalism.

Although proto-industrialization had emerged out of the disruption of the traditional peasant economy—and by the end of the eighteenth century the independent peasantry had more or less disappeared—it nevertheless retained its commitment to production for use-value: commodities were still produced and exchanged in order to meet the immediate (and in some sense determinate) needs of the family. There were two aspects to this.

(a) The rhythms of production continued to be set by the pace of manual labour. This was hardly surprising, because one of the consequences of breaking the tie to the land had been to bring down the age at which the young artisan could afford to support a family and, moreover, a wife and children were now strategic elements in the labour process. Population growth therefore developed a self-sustaining impetus which militated against technological innovation. [5]

(b) The rhythms of production continued to be set by the pangs of the belly. If a family had difficulty in making ends meet then its members had little alternative but to redouble their efforts and work longer hours but, equally, once they had found their means of subsistence then they were free to divert their energies out of the labour process and into feasting, playing and dancing, the familiar celebrations of the moral economy.

Both of these were clearly in the way of further industrial change, and to understand how the barriers were eventually dismantled we have to move up to the macro-level.

Proto-industrialization relied on the ability of merchant capitalists to bring together the activities of individual households in a common market, and the various forms of integration which they employed all revolved around the realization of speculative gains. In the end, therefore, and unlike the artisans, they were committed to production for exchange-value. But at the very moments when opportunities for mercantile profits were at their greatest, artisan families were able to satisfy their needs most easily and so production slowed down. How true this was at any one time depended on the conditions obtaining in different production systems and on the web of trading relationships which had been established between them. This made the pattern a complex one, but in general these structural oppositions between merchant capitalist and artisan either led back to an uncertain version of the traditional economy or pushed forward to a much more clearly defined system of industrial capitalism.

Where proto-industrialization moved towards production for exchange-value one of its most common forms was the controlled chain. Whether the artisans were gathered under the roof of a single workshop or strung out across the countryside their work was now determined by the efforts of those in front of them and in turn determined the efforts of those behind them. Manufacturing rhythms were still in some measure geared to those of the seasons, but as far as possible these 'natural' cycles were over-ridden by the unrelenting motions of the labour process itself. Although this gradually brought production under the control of the merchant capitalist his remained in large measure a nominal authority, inasmuch as industry also came to rely on the specialized skills of the detailed labourer and his pivotal role allowed him to restrict the entry of apprentices to his trade and to retain considerable direct control over the conditions of his work. It was at this point that the moral economy intervened to establish an accepted labour discipline through which relations between master and man could be mediated. Its ethic of paternalism provided a grid of intersecting responsi-bilities and deferences: it obliged the squire, the parson and the merchant capitalist to recognize the status of the skilled craftsman and at the same time defined what was required of the artisan in return, both in and, just as important, out of the labour process. In this way the moral economy circum-scribed, even if it did not entirely remove, the traditional disjunctures between production and consumption within the household economy and, through this, helped to accelerate the process of capital accumulation.

Alienation and Technological Innovation [6]

Technical change transformed the labour process and increased the rate of capital accumulation, but the fragmentary evidence makes it difficult to reconstruct the pathways traced by innovations through the space-economy. Much of the available information relates to the early adoption of the stationary steam-engine, [7] but this is secondary to the discussion. As Marx realized,

> the steam-engine itself, such as it was at its invention during the manufacturing period at the close of the seventeenth century, and such as it continued to be

down to 1780 did not give rise to any industrial revolution. It was, on the contary, the invention of machines that made a revolution in the form of steam-engines necessary. [8]

And although converting the steam-engine from reciprocal to rotary motion took it into the mill as well as the mine, many of the early surges in its adoption curve were temporary advances, intended to supplement rather than supplant waterpower; the most dramatic expansion of steampower did not occur until after 1870. [9]

We cannot turn to conventional diffusion theory to fill the gaps in the record: its models are based on assumptions which are scarcely tenable in the Industrial Revolution. The early entrepreneur's information field was a spatially discontinuous, socially biased array of regular and occasional contacts, some far more reliable than others; many of his subsequent experiments were made on the basis of trial and error, whose results prompted him to reject or discontinue an innovation as often as they persuaded him to accept or develop it; and in any case much of his time was taken up in tinkering with old machines, modifying a fly-wheel here and adjusting a shuttle there, in a more or less continuous process of technical evolution. These realities cannot be collapsed into the contagious-cum-hierarchical spread of a series of technologically discrete innovations out from a limited set of locations without removing the very uncertainties and complexities which shaped investment patterns during the Industrial Revolution. But, more than this, any attempt to do so would distil out the specificities of the labour process in which the machines were put to work, and this would mean obscuring strategic links at the micro-scale between technological innovation and the relations of production and at the macro-scale between technological innovation and the competitive structures of industrial capitalism.

Innovation and the Relations of Production

Technological innovation undermined the status of the skilled man, and as the labour process came to be dominated by simple and essentially repetitive sequences his place was (in part) challenged and (in part) usurped by the women and children who came to work alongside him and who in some cases were eventually to displace him. This did not happen without a struggle, and its successes and failures played a major part in structuring the geography of industrial change. There were two interrelated ways in which the resilience of the working class helped to blunt the advance of technological innovation and to weaken its transformation of the relations of production: social protest and kinship cohesion.

The protests which flared up in the manufacturing districts of England and Wales between the 1780s and the 1840s were not simply time-honoured rebellions of the belly, however, and their contours cannot be read off from a map of economic distress. Whether machine-breaking is regarded as 'collective bargaining by riot' or whether it is seen as part of a radical tradition, [10] it had a political dimension whose implications resonated well beyond the communities in which it took place. This cannot be explained solely by the importance of the industrial sector to the national economy, great though this was, because the state was clearly concerned to monitor working-class movements for reasons other than the narrowly economic. To understand industrial change, therefore, we have to understand its political context as well.

An example should clarify what was at stake. In the West Riding of Yorkshire master clothiers had petitioned Parliament several times by the early 1800s in an attempt to enforce existing apprenticeship regulations, to restrict the number of looms worked under one roof and to outlaw the gig-mill and shearing-frame. These constitutional moves to reassert the traditional organization of the woollen industry were articulated through various institutions, societies and clubs, and given more force by contacts with similar movements in the West Country, but the passage of the Combination Acts in 1799 and 1800 inevitably made many of their activities tremble on the edges of the law. In pursuing their demands for the formal recognition of statuses and practices which before had always been legitimized by the moral economy, they found themselves beaten about the head by a statute book which was now written in the unfamiliar language of a political economy. As a broadsheet circulating in 1801 put it, 'petitioning Parliament to redress these grievances [is] like petitioning a corrupt agent to remove himself'. And in 1806 a Select Committee finally rejected their submissions, so that where economic rationality had long been nibbling through the bonds of paternalism, it could now gnaw away without restraint. [11]

This was all the more serious because technical change had played an important role in increasing output, and as regional commodity production had grown so the industry had had to turn to ever more distant markets which were notoriously liable to sudden and spectacular interruptions. If employers were unwilling to accept their traditional responsibilities to their men during a recession, then the family economy would be hard hit: and, in relative terms at least, the skilled artisan would be hit hardest. But it would be a mistake to see the Luddism of 1811–12 as no more than the work of croppers and shearmen desperate to retain their control over the labour process and so safeguard their livelihood, because the position of the small-scale *independent* clothier was no less precarious. Technical change had accelerated the pace as well as the volume of production, and in order to keep up with the advances being made in the mills and the large domestic workshops the small clothier had been obliged to devote more and more time and money to the woollen industry and consequently found himself with fewer and fewer opportunities to engage in the ancillary occupations which had in the past provided a portfolio of investments on which to draw in times of hardship. Many failed to meet their competitors and were reduced to the ranks of the dependent clothworkers, while many more were never far from the ruin that a trade recession would spell. The Orders in Council brought matters to a head, and an embargo on American trade plunged the industry into a protracted crisis. Its effect was to increase the concentration of capital and this prompted the croppers and shearmen and the small clothiers to make common cause against the relations of production which were emerging in the industry. Whatever their immediate objectives in attacking particular mills and machines, and however much they were informed by the claims of contemporary radical critiques, their efforts were obviously directed at *both* control over *and* ownership of the means of production, and in this sense they were necessarily part of a wider political movement. [12]

But by the 1820s and 1830s most of the struggles which took place were about control over the labour process alone. In the Lancashire cotton industry, for example, the position of the adult male spinner was threatened by the invention of the automatic mule in the 1820s, and its diffusion in the 1830s and 1840s was accompanied by a sustained battle to defend the spinners' position. These were, of course, still class confrontations, and in towns like Oldham they spilled over into an arena outside the labour process itself. The earlier attacks on mills and machines gave way to a more effective use of the strike weapon, [13] made all the more powerful as it became more general, and to systematic boycotts of shopkeepers who refused to support radical candidates in elections. But for all these bids to secure a wider hold on the institutions of local government, the effects of technical change were never very far from men's minds. Cutting wages and putting workers on short-time was only half the story: 'More dangerous in the long run (because they represented losses which could not be regained) were attempts to dilute the labour force, cut down the number of well-paid jobs, and substitute women and children for men.'[14]

These attempts met with some success, at least in the medium term, and many branches of industry—not just cotton spinning—recorded increases in female and juvenile employment for substantially similar reasons: a desire to break the bargaining power of the skilled artisan and thereby to complete capital's subordination of labour. Thus in 1844, the year of Engels' classic survey of the condition of the working class,[15] the military commander in Lancashire could report to the Home Office that 'in certain places the adult male population has been thrown out of work to a much greater extent than had been supposed by the improvement of machinery. . . and the employment of women', and the spinners appeared set to follow in the steps of the hand-loom weavers.[16]

But stark though the prospects were, none of this meant, as Smelser once supposed, that the technical changes of the 1820s and 1830s 'pressed for a thorough-going reorganisation of family relationships'.[17] Where family recruitment had existed before (and it is by no means clear how common this had been in the early mills) it probably continued beyond the 1830s. The authority of a father over his children was certainly disrupted by the discipline of the factory system, since his position was obviously a subordinate as well as a superordinate one, but in most towns this had occurred well before 1820. What was happening in the 1830s and 1840s, and therefore what made the protests so urgent, was a sustained attack on the *livelihood* of existing cotton workers which simultaneously posed a threat to the *status* of the newly proletarianized artisans entering a factory for the first time.[18] It seems more likely that the spinners were fighting to maintain their control over recruitment to the industry rather than over the deployment of their families within it.

Indeed, the arrows could just as easily be made to go the other way, to argue that far from technical change splintering traditional family structures it was in fact the cohesion of primary kinship groups which helped to sustain many individuals through the successive crises of early industrialization. This is not to attribute a unique, much less a single role to the family, of course: in some cases it proved to be a means of accommodating its members to the discipline of industrial capitalism, a ready way of admitting them to the housing market and the labour market; but, just as often, it functioned as a means of resisting its encroachments, and of upholding a network of reciprocities which flew in the face of the starkly economic calculus of supply and demand.[19] In moving from one town to another, for instance, artisans frequently relied on their relations to put them up for a few weeks or even months, to help them find more permanent lodgings, and to introduce them to the charge-hand at the factory gate; but, again, during trade recessions and strikes it was often the extended family which provided the most reliable and certainly the most clearly defined matrix of material and even ideological support.

The incidence of these 'critical life situations' was not geared solely to the cycle of technical change, but it is clear that technological innovation was responsible for some remarkable economic fluctuations which required the kind of assistance that the family was often best placed to provide.

Innovation and the Competitive Space-economy

Not all of the barriers to diffusion were located at the micro-level of the labour process, and many were found at the macro-level of the space-economy. The outlines are fairly easy to sort out. Technological innovation was only entertained where it appeared to open the door to greater profits,[20] and once a particular cycle of technical change was under way differential patterns of adoption would have ensured that some firms were able to realize greater profits than others. All the time that the market was *expanding* at least as fast as the innovating firms—and, after all, it was in circumstances like this that working-class resistance to technical change was at its lowest ebb—there was little incentive for them to grow at the expense of their competitors. In fact, as Levine points out, price-cutting is especially undesirable in these situations because the high rates of internal expansion are financed by the high gross margins which result from the difference between prices and productivity. In so far as competition was important, therefore, it was likely to occur mainly through the entry of new firms. But once an industry moved into *recession* continued growth took place through the elimination of high-cost (i.e. marginal) producers.[21] In the past, and more particularly in the eighteenth century, several industries had tried to contain these price-cutting wars through the formation of oligopolies, whose members agreed to restrict output and so maintain their rate of profit. The classic case was the 'Limitation of the Vend' which operated among Tyneside coal owners in various forms down to 1828. [22] But associations of this kind were often in fact highly unstable in these periods of market contraction, and it may be that the recurring commercial crises of the early nineteenth century were instrumental in firms breaking price agreements so as to avoid financial disaster: at any rate, it has been suggested that this could explain the collapse of price associations in Adam Smith's famous pin industry of the Midlands and the South-West and the persistent failure of cartels among the ironmasters of South-Wales, and it could prove to be of more general application. [23]

In the long run, then, technical change was closely tied to the dynamics of a competitive space-economy and thus, it might be argued, tended to promote (i) an increase in the average size of firms (which meant a corresponding increase in the height of entry barriers) and, connected to this, (ii) an increase in the concentration of capital within and between industries (which meant a corresponding polarization of economic growth). [24] These bare bones make up a reasonably convincing skeleton, but it is one which has to move into different postures in different places. Again, an example will reveal some of the necessary qualifications.

As Gattrell notes, by the early 1840s increases in firm size and in capital concentration were something of a commonplace in contemporary depictions of the cotton industry and its society. [25] Many of the early water-powered mills of the 1770s had been built on the Arkwright model, and with the possible exception of Lancashire there was little variation in the capital requirements from one place to another. These were typically of the order of £3000. During the 1790s a dispersion about the mean became more noticeable, as many small (and, as it turned out, marginal) producers entered the industry, relying on the advance of credit from merchants or wholesalers and on the use of hired or shared premises and machines. Although at about the same time much larger steam-powered mills were coming into operation as well, running perhaps 3000 spindles from a 30 hp engine and valued (at a conservative estimate) at some £10,000, it is clear that ease of entry continued to promote a hierarchical distribution of firms within the industry. Soon afterwards, however, technical change started to close the doors, and by the 1840s mean capital investment was hovering between £20,000 and £30,000 per mill. [26]

Even so, many of these giant firms had experienced their most rapid growth during the first two decades of the nineteenth century, through the investment of retained profit and the innovative exploitation of new technology, and in the years which followed the trend to size had been limited in a number of ways. There were three main constraints:

(a) larger firms often had to bear higher fixed charges on capital (through rent, depreciation and maintenance) and since these could be high enough to force them to carry on working during a recession and stock the surplus until the market recovered, the larger firms were particularly vulnerable to a prolonged fall in prices;[27]

(b) larger firms were sometimes unable to keep up with successive cycles of technical change, partly because their owners could be screened from innovatory flows by accumulated information which supported existing strategies in a way which was not true of newer entrants to the industry,[28] and partly because continuous innovation imposed high obsolescence costs in writing-off capital equipment;[29]

(c) larger firms could come up against acute management problems, and it has been claimed that 'the character and success of those who survived the very high failure rate among the early industrialists can be explained not so much in terms of differences in the quality of labour or of machines, but more in terms of differences in the quality of management'.[30] Certainly, contemporaries believed that men of modest means did best in cotton, and many of the wealthiest entrepreneurs sunk their capital in several medium-sized plants, accepting the spatial fragmentation which resulted as the necessary price to pay for effective internal organization.[31]

What was more, if the failure rate of small firms during recession was high, they nevertheless showed a marked propensity to come back in again once the market picked up, and this weakened the concentration of capital still further.

This was especially characteristic of the textile trades, but it was typical of many other industries as well. In some cases small firms could even maintain their traditional organization of the labour process by exploiting the more specialized sectors of the market, relying on good intelligence networks to switch them from one line to another in time to meet sudden shifts in demand, and working on sub-contracts for the large firms unable to meet unexpected market explosions or unwilling to divert investment into product experimentation. This placed local industrial linkages at a premium, both within and between industries; so much so that Hannah has maintained that many of the scale economies which were possible, at least before the 1860s, were *external* to the firm, generated through progressive differentiation and almost invariably realized through agglomeration, and that where there were internal economies they appear to have been exhausted well below the full extent of the market, so that no firm had a dominant share of production. There were large plants of course, particularly in the 'heavy' industries, [32] and firm size did increase over the course of the century, but by 1871

> when over half of the working population were employed in factories (and considerably more than half of the output was produced in factories) it could be argued not only that the degree of competition was no less than it had been previously, but even (given larger markets and greater competition between larger numbers of firms) that it had become more intense. [33]

In short, the rise of the corporate economy did not begin to gather momentum until after 1871, and it only really accelerated once the First World War was over. The competitive mechanisms were therefore maintained, and although technological innovation was no longer trammelled by the obligations of a moral economy, it did not leave the way clear for the elimination of the small producer. If these years witnessed the triumph of the bourgeoisie, as Hobsbawm has suggested, then it was a triumph which was shared (albeit in different ways) by the petty bourgeois as much as the captain of industry. [34]

Restabilization and Technological Differentiation

Specialization, then, was an important way in which the concentration of capital could, in certain circumstances, be constrained. It had two major effects, one at the micro-scale and one at the macro-scale. The first of these was located within the labour process and related to the work discipline enforced through a so-called 'labour aristocracy' and the second was located at the level of the space-economy and related to the intensification of regional clusters of industrial production for much of the nineteenth century and the changes this demanded in the structure of the circuits of capital transfer.

Differentiation and the Labour Aristocracy

The working-class militancy which had dominated the opening decades of the nineteenth century had all but collapsed by 1851, the year of the Great Exhibition. The coincidence between this restabilization of the labour force and the emergence of these giant rituals of self-congratulation was not entirely accidental, but it is one which conceals as much as it reveals. Economic recovery undoubtedly played its part, but it was a process discontinuous in both space and time. Church has shown that although the rate of economic growth in the nineteenth century reached its secular maximum some time between 1851 and 1871, 'overall, the period brought alternating, but not all simultaneous, spells in most industries of high and low levels of output, employment and profits, while technical changes added problems of industrial relocation to these difficulties.' [35] As Church goes on to say, such a situation was hardly conducive to entrepreneurial complacency; and it was unlikely to promote working-class acquiescence either.

And yet, if restabilization (or 'liberalization') extended beyond the workplace, if it relied on a multiplicity of social controls, which it clearly did, [36] it can still be argued that the workplace had a strategic role, and that changes in industrial authority systems, and particularly the appearance of a privileged group within the workforce implementing technically phrased instructions on behalf of the management and acting as its messenger boys and interpreters in the labour community, was in many respects the crucial dimension of the mid-century working-class subculture. This thesis has a long history in various guises, but it has been advanced most recently by Foster. [37] It rests on the assumption that technological differentiation within the labour process allowed internal sub-contracting and pace-making to create a hierarchy of skilled and unskilled tasks defined on a new and essentially *technological* basis. This meant that immediate advances, necessarily of a highly sectional kind, could be won by accepting the wage-contract as the starting-point and bargaining within the labour process. Further, it was possible to restore (or at least to reduce future threats to) the customary authority of the adult male worker, and female labour rates remained remarkably constant for the rest of the century. [38] Thus, according to Foster, 'By the 1860s about one-third of all workers in engineering and about one-third of all male workers in cotton were acting as pacemakers and taskmasters over the rest; and in doing so made a decisive break with all previous traditions of skilled activity.' [39]

As he himself admits, however, it is not at all easy to transfer these conclusions from Oldham to the national stage. Although engineering was without doubt the *locus classicus* of a work-discipline based upon the interaction of machines rather than the co-operation of specific groups of detailed labourers, and although it expanded dramatically and became much more specialized in the years after 1850, [40] the existence of similarly convincing developments in other industries is more debateable. What is clear is that no direct correlation can be made between the restabilization of the post-1850 period and the emergence of a labour aristocracy based on sub-contracting and pace-making. For Stedman Jones, therefore, the explanatory burden has to be borne (in part) by the structural requirements of technological differentiation *per se*, rather than by 'the establishment of a pace-making form of sub-contracting, which was only one among many other possible forms of organisation of a socialised labour force—and a rather primitive one at that'.[41] An adequate cultural geography of mid- and late-Victorian Britain would thus have to explore the range of possibilities which existed within particular labour processes and would also have to examine their relations to the fabric of community life conducted outside the factory-gates.[42] The two were closely connected; a new paternalism was abroad, which muted many of the divisions between skilled and unskilled by tying the labour force *as a whole* into the employer family's life-cycle. This still left room for differential rewards of course, but

> the whole body was involved too—at Christmas treats, those marking upswings in trade, and presentations to old hands and managers. The largest and most revealing were those celebrating the employers themselves, none more so than a son's coming-of-age. At these work people were often reported as mounting the jamboree themselves, sometimes contributing to the cost.[43]

But it would be quite wrong to assume that any of this made for a wholly passive working-class response to industrial change. Inasmuch as restabilization rested on a consensus at all (and there were clearly elements of coercion present), it was a fragile agreement which demanded continuous renegotiation. This was, by definition, a two-way affair, and there was a constant tension between the aspirations of the middle class and the attitudes of the working class; in many ways the subculture which resulted was one which successfully resisted middle-class intrusions, one of consolation rather than collaboration. By the close of the nineteenth century the dominant cultural institutions of the urban working class 'were not the school, the evening class, the library, the friendly society, the church or the chapel' but instead 'the pub, the sporting paper, the racecourse and the music hall'.[44] It is therefore doubly important to reconstruct the rhythms and imperatives of local community life, and to locate the social meaning of residential differentiation in the wider structures of industrial capitalism.

Differentiation and the Circuits of Capital

In the *Wealth of Nations*, first published in 1776, Adam Smith had argued that 'the division of labour is limited by the extent of the market' and that an increase in demand 'encourages production and thereby increases the competition of the producers, who, in order to undersell one another, have recourse to new divisions of labour'.[45] It was rather more complicated than that, but even in their prophetic form these remarks indicate that technological differentiation intersects with the generalization of the market. While specialization increased the importance of local *production* linkages and thereby accentuated the regional organization of industry and the rise of the great industrial city-systems, it also increased the importance of non-local *consumption* linkages and thereby accentuated the extra-regional organization of markets and the development of overseas trade. With production becoming more localized and consumption becoming more generalized then, as Harvey observed, some sort of centre-periphery relation was bound to arise out of the tension between concentration and geographical expansion.[46] In fact centre-periphery relations existed at a whole series of interlocking scales, both within and between city-systems, but at the national level they were underpinned by two basic processes.

First, as the web of inter-regional and international trade was periodically broken and recast, continually moving outwards, so capital took longer and longer to return to the labour process. This restricted the accumulation of capital, and in order to reduce circulation time three functionally distinct circuits of capital were gradually established:[47]

(1) the circuit of *industrial* capital, which involved the process through which value was produced: it is this with which we have been concerned so far;

(2) the circuit of *commercial* capital, which involved the circulation of value in its commodity form. Hence Clapham noted that by the 1860s 'the growing size and intricacy of commercial operations of all kinds had called for additional specialisation and so perhaps for new links in the commercial chain'. The traditional home-trade merchant had begun to disappear by mid-century as producers of primary commodities established their own contacts with corporate and domestic consumers and as manufacturers of standardized commodities started to deal with retailers direct, but the importance of the wholesaler was guaranteed by the complexity of the linkages which were forming: 'as one door was shut in the middleman's face another often opened on his left hand'.[48] The same was true of merchants engaged in overseas trade: although they rarely 'adventured' as they had done in the past, their pivotal role was

assured through the growth of networks of branch agents and local correspondents sending them specialized market intelligence; [49]

(3) the circuit of *financial* capital, which involved the circulation of value in its money form. After 1826 the diffusion of provincial joint-stock banking networks, particularly through the industrial towns of the Midlands, the North-West, the West Riding and the North-East, had allowed a greater articulation of intra-regional capital transfers than had been possible through the localized, cellular structures of country banking, but the joint-stock organizations were still inadequate when it came to inter-regional transfers. But as the century wore on national networks of banking were established, and although cohesion was still imperfect by the 1870s and 1880s a firmer, more hierarchical structure to the circuit was discernible. [50] Much the same was happening on the world stage, particularly after the 1840s, and the British economy was tied to those of its colonies in a process of 'interdependent development'. [51]

These three circuits meshed in the towns and the cities, where value was switched from one form to another and from one location to another, and in a very real sense the transfers which they affected were responsible for changes in the industrial geography of Britain.

Second, and following from this, such a process of sustained *differentiation* demanded the concomitant emergence of modes of economic *integration*. [52] There had always been leads and lags between regional sub-systems, and to some extent the space-economy had relied on these to move capital or labour from one sector to another. But the process of industrial change disrupted the pre-existing pattern of exchanges because different production systems were transformed at different times. The sequence of events which have been described in this essay therefore cannot be applied across England and Wales as a whole, to generate some sort of neat chronological sequence at the national level, because, as Samuel has reminded us, hand and steam-powered technologies represented *concurrent* phases of capitalist growth, 'feeding on one another's achievements, endorsing one another's effects'. [53] Each circuit of capital marked out its own 'space-times', but industrialization sent new rhythms oscillating through the economy, which had to be accommodated alongside the old ones. In doing so, acute 'packing problems' appeared, [54] and even with the growth of more responsive marketing mechanisms, the development of new communications systems and the extension of credit arrangements, they never fully resolved during this period.

In the long run, perhaps, it was an unequal struggle, but at the close of the nineteenth century the space-economy was still made up of regional mosaics. Many of the traditional parochialisms had been dissolved by the processes of industrial change, but they were yet to be reconstituted at the national level.

References

1. E. A. Wrigley, 'The process of modernisation and the Industrial Revolution in England', *Journal of Interdisciplinary History*, **3** (1972), pp. 225–59.
2. See E. P. Thompson, *The Making of the English Working Class*, (Harmondsworth, 1968); E. P. Thompson, 'Patrician society, plebeian culture', *Journal of Social History*, **7** (1974), pp. 382–405.
3. This essay is primarily concerned with manufacturing industry; I have attempted a more detailed analysis in *Industrial Capitalism and the Industrial Revolution in England*, (Folkestone, 1979).
4. This section draws on F. Mendels, 'Proto-industrialisation: the first phase of the process of industrialisation', *Journal of Economic History*, **32** (1972), pp. 241–61; F. Mendels, 'Social mobility and phases of industrialisation', *Journal of Interdisciplinary History*, **7** (1976), pp. 193–216; H. Medick, 'The proto-industrial family economy: the structural function of household and family during the transition from peasant society to industrial capitalism', *Social History*, **3** (1976), pp. 291–315.
5. D. Levine, *Family Formation in an Age of Nascent Capitalism*, (London, 1977).
6. The most invigorating account of these themes is still that of Karl Marx in *Capital: a Critique of Political Economy*, (Penguin/New Left Review edn.), (Harmondsworth, 1976), pp. 492–639.
7. See, for example, J. S. Allen, 'The introduction of the Newcomen Engine, 1710–1733', *Transactions of the Newcomen Society*, **42** (1970), pp. 169–90; J. R. Harris, 'The employment of steam power in the eighteenth century', *History*, **52** (1967), pp. 29–44; E. H. Robinson, 'The early diffusion of steam power', *Journal of Economic History*, **34** (1974), pp. 91–107; J. Tann, 'The employment of power in the West of England wool textile industry, 1790–1840', in N. B. Harte and K. G. Ponting (eds.), *Textile History and Economic History: Essays in Honour of Miss Julia de Lacey Mann*, (Manchester, 1973), pp. 196–224.
8. Marx, *Capital*, pp. 496–7.
9. J. R. Harris, 'Skills, coal and British industry in the eighteenth century', *History*, **61** (1976): p. 170n suggest that although there were probably over 2000 steam-engines in Britain by 1800, over half of the power employed was still at coal mines. On the comparative costs of water- and steam-

power, see S. D. Chapman, 'The cost of power in the Industrial Revolution: the case of the textile industry', *Midland History*, **1** (1971), pp. 1–23 and G. N. von Tunzelmann, *Steam Power and British Industrialisation to 1860*, (Oxford, 1978), and on the post-1870 expansion, see A. E. Musson, 'Industrial motive power in the United Kingdom, 1800–1870', *Economic History Review*, 2nd ser., **XXIX** (1976), pp. 415–39.

10.   E. J. Hobsbawm, 'The Machine Breakers', *Past and Present*, 1 (1952), pp. 57–70; E. P. Thompson, *The Making of the English Working Class*, (Harmondsworth, 1968), pp. 515–659.

11.   D. Gregory, 'From moral economy to political economy: a geography of class struggle in the early Industrial Revolution', in A. R. H. Baker and D. Gregory (eds.), *Explorations in Historical Geography: Some Interpretative Essays*, (Folkestone, 1979).

12.   *Ibid.*

13.   J. R. Cuca, 'Industrial change and the progress of labor in the English cotton industry', *International Review of Social History*, **XXII** (1977), pp. 241–55.

14.   J. Foster, *Class Struggle and the Industrial Revolution: Early Industrial Capitalism in Three English Towns*, (London, 1974), p. 83.

15.   F. Engels, *The Condition of the Working Class in England*, (Panther edn.), (London, 1969).

16.   Foster, *Class Struggle and The Industrial Revolution*, p. 296; D. Bythell, *The Handloom Weavers* (Cambridge, 1969).

17.   N. J. Smelser, *Social Change in the Industrial Revolution: an Application of Theory to the Lancashire Cotton Industry, 1770–1840*, (London, 1959), p. 406.

18.   M. M. Edwards and R. Lloyd-Jones, 'N. J. Smelser and the cotton factory family: a reassessment', in Harte and Ponting, *Textile History and Economic History*, pp. 304–19; M. Anderson, 'Sociological history and the working-class family', *Social History*, **3** (1976), pp. 317–34.

19.   This is intended to qualify the economism of M. Anderson, *Family Structure in Nineteenth-Century Lancashire*, (Cambridge, 1971); see also J. Humphries, 'Class struggle and the persistence of the working-class family', *Cambridge Journal of Economics*, **1** (1977), pp. 241–58.

20.   This puzzle is discussed in E. J. Hobsbawm, *Industry and Empire*, (Harmondsworth, 1968), pp. 34–55.

21.   D. Levine, 'The theory of the growth of the capitalist economy', *Economic Development and Cultural Change*, **24** (1975), pp. 47–74.

22.   P. Cromar, 'The coal industry on Tyneside, 1771–1800: oligopoly and spatial change', *Economic Geography*, **53** (1977), pp. 79–94.

23.   S. R. H. Jones, 'Price associations and competition in the British pin industry, 1814–1840', *Economic History Review*, 2nd ser., **XXVI** (1973), pp. 237–53.

24. Levine 'Growth of the capitalist economy', pp.47–94.
25. V. A. C. Gattrell, 'Labour, power and the size of firms in Lancashire cotton in the second quarter of the nineteenth century', *Economic History Review*, 2nd ser., **XXX** (1977), pp. 95–139.
26. S. D. Chapman, 'Fixed capital formation in the British cotton industry, 1770–1815', *Economic History Review*, 2nd ser., **XXIII** (1970), pp. 235–66; for comparable estimates for the woollen industry, see D. T. Jenkins, *The West Riding Wool Textile Industry, 1770–1835: a Study of Fixed Capital Formation*, (Edington, 1975).
27. Gattrell, 'Labour, power, and the size of firms in Lancashire cotton'.
28. For a theoretical discussion, see P. Converse, 'Information flow and the stability of partisan attitudes', *Public Opinion Quarterly*, **26** (1962), pp. 578–99, and K. R. Cox, 'The spatial structuring of information flow and partisan attitudes', in M. Dogan and S. Rokkan (eds.), *Quantitative Ecological Analysis in the Social Sciences*, (Cambridge, 1969), pp. 157–85.
29. M. Frankel, 'Obsolescence and technical change in a maturing economy', *American Economic Review*, **45** (1955), pp. 269–319.
30. R. M. Hartwell, 'Business management in England during the period of early industrialization: inducements and obstacles', in R. M. Hartwell (ed.), *The Industrial Revolution*, (Oxford, 1970), p. 31.
31. Gattrell, 'Labour, power, and the size of firms in Lancashire cotton'; S. Pollard, *The Genesis of Modern Management*, (London, 1965).
32. See K. Warren, *The Geography of British Heavy Industry since 1800*, (Oxford 1976).
33. L. Hannah, *The Rise of the Corporate Economy*, (London, 1976), p. 11.
34. E. J. Hobsbawm, *The Age of Capital, 1848–1875*, (London, 1975); see also G. Crossick (ed.), *The Lower Middle Class in Britain, 1870–1914*, (London, 1977).
35. R. A. Church, *The Great Victorian Boom, 1850–1873*, (London, 1975), p. 56.
36. See T. Tholfsen, *Working-class Radicalism in Mid-Victorian England*, (London, 1976); R. Gray, 'Bourgeois hegemony in Victorian Britain', in J. Bloomfield (ed.), *Class, Hegemony and Party*, (London, 1977), pp. 73–93.
37. Foster, *Class Struggle and the Industrial Revolution*.
38. For a more detailed discussion, see E. Richards, 'Women in the British economy since about 1700: an interpretation', *History*, **59** (1974), pp. 337–57.
39. Foster, *Class Struggle and the Industrial Revolution*, p. 237.
40. S. B. Saul, 'The market and the development of the mechanical engineering industries in Britain, 1870–1914', *Economic History Review*, 2nd ser., **XX** (1967), pp. 111–30; R. Floud, *The British Machine-Tool Industry, 1850–1914*, (Cambridge, 1976).
41. G. Stedman Jones. 'Class struggle and the Industrial Revolution', *New Left*

Review, **90** (1975), pp. 35–69; this manoeuvre does not exhaust all the problems: for a useful review, see H. F. Moorhouse 'The Marxist theory of the labour aristocracy', *Social History*, **3** (1978), pp. 61–82.

42. See M. Billinge, 'Towards a cultural geography of industrialisation in nineteenth-century Britain', in Baker and Gregory, *Explorations in Historical Geography*.

43. P. Joyce, 'The Factory politics of Lancashire in the later nineteenth century', *Historical Journal*, **XVIII** (1975), pp. 525–53; the effects of community structure on class consciousness are also examined by D. Harvey, 'Class structure in a capitalist society and the theory of residential differentiation', in R. Peel, M. Chisholm and P. Haggett (eds.), *Processes in Physical and Human Geography: Bristol Essays*, (London, 1975), pp. 354–69.

44. G. Stedman Jones, 'Working-class culture and working-class politics in London, 1870–1900: notes on the remaking of a working class', *Journal of Social History*, **7** (1974), pp. 460–508.

45. A. Smith, *An Inquiry into the Nature and Causes of the Wealth of Nations*, (London, 1776).

46. D. Harvey, 'The geography of capitalist accumulation: a reconstruction of the Marxian theory', *Antipode*, **7** (1975), pp. 9–21.

47. F. Lamarche, 'Property development and the economic foundations of the urban question', in C. Pickvance (ed.), *Urban Sociology: Critical Essays*, (London, 1976), pp. 85–118; see also J. Carney, R. Hudson, G. Ive and J. Lewis, 'Regional underdevelopment in late capitalism: a study of the Northeast of England', in I. Masser (ed.), *Theory and Practice in Regional Science*, (London, 1976), pp. 11–29.

48. J. Clapham, *An Economic History of Modern Britain: Free Trade and Steel, 1850–1886*, (Cambridge, 1932), pp. 298, 308; see also R. B. Westerfield, *Middlemen in English Business, 1660–1760*, (New Haven, 1915; D. Alexander, *Retailing in England during the Industrial Revolution*, (London, 1970), and J. E. Vance, *The Merchant's World: the Geography of Wholesaling*, (Englewood Cliffs, 1970).

49. These various developments were closely connected to changes in transportation systems: see below, Chapter 14.

50. There were many institutions involved in articulating this circuit; see L. Pressnell, *Country Banking in the Industrial Revolution*, (Oxford, 1956), S. E. Thomas, *The Rise and Growth of Joint Stock Banking*, (London, 1934), R. Cameron, *Banking in the Early Stages of Industrialisation*, (New York, 1967), J. R. Killick and W. A. Thomas, 'The Provincial Stock Exchanges', *Economic History Review*, 2nd ser., **XXIII** (1970), pp. 96–111. Again, these developments were closely connected to changes in transportation systems: see, for example, J. R. Ward, *The Finance of Canal Building in Eighteenth Century England*, (London, 1974), and M. C. Reed, *Investment in Railways in*

Britain, 1820–1844 a Study in the Development of the Capital Market, (Oxford, 1975).

51. H. Brookfield, *Interdependent Development*, (London, 1975); hence, as E. J. Hobsbawn, *Industry and Empire*, (Harmondsworth, 1968), p. 14 notes, 'perhaps because it was so largely built around Britain, the world economy of nineteenth-century capitalism developed as a single system of free flows, in which the international transfers of capital and commodities passed largely through British hands and institutions, in British ships between the continents, and were calculated in terms of the pound sterling.'

52. This should not be understood in the idealist sense used in D. Harvey, *Social Justice and the City*, (London, 1973), pp. 206–15 and 240–84.

53. R. Samuel, 'Workshop of the world: steam power and hand technology in mid-Victorian Britain', *History Workshop*, **3** (1977), p. 60.

54. For a simple theoretical discussion, see N. Thrift, 'Time and theory in human geography', *Progress in Human Geography*, **3** (1977), pp. 413–57; until we have more detailed analyses of regional production series, the application of these concepts to nineteenth-century Britain will remain at this abstract (and unsatisfactory) level: but see N. Thrift, 'The diffusion of Greenwich Mean Time in Great Britain', *Working Paper* **188**, School of Geography, University of Leeds, (1977).

12
Population and Society
1730–1900

R. Lawton

The transformation of Britain from the mainly rural, pre-industrial society of the early eighteenth century to the predominantly urban, manufacturing society of what has been described as the first industrial nation[1] provides a model of the process of modernization, or 'development' against which similar processes in other countries and at other times are often measured.[2] That development process involved several major transitions. First, there was an economic and technological transition from a slowly changing agricultural way of life with a widely dispersed, handicraft industry to an innovative, increasingly mechanized and regionally concentrated manufacturing and commercial economy. Secondly, there was a massive social transition from rural to urban living, from small communities, with a more cohesive society, to a new and much less coherent urban society with a quite different class structure and life-style. Thirdly, a demographic transition from relatively slow population growth to a rapid natural increase which was also accompanied by a major regional redistribution brought about largely by greatly increased population mobility.

Population change reflects, in various ways, all these transitions and the processes which underlie them. Changes in the total and structure of the national population reflect demographic changes in the components of population growth. Changes in regional distribution due to differential population growth reflect shifts in the relative economic importance of town and country and of regional economies. At the local scale, changing patterns of population—both in terms of its demographic and socio-economic structure—reflect the continuing process of adjustment of society to the changing patterns of life in both town and country. The main emphasis in this chapter is on changing population growth and distribution

313

at national and regional level, though in discussing changes within rural and urban society reference will be made to internal contrasts in demographic and social characteristics, particularly within the cities.

National Population Trends

Slow population growth rates of less than 0·25 per cent per annum persisted in England and Wales up to about 1740. But over the next century a demographic transition was initiated: population increases accelerated to an estimated 0·6 to 0·8 per cent per annum leading, in the 1780s to 1820s, to a phase of hitherto unprecedented population growth averaging 1·45 per cent per annum in England and Wales and reaching a peak of 1·8 per cent per annum in the census decade 1811–21. [3] Relatively high rates of growth were maintained until the end of the nineteenth century, though they slackened somewhat after 1851, and, right up to the First World War, increments were progressively greater averaging 338,000 per annum in England and Wales between 1871 and 1911. [4] Cumulatively, the population of England increased four-fold from around 9 million in 1801 to 36·1 million in 1911: this was indeed a population revolution.

The precise reasons for this relatively rapid growth from the mid-eighteenth century have been and still are being debated, but a substantial reduction in mortality was achieved due to better diet, better hygiene, and more effective control of epidemic disease, particularly smallpox. Together these contributed to a substantial reduction in general mortality from around 33 per 1000 in the early eighteenth century to 22–23 per 1000 in the early nineteenth. [5]

This increased expectation of life may not have been the only factor in the onset of the British demographic transition. There is a good deal of evidence of a younger marriage age and, perhaps, a higher incidence of marriage in the late eighteenth century in both rural areas—where it has been associated with the system of outdoor poor relief (the so-called Speenhamland system of 1795–1834) [6]—and in urban and industrial areas, where there was employment for women and children in handicraft and the early factory industry. [7] The estimated increase in corrected crude birth rates to 40–42 per 1000 around the turn of the century as compared with 35–37 per 1000 in the mid-eighteenth and mid-nineteenth centuries may have resulted from earlier marriage and reduced maternal mortality rather than increased standardized fertility: Habakkuk has calculated that a reduction of only one year in the mean marriage age would increase family size by 8 per cent, [8] helping to accelerate population growth in the second stage of demographic transition from around 1780 to 1830.

From the 1830s to the 1880s the rates of population increase slackened. Unhealthy conditions in urban and industrial areas prevented further improvements in mortality rates, which remained around 22 per 1000 till about 1880. [9] Only with improved housing, sanitation and public health, and better scientific and medical knowledge, especially of such infectious diseases as cholera and typhoid, did the towns become safer places—especially for the working classes—a fact reflected in the rapid improvement in infant mortality after the turn of the century.

A decline in the birth rate from the late 1870s initiated the third phase of the British demographic transition. While there had been advocates of restraint of fertility from Malthus onwards there is little evidence of birth control in the modern sense of the term until the 1870s. The restriction in the size of middle-class families became evident from the 1880s. [10] Around 1860 the average family was nearly seven children for women marrying at between 20 and 24 years of age but after 1870 fewer children were born and there were fewer mothers bearing children in their late 30s and early 40s. [11] Restrictions in the employment of child labour from mid-century in both factory and field and, after the 1870 Education Act, compulsory education began to prevent working-class children from earning. More employment for women (in workshops and offices) may have been a further disincentive to prolonged years of child-bearing. Whatever the causes, the average size of family fell by about 1910 to around 3·5 for women marrying young, though there were regional and class differences which would repay further investigation. [12]

The general growth of population would have been faster in the mid- and late nineteenth century had it not been for overseas migration. Though the net loss by migration throughout the nineteenth century was relatively unimportant, varying from 0·05 to 0·23 per cent per annum between 1841 and 1910 (Table 12.1A), overseas migration affected both rural and urban areas, the level of overseas emigration rising during periods of economic depression when migration, especially to North America, was an alternative to internal migration to the growing towns and industrial regions. [13] In the mid-Victorian period 50 per cent of emigrants from England were unskilled labourers; by the late nineteenth century this proportion dropped to one-third or less. Certainly by then four out of five

Table 12.1A: Population trends, England and Wales, 1700–1921.

	Population		Natural increase		Births		Deaths		Net migration	
	000s	Per cent increase p.a.	000s	Per cent p.a.	000s	Per cent p.a.	000s	Per cent p.a.	000s	Per cent p.a.
1701[a]	5826	—	—							
1751[a]	6140	0·11	317	0·11	N.A.		N.A.		−3	−0·00
1781[b]	7531	0·76	1390	0·75	N.A.		N.A.		+1	+0·01
1831[b]	13,897	1·69	6522	1·73	N.A.		N.A.		−155	−0·04
1881[b]	25,974	1·74	11,332	1·63	32,362	4·66	21,030	3·03	−745	−0·11
1921[b]	37,887	1·15	14,188	1·37	35,440	3·41	21,252	2·05	−2275	−0·22

Table 12.1B: Vital trends, England and Wales, 1841–1920.

(Average annual)[b]	Births/1000	Fertility rate B/F. 15–44	Deaths/1000	Infant mortality (D<1/1000 live births)
1841–50	32·6	136·9	22·4	154
1851–60	34·2	145·1	22·2	153
1861–70	35·2	151·3	22·5	154
1871–80	35·4	153·9	21·4	149
1881–90	32·5	139·3	19·1	142
1891–1900	29·9	123·1	18·2	154
1901–10	27·2	109·3	15·4	127
1911–20	23·8	104·1	14·4	101

Sources:
[a] Phyllis Deane and W. A. Cole, *British Economic Growth, 1688–1959*, (2nd edn.) (Cambridge, 1969).
[b] B. R. Mitchell and Phyllis Cole, *Abstract of British Historical Statistics*, (Cambridge, 1962).

emigrants from England and Scotland were predominantly from large towns and industrial areas, and included a considerable and increasing proportion of skilled handicraft, industrial and tertiary workers, who formed nearly half (48·6 per cent) of British passengers in ship lists of vessels arriving in the U.S.A. in 1878 and 59·1 per cent in 1897.[14]

The consequences of these various demographic and structural changes for the population of nineteenth-century Britain were two-fold. First, they led to changes in the age structure and, secondly, in the growth potential and size of the workforce. While lowering of mortality rates produced more people in the older age groups, a relatively high birth-rate maintained a structure favourable to population growth. Nevertheless, until the late-Victorian period there was a high dependency rate. Until the 1880s around 35 per cent of England's population was in the under-15 age group and rather less than 5 per cent in the over-65s.[15] By the end of the century a falling birth-rate was reflected in the population structure: juvenile dependency fell while improvements in mortality of the late nineteenth century helped to increase the proportion of the over-65s.

While these trends show all the features associated with the classic demographic transition model, the passage to phase III from a lengthy phase II in which reduced mortality led to substantially increased natural increase of population was prolonged in England and Wales by rural-urban migration.[16] The decline in rural birth-rates is late (in contrast to the situation in France) since early industrial development and urbanization, together with emigration, successfully absorbed surplus rural population. Hence, differentials in regional rates of national increase were offset by even wider contrasts in levels of internal migration: not only did England experience an early *vital* transition, but it embarked early on the second stage of what has been described as the *mobility* transition.[17]

From the later eighteenth century there was a relative and, from the mid-nineteenth century, an absolute movement of people from rural to urban and industrial areas permitting natural increase, due largely to a relatively high birth-rate, to persist in most rural areas until late in the nineteenth century.[18] Out-migration from the rural reservoirs of very large numbers of young adults—both men and women—provided the stock from which, in the eighteenth century, the large towns, London in particular, were able to sustain relatively rapid growth despite high mortality. During the nineteenth century rural migrants gave momentum over short periods of very rapid growth to individual areas from which, subsequently, high rates of growth could be sustained largely by natural increase.

There has also been a continuing redistribution of population between peripheral areas and a core of maximum economic and population concentration focused upon the area from south Lancashire and west Yorkshire, through the industrial Midlands to Greater London, together with secondary nodes of rapid population increase in north-east England and South Wales, all areas of high levels of urbanization and industrialization by the later nineteenth century. Table 12.2 shows the broad features of population trends, 1750–1901 in the *present* standard regions of England and Wales as compared with Britain as a whole.

South-east England grew at the national rate throughout the eighteenth century: though growth was focused largely on London, the south-coast towns—particularly resorts such as Brighton—experienced rapid growth from the later eighteenth century, as reflected in the population trends in Hampshire and Sussex. From 1851 the South-East's rate of population increase was much above the national level and its share of Britain's population increased markedly as it was increasingly dominated by the spreading growth and influence of Greater London.

The West Midlands experienced early industrialization and relatively rapid population growth in the eighteenth and early nineteenth centuries. But the relative decline of the Black Country after 1870 is reflected in the slight fall in the region's share of the national population by 1901.

The other regions south of the Humber-Mersey all experienced a relative decline in population throughout this period, particularly in the later nineteenth century. Indeed in East Anglia and the South-West decline of rurally based industries and persistent nineteenth-century migration from the countryside, together with relatively slow urban development, led to a marked reduction in their share of the national population. The more modest decline in the East Midlands' share of population reflects a more diversified economy. Indeed in the later nineteenth century the towns and industries of the East Midlands attracted population from adjacent and northern areas, leading to an acceleration in population growth which has been reflected in the twentieth century in the increased proportion of the national population living in the region.

Of the remaining regions of England, the profiles of the North-West and Yorkshire are similar. Rapid growth of the specialist textile districts in the eighteenth and early nineteenth centuries are reflected in large population growth, absolutely and relatively. But, despite increasing

Table 12.2: Regional population trends, 1701–1901.

REGION	Total population (000)					Share of Great Britain (per cent)				
	1701[a]	1751[a]	1801[c]	1851[c]	1901[c]	1701	1751	1801	1851	1901
ENGLAND	5413	5691	8305	16,764	30,515	78·7	76·8	79·1	80·6	82·5
South-East	1609	1690	2503	5111	10,523	23·4	22·8	23·8	24·3	28·4
West Midlands	516	558	858	1713	2987	7·5	7·5	8·2	8·2	8·1
East Midlands	486	472	640	1152	2013	7·1	6·4	6·1	5·5	5·4
East Anglia	516	484	626	1049	1131	7·5	6·5	6·0	5·0	3·1
South-West	1061	1109	1344	2243	2570	15·4	15·0	12·8	10·8	6·9
Yorks/Humberside	409	461	817	1808	3514	6·0	6·2	7·8	8·7	9·5
North-West	339	425	882	2525	5278	4·9	5·7	8·4	12·1	14·3
North	480	494	634	1163	2498	7·0	6·7	6·0	5·6	6·8
WALES	413	449	588	1164	2013	6·0	6·1	5·6	5·6	5·4
SCOTLAND	1048[b]	1265[b]	1608	2889	4472	15·2	17·1	15·3	13·9	12·1
GREAT BRITAIN	6974	7405	10,501	20,816	37,000	100	100	100	100	100

Table 12.2: Regional population trends, 1701–1901 (continued).

REGION	Percentage increase				Percentage regional change — Percentage G.B. change			
	1701–51	1751–1801	1801–51	1851–1901	1701–51	1751–1801	1801–51	1851–1901
ENGLAND	5·2	32·6	101·9	82·0	68	72	104	106
South-East	5·0	51·9	104·2	105·9	65	114	106	136
West Midlands	8·1	56·1	99·7	74·3	105	126	102	96
East Midlands	−2·9	47·2	79·9	74·8	−38	104	81	96
East Anglia	−6·3	30·3	67·6	7·8	−82	68	69	10
South-West	4·6	26·1	66·9	14·6	60	57	68	19
Yorks/Humberside	12·6	82·5	121·2	94·4	164	182	123	121
North-West	25·5	109·7	186·4	109·0	331	242	190	140
North	2·8	32·6	83·3	114·9	36	72	85	148
WALES	8·7	34·9	98·0	73·0	113	77	100	94
SCOTLAND	20·7	27·1	79·6	54·8	269	60	81	71
GREAT BRITAIN	7·7	45·4	98·2	77·7	100	100	100	100

The regions are the revised Standard Regions of 1971.

Sources:

[a] Phyllis Deane and W. A. Cole, *British Economic Growth, 1688–1959*, (2nd edn.) (Cambridge, 1969).

[b] T. C. Smout, *A History of the Scottish People, 1560–1830*, (London, 1969), quoting Sir John Sinclair (1805) for 1707 estimate and A. Webster for 1755 estimate.

[c] Department of the Environment, *Long Term Population Distribution in Great Britain—a study*: Report by an inter-departmental Study Group, (H.M.S.O., 1971), Tables 1.4, 1.5, 1.6 and 1.12.

industrial diversification, there was a considerable fall in rates of increase in the late nineteenth century reflecting out-migration from many of the older industrial districts.

Despite the early development of coalmining, especially in north-east England, the northern region and Wales did not experience the full impact of mining and heavy industry until the mid-nineteenth century. Thereafter high rates of population growth led to an increase in their relative regional importance, though the upsurge of population in the South Wales coalfield in the later nineteenth century is obscured in Table 12.2 by massive migrational losses from the rest of the region.

Spatial Patterns of Population Development 1730–1911

The broad view of regional population trends during the eighteenth and nineteenth centuries given above indicates the general population response to changing economic prosperity. These are now analysed in greater regional detail and within a chronological framework more closely related to significant fluctuations in the demographic components of change.

Detailed, exact and directly comparable analysis of vital and migrational components of population change in England and Wales over this period is not easy. Prior to the development of civil registration of vital statistics with the creation of the Office of Registrar General in 1837, vital trends must be assessed from baptismal and burial registers both of which are deficient in a number of ways. Even after the adoption of civil registration, vital data, especially on births, were defective and, despite the much increased census data on age and sex composition from 1841, it is difficult to calculate standardized measures of fertility and mortality.[19] Migration must be calculated indirectly: first, by comparing natural change with total change to give net migration; and, secondly, from the 1841 census onwards by using census information on birthplace to give lifetime migration into a particular area[20] or to estimate inter-censal migration from changes in birthplace figures in successive censuses adjusted for mortality.[21] Changing areal units for which population data are available also create problems: in this section change is analysed for geographical counties up to 1830 (Figs 12.1–12.3); thereafter the registration districts created under the Civil Registration Act of 1836 are used (Figs 12.4–12.6).

1730–80

From the mid-eighteenth century population growth in England and Wales accelerated. The 1730s were years of stagnation, continuing the relatively high mortality which kept the general rate of natural growth during the early eighteenth century to a very low level. [22] In London and the south-eastern counties there was a considerable excess of deaths over births, population growth being sustained by considerable in-migration. In a number of rural counties of midland, southern and northern England natural growth was negligible and, indeed, there were some areas of decline; in many such areas total numbers fell because of out-migration. [23]

Relatively heavy mortality persisted until the 1740s, but between 1740 and 1780, the beginnings of a period of sustained growth in a demographic as well as an economic sense, [24] population increased nationally by 27·1 per cent due mainly to a substantial reduction in death rate coupled, perhaps, with a slight increase in birth rate. [25] Indeed, there was a considerable acceleration in rates of natural increase in all parts of the country outside London between 1750 and 1780 (Fig. 12.1). These were particularly marked in areas of early industrial development—such as the West Midlands and the textile districts of east Lancashire, west Yorkshire, and Notts-Derby—where birth rates seem to have been relatively high, and in adjacent counties. [26] Already, it seems, there may have been a demographic gradient from areas of higher fertility and mortality in the north and west to lower rates in the south and east, though with notable exceptions, particularly in the Metropolis with its very high mortality and in Wales and the northern counties with their relatively low birth-rates.

While calculations of net migration from such estimates of natural and total change must be somewhat speculative, the few areas of gain, dominated by the metropolitan counties and the new industrial areas of the West Midlands and textile counties, are in keeping with the concept of a growing redistribution of population resulting principally from short-range movement. Seasonal migration of labour, local mobility (encouraged by movement of labour from 'closed' parishes to 'open' parishes), [27] annual hirings of farm servants and migrant (including itinerant) craftsmen, all contributed to a rural population which was much less stable than once thought. Comparison of parish 'listings' and persistence of families in parish registers suggest a relatively high turnover. [28] Studies of marriage distance have also confirmed a considerable level of local movement and, among higher social groups and

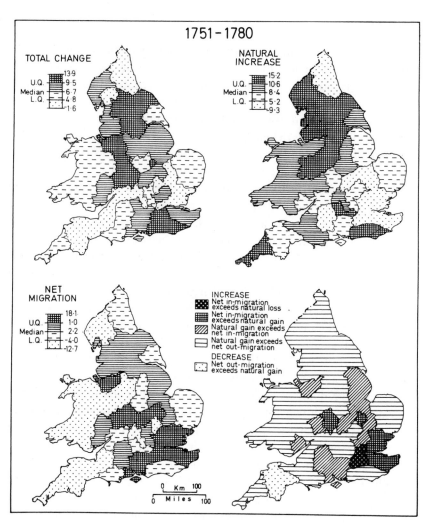

Fig. 12.1. Components of population change in England and Wales by counties, 1751–80. The average annual rate of change per 1000 over the 30-year period is shown in four quartile groups and is comparable with Figs 12.2 and 12.3. Based on estimates of population change as given by Phyllis Deane and W. A. Cole, *British Economic Growth 1688–1959* (2nd edn.) (Cambridge, 1969), Table 26 (p. 115).

their servants and in particular occupations, there was an important element of long-distance migration. [29]

Studies based on apprenticeship registers [30] and Poor Law records [31] also point to a considerable level and range of migration to a wide spectrum of towns. There were significant long-distance movements of skilled craftsmen in a wide range of industries (for example, in metallurgy, chemicals and glass-making), while textiles and coalmining attracted not only considerable short-range but also medium- and long-distance migration. [32]

Migration, often from considerable distances, was needed to sustain the rapid growth of London and the major provincial cities in the early- and mid-Georgian period, and was a key factor in the growth of new towns, such as the spas and seaside watering places, and the emerging industrial centres. In London, deaths remained above births until the 1780s and indeed were intermittently so—as in provincial cities—until mid-Victorian times: hence the unique combination of net in-migration in excess of natural loss of population (Fig. 12.1).

At the beginning of the eighteenth century London, with a population of nearly 600,000, already housed one-tenth of the country's population. Over the next half-century, despite an estimated net migration gain of 500,000-600,000, population increased only to some 675,000, due to high mortality. [33] An estimated migration gain in the metropolitan counties of 404,720 (according to Deane and Cole) [34] between 1750 and 1780 saw London's population increase to around three-quarters of a million in 1780. The attractive power of the capital in a demographic as well as an economic sense was nation-wide. It included people from all parts of England and Wales, with town dwellers probably important among long-distance migrants, and from Ireland, Scotland and overseas: indeed, of married people treated at the London Dispensary between 1774 and 1781, 1 in 11 were Irish-born, 1 in 15 Scots, and 1 in 60 foreign. [35] London was at the head of a hierarchical system in which its dominance was more pronounced than in the nineteenth century, the capital's primacy over the next large city being some 20 to 1.

Population surpluses from areas of high natural increase moved to adjacent industrial and urban areas, while the larger urban centres drew upon the smaller to sustain their accelerating increase, producing a substantial increase in urban growth from the mid-eighteenth century, the population and social implications of which have yet to be examined for mid- and late-Georgian England. Chalklin has estimated that the total urban population increased from 22 or 23 per cent of the total in 1700 to one-quarter by 1750, [36] and Law estimated that over 3 million people (or 33·8 per cent) were town dwellers in 1801. [37] There was a substantial increase in general population growth and in the numbers of migrants to towns in the mid-Georgian period.

Not all towns were equally affected. Traditional regional centres, especially in predominantly agricultural districts and those which lost craft industry, grew relatively slowly. So did the country towns whose modest growth at best paralleled that of the surrounding rural areas. But industrial towns, ports and spas and seaside resorts grew rapidly in the early industrial and transport revolutions. The practical problems of rapid population growth in the towns, especially those of health, sanitation and the levying of rates, produced a considerable number of local censuses in the later eighteenth century. Of over 120 listed by Law, from 1750 to 1790, 102 relate to 81 towns ranging from market centres to major provincial cities. [38] Of the 12 places for which there is more than one listing, some larger cities doubled their population—for example, Manchester from 19,839 in 1758 to 42,821 in 1788—Birmingham grew from 23,688 in 1750 to 30,804 in 1770 and Nottingham from 10,020 in 1739 to 17,711 in 1779, while new industrial towns mushroomed as with Bolton which grew from 5339 to 11,739 between 1773 and 1789. However, as Chalklin notes, the smaller market and county towns grew more slowly: for example, Cambridge with 6422 people in 1728 had reached only 9868 by 1794.

Information on population structure in such local censuses, though mainly related to sex and household structure with a few giving age and marital status, indicates fewer children and old people and more young adults in the towns than in rural areas, evidence of active in-migration and future growth potential which was already reflected in large towns in pressure on housing.

1780–1831

During this half-century population increased sharply by 83·2 per cent (Table 12.1A). The balance between agriculture and industry shifted, as reflected in increased levels of urbanization in which the draw of London and the big provincial cities was reflected in considerable in-migration. [39] However, natural increases were often higher in rural areas, due mainly to a lower death rate, while extension of the cultivated area and intensification of farming, together with a wide range of rurally based industries, retained much of the increment in the countryside. The main pull of migrants up to the early nineteenth century was to London and the metropolitan counties: Deane and Cole believe that 'not until 1800 [was there] a general movement of population to . . . new industrial centres', [40] which grew mainly by natural increase fed also by short-range movement from adjacent areas.

Nevertheless, the modern pattern of population distribution was taking shape by the first census of 1801 (Fig. 12.4). A zone of relatively high population density extended from London to the textile districts of Lancashire and west Yorkshire. [41] Though early nineteenth-century England was still predominantly rural, with one-third of its population dependent on agriculture, industrial and commercial activity accounted for population concentrations in Greater London, the Black Country, south Lancashire—west Yorkshire and Tyneside and parts of the north-east coalfield. While remote rural areas of upland Wales and northern England had low densities, in much of lowland England a growing agriculture and diversified economies, including a considerable range of craft industries, were reflected in population increases rivalling those of many towns and in relatively high population densities. [42] Indeed it has been correctly said that, in the early nineteenth century, 'the man of the crowded countryside was still the typical Englishman'. [43]

Between 1780 and 1830 the highest rates of population increase were, first, in the metropolitan and south-eastern counties, including the rapidly growing towns along the south coast; secondly, in the industrial north (especially Lancashire and south Yorkshire), the West and parts of the East Midlands; and, thirdly, the mining and industrial districts of Cornwall, Monmouth and south-east Wales, and north-east England (Figs 12.2 and 12.3). Low-growth areas included both relatively populous farming districts in East Anglia and the south Midlands and thinly peopled uplands in the South-West, Wales and northern England. All were increasingly dependent on farming and many had suffered a decline in handicraft manufacture, especially textiles. However, rural areas in general experienced a population growth not dissimilar from the national rate, and enclosure and reclamation often greatly benefited hitherto marginal lands, especially during the plough-up campaign of the Napoleonic Wars, in both uplands [44] and in areas of more intensive farming such as the Fenland and heathlands of eastern England. [45]

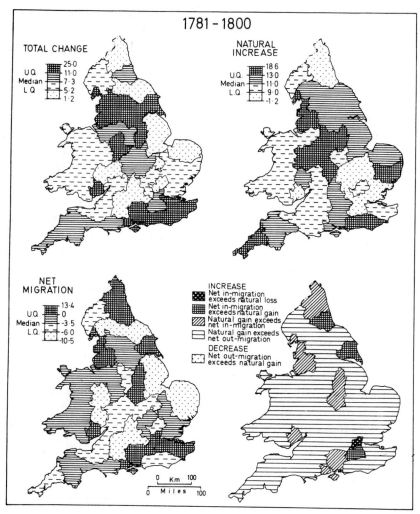

Fig. 12.2. Components of population change in England and Wales by counties, 1781–1800. The average annual rate of change per 1000 over the 20-year period is shown in four quartile groups and is comparable with Figs 12.1 and 12.3. Based on Deane and Cole, see Fig. 12.1.

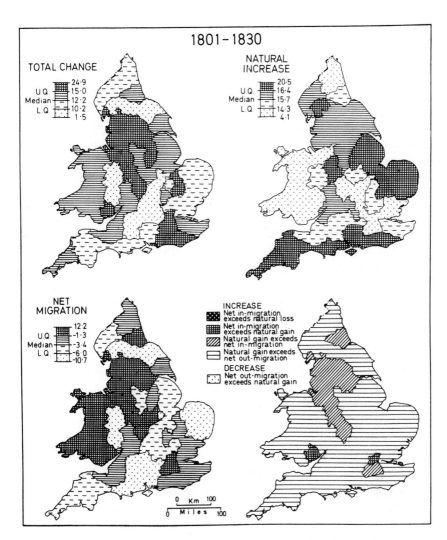

Fig. 12.3. Components of population change in England and Wales by counties, 1801–30. The average annual rate of change per 1000 over the 30-year period is shown in four quartile groups and is comparable with Figs 12.1 and 12.2. Based on Deane and Cole, see Fig. 12.1.

Natural components of population change do not always accord with these total trends, though deficiencies in parochial registration especially of births make detailed analysis of regional fertility and mortality hazardous. [46] On the one hand, above-average rates of natural increase seem to characterize both low-growth areas such as East Anglia, the South Midlands and Wales and also such rapidly growing regions as the Metropolis, the West Midlands and the industrial north. In London, though mortality fell in the late eighteenth century, [47] birth rates remained low. In the North-West and the industrial Midlands a rising birth-rate and a falling death-rate led to an acceleration of natural growth. In most rural areas mortality continued to fall and was probably more important than additional births in maintaining high local rates of natural increase, notably in the southern and south-western counties, and in parts of East Anglia and eastern England. While there may have been increases in family size in some rural areas and, perhaps, some slight increase in general fertility in the late eighteenth and early nineteenth centuries, there seems little to support the contentions of Malthus and the 1834 Poor Law Commissioners that the so-called Speenhamland system of outdoor poor relief led to earlier marriage and increased families among the rural poor, though it may have contributed to reduced infant mortality. [48]

In sum, reduced mortality was a more significant agent of population change in the late eighteenth and early nineteenth centuries than fluctuations in birth rate. This was especially true of London and the large provincial cities, but also the case in rural areas. Nevertheless, there are interesting regional and temporal differences in the levels of fertility and mortality suggested by the calculations based on the Parish Register Abstracts of the early censuses (1801–41) which have yet to be fully examined in the light of more recent work on parish registers. [49]

The greater part of population growth in London and the metropolitan area during this period—perhaps three-quarters of a million out of an estimated total increase of 1,364,000—was contributed by net migration, though the natural growth rate generally exceeded migration from the early nineteenth century. [50] In contrast, the industrial regions of England largely depended for their growth on their own natural increase and that of adjacent counties, though the major provincial cities began to attract population from farther afield, as witness the number of Irish, Scots and overseas-born in the population of late-Georgian Liverpool. [51] However, while there was growing short-range movement of population there was no sudden transfer of population from the south to the midlands and north of England. [52] By far the greatest migration gains were to the metropolitan region: between 1781 and 1830, besides London, only Lancashire, Durham and Monmouth enjoyed continuous net in-migration while Yorkshire and parts of the West and East Midlands showed intermittent gain: indeed in 1780–1800 only twelve counties and in 1800–30 only nine counties gained by migration. Though such estimates of net migration are certainly defective, they point to a focusing of movement on a relatively few areas. For the most part rural areas suffered net migrational losses, though the local situation was complex: areas with craft industry often retained their natural increase and also attracted labour from adjacent districts, producing a considerable ebb and flow of population. Nevertheless, the greatest tides of migration were setting towards the towns and new industrial regions in what Redford described as 'a complex wavelike motion'. [53] Though less sharply contrasted, population trends in both 1780–1800 (Fig. 12.2) and 1800–30 (Fig. 12.3) anticipate those of the later nineteenth century (Fig. 12.6) in the combination of the surrender of the natural increases of the agricultural areas through movement of population towards the urban and industrial areas in which migrational and natural increases of population combined to produce rapid total growth.

From the late eighteenth century the acceleration in the growth of urban population was as great as any experienced in modern times and, particularly in London and the larger provincial cities, it led to major health and social problems and to marked changes in the characteristics of the towns and their populations. London, in 1801 with a population of some 960,000 and the only truly large city, continued its dominance but at a slower rate of growth to reach 1,776,556 in 1831 in a metropolitan area 'some 8 miles around St. Pauls'. The provincial capitals expanded rapidly and the impact of industrialization spawned new towns, particularly in the textiles and metal-working districts. Whereas in 1780 little more than one-quarter of the country's population were town dwellers, by 1801 33·8 per cent were urban and the proportion grew rapidly to 44 per cent in 1831. [54] Between 1801–31 urban population doubled, as compared with the total population increase of 48 per cent, and 3·14 million—62·8 per cent of the total increase of 5 million—were added to it (Table 12.3).

Compared with the eighteenth century when London dominated the national pattern of urban growth, the gap between the capital and regions was narrowed and the rank order of cities began to assume a more regular gradient (see Fig. 13.2). [55] The pattern of urban growth, 1780–1830, points

Table 12.3: The growth of population in England and Wales, 1841–1911.

	Population in 1841	Population in 1911	Natural increase 1841–1911	Net gain (+) or loss (−) by migration 1841–1911	Ratio of migrational gain or loss to natural increase (per cent)	Total percentage increase 1841–1911
1. Towns						
(a) *Large*						
London	2,261,525	7,314,738	3,802,252	+1,250,511	+32·9	223·7
8 Northern	1,551,126	5,191,769	2,747,306	+893,337	+32·5	234·7
(b) *Textile*						
22 Northern	1,386,670	3,182,382	1,705,779	+89,933	+5·3	129·5
(c) *Industrial*						
14 Northern	603,214	1,812,219	1,361,999	−152,994	−11·2	200·4
11 Southern	296,009	708,693	428,363	−15,679	−3·7	139·4
(d) *Old*						
7 Northern	289,819	648,769	343,006	+15,944	+4·6	123·9
13 Southern	664,782	1,375,651	732,973	−22,004	−3·0	107·0
(e) *Residential*						
9 Northern	206,897	559,022	211,895	+140,230	+66·2	170·2
26 Southern	692,185	1,770,030	750,483	+327,362	+43·6	155·7

(f) Military						
16 Southern	470,821	1,212,413	616,644	+124,948	+20·3	157·5
Northern Towns	4,031,725	11,394,161	6,369,985	+986,450	+15·5	188·2
Southern Towns	4,385,222	12,381,525	6,331,165	+1,665,138	+26·3	182·3
	8,669,167	23,775,686	12,701,150	+2,651,588	+20·9	174·3
2. Colliery Districts						
9 Northern	1,320,342	5,334,002	3,363,112	+650,548	+19·3	304·0
3. Rural Residues:						
12 Northern	2,425,614	2,875,113	2,093,257	−1,643,770	−78·6	18·5
12 Southern	3,740,228	4,085,691	3,208,729	−2,863,266	−89·2	9·2
	6,165,842	6,960,804	5,301,986	−4,507,036	−85·0	12·9
North of England	7,783,682	19,602,876	11,825,942	−7648	−0·1	151·8
South of England	8,125,450	16,467,616	9,540,294	−1,198,128	−12·6	102·7
Total	15,914,148	36,070,492	21,366,236	−1,209,892	−5·7	126·6

Based on Cairncross (1953) using T. A. Welton's classification of 1911 but with a modification in the division between north and south.

to a number of regional sub-systems with high rates of population increase particularly in the textile areas of south Lancashire and west Yorkshire and the metal-working areas of the West Midlands, while the rapid growth of towns along the south coast was also marked. [56] Many textile towns achieved spectacular growth, up to ten-fold in places like Bury, Bolton, Bradford and Huddersfield, while of the regional capitals Manchester grew from 27,246 in 1773 to some 182,000 in 1831 and Leeds from 17,121 in 1775 to 123,000. There were similar increases recorded in the metallurgical centres: Birmingham grew from 50,000 in 1781 to 144,000 in 1831; Wolverhampton from 11,368 in 1788 to 25,000; and Sheffield from 26,538 to 92,000. Some notable increases were also recorded in the seaports, particularly a large commercial port such as Liverpool which grew from 34,407 in 1773 to 202,000 in 1831, though specialized ports also boomed, for example, Sunderland which increased its population from around 10,000 in 1760 to 39,000 in 1831. Rapid development of naval bases such as Plymouth and Portsmouth, together with resorts such as Brighton, also had much to do with rapid urbanization along the south coast. [57]

In contrast, many older regional centres and, in particular, market and county towns achieved only modest population increases, especially in the south and east of the country. Norwich, one of the largest of pre-industrial cities in England with a population of 40,050 in 1786 had only 62,000 in 1831, while Exeter, despite its growing regional functions, was affected by its decline as a port and centre of an important regional textile trade and its 1831 population of 28,000 was little more than twice that of the late seventeenth century.

The acceleration of urban growth drew many newcomers to the towns. Chalklin suggests that the bigger provincial towns added an average of some 500–1000 new migrants to their population every year. [58] Many of these came from the surrounding countryside. Birmingham, where population grew by some 20,000 in the 1780s and 1790s attracted people from rural Warwickshire and Matthew Boulton, the founder of the Soho works at Handsworth, claimed that, 'I have trained up many, and am training up more, plain country lads into good workmen.' [59] Most of the migrants to the growing textile towns came from adjacent handicraft producers. [60]

However, especially in London but also in the major provincial cities, there were growing numbers of long-distance migrants. The largest group were the Irish who numbered 284,128, or 1·9 per cent of the population of

England, in the 1841 census. However, London, Liverpool and Manchester had between them over half of the Irish-born in the country at that time and there were areas in all three in which over 10 or even 20 per cent of inhabitants were of Irish origin.[61] In London these included St Giles, Whitechapel and Shadwell. In Liverpool the numbers of Irish increased rapidly after the 1798 uprising, according to contemporaries. Already certain districts in the town centre and in the working-class 'North End' held significant concentrations of Irish, which increased as the proportion of Irish built up to 17·3 per cent of the Borough's population in 1841 and which were reflected in the spread of Catholic churches in the early nineteenth century.[62] These areas were reflected in growing overcrowding to which the increasing average household size, the frequent presence of lodgers and the testimony of the Poor Law records bear witness.[63] These conditions led to a worsening of living conditions in the inner areas of towns that was reflected in relatively high levels of urban mortality even before the marked deterioration of the 1830s.[64]

Despite growing migration from the countryside to the town, much of the rural increment was retained in the period 1780–1830. Almost without exception rural population growth accelerated to a peak in 1811–21, the decade of most rapid increase in the country as a whole.[65] The increased demand for labour, not least on newly reclaimed and enclosed land, usually more than compensated for the decline in small farms and the increase in landless labourers.[66] However, while the *numbers* of those engaged in primary pursuits continued to rise, they formed a diminishing *proportion* of the rurally employed, although in 1831 half the population of rural England was still engaged in agriculture, horticulture and forestry.[67] In contrast to widespread depopulation associated with earlier enclosures for pasture (see above, pp. 154–9) there is little evidence of widespread depopulation following parliamentary enclosure. A more likely local cause of slow population growth was the restriction on labourers' cottages in 'closed' parishes.[68] Gonner[69] saw little evidence of specific links between parliamentary enclosure and population trends, 1750–1811, and recently Yelling,[70] while admitting that there was considerable local variation, has argued that in most parishes involved in enclosure during this period there was— to use the conclusion from one study of the effect of enclosure on 200 parishes in the East Midlands—'no necessary accompaniment of population decline or even of very slow growth'.[71]

Nevertheless, by 1830 this phase of relatively rapid rural population growth was coming to an end. Though population continued to increase throughout rural England up to mid-century, three Welsh counties declined and there was slow growth along the Welsh border and in south-west England and the grazing areas of the Midlands, and very limited growth in many parts of upland Wales and northern England.

The relatively high rural growth rate was due to relatively high fertility. There is little support for the view that that was the *direct* result of Poor Law family allowances (see above, p. 330), either due to their effects on the age or numbers of those marrying—which were broadly in line with the national situation—or in increased size of families.[72] However, the restrictive settlement clauses of the Old Poor Law helped to keep in remoter rural areas surplus labour which was released from the 1830s.[73] A more important factor was the diversity of employment offered by the 'dual economy' in many rural areas during this period: local craft trades in village and market town, and a considerable amount and range of rurally located cottage, workshop and extractive industry gave great diversity to the employment structure,[74] while the transport improvements of the turnpike and canal age brought new jobs to the countryside in addition to giving a new nodality to towns.

The drift of rural industry towards new industrial regions in fact often contributed to *rural* growth in this period. Nevertheless, it also promoted accelerated urban increase and was instrumental in initiating a substantial redistribution of population, the full impact of which was to be experienced only in Victorian times: as Francis Galton later observed 'the population of towns decays and has to be recruited by migrants from the country'.[75]

1831–1911

Between 1831 and 1881 the rural increment of population slackened and migration from the countryside accelerated: though rural fertility and natural increments remained relatively high, they were progressively directed towards rapidly growing industrial areas, to the coalfields of the midlands and north and to the rapidly growing towns among which London dominated. Much of the transfer of population was short-range, though major cities always had a strong pull which reached out to more distant regions. Moreover, fed by young adults, the towns and industrial regions provided much of their population increment from their own natural growth.

Although during the years from the 1880s to the First World War, rural depopulation and the fuller concentration of population in the towns and industrial regions continued, some new features affected regional trends. As the rural reservoirs were drained of younger people natural increase of population declined, due especially to falling births. In complementary fashion the towns and, especially, the coalfield areas derived more and more of their increment from natural increase to which the rapidly falling death-rates of the late nineteenth century (due mainly to falling infant mortality) largely contributed. Changing patterns of industry, including a relative decline of staple industries in areas of early industrialization, shifted the balance of attraction towards the South-East and, to some extent, the West and East Midlands in which many of the newer industries were developing most rapidly. Moreover, as the rural reservoir drained, the emphasis shifted from mainly short-range rural-urban movements to inter-regional movements of population, much of it urban-urban in character and including longer-distance migrations.

In 1851, while half the population of England and Wales still lived in rural areas, only one-fifth was dependent on agriculture. The considerable increases in population since 1801 (Fig. 12.5), both in areas of early industrialization and in newer industrial regions such as the North-East and South Wales coalfields, are reflected in the marked extension of areas of high population density (Fig. 12.4). In the later nineteenth century, however, out-migration reduced rural populations and there were widespread areas of decline. By 1911, only 21 per cent of the population was rural and a mere 8 per cent worked on the land: much rural industry which, up to mid-century, had given diversity to the countryside, had been lost to the towns.

Of the four-fifths who were town dwellers, a high proportion was crammed into large cities and rapidly expanding conurbations. The areas of most rapid increase, 1851–1911 (Fig. 12.5), were often peripheral to the regions of earliest industrial growth, many of which had passed their climax and were losing population to newer industrial areas. The resultant pattern of population distribution (Fig. 12.4) is more complex and reflects varying regional responses both to industrial change and to the emergence of a more diversified economy in which building, transport and services of all kinds were growing more rapidly than manufacturing. Many of the features associated with the economic and population trends of the twentieth century were already present from the 1880s. The pull of the coalfields was giving way to the attraction of the ports and the major urban markets; while greater regional concentration of industry and a shift to larger production units continued to shift the centre of gravity of

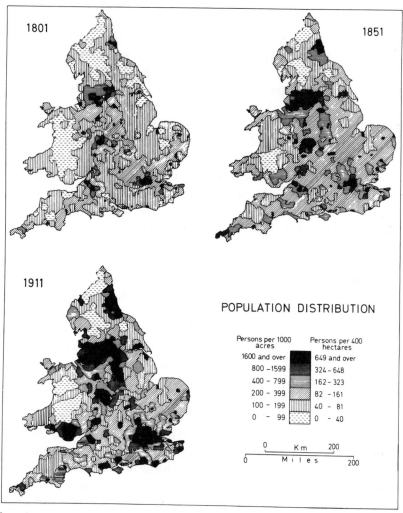

Fig. 12.4. Population distribution in England and Wales, 1801, 1851 and 1911. The density of population is shown for registration districts. Based upon the *Census of Great Britain*, 1851 and the *Census of England and Wales*, 1911.

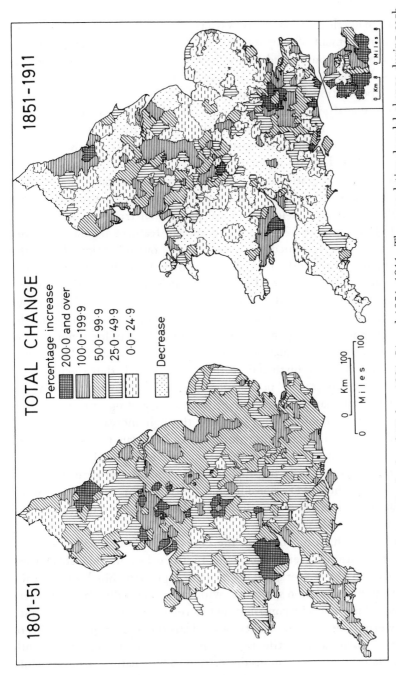

Fig. 12.5. Population change, England and Wales, 1801–51 and 1851–1911. The cumulative decadal change during each period is shown for registration districts. The inset map is of districts in London, 1851–1911, which is shown as a single unit, the registration county, in the national map. Based upon the *Census of Great Britain*, 1851 and the decennial *Census of England and Wales*, 1861 - 1911.

population north and west, there was a reversal of internal migration and a growing movement of people to the midlands and south which added to the accelerating countrywide movement to Greater London: so began 'the drift to the south-east' which has been such a marked feature of recent regional population trends in Britain. [76]

Regional analysis of natural and migrational components of population change becomes more secure from the 1840s with the more detailed censuses from 1841 and civil registration of vital events from 1837, though births continued to be under-registered until mid-Victorian times. [77] Estimates of net migration can be made from a comparison of vital changes from registration data with census figures of total change, so that it is possible to analyse regional and intra-regional population trends in some detail from 1841 (Figs 12.4–12.6). [78] The dominant features are those of rapid urbanization accompanied by large scale out-migration from the countryside. Whereas the rural areas lost over 4·5 million people by net migration between 1841 and 1911, absorbing 85 per cent of their natural increment, the towns and 'colliery districts' gained 3·3 million, about one-sixth of their total increase. Fluctuations in migration differentials, over time and from region to region, account largely for temporal and spatial variations in population trends in the period since 1831. Though regional variations in birth and death rates persisted, they seem to have been less significant in producing differential growth than in the eighteenth and early nineteenth centuries suggesting that population responded to economic forces mainly through increased mobility. [79] Natural changes in population during the Victorian period fluctuated much less than migrational, both nationally and regionally. Urban and industrial areas generally had higher rates of natural growth than rural areas, though there were considerable contrasts, for example, between the high natural increase in coalmining and heavy industrial areas and the low rates in textile areas.

Despite the high mortality in the cities, which did not begin to fall nearer the national average until the 1880s, urban and industrial areas generally had above-average rates of natural growth. Much of this they owed to their population structure, with migration adding large numbers of young adults, thereby contributing to a relatively high crude birth-rate and lowering the crude mortality rates. Thus the high migration gains of the large towns and textile regions in the early and mid-nineteenth century later gave a built-in predisposition to high natural growth, while heavy in-migration to the coalfields from the mid-nineteenth century onwards provided the basis for the large families and high natural growth of the end of the century.

The level of births remained relatively high in rural areas until well into the nineteenth century. Nevertheless prolonged outflow of young men and women, the potential parents of the next generation, reduced the growth, despite relatively low mortality, so that there was a sharp downturn in natural increase in rural areas after 1891. Rural births peaked in the south of the country in the 1860s and in northern areas in the 1870s. By the early twentieth century rural birth-rates were 30 per cent below their nineteenth-century peak and an ageing rural population had little potential for natural growth;[80] the draining of the rural reservoir was reflected in reduced levels of out-migration.

The vital experience in the urban and industrial areas varied considerably, not least within individual regions. The major cities were areas of relatively high natural growth, though an above-average birth-rate was offset by relatively high mortality until after 1900. London, however, had below-average birth-rates until the period 1901–10, again with slightly above-average mortality. Moreover, within the cities there were marked contrasts: in the inner areas, because of high mortality, often relatively low fertility and persistent out-migration, population declined rapidly after the mid-century; the suburbs on the other hand gained by in-movement of young people, by birth rates being relatively high and mortality moderate to low. Similar contrasts exist between 'residential' districts and poorer-class areas of the industrial regions but require detailed analysis of the contrasts in the components of population change which vary much more widely than suggested by Table 12.3. The textile areas showed considerable evidence of demographic decline by the late nineteenth century. Not only did they generally lose population by migration, but birth rates declined from the 1880s to a figure well below the national average. In contrast, despite relatively high mortality rates, colliery districts maintained a strong late nineteenth-century growth largely from a high natural increase, in turn the produce of high fertility, relatively early marriages and large families.[81]

Table 12.4 underlines the extent of the slackening in the rate of increase and the considerable scale of net out-migration from the rural areas. Such movements were large and sustained, though they fluctuated from decade to decade depending largely on the power of urban labour markets to absorb this largely unskilled labour. In aggregate they led to massive concentration of population into a relatively few areas. Net migration

Table 12.4: Urban and rural populations in England and Wales, 1801–1911.

	TOTAL		RESIDUAL			URBAN			Per cent of total in towns of			
	Million	Per cent change	Million	Per cent change	Per cent of total	Million	Per cent change	Per cent of total	<10,000	10–50,000	50–100,000	>100,000
1801	8·9		5·9		66·2	3·0		33·8	9·9	9·5	3·5	11·0
1811	10·2	14·0	6·4	9·5	63·4	3·7	23·7	36·6	10·8	8·4	3·7	13·7
1821	12·0	18·1	7·2	11·7	60·0	4·8	29·1	40·0	11·0	9·2	4·3	15·6
1831	13·9	15·8	7·7	7·8	55·7	6·2	28·0	44·3	10·6	11·1	4·0	18·6
1841	15·9	14·3	8·2	6·2	51·7	7·7	25·0	48·3	10·0	12·1	5·5	20·7
1851	17·9	12·6	8·2	1·4	46·0	9·7	25·9	54·0	9·9	13·4	5·8	24·8
1861	20·1	11·9	8·3	0·5	41·3	11·8	21·6	58·7	9·8	14·1	6·1	28·8
1871	22·7	13·2	7·9	−4·5	34·8	14·8	25·6	65·2	10·8	16·2	5·6	32·6
1881	25·9	14·7	7·8	−1·5	30·0	18·2	22·8	70·0	10·5	16·0	7·3	36·2
1891	29·0	11·6	7·4	−5·0	25·5	21·6	18·8	74·5	10·2	16·2	8·6	39·4
1901	32·5	12·2	7·2	−3·3	22·0	25·4	17·5	78·0	8·9	18·0	7·4	43·6
1911	36·1	10·9	7·6	6·2	21·1	28·5	12·2	78·9	8·8	18·3	8·0	43·8

Based on Law, 'The growth of urban population', (1967), Tables V, VI and XI. The urban category is based on three criteria: minimum size, density and degree of nucleation. Hence the 'residual' category is not confined to purely agricultural rural areas. Estimates of the truly rural vary, some arguing that it was as low as one-third in 1841 and one-eighth by 1911: for a summary see Lawton, 'Rural depopulation in nineteenth-century England' (1967).[92]

accounted for over one-sixth of the population increase of 15·1 million in the urban areas of England and Wales between 1841 and 1911: migration to London contributed one-quarter of its total increase, and there were similar proportions in the large northern towns. Yet fluctuations in prosperity in industrial areas tended to off-set phases of high migrational gain, so that while 160 registration districts (about 26 per cent of the total) gained by migration over the period 1851–1911, in only 53 districts was there migration gain in every decade. Areas of migrational gain throughout 1851–1911 were confined principally to London and the South-East, the North-West and Yorkshire, parts of the North-East and South Wales coalfields and the West and East Midlands industrial areas (Fig. 12.6).

Within such areas, cycles of population change are reflected in fluctuations in growth rates and, particularly, in changes in net migration. In phases of expansion, developing regions drew a considerable proportion of their labour force from other areas. After the initial in-migration population growth was often self-sustaining, though if economic growth slackened, attraction for migrants diminished and labour moved to other areas. Thus, in the 1890s and 1900s many northern industrial areas, particularly the textile towns, lost population to London and the south. Hence, the relative contribution to total population growth made over the period 1841–1911 differs considerably from one type of area to another: it was considerable in London and the larger towns; very marked in the residential towns; persistent, but not pronounced, in the colliery districts; and limited and, after 1881, negative in the industrial towns. Brinley Thomas has argued that migration is a sensitive index of British economic conditions, in particular as measured by building fluctuations, which are in turn inversely related to those of the United States. [82] When growth was strong in Britain, levels of internal migration were high (as in the decades 1861–70, 1871–80 and 1890–1901) but when growth was weak in Britain, external migration increased particularly to North America, as in the decades 1881–90 and 1901–10. Moreover, by the late nineteenth century a great deal of population movement was intra-regional (especially intra-urban) rather than inter-regional.

Thus, while differential natural growth to some extent helps to account for regional differences in population change, the major determinant of fluctuations in the rate of change was migration. In a period when individual economic necessity often compelled movement, migration trends may be seen as one of the best indicators of long-term shifts in

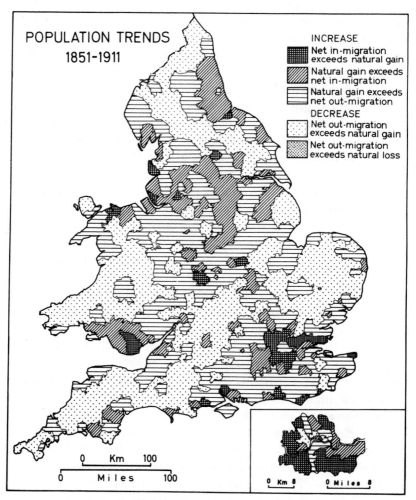

Fig. 12.6. Population trends in England and Wales, 1851–1911. The relationship between natural and migrational components of change is shown for registration districts and is comparable with similar maps for counties included in Figs 12.1–12.3. Based upon the decennial *Census of England and Wales*, 1861–1911.

regional economic growth. As their growth rate slackened, many older industrial and coalfield areas lost population by migration. Such areas (e.g. south-west Durham, the Black Country, parts of east Lancashire and west Yorkshire, and the northern fringes of the South Wales coalfield) show migration gain followed by loss or a fluctuating migration trend. In contrast, within south-east England, the East Midlands and the Birmingham areas there is a greater tendency for migrational gain in the late nineteenth century to follow earlier losses. A summary of natural and migrational components of change in the period 1851–1911 (Fig. 12.6) indicates that in most areas (three-quarters of all registration districts) natural gain was coupled with migrational loss. Areas of migrational loss exceeding natural gain may be equated with severe rural depopulation, as in rural lowland England, the South-West and Wales. Natural gain exceeded migrational loss in 41 per cent of all districts, many of which avoided the worst effects of out-migration because of proximity to towns and which, especially in the late nineteenth century, were affected by suburban growth. In only 20 per cent of registration districts was there both natural and migrational gain over the period as a whole, principally in the major conurbations of the late nineteenth century (London, South Wales, the West Midlands, Merseyside, Greater Manchester, west Yorkshire and north-east England), together with the major cities of the East Midlands. Elsewhere the picture is more confused, the concentration of high natural growth and migrational gain in each of the major urban regions as a whole being masked to some extent by complex short-distance migration within them.

Net migration conceals a complex ebb and flow of population movement which, in the absence of population registers recording migration, must be studied from census birthplace tables. These only summarize 'lifetime migration'—usually for geographical counties—at each census from 1851, though there are some more rudimentary data in the 1841 census tabulations. Such birthplace data can be manipulated to yield a certain amount of information on migration flows, [83] while age and sex tables, available from 1841, may be used to estimate the effects of movement on the population structure and composition of both sender and receiver areas.

In 1885 Ravenstein drew attention to a complex pattern of internal migration, mainly based on short-range movements, from rural areas of dispersion to urban and industrial areas of population absorption. [84] By 1861 most rural counties had lost over 20 per cent of their native-born population and in Wales and the rural midlands the proportion was as much as 30–40 per cent. By 1911 it was not uncommon for such counties or those in the South-East affected by the suburbanization of London to have lost over 50 per cent of their natives. In contrast, these migrants were attracted to a relatively few targets. For example, in 1861, in London, the South Wales and Durham coalfields, the West Midlands and Cheshire, over 30 per cent of the population were born outside the county of residence, while the towns often had much higher proportions of non-natives. By 1911 in much of south-east England over 40 per cent were non-natives and in nearly all the towns of the Greater London area the proportion was over 50 per cent. By recalculating those birthplace statistics, to allow for the effect between censuses of death and remigration of people living outside their native county, Friedlander and Roshier have been able to estimate new migration for each decade between 1851 and 1911.[85] Disregarding movements between adjacent counties, their analysis shows that up to the First World War the areas of persistent loss were in rural Wales, northern England, the South-West, East Anglia and, perhaps surprisingly, Staffordshire. The main areas of gain were Greater London and South Wales (especially Glamorgan). Those that initially gained then lost from the late nineteenth century included Lancashire, Yorkshire and Durham. The counties around London tended to lose in the mid-nineteenth century to the capital but by the end of the century were gaining by overflow from the capital and by direct movement from all other regions of Britain.

One final but important aspect of migration is its influence on population structure and vital trends in both sender and receiver areas. There is little direct information from birthplace statistics, though the break-down by age of persons born and enumerated in selected counties in 1911 indicates that lifetime migrants generally exceeded the proportion of the total adult population under 35 years. Contemporaries were in no doubt that Victorian migration was to a considerable degree age- and, sometimes, sex-selective. Ravenstein noted that 'females are more migratory than males'.[86] Welton's analysis of the estimated net migration gain or loss by age groups,[87] for the areas listed in Table 12.3, showed that in 1881–1900 towns made considerable gains in the 15–35 groups and the over 65 groups; in the 'old towns' the gains were mainly of young females (no doubt for domestic service) and older ages of both sexes. In the colliery and heavy industrial districts the largest 'gains' were of men under 35 and of women between 25 and 40. In residential towns the age-migration gain among men was in the over-35 groups but among women in most age groups with an emphasis on ages 15–25 and over 40. In rural areas there was a loss in nearly all age groups except the 70–75, but especially of men aged 15–30 and of women up to the age of 50. [88] Thomas's analysis of a number of urban areas, 1871–1900, reveals the declining attraction of many older industrial regions for the younger adult population (aged 20–44). [89] Within the rapidly expanding urban regions of the mid- and later nineteenth century, migrants to inner city areas tended to be dominated by single persons among the younger age groups. Family migration towards the surburbs often occurred after marriage and at distinctive stages in the family cycle, creating different demographic structures within the urban region which, by the later nineteenth century, were made more distinctive as longer journeys to work developed. [90]

Rural and Urban Society

One crucial aspect of differential population growth was the movement of labour from rural to urban areas throughout Britain. The growing concentration of industrial employment, the greater mobility permitted by the railways and the relative decline of employment in the countryside led to a reduction in the rate of population increase in agricultural areas from the 1830s. [91] From the 1840s, net out-migration became general leading to a general decrease in population after 1851, a fall arrested only in the early 1900s and then only in areas affected by residential growth around the cities. The reasons for those losses, though complex, were basically economic: the decline of employment in agriculture, especially for farm labourers, the loss of craft industries to urban factories and workshops, and the increasing accessibility of the big towns all pushed people from the countryside, while higher wages and more varied job opportunities pulled them towards the towns. [92]

Rural out-migration was severe and sustained throughout the period of 1841–1911, though it fluctuated in intensity from decade to decade. By the 1850s, there were few places in England more than ten miles from a railway station and most parts of the country had contact with large towns. Though most rural migrants went only a short distance at any stage of movement, the currents of migration engendered were directed toward the populous areas and the new industrial and urban centres. As local population declined, small market towns lost business and, by the late nineteenth century, their decay was hastened by improved accessibility to large towns.

Heavy population losses resulting from the fall in demand for agricultural labour were experienced in all types of farming, arable and stock alike, and on all but the highest quality cash crop soils.[93] Initially caused by replacement of seasonal labour by machinery, this was accentuated by agricultural depression from the 1870s, especially in the arable districts.[94] Only in those rural areas close to growing towns or industrial regions were losses from land offset by a growth of an adventitious population not dependent upon primary activities.[95]

Urban Growth

In 1831, 44·3 per cent—6·15 million of the total population of 13·9 million—was urban (Table 12.4).[96] London was by modern standards a great city of 1·78 million[97] but there were five other cities of over 100,000—Manchester-Salford (235,000), Liverpool (210,000), Birmingham (144,000), Leeds (123,000) and Bristol (104,000).[98] By 1851 just over half the population were town dwellers, London a giant of 2·5 million and a number of provincial cities exceeding one-quarter of a million. In 1911, even at a conservative estimate 80 per cent of England and Wales' 36 million people were urban and probably nine-tenths depended on towns for a living. Over half the urban population—15·8 out of 28·5 million—was in 36 large towns of over 100,000 headed by London with 7·25 million within the conurbation.[99]

Towns of various types and sizes varied in their rates of growth during the nineteenth century (Table 12.4 and Chapter 13, pp. 373–84). The sheer volume of growth brought people to the towns from near and far, shaped their future growth and moulded the character and composition of the new society of Victorian times. Of the 27 million added to the population of England and Wales, 1801—1911, 94 per cent (25·5 million) was absorbed by towns. The differential growth between urban and rural populations became marked from the 1830s: rural areas added only 13 per cent to their population between 1841 and 1911, but the urban dwellers nearly trebled (+ 182 per cent) (Table 12.3). Nearly one-third of the urban gain was from net migration,[100] much of it of young people with high fertility potential so that natural increase quickly came to dominate urban growth rates: thus in London, the biggest attraction for migrants, three-quarters of the total increase, 1841–1911, was from natural growth.

Though inter- and intra-urban variations in fertility exist, particularly where birth rates were affected by differences in migration experience, the major factor in differential natural growth until the late nineteenth century was mortality. For most of the century natural increase was restrained by high mortality, especially in the large industrial cities (Table 12.IB). Poverty, bad water supply and sanitation and poor housing are reflected in the contrasts between 'Healthy Districts', where the average expectation of life at birth in the 1880s was 51·5 years as compared with 43·7 in England and Wales, and the 'Poor Districts' (e.g. Manchester, where life expectation was only 28·8 years).[101] This gap, which did not begin to narrow until the 1880s, was pronounced at all ages and in both sexes ranging from a ratio of 134 to 74 (England and Wales = 100) for males aged 0–4 between Manchester and the healthiest areas, to 124 to 90 for men aged 15–24 (the most favourable comparison for towns) but deteriorating to 153 as against 78 in ages 55–64.[102]

Infant mortality was particularly bad in the poor districts of the large cities, a class disparity which may have worsened between the early 1800s and the 1840s when 'a quarter of all children died before their fifth birthday'.[103] In the 1890s infant mortality was as high as in the 1860s (Table 12.IB) and mortality in industrial towns was markedly worse than in rural counties at all stages during the first year of life.[104]

Such marked contrasts have been ascribed primarily to neglect and infection. The latter was principally related to poverty and poor environment, particularly bad water supply, sanitation and housing. Conditions improved with better public health from the 1870s and improvements in housing in the later nineteenth century but also with better nutrition as standards of living rose in the late nineteenth and early twentieth centuries.[105] In medical terms, McKeown has argued that, around 1840, 'a large majority of infectious deaths were due to . . . tuberculosis, scarlet fever, diphtheria and the intestinal infections'.[106] These, together with epidemics of cholera, typhoid and typhus which periodically raised mortality in the poor areas of large cities to crisis proportions in the 1830s to 1860s, were the main causes of the marked rural-urban and, within cities, of poor area-rich area mortality differentials which were such a feature of the Victorian period. The improvement in mortality in the later nineteenth century has been largely ascribed by McKeown to a reduction in airborne diseases, especially following housing improvement, and in water- and food-borne disease, due mainly to better sanitation and hygiene, not least the improved quality of milk supply from the turn of the century.[107]

Within Victorian cities, mortality experience varied widely and directly reflected environment, housing quality and social status. In a pioneer study of York, Armstrong has shown marked contrasts in mortality in the 1840s, which he ascribes mainly to environmental conditions, especially drainage.[108] However, both in the city centre and the suburbs, the highest social classes were longer-lived and less susceptible to epidemic and contagious diseases: whereas the mean age of death in 1844 ranged between 35·3 and 22·6 years in the 'best' and 'worst' parishes in York, it was 49·2 and 20·7 years for gentry/professional people and for artisans, respectively, with little difference between city and suburb. Such contrasts were more marked in the large industrial cities. In London in 1886–9, the general death rate was 19·6 per 1000 and infant mortality 188 per 1000: the poor districts of the East End had rates of 25·6 and 175 respectively, but working-class people housed by the Peabody Trust were below the *general* mortality levels at 18·6 and 141 respectively.[109] Similarly, Woods has shown that in Birmingham, a city with a good health record and near to the national death rate in the 1880s, there were marked internal differences in mortality from such diseases as measles, scarlet fever and typhoid.[110] Such contrasts echo the intra-urban contrasts in the impact of cholera and typhoid epidemics of the mid-nineteenth century (see above, p. 349)[111] and support the view that sanitary reform and, especially, improved living standards did most to lower mortality in the late nineteenth century.[112]

Towns depended both for much of their short-term growth and their long-term potential for natural increase on migrants and, though less dominant than in the cities of the United States,[113] the new town-dwellers were sufficiently numerous and distinctive to create immigrant 'colonies' in all the large cities of Victorian England. Most movement to cities was short-range, described by Ravenstein in 1885 as 'a uniform shifting and displacement of the population, which produces "currents of migration" setting in the direction of the great centres of commerce and industry'.[114] In aggregate, such migration had many features of a simple gravity model. Movement to each centre of attraction decreased in inverse proportion to distance, though where there were few intervening opportunities or where, as in large cities, social and economic attractions to migrants were great, the migration hinterland widened and long-distance movements were accentuated.

Most labour recruited by nineteenth-century cities was unskilled and largely drawn from the immediate rural hinterland though in certain cases, as with the Irish in both the pre- and post-famine period, powerful 'push' forces in the home area caused massive long-distance movements.[115] Specialist skilled workers and professional people often moved farther and more directly to new jobs. Thus, the general pattern of migration into the West Midlands was dominated by short-distance migration but the range and intensity of movements into Birmingham and the Black Country towns was much greater up to 1861 and birthplace origins much more varied.[116] Occupationally related migration often reflects expansion of trade, increased job opportunities and higher wages in receiving areas. Thus while the population of Saltley, an industrial suburb of Birmingham, was dominated in 1851 by those born in the city and adjacent areas of the West Midlands, the skilled workers of the relatively new railway carriage-building industry were recruited from coach-builders, wheelsmiths and the like born in towns throughout the British Isles.[117] Similarly, technological changes in glass-making in the mid-nineteenth century were reflected in considerable movement of skilled labour between glass-making centres: many migrants to St. Helens, Lancashire, whose glass-makers were expanding rapidly from the mid-1840s to 1861, came mainly from Tyneside and Clydeside with others from the West Midlands.[118] Occupationally related migration contributed substantially to skilled trades and the social characteristics of parts of mid-Victorian Merseyside. Many of the substantial Welsh community—over 20,000 between 1851 and 1871, forming 4 to 5 per cent of Liverpool's population—were builders or building workers who originated in the slate- or stone-quarrying areas of North Wales, or were in shipping or commerce, reflecting the considerable maritime links between Liverpool and small Welsh ports. Similar direct occupational links are evident in the Scots-born population of the city (some 4 per cent of the total in the mid-Victorian period): one cluster was mainly resident in north Liverpool and worked in metal manufacture and shipbuilding, and a second group of merchants and professional men lived in the high-status residential area to the south-east of the city centre (Fig. 12.7).[119]

Many of the characteristics of individual districts within nineteenth-century cities were shaped by the character of such migrant groups, not only their occupational status but age and sex structure and cultural characteristics. These were often reflected in patterns of residential segregation which were further shaped by social sifting in the process of intra-urban movement. Part of this process was the outcome of city growth, the development of new suburbs, and the internal movements of population consequent on this, and the decay of the centres of cities as

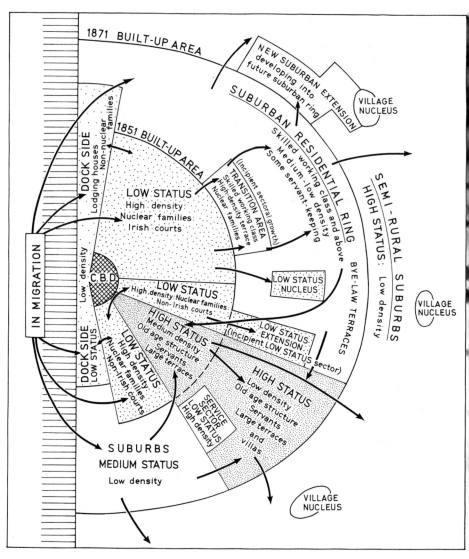

Fig. 12.7. The urban structure of mid-Victorian Liverpool. This schematic diagram, which is not to scale, attempts to summarize the main residential and social areas within Liverpool in 1871 and the associated processes of migration to the city and of residential mobility within it. The high-status sector south-east of the Central Business District should be noted and the contrasting working-class residential areas of the dock-side and the North End. Stages of growth may be seen in the sequence of suburban zones around the historic core, the CBD of 1871. Based on R. Lawton and C. G. Pooley, *The Social Geography of Merseyside in the Nineteenth Century*, (Liverpool, 1976), Fig. 26.

residential areas. This process is illustrated from Liverpool but is common to all nineteenth-century towns.

The inner areas of English cities began to lose population in early-Victorian times: for example, in Liverpool high mortality and relatively low fertility combined with movement from the centre to shift progressively outwards the areas of most rapid population increase. Though the development of mass transport systems did not come till the 1890s, except in London,[120] there was considerable growth of working-class, as well as middle-class suburbs from the 1860s creating successive residential belts of distinctive physical and social character wrapped around the older city—within which were individual sectors deriving much of their character from adjacent areas. While in favoured areas some middle-class residential sectors remained, many were swamped by the advancing tide in a classic process of invasion and succession.

The extent to which such differentiation, based on class consciousness, occupational clustering near to places of work, social stratification and demographic change—relating both to the family life-cycle and to movement to and within the city—produced a 'modern' pattern of social areas in the nineteenth-century city is still a subject of debate.[121] However, a growing number of studies of nineteenth-century cities show that residential, cultural and social contrasts within the city produced 'natural' or 'social' areas characterized by considerable homogeneity of population and socio-economic status.[122] Multivariate analyses based on census enumerators' books, rate books and information on housing and environment have indentified three principal sets of characteristics in such social areas: socio-economic status (based on occupation); family status (relating to age structure and to family and household composition); and ethnicity (derived from information on birthplace). Individual districts within cities were characterized not only by distinctive housing and environmental conditions but also by population characteristics relating to demographic, occupational and cultural features.

A key factor in shaping the character of such neighbourhoods was migration. In the case of mid-Victorian Liverpool over half the population was born outside the area and distinctive migrant groups, often strongly associated with particular occupations, dominated particular parts of the city. Many were Irish, part of the vast out-pouring of poor, unskilled labour which flocked to the industrial towns and seaports of Britain especially after the famine of the late-1840s. Between 1841 and 1851, when the numbers of Irish-born in Britain increased from 416,000 to

727,000, Liverpool's Irish-born population increased from 50,000 to 84,000 (over 24 per cent of the total population) and Ireland continued as the major supplier of unskilled labour until the First World War. In many of Liverpool's dockside working-class areas 40 per cent or more of all people were Irish by birth, and in some individual enumeration districts as many as 70 per cent or more of heads of household. By 1871 a residential pattern was emerging in Liverpool in which the Irish were principally concentrated in the North End and dock-side areas, areas of poor and overcrowded housing, low socio-economic status, high measures of social malaise and unskilled, casual labour. The Catholic, southern Irish mainly congregated in the poorest areas between the north docks and Scotland Road, while inland the Protestant, northern Irish overlapped the Welsh in the Everton area.

As previously noted (p. 351) the Welsh, though having a stronger cultural and linguistic sense of community, were residentially less segregated—as were also the Scots—than the Irish. One important factor in the contrasting residential pattern of these groups was their different socio-economic structure. The mainly semi- and unskilled Irish lived in the cheapest accommodation close to the main source of jobs on the docks.[123] The Welsh and Scots were over-represented in the skilled manual and non-manual groups in mid-Victorian Liverpool and, like many born in other regions of England, seem to have been occupationally selective migrants. For example, by 1871, many migrants to Liverpool from the West Midlands were engaged in metal dealing or manufacturing, whereas among those born in eastern and southern England professional, managerial and skilled non-manual jobs were relatively important.

By 1871, Liverpool had a clearly identifiable social structure with a distinctive spatial expression (Fig 12.7). High-status, merchant and professional class areas extended south-east from the city centre. Working-class communities dominated most of the inner residential areas, though there was a clear distinction between low-status, unskilled working-class disticts in the dock-side and 'North End' areas and a zone of mid-Victorian bye-law terraces shared between skilled working-class families[124] and clerks and small traders, many of whom aspired to lower middle-class status.[125]

The progressive spatial differentiation of communities in nineteenth-century cities involve not only housing and physical surroundings, patterns of job availability, and levels of social and cultural identity, but also individual perceptions of the urban environment. Together these underlie the process of intra-urban residential mobility which is focal to the development of social areas in the city. There have been relatively few studies of internal mobility in English cities, especially among the working classes, though these can be based on analysis of successive censuses, directories or rate books. In a study of Leicester, Pritchard noted frequent, short-range mobility both in the early industrial period to 1868 and between 1865 and 1914 when the contrast between working-class and middle-class areas was firmly established with the rapid expansion of housing and the development of more complex ideas on class and social status. [126] Dennis found that of the 58 per cent of his sample that persisted in Huddersfield between 1851 and 1861, about two-fifths moved within the town, mainly and often frequently over short distances. [127] In a study of Liverpool over two decades, only 18 per cent persisted for ten years at the same address out of 46 per cent who remained in the city (again around two-fifths). [128]

The factors which seem to be most important in intra-urban mobility are (as in American studies) [129] life-cycle stage, social status and home ownership. Mobility was greatest among young adults in the early stages of family building, while mobility decreased with age and was lowest among high-status families who owned their own home. Manual workers with low incomes, casual jobs with little security, and few possessions moved frequently from one rented property to another, usually over very short distances in the same area of the city. They dominated residential mobility in Liverpool where 70 per cent of moves were less than one mile and one-third under quarter of a mile. But if the higher-status professional and intermediate classes moved less often, they tended to move over longer distances, often to new suburbs.

The precise reasons for such mobility require personal information only rarely available from diaries [130] or through oral accounts [131] but such individual life histories are important to an understanding of mobility and the shaping of the internal structure of the city in the nineteenth century. The tendency for upward social mobility to be reflected in residential mobility, bringing together those who sought the higher-status areas, progressively led to the development of higher-status residential areas in most towns during the nineteenth century. Within the mass of working-class housing areas there was equally differentiation based on housing quality, the occupational and social background of the inhabitants and cultural factors such as religion, regional or ethnic origin and, sometimes, language.

Mobility, both inter-regional and within the city, was thus a key factor in the social and spatial transformation of nineteenth-century populations in England and Wales. Within a lifetime the same individual could be a migrant several times over: as an itinerant worker; on moving from a rural to an urban area, usually involving a change of job; as an inter-urban migrant to a larger city with perhaps greater job opportunities; then in a series of short-distance movements within the city of his final choice perhaps occasioned by changes in job, or family status or changing economic fortunes. Clearly the aggregate of such individual decisions produces flows of people to and within the city which shape its changing social character: areas of instability, such as decaying city centres, will change rapidly as transients pass through it to more established housing areas; working-class residential areas may change slowly as newcomers are absorbed, both from other regions and by movement from the city centre or within the immediate neighbourhood, though such stability in character is accompanied by very high turnover of population; middle-class residential areas near to the city often persist throughout the nineteenth century but, where invaded or surrounded by working-class areas, may collapse and give way to rapid deterioration in social status accompanied by multiple occupation while new high-status suburbs further out in the same sector of the city or on the semi-rural periphery receive those displaced. Thus the social structuring within a city reflects processes of internal population change (see Fig. 12.7 for a schematic representation of these processes in mid-Victorian Liverpool). It is appropriate, in a chapter in which the main emphasis has been on the general characteristics of population at a regional level—the resultants of processes of change—that we should end with the individual: for an understanding of individual decisions and actions is crucial to an understanding of the transitions outlined at the outset of this chapter which involve the fundamental processes of change in population and society experienced during the eighteenth and nineteenth centuries.

References

1. For general accounts see P. Mathias, *The First Industrial Nation: An Economic History of Britain, 1700–1914*, (London, 1969) and Phyllis Deane, *The First Industrial Revolution*, (Cambridge, 1965).
2. A. R. de Souza and P. W. Porter, *The Underdevelopment and Modernization of*

the Third World, Commission on College Geography, Resource Paper 28, Association of American Geographers, (Washington D.C., 1974).

3. An excellent general summary is given by M. W. Flinn, *British Population Growth, 1700–1850*, (London, 1970).

4. These national changes are reviewed by Rosalind Mitchison, *British Population Change since 1860*, (London, 1977).

5. T. McKeown, *Modern Rise of Population*, (London, 1976) ascribes the main changes in natural growth to reduced mortality. For an alternative view, indicating the possible significance of an upward trend in births in the late eighteenth and early nineteenth centuries see J. T. Krause, 'Changes in English fertility and mortality, 1781–1850', *Economic History Review*, 2nd ser., **XI** (1958), pp. 52–70.

6. For a detailed examination of this question see M. Blaug, 'The Poor Law Report re-examined', *Journal of Economic History*, **XXIV** (1964), pp. 229–45 and for a detailed case study see J. P. Huzel, 'Malthus, the Poor Law, and population in early nineteenth-century England' *Economic History Review*, 2nd ser., **XXII** (1969) pp. 430–52.

7. See J. D. Chambers, 'The Vale of Trent, 1670–1800: a regional review of economic change', *Economic History Review*, Supplement No. 3 (London, 1957) for an example of the impact of early industrial development on family size. The wider context is given in his *Population, Economy and Society in Pre-industrial England*, (London, 1972).

8. H. J. Habakkuk, *Population Growth and Economic Development since 1750*, (Leicester, 1971).

9. S. E. Finer, *The Life and Times of Sir Edwin Chadwick*, (London, 1952) outlines the background to and developments in public health in the early- and mid-Victorian period.

10. J. A. and Olive L. Banks, *Feminism and Family Planning in Victorian England*, (Liverpool, 1964).

11. W. V. Hole and M. J. Pountney, *Trends in Population, Housing and Occupancy Rates*, (H.M.S.O. London, 1971), pp. 13–19.

12. For a general review see P. Laslett, 'Size and structure of the household in England over three centuries' *Population Studies*, **XXIII** (1969), pp. 199–223. An approach to the study of household and family in one region in the late nineteenth century is M. Anderson, *Family Structure in Nineteenth-century Lancashire*, (Cambridge, 1971).

13. B. Thomas, *Migration and Economic Growth: a study of Great Britain and the Atlantic Economy*, (Cambridge, 1954), and *Migration and Urban Development*, (London, 1972), especially Chapter 2.

14. J. Erickson, 'Who were the English and Scots immigrants to the United States in the late-nineteenth century', in D. V. Glass and R. Revelle (eds.), *Population and Social Change*, (London, 1972), pp. 347–81.

15. D. C. Marsh, *The Changing Social Structure of England and Wales, 1871–1961*, (Revised edn., London, 1965).

16. This point has been stressed by D. Friedlander, 'Demographic responses and population change', *Demography*, **6** (1969), pp. 359–81.

17. W. Zelinsky, 'The hypothesis of the Mobility Transition', *Geographical Review*, **61** (1971), pp. 219–49; five stages were outlined in such a transition.

18. J. Saville, *Rural Depopulation in England and Wales, 1851–1951*, (London, 1957).

19. For an authoritative review see D. V. Glass, 'A note on under-registrations of births in Britain in the nineteenth century', *Population Studies, V* (1951–2), pp. 70–88. More recently this has been discussed by J. T. Krause, 'The changing adequacy of English registration, 1690–1837', pp. 379–93 in D. V. Glass and D. E. C. Eversley (eds.), *Population in History, Essays in Historical Demography*, (London, 1965), and M. S. Teitelbaum, 'Birth under-registration in the constituent counties of England and Wales: 1841–1910' *Population Studies*, **28** (1974), pp. 329–43.

20. The classic study is E. G. Ravenstein, 'The laws of migration', *Journal of the Statistical Society*, **XLVIII** (1885), pp. 167–235.

21. See D. Friedlander and F. J. Roshier, 'A study of internal migration in England and Wales. Part I', *Population Studies*, **XIX** (1966), pp. 239–79. Methods of calculation of nineteenth-century internal migration are discussed by D. E. Baines in 'The use of published census data in migration studies', pp. 311–35 in E. A. Wrigley (ed.), *Nineteenth Century Society*, (Cambridge, 1972).

22. G. T. Griffith, *Population Problems of the Age of Malthus*, (Cambridge, 1926).

23. E. C. K. Gonner, 'The population of England in the eighteenth century', *Journal of the Royal Statistical Society, * **LXXVI** (1913), pp. 261–96. A more recent study is H. J. Habakkuk, 'English population in the eighteenth century', *Economic History Review*, 2nd ser., **VI** (1953), pp. 269–84.

24. W. W. Rostow, *The Process of Economic Growth*, (Oxford, 1960).

25. D. V. Glass, 'Population and Population Movements in England and Wales, 1700 to 1850', in Glass and Eversley, *Population in History*, pp. 221–46.

26. Phyllis Deane and W. A. Cole, *British Economic Growth, 1688–1959* (2nd edn.) (Cambridge, 1969): Chapter 3 is a concise and careful review of population changes in England and Wales in the eighteenth and early nineteenth centuries. For a critique of their estimates see L. Neal, 'Deane and Cole on industrialization and population change in the eighteenth century', *Economic History Review*, 2nd ser., **XXIV**, pp. 643–7.

27. The question of the effect of the type of parish on population trends is discussed by D. R. Mills, 'The Poor Laws and the distribution of population, *c.* 1600–1860 with special reference to Lincolnshire',

Transactions, Institute of British Geographers, **26** (1959), pp. 185–95. For a case study see B. A. Holderness, ' "Open" and "Close" ' parishes in England in the eighteenth and nineteenth centuries', *Agricultural History Review,* **20** (1972), pp. 126–39.

28. Such listings are discussed by P. Laslett, *The World we have lost*, (London, 1965). For a case study see N. Tranter, 'Population and social structure in a Bedfordshire parish: the Cardington Listings of Inhabitants, 1782', *Population Studies,* **XXI** (1967), pp. 261–82.

29. An early study of marriage migration is by A. Constant, 'The geographical background of inter village population movements in Northamptonshire and Huntingdonshire, 1754–1943', *Geography,* **XXXIII** (1948), pp. 78–88. Current work on the Welsh Border is reported by W. J. Edwards in *Local Population Studies,* **17** (1976), pp. 25–41 and **19** (1977), pp. 23–7.

30. See, for example, E. J. Buckatzsch, 'Places of origin of a group of immigrants into Sheffield, 1624–1799', *Economic History Review*, 2nd ser., **II** (1950), pp. 303–6.

31. An interesting case study is H. A. Randall, 'Some aspects of population geography in certain rural areas of England during the eighteenth and early nineteenth centuries', unpublised Ph.D. thesis, University of Newcastle upon Tyne, (1971).

32. Further studies of Poor Law Records and Parish registers are needed to supplement the literary evidence. Randall, 'Some aspects of population geography', has shown movement of textile workers over considerable distances to Kettering (Northants) in the late eighteenth century, and J. Langton, *Geographical Change in the Industrial Revolution: the South-West Lancashire Mining Industry, 1590–1799*, (Cambridge, 1978), has indicated a good deal of migration of colliers into and within the Lancashire coalfield in the seventeenth and eighteenth centuries, while B. Trinder, *The Industrial Revolution in Shropshire*, (London, 1973), discusses migration to an early centre of the metallurgical industry. For a general review see P. Spufford, 'Population mobility in pre-industrial England', *Genealogists Magazine,* **17** (1973), pp. 420–9; 475–81; and 537–43.

33. It is difficult to give exact figures for London's population in the eighteenth century. M. Dorothy George, *London Life in the Eighteenth Century,* (London, 1925), following the contemporary estimates of Dr Price (1779) gives the total for the Metropolis (the area covered by the Bills of Mortality together with five out-parishes) as 674,350 in 1700 and 676,250 (George, *London Life,,* p. 329). In a recent review G. Rudé, *Hanoverian London 1714–1808*, (London, 1971), follows E. A. Wrigley, 'A simple model of London's importance in changing English economy and society, 1650–1750', *Past and Present,* **37** (1967), pp. 44–70, in estimating the population of the area as 575,000 in 1700, 675,000 in 1750 and 900,000 in 1800.

34. Deane and Cole, *British Economic Growth*, Table 25 (pp. 108–9) and p. 111.
35. George, *London Life*, p. 111. The great majority of London's 14,000 Roman Catholic households listed in the Returns of Papists of 1767 and 1789 were Irish, according to Rudé (*Hanoverian London*, p. 7), while many of the recent overseas immigrants were German and Polish Jews.
36. C. W. Chalklin, *The Provincial Towns of Georgian England. A Study of the Building Process 1740–1820*, (London, 1974), Chapters 1 and 2, reviews population trends from 1700 to 1820.
37. C. M. Law, 'The growth of urban population in England and Wales, 1801–1911', *Transactions, Institute of British Geographers*, **41** (1967), pp. 125–43.
38. C. M. Law, 'Local censuses in the eighteenth century', *Population Studies*, **23** (1969), pp. 87–100.
39. *Ibid.* See also T. A. Welton, 'On the distribution of population in England and Wales and its progress in the period of ninety years from 1801–1891', *Journal of the Royal Statistical Society*, **LXIII** (1900), pp. 527–89.
40. Deane and Cole, *British Economic Growth*, p. 113.
41. J. W. Watson and J. B. Sissons (eds.), *The British Isles. A Systematic Geography*, (London, 1964), Chapters 12 ('The Industrial Revolution') and 18 ('Population').
42. D. R. Mills (ed.), *English Rural Communities: The Impact of a Specialized Economy*, (London, 1973), especially Part Two: 'Specialisation in Industry'.
43. J. H. Clapham, *An Economic History of Modern Britain*: Vol. I *The Early Railway Age, 1820–1850*, (2nd edn.) (reprinted, Cambridge, 1967), p. 66.
44. D. Thomas, *Agriculture in Wales during the Napoleonic Wars. A Study in the Geographical Interpretation of Historical Sources*, (Cardiff, 1963).
45. For a case study see M. B. Gleave, 'Dispersed and nucleated settlement in the Yorkshire Wolds, 1770–1850', *Transactions, Institute of British Geographers*, **30** (1962), pp. 105–18.
46. Krause, 'The changing adequacy of English registration'.
47. George, *London Life*.
48 For a specific case study see Huzel, 'Malthus, the Poor Law, and population'. For the debate on the level of poor relief under this system see M. Blaug, 'The Myth of the Old Poor Law and the making of the new', *Journal of Economic History*, **XXIII** (1963), pp. 151–84, and for a recent case study, D. A. Baugh, 'The cost of Poor Relief in south-east England, 1790–1834', *Economic History Review*, 2nd ser., **XXVIII** (1975), pp. 50–68.
49. The Parish Register Abstracts were compiled by John Rickman who was in charge of the early censuses and whose county tabulations are the basis of the extensive recalculations of county populations, 1730–1830, by Deane and Cole, *British Economic Growth* on which Figs 12.1–12.3 are based. The

background is given in D. V. Glass, *Numbering the People. The Eighteenth-century Population Controversy and the Development of Cenus and Vital Statistics in Britain*, (Farnborough, 1973). The ongoing work on aggregative analysis and family reconstitution for individual parishes carried out in association with the Cambridge Group for the History of Population and Social Structure is summarized from time to time in *Local Population Studies 1968*, proceeding. See also Chapter 8, this volume.

50. Dean and Cole, *British Economic Growth*, Table 27, p. 118.

51. R. Lawton, 'Genesis of population', in W. Smith (ed.), *A Scientific Survey of Merseyside*, (Liverpool, 1953), pp. 120–31.

52. Deane and Cole, *British Economic Growth*, pp. 106–22, argue that the view of A. K. Cairncross that 'the north triumphed over the south mainly by superior fertility (and not . . . by attracting migrants)', *Home and Foreign Investment, 1870–1913*, (Cambridge, 1953), p. 79, is as true of the eighteenth and early nineteenth century as of the period from 1840.

53. A. Redford, *Labour Migration in England, 1800–1850*, (Manchester, 1926).

54. C. M. Law, 'The growth of urban population in England and Wales, 1801–1911', *Transactions, Institute of British Geographers*, **41** (1967), pp. 125–43.

55. B. T. Robson, *Urban Growth: An Approach,* (London, 1973), especially p. 30 and pp. 63–89.

56. Robson, *Urban Growth*, pp. 99–127 and Law, 'The growth of urban population', pp. 132–40.

57. See Chalklin, *Provincial Towns of Georgian England*, pp. 32–54 for a general description of late-Georgian urban expansion.

58. *Ibid*, p. 54.

59. Quoted by R. Lawton, 'Population movements in the West Midlands, 1841–1861', *Geography*, **XLII** (1958), p. 168.

60. See Redford, *Labour Migration in England*, for a full analysis using the Poor Law records. The social impact of the change from handicraft to factory industry is discussed by N. J. Smelser, *Social Change in the Industrial Revolution, an application of theory to the Lancashire Cotton Industry*, (London, 1959).

61. T. W. Freeman, *Pre-famine Ireland. A Study in Historical Geography*, (Manchester, 1957), pp. 37–46.

62. For a discussion of the society of late-Georgian Liverpool see I. C. Taylor, 'Black Spot on Mersey', unpublished Ph.D. thesis, University of Liverpool (1976), Chapter 1; for the development of churches see Janina Klapas, 'The religous geography of Victorian Liverpool', unpublished M.A. thesis, University of Liverpool, (1977).

63. H. C. Prince, 'England *c.* 1800', in H. C. Darby (ed.), *A New Historical Geography of England*, (Cambridge, 1973), Chapter 8, p. 394.

64. A full analysis of early nineteenth-century mortality awaits detailed study of

parish registers and bills of mortality for representative towns. The general position is reviewed in Flinn, *British Population Growth*.

65. R. P. Williams, 'On the increase of population in England and Wales', *Journal of the Royal Statistical Society*, **XLIII** (1880), pp. 462–96.

66. A. H. Johnson, *The Disappearance of the Small Landowner*, (London; 1909).

67. S. W. E. Vince, 'The rural population of England and Wales', 1801–1951', unpublished Ph.D. thesis, University of London, (1955).

68. B. A. Holderness, 'Open and Closed parishes in England in the eighteenth and nineteenth centuries', *Agricultural History Review*, **XX** (1972), pp. 126–39 and D. R. Mills (ed.), *English Rural Communities*.

69. E. C. K. Gonner, *Common Land and Inclosure*, (London, 1912).

70. J. A. Yelling, *Common Field and Enclosure in England 1450–1850*, (London, 1977), Chapter 11.

71. R. H. Osborne, 'A general view of the population changes in the middle Trent counties, 1801–1861', *East Midlands Geographer*, **5** (1970), pp. 39–51.

72. A recent regional study rejects the notion of 'associating imprudent marriage with Poor Law practice', J. M. Martin, 'Marriage and economic stress in the Felden of Warwickshire during the eighteenth century', *Population Studies*, **31** (1977), pp. 519–35.

73. W. Hasbach, *A History of the English Agricultural Labourer*, (Trans. by Ruth Kenyon) (London, 1908).

74. See Mills, *English Rural Communities*, Part Two; for case studies see R. Lawton, 'The economic geography of Craven in the early nineteenth century', *Transactions, Institute of British Geographers*, **20** (1954), pp. 93–111, and R. Hall, 'Occupation and population structure in part of the Derbyshire Peak District in the mid-nineteenth century', *East Midland Geographer*, **6** (1974), pp. 66–78.

75. F. Galton, 'The relative supplies from town and country families to the population of future generations', *Journal of the Statistical Society of London*, **XXXVI** (1873), pp. 19–26.

76. R. H. Osborne, 'Population' in Watson and Sissons, *The British Isles*, Chapter 18.

77. See Glass, 'A note on the under-registrations of births', (1951–2), and Teitelbaum, 'Birth under-registration', (1974).

78. For a review of spatial changes see R. Lawton, 'Population changes in England and Wales in the later nineteenth century: an analysis by Registration Districts', *Transactions, Institute of British Geographers*, **44** (1968), pp. 55–74.

79. Deane and Cole, *British Economic Growth*, p. 289, observe that by the nineteenth century 'the regional variations in birth and death rates were no longer so significant' and that national increase is of less significance in relation to 'economic growth than the changes in the rates of migration'.

80. A. K. Cairncross, *Home and Foreign Investment, 1870–1913*, (Cambridge, 1953) especially Chapter 4. The effect of rural depopulation on population structure is discussed by J. Saville, *Rural Depopulation in England and Wales, 1851–1951*, (London, 1957).

81. D. Friedlander, 'Demographic patterns and socio-economic characteristics of the coal mining population in England and Wales in the nineteenth century', *Economic Development and Cultural Change.*

82. Thomas, *Migration and Urban Development*, Chapter 2.

83. See D. E. Baines in Wrigley, *Nineteenth-Century Society*.

84. E. G. Ravenstein, 'The laws of migration', *Journal of the Statistical Society of London*, **XLVIII** (1885), pp. 167–227. For a review of his work see D. B. Grigg, 'E. G. Ravenstein and the "laws of migration"', *Journal of Historical Geography*, **3** (1977), pp. 41–54.

85. D. Friedlander and R. J. Roshier, 'A study of internal migration in England and Wales, Part I', *Population Studies*, **19** (1966), pp. 239–79.

86. Ravenstein, 'The laws of migration'.

87. T. A. Welton, *England's Recent Progress . . . in the twenty years from 1881 to 1901*, (London, 1911), Appendix B.

88. Saville, *Rural Depopulation*, discusses the impact of differential migration on the countryside, especially in producing a progressively ageing population.

89. Thomas, *Migration and Urban Development*, Chapter 2, Appendix B.

90. An increasing number of studies based on rate books, directories and the enumerators' books of the 1841–71 censuses illustrate aspects of intra-urban migration: for example see R. J. Dennis, 'Intercensal mobility in a Victorian city [Huddersfield]', *Transactions, Institute of British Geographers*, New Series, **2** (1977), pp. 349–63 and R. M. Pritchard, *Housing and the Spatial Structure of the City*, (Cambridge, 1976).

91. An additional factor, the easing of the Laws of Settlement by the Poor Law Amendment Act of 1834, has been held to be a substantial factor in increased rural mobility: for a recent critical case study see Anne Digby, 'The labour market and the continuity of social policy after 1834: the case of the eastern counties', *Economic History Review*, 2nd ser., **XXVIII** (1975), pp. 69–83.

92. There is a considerable literature on rural depopulation in Victorian Britain. For a general review see Saville, *Rural Depopulation*, and for a summary of its effects on society and regional population trends see R. Lawton, 'Rural depopulation in nineteenth-century England', in R. W. Steel and R. Lawton (eds.), *Liverpool Essays in Geography: A Jubilee Collection*, (London, 1967), pp. 227–55.

93. G. B. Longstaff, 'Rural depopulation', *Journal of the Royal Statistical Society*, **LVI** (1893), pp. 380–442.

94. E. J. T. Collins, 'Harvest technology and labour supply in Britain, 1790–1870', *Economic History Review*, 2nd ser., **XXII** (1969), pp. 453–73, notes that between the 1840s and 1870s harvest labour shortages became acute in many areas as migrant seasonal labour (especially Irish) declined— this was alleviated by technical improvement.

95. See Vince, 'Rural population of England and Wales'.

96. Law, 'The growth of urban population', Table V.

97. This is the figure for the area later incorporated in the London Administrative County.

98. These figures include some suburbs later incorporated into the city boundaries and are taken from B. R. Mitchell and Phyllis Deane, *Abstract of British Historical Statistics*, (Cambridge, 1962), Table 8.

99. J. T. Coppock, 'The changing face of England, 1850–c. 1900' in H. C. Darby (ed.), *A New Historical Geography of England*, (Cambridge, 1973), Chapter 11, p. 655.

100. Cairncross, *Home and Foreign Investment*.

101. Weber, *The Growth of Cities.*, p. 347. The mortality experience of these areas, designated by the Registrar General, is analysed by W. Farr, *Vital Statistics*, (London, 1885).

102. T. A. Welton, 'Local death-rates in England and Wales in the ten years 1881–90', *Journal of the Royal Statistical Society*, **LX** (1897), pp. 33–75.

103. Habakkuk, 'English population in the eighteenth century', p. 62.

104. In a study by the Registrar General, Preston, Leicester and Blackburn were compared with the rural counties of Hereford, Wiltshire and Dorset: at virtually all stages the towns' infant mortality as compared with the counties (= 100) was markedly worse, the ratio ranging from 164 to 95 at 0–6 days, 197 to 123 at 0–3 weeks and 275 to 127 at 0–11 months. Quoted by Weber, *The Growth of Cities*, pp. 363–4.

105. For a general discussion see R. Mitchison, *British Population Change since 1860*, (London, 1977).

106. T. McKeown, *The Modern Rise of Population*, (London, 1976), p. 15.

107. *Ibid*, Tables 3.1 and 3.2 show that these declined by 35 per cent, 1848–1901, as compared with a 22 per cent fall in deaths from all diseases, and that there was a particularly sharp fall in mortality from tuberculosis (by 56 per cent) and scarlet fever and diphtheria (by 60 per cent).

108. A. Armstrong, *Stability and Change in an English County Town. A Social Study of York 1801–51*, (Cambridge, 1974), especially Chapter 5.

109. Weber, *The Growth of Cities*, p. 352. For a fuller discussion of health in relation to housing in London see A. S. Wohl, *The Eternal Slum, Housing and social policy in Victorian London*, (London, 1977).

110. R. Woods, 'Mortality and sanitary conditions in the "best governed city in the world"—Birmingham 1870–1910', *Journal of Historical Geography*, **4** (1978), pp. 35–56.

111. E. W. Gilbert, 'Pioneer maps of health and disease in England', *Geographical Journal*, **CXXIV** (1958), pp. 172–83.
For a general review, see G. M. Howe, *Man, Environment and Disease in Britain, A Medical Geography through the Ages*, (Harmondsworth, 1976), Chapters 11 and 12.

112. *Ibid.*

113. For comparative studies see Weber, *The Growth of Cities*: the role of the migrant in U.S. cities is discussed by D. Ward, *Cities and Immigrants. A Geography of Change in Nineteenth-century America*, (London, 1971).

114. Ravenstein, 'The laws of migration', p. 198.

115. For general reviews see J. A. Jackson, *The Irish in Britain*, (London, 1963), and R. Lawton, 'Irish migration on to England and Wales in the mid-nineteenth century', *Irish Geography*, **4** (1959), pp. 35–54.

116. R. Lawton, 'Population movements in the West Midlands, 1841–1861', *Geography*, **42** (1958), pp. 164–77.

117. R. Lawton, 'An age of great cities', *Town Planning Review*, **43** (1972), pp. 199–224, especially Figs 5 and 6.

118. I am indebted to Dr J. T. Jackson for this information: for details see his 'Migrant glass workers to St. Helens in the nineteenth century', (in preparation.)

119. C. G. Pooley, 'The residential segregation of migrant communities in mid-Victorian Liverpool', *Transactions, Institute of British Geographers*, New Series, **2** (1977), pp. 364–82. For a fuller discussion of such occupationally-related long-distance migration to Liverpool see: R. Lawton and C. G. Pooley, *The Social Geography of Merseyside in the Nineteenth Century: Final Report to the SSRC*, (Liverpool, 1976).

120. C. Booth, *Life and labour of the People of London*, (London, 1903), describes the impact of suburban railways on development from the 1860s. See also J. R. Kellett, *The Impact of Railways on Victorian Cities*, (London, 1969) and for a case study H. J. Dyos, *Victorian Suburb. A Study of the Growth of Camberwell*, (Leicester, 1961, reprinted 1973).

121. For the view that until the late nineteenth century cities were 'transitional', see D. Ward, 'Victorian cities: how modern?', *Journal of Historical Geography*, **1** (1975), pp. 135–51. A counter-argument is by D. Cannadine, 'Victorian cities: how different?', *Social History*, **1** (1977), pp. 457–82.

122. A convenient summary is in R. Lawton, 'An age of great cities', (1972); a number of aspects of the process are dealt with by papers on nineteenth-century towns in 'Change in the town', *Transactions, Institute of British Geographers*, New Series, **2**, No. 3 (1977).

123. A similar relationship between sources of unskilled work and Irish districts has been established in many other British cities: for example, L. H. Lees, 'Patterns of lower-class life: Irish slum communities in nineteenth-century

London', in S. Thernstrom and R. Sennett (eds.), *Nineteenth-century Cities: Essays in the New Urban History*, (New Haven, 1964), pp. 359–85; R. D. Lobban, 'The Irish community in Greenock in the nineteenth century', *Irish Geography*, 6 (1971), pp. 270–81; and C. Richardson, 'Irish settlement in mid-nineteenth-century Bradford', *Yorkshire Bulletin of Economic and Social Research*, 20 (1968), pp. 40–57.

124. C. G. Pooley, 'The residential segregation of migrant communities in mid-Victorian Liverpool', *Transactions, Institute of British Geographers*, New Series, 2 (1977), pp. 364–82. For a full discussion of the residential pattern of different types of worker see R. Lawton and C. G. Pooley, 'David Brindley's Liverpool', *Transactions, Historic Society of Lancashire and Cheshire*, 125 (1975), pp. 58–63.

125. See E. J. Hobsbawm, *Labouring Men*, (London, 1964) for a discussion of the 'labour aristocracy'.

126. Pritchard, *Housing and the Spatial Structure of the City*.

127. R. J. Dennis, 'Intercensal mobility in a Victorian city', *Transactions, Institute of British Geographers*, New Series, 2 (1977), pp. 349–63.

128. R. Lawton and C. G. Pooley, 'Problems and potentialities for the study of internal population mobility in nineteenth-century England' (in preparation); the figure is based on Mr Pooley's study of a sample of 2446 households.

129. For example, P. R. Knight, *The Plain People of Boston, 1830–60* (New York, 1971); M. B. Katz, *The People of Hamilton, Canada West: Family and Class in a Mid-nineteenth Century City*, (New Haven, 1976).

130. Lawton and Pooley, 'David Brindley's Liverpool', pp. 58–63. J. Burnett, *Useful Toil*, (London, 1974).

131. P. Thompson, 'Voices from Within', Chapter 2 of H. J. Dyos and M. Wolff (eds.) *The Victorian City. Images and Reality*, 2 Vols, (London, 1973).

13
Towns and Urban Systems 1730–1900

H. Carter

The Urban System 1730–1900

Large-scale urbanization has been a process common to all the countries of the western world in modern times. More recently it has become characteristic of developing countries. Britain was the first to be subject to this critical transformation, critical not only because it changed the settlement pattern but because it revolutionized the whole socio-economic system. Between 1730 and 1900 England and Wales shifted from being primarily rural to being predominantly urban counties. The significance of the process was immediate and obvious, and recognized as much by poets as by those concerned with social welfare. [1] Even before the end of the nineteenth century the first major study of urbanization had been published in Adna Ferrin Weber's book, *The Growth of Towns in the Nineteenth Century*. [2] Weber began by noting that it was a common observation that the most remarkable social phenomenon of the century had been the concentration of population in cities. But on the same first page he poses more pertinent questions: 'What are the forces that have produced a shifting of population? Are they enduring? What is to be the ultimate result?'

There have been numerous attempts since Weber's pioneer work to consider these questions and, in general, they fall into two categories. The first comprises studies directed at the first of Weber's questions. In approach, they constitute a narrative, though explanatory account of the growth of towns related to specific causes. They are usually carried out region by region or according to functional type. A recent example is made up of those sections of chapters subtitled 'Towns and Cities' in the volume entitled *A New Historical Geography of England*, edited by Darby. [3]

Studies in the second category are more concerned with Weber's last two questions and can be identified as theoretical, national and system based. Their approach is dominated by an attempt to evaluate structural transformations in the whole system of cities, transformations which are related to rank–size relationships of varying descriptions. These works are best exemplified by Robson's book *Urban Growth*. [4] It must be admitted that neither approach has been greatly productive. The first has given rise to a large number of very similar descriptive accounts but little in the way of synthesis, while the second has given some relevant insights into the emergence of size relationships but of a restricted kind.

In this present review of changes in the urban system over some 170 years a three-fold division will be adopted. To begin with a general review of the facts of urban growth 1730–1900 will be presented. This will be followed by a review of the regional and functional components of that growth, and finally the possibility of extracting some generalizations will be considered.

In measuring city size one is compelled to use population as the sole criterion, for any more esoteric basis would be far too difficult to develop. The sources available divide themselves in two. Before 1801, and the first census, one is forced to employ a miscellany of sources, standardizing and integrating their material to derive an overall perspective. After 1801, the availability of the census allows one to take sources for granted and to concentrate on the problems of interpretation and analysis. Amongst the varied sources used to construct a view of the urban system before 1801, the most valuable include parish registers, bills of mortality, taxation assessments, especially the Hearth Tax, and, when available, local censuses. [5] Most of these imply the use of a multiplier to convert partial information into population. There are problems both of accuracy and of uniformity, for it is unusual to obtain figures relating to all towns at one date. Again, prior to the municipal reforms of the early nineteenth century it is difficult to know what to count as urban. The famous list, *Index Villaris or an Alphabetical list of all Cities, Market Towns . . .* of 1680 included a large number of decayed towns where markets were no longer held. [6] Definition is also a problem when the censuses become available. Administrative character has always been used as the identifier of urban status in England and Wales, but that counted for little in a period of rapid change, and especially when the administrative system was itself changing. The early censuses made no attempt to identify urban and rural and it was not until 1851 that the population of municipal and parliamentary boroughs were added to those of unincorporated places of over 2000 to isolate an urban component. By 1871 figures for municipal boroughs and places with either an Improvement Commission or a Local Board were used and after 1881 the Urban Sanitary Districts provided the basis. Census data, therefore, do not provide the simple foundation which at first might appear to become available in 1801. Fortunately, Law has attempted to provide a uniform set of figures by deriving a definition of urban areas from a combination of a minimum size criterion (2500), a measure of density (over one per acre) and a nucleation principle. [7] Using these bases he has calculated urban populations for each census and his figures will be used in the discussion of the facts of urban growth. This will limit initial consideration to the major period of change between 1800 and 1900.

Table 13.1 sets out various measures of change in the urban population of England and Wales for all the census years of the nineteenth century. It reveals the extent and character of change. The urban population itself increased eight-fold during the period, while the proportion of the population living in towns rose from a third in 1801 to over three-quarters by 1901. In 1801, London was the only city with a population of over 100,000; by the end of the century there were 33 cities over that figure. If Law's base of 2500 be taken as the threshold of urban status, then the total number of urban places increased from 253 to 908, that is by over three and a half times. But if the system of cities was extended in number, it was also changed in structure for the largest towns accounted for an increasingly greater proportion of the total urban population. Thus if the smallest group with populations between 2500 and 10,000 is examined it will be seen that the proportion of the urban population accounted for by them actually fell from 29·1 per cent in 1801 to 11·2 per cent in 1901, while the proportion of the total population accounted for by this size class declined from 9·9 per cent to 8·9 per cent over the same period. In complete contrast, the proportion of the urban population in towns of over 100,000 rose from 32·6 per cent to 55·5 per cent and the proportion of the national population in these largest towns increased from 11·0 per cent to 43·8 per cent. Indeed, the percentage of the urban population accounted for by all size groups below 100,000 fell between 1801 and 1901. The implication is that the hierarchy of town was taking on a different structure.

In terms of change during the century there was a fairly even decennial increase as measured by the percentage urban change, but with small peaks in the early part in 1821 and in the latter part of the century in 1871, and a

Table 13.1: Urban populations in England and Wales, 1801–1901 (after C. M. Law).

England and Wales

	Total population	Urban population	Percentage urban	Percentage urban change in previous decade	Index of urban population, 1801 = 100	Urban change as percentage of total change in previous decade	Number of places with population greater than 2500	100,000
1801	8,829,536	3,009,260	33·8	—	100	—	253	1
1811	10,164,256	3,722,025	36·6	23·7	124	56·0	302	3
1821	12,000,236	4,804,534	40·0	29·1	160	59·0	352	4
1831	13,896,797	6,153,230	44·3	28·0	204	71·1	397	6
1841	15,914,148	7,093,126	48·3	25·0	256	76·3	450	7
1851	17,927,609	9,687,927	54·0	25·9	322	99·1	522	10
1861	20,066,224	11,784,056	58·7	21·6	392	98·0	577	13
1871	22,712,266	14,802,100	65·2	25·6	492	151·8	697	17
1881	25,924,434	18,180,117	70·0	22·8	604	103·5	754	20
1891	29,002,525	21,601,012	74·5	18·8	718	113·0	845	24
1901	32,527,843	25,371,849	78·0	17·5	843	107·0	908	33

tailing off towards 1901. In terms of urban change related to total change, however, there is a marked dominance in the last quarter of the century when the metamorphosis of the country to an urban basis was completed with the onset of gross rural depopulation, so that urban increase became greater than total increase, with rural losses making up the difference.

Table 13.1 and the foregoing exegesis of it outlines the essential facts of urbanization as a national process. But urbanization did not operate uniformly over the country and a brief account of regional and functional variation is also needed in this analysis. Moreover, moving away from the general statistical scale allows a brief review of the situation during the eighteenth century before census figures are available.

In the first half of the eighteenth century the urban system in England and Wales was largely that which had emerged from the late medieval period. It reflected local wealth and density of population supported by agriculture, rural industry and the trade based on their products. It also represented political clout as expressed through an administrative system still concerned with the security of the realm and the preservation of an united kingdom. At the lowest level in the urban hierarchy, it is estimated that there were between five and six hundred market towns, many possessing extremely small populations with a minimum about 500 and a maximum about 1800. [8] These were the survivors of that complex web of market towns which had characterized the late medieval period. Change at this level had been considerable as the sorting-out process eliminated those less able to compete. [9] Communication, especially along rivers and around the coast, had certainly improved, but to no revolutionary extent and those towns which had been lifted out of this level owed a great deal to the administrative system, both lay and ecclesiastical, based on the counties. For its operation, especially for the administration of justice, designated centres were needed and these were raised to a level above that of the market town. In that designation, advantages in location and size, derived from centrality and agricultural wealth, were critical. But to a large degree the towns which had counties named after them, such as Nottingham, Derby, Leicester, Northampton and Bedford, still retained their status. Raised still further above this level were those centres which can be termed 'provincial capitals'. All commentators agree that five stood out—Norwich, Bristol, York, Exeter and Newcastle. [10] Moreover these towns maintained this status over a period of some 200 years, suggesting an area of stability at least in the upper ranges of the hierarchy. It is not possible to consider them individually, but a number of general points can be made. The first and obvious one is that wealth of surroundings and location on navigable rivers or function as ports, had played signficant roles in enhancing their status. But at the same time there is a political, administrative and ecclesiastical backing. None of these towns lay within competing distance of London. They represent the last phase in the importance of the provincial capitals of less stable areas of the United Kingdom. Newcastle, in particular, was still, at the outset of the period, a major bastion against the Scots. In contrast, towns close in to London suffered from competition with that primate city at a time when its population was some 20 times that of its nearest in size. There were two provincial areas significantly without capitals at this higher level. The first was Wales where the general poverty of the country, together with its physical nature of a mountain core and a thin periphery, had produced no chief city. The same physical character meant that there was no one focus in the marchlands. Potential candidates like Chester, Shrewsbury, Hereford, Worcester and Gloucester remained all at the county town level. But in the extreme south, Bristol was the effective capital of southern Wales, just as the rapidly growing port of Liverpool was later to become the capital of the north. The Welsh situation was, to a degree, echoed in north-west England. In Lancashire the county town of Preston, and the older capital city at Lancaster, were locally effective but lacked regional command. Chester was in decline and Liverpool growing, as was Manchester. A transition situation characterized the area even at this early date. Moreover, Cumberland and Westmorland were as thinly peopled and incapable of generating a regional capital as was Wales. It is a significant reflection on the pre-industrial situation that whereas the east coast had three provincial capitals in Norwich, York and Newcastle, in addition to London, the west had only Bristol. This contrast reflected their differences of agricultural wealth and the industry and trade derived from its products. Finally, at the head of the hierarchy, there was London, a primate city which was the centre not only of trade and commerce, but pre-eminently of government and adminstration.

This classification of towns in the mid-eighteenth century is admittedly incomplete. It fails to include those already characterized by special industry, such as Birmingham, and takes no account of the spas and the naval ports. Even so, it represents the critical system upon which industrialization was to make major changes. These changes are best introduced by a tabulation of the largest towns at the first census of 1801 (see Table 13.2).[11]

Table 13.2: The largest towns of England and Wales, excluding London, in 1801 and 1851.

	1801		1851
Manchester	84,000	(includes Salford)	367,955
Liverpool	78,000		375,955
Birmingham	74,000		232,841
Bristol	64,000	(includes Barton Regis Hundred)	137,328
Leeds	53,000		172,270
Plymouth	43,000		
Norwich	37,000		
Bath	32,000		
Portsmouth	32,000	(includes Portsea)	
Sheffield	31,000		135,310
Hull	30,000		
Nottingham	29,000		
Newcastle	28,000		
		Bradford	103,310

After Prince and Harley, in H. C. Darby (ed.), *A New Historical Geography of England*, pp. 459, 578.

From about 1730, a period of stability, at least in the upper echelons of the urban hierarchy, was replaced by one of quite fundamental change. If London be excluded, only Bristol retained its place amongst the five largest towns in 1801. Norwich had moved down to seventh, Newcastle to thirteenth, Exeter to fourteenth and York to sixteenth. The newcomers which had displaced them rested unequivocally on industry as a basis for their growth. Appropriately the incoming members epitomize the new areas of urban growth. Manchester and Liverpool, the first the regional centre of commerce, the second the port, were the cities being created by cotton textiles: Birmingham was the largest of a group of West Midland towns concerned with metalware and miscellaneous engineering products: Leeds was the capital of the woollen manufactures of Yorkshire's West Riding. Lower down in the hierarchy Sheffield, at tenth, was the centre of a steel industry and the other specialized trades such as Sheffield plate, while Nottingham, twelfth in rank, represented in its hosiery and lace industries the growing area of the East Midlands. High in the ranks were Bath, still representing the spas and foreshadowing the resorts, and Plymouth and Portsmouth, the naval bases. It is necessary to record at this point that in spite of the overturning of the rank order of towns highest in status, nevertheless those coming to supremacy were already settlements of some size with a long standing industrial tradition based on earlier mercantile activity. Although changes were 'fundamental' even so there was an element of continuity. One of the bases for the successful take-off of the new industrialism would seem to have been a good urban foundation. Industrialization and urbanization would seem to have been mutually reinforcing, rather than to have acted in a simple unilateral cause-effect fashion.

Each of the major industrial cities was associated with an aureole of smaller towns the sizes of which were closely related to their industrial development. This is best illustrated by Lancashire where the smaller cotton towns grew as rapidly between 1801 and 1821 as the larger centres (see Table 13.3).

Space precludes a narrative description of the causal factors behind the growth of individual members of a hierarchy which was being both extended in length and modified in structure. However, an overall picture can be given in a series of maps derived from a set produced by Robson (Fig. 13.1).[12] These maps show those towns whose growth in the specified decade was one standard deviation above the mean for its size group. It must be emphasized that these are not absolute growth rates, but rates related to the means for size groups, so that at any one time only a proportion of any size group can appear. The size groups are not identified on the maps but are indicated in the key. The main conclusions which can be drawn from this series of maps reinforce the fairly standard view on the

Table 13.3: Population growth of cotton towns.

	1801	1821
Wigan	10,989	17,716
Bury	7072	10,583
Oldham	12,024	21,662
Blackburn	11,980	21,940
Bolton	12,549	22,037
Preston	11,887	24,575
Stockport (Cheshire)	14,850	21,726

After Chalklin, *Provincial Towns of Georgian England*, p. 35.

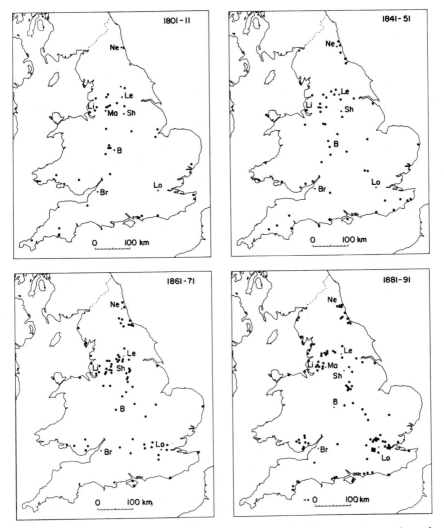

Fig. 13.1. The pattern of urban growth in England and Wales in four selected decades (after Robson). Those cities registering high rates have been abstracted. Standardized growth rates are represented where

$$zi = \frac{Gi.n - \bar{G}n}{\sigma n}$$

where $Gi.n$ is the growth rate of the ith town the population of which puts it within the nth size group of towns: Gn and σn are the mean and standard deviation of the nth size group. Lower limits of size groups used are 2500, 5000, 10,000, 20,000, 40,000, 80,000, 160,000, 320,000. B. T. Robson, *Urban Growth*, (1973), pp. 82, 98–111.

evolution of industrial and urban England and Wales. Even so, some interesting points emerge. The earliest decade from 1801 to 1811 appears transitional between the pre-industrial state and the new order being ushered in by industry. County towns, such as Bridgwater in the South-West, Carmarthen in South Wales and Boston in East Anglia, reflect both the significance of the regional centre and the role of the port as a distributor of shop goods, a role which was to continue until the coming of the railway. The Severn Valley has only one representative of high growth but there were others in the West Midlands area generally. The newer seaside resorts, such as Ramsgate appear, although the war with France gave a distorted stress to south-east coast ports. But the main growth area was Lancashire. The high growth rate of its towns was sustained into the next decade when a clear dominance is evident in both Lancashire and the West Riding of Yorkshire. Elsewhere the occurrence of high growth is sporadic apart, perhaps, from the south coast towns. By 1831–41 and 1841–51 a new influence begins to operate through the development of the railway system and the rapid growth of the ports dealing with the import of raw materials and the export of manufactured goods. The West Midlands appears more firmly as an area of rapid growth as the railway mitigated the problem of distance from the coast, while in the North-East and South Wales the ports themselves show rapid increase. By the decade 1851–61 the main industrial areas of the country were clearly established and marked by growth, the only exception being South Wales. But the North-East, Lancashire, the West and South Ridings of Yorkshire, Nottingham-Derby and the West and East Midlands were outstanding cores of high urban increase. During the decade 1861–71 three features were added to this complex. The first was a distinct scatter of growth in the London basin as Greater London was created out of suburban extension. The second was the appearance of a new generation of seaside resorts created by the demand of the industrial population and of which Blackpool was the epitome. The third was the clear entry of South Wales into the high growth areas as coalmining and export expanded. By 1881–91, the patterns of growth show up that axial belt of population lying south-east to north-west from London to Lancashire-Yorkshire which was to be the outstanding feature of the population distribution of England until after the Second World War. High growth can also be discerned in the two major industrial areas outside this dominant belt, north-east England and South Wales.

The crucial issue for the historical geographer is whether the pattern of growth which characterized the period 1730–1900 can be shown to demonstrate any general principles of city-system development. The standard types of analyses have been carried out by Robson for the period when reasonably accurate census data are available.[13] In these rank order was plotted against population size for decennial censuses (Fig. 13.2) and also the rank changes of individual towns between censuses were plotted. The progressive horizontal shift to the right in the rank-size array (Fig. 13.2) demonstrates the simple additon of extra members into the array, while the vertical shift indicates the growth of the size of individual members. The general form of the graph remains surprisingly similar, thereby reflecting some form of allometric growth, that is, there is a relationship between the addition of extra cities and the size of cities. This confirms the conclusions drawn earlier (p. 369) regarding the concentration of growth in the upper ranks of the settlement array, but it does not signify that a structural transformation was in progress. As regards those towns which were the largest in 1801, the examination of change in rank supports the view that there was comparatively little shift of rank order amongst the top places, but that fluctuations became greater the further down the hierarchy of towns one moves. Robson writes,

> All of these larger places (London, Liverpool, Manchester, Birmingham), indeed, show relatively little change in their rank orders over the whole period. On the other hand, with the smaller places there is a tendency for increasingly large flucuations to occur at smaller city sizes. Some places move rapidly up the rank hierarchy: Leicester, for example, was 21st in 1801, had moved to 13th by 1891 and retained this rank up to 1911. Other places moved rapidly down the hierarchy: Exeter, for example, began at 20th position, and had fallen to 65th by 1911.[14]

These analyses, therefore, suggest that over a short time period the largest cities captured, in direct and simple terms, a disproportionate amount of growth, thereby maintaining their highest ranking and confirming an allometric growth characteristic. At the lower end of the scale there was considerable change and jockeying for position.

At this point it is appropriate to consider other interpretations of the same problem. Haggett, Cliff and Frey in *Locational Models* briefly review historical changes in city-size distributions.[15] They conclude that although the Industrial Revolution administered a severe shock to the system, there may be a general tendency for the urban system to move towards a dynamic equilibrium, maximum entropy, distribution.[16] Presumably this simply means that the rapid creation of new towns during the century

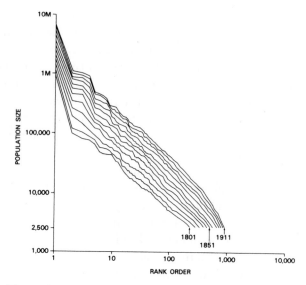

Fig. 13.2. The rank-size array of towns in England and Wales, 1801–1911 (after Robson). [4]

shook up the existing hierarchy, but that eventually it settled back to a condition of relative stability after the maximum period of town creation was over. This was largely achieved by towns, constrained by the threshold populations needed to generate services and by the limited range over which they could operate, eventually achieving a settled relationship in the context of the total population distribution. It appears that two forces were at work, in addition to the direct, aggregating influence of industry and mining. The first of these was those agglomeration economies in the offering of goods and services which favoured the largest settlements. The second was those constraints of the traditional central-place concept, threshold and range, which sorted out the smaller centres. The separation of all these into two distinct influences is, however, quite arbitrary.

The most pertinent contribution to the role of agglomeration economies has been that of Pred. [17] Over a number of years he has developed and extended the notion of cyclical cumulative growth put forward by Myrdal. Figure 13.3 reproduces his diagram which outlines the circular and feedback process of local urban-size growth for individual large cities during a period of industrialization. It is based on new or enlarged industry providing the most likely environment for invention and innovation. This not only further stimulates industry but generates a

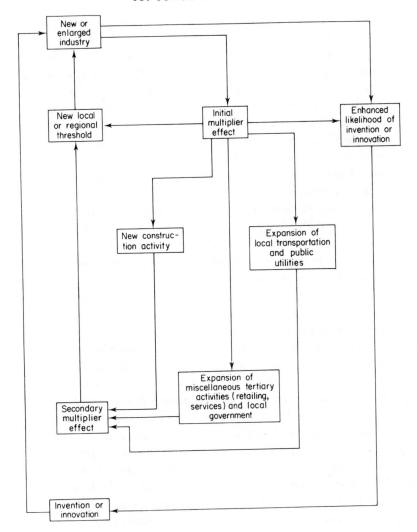

Fig. 13.3. The circular and cumulative feedback process of local urban size-growth for individual large cities during periods of initial modern industrialization (after Pred).[17]

multiplier which is expressed in the extension of construction, transport and public utilities and in tertiary services. These in turn attract new investment and provide a stimulus to further industrial growth. It is this process which explains two distinctive features of urban growth in the period under discussion; most of the large towns were early centres of mercantile activity in which the critical thresholds were met and new activity generated; those towns which grew most rapidly were the largest towns with few fundamental changes in rank at the top occurring during the nineteenth century. It must, however, be noted that these statements are only true if a limited time span is taken. If reference is made to the hierarchy of towns in the first half of the eighteenth century there is a complete transformation at the top of the size-rank array. By 1801, with the sole exception of London, all of the top towns have disappeared, apart from Bristol (which does not appear in Robson's array). In other words much of the real transformation at the higher levels is concealed before the first British census of 1801. Again the dominance in growth by the largest towns is lost by the end of the nineteenth century, probably due to the onset of suburbanization, although that could well be regarded as indistinguishable from the growth of the largest centres. Even so, it must be conceded that viewing the problem over a longer time period arouses reservations as to the role of agglomeration economies. But once growth at a point is begun, for whatever reason, then size generated a size increase and encouraged innovation and the achievement of new thresholds. But a further problem arises in a critical review of this notion for it is essentially *ex post facto*, virtually teleological, in its structure. This can be revealed by a review of some of the detail of urban growth in any one area.

South Wales can be regarded as exceptional in the British context of industrial urbanization for its critical development was late; there was no strongly developed urban system, no mercantile capital, and the basic investment came from sources outside the area. It is possibly an example of internal colonialism rather than of growth generated from within. But however it be regarded, a number of problems arise which cut across the idea of agglomeration, innovation and invention as the controllers of the city system's growth. The earliest eighteenth-century core of industry was about Swansea Bay, but that area was rapidly superseded by Merthyr Tydfil, the centre of the iron industry after 1750. Merthyr was the largest town in Wales for most of the period under review, and certainly in all the censuses from 1801 to 1881. In 1881 it lost its supremacy to Cardiff and fell below Swansea and the Rhondda, although to regard the last area as a single settlement demands an array of presumptions. Merthyr did not fall rapidly in population until the present century but even so according to all the principles it should have grown apace. In 1821 it was five times as large as Cardiff and even in 1851 it was still more than twice the size of Cardiff and Swansea. Moreover, it was the centre of significant innovation in the iron industry and above all else, in transportation. In 1801 Richard Trevithick's steam engine ran from Penydarren to Abercynon, so inaugurating the age of the steam locomotive. And yet by 1881 Merthyr had been overtaken by a town which had only 1870 inhabitants in 1801. The success of Cardiff also raises questions, for it never achieved the size and significance of equivalent capitals of other industrial areas such as Birmingham or Manchester, when according to the principles of cumulative agglomeration it should have. The reasons for the situations described are neither obscure nor surprising. Merthyr lost its supremacy in the Welsh hierarchy because the basic local raw material, iron ore, was exhausted and the transport costs of importing ore to an inland and upland location became prohibitive. Again, after 1860 the main characteristic of South Wales was the export of coal and the bulk of this went through the port of Cardiff. But Cardiff failed to generate a real industrial base. [18] This can be attributed in part to the attitude of the Bute family who owned the docks but did little to enhance the facilities which might have attracted shipbuilding. Further, the late development of Cardiff meant that it could not gain a place in the manufacturing sphere and, like a true colonial city, it exported the raw material wealth of the hinterland without establishing raw material using industries of its own. This brief review of South Wales reverts to the particular which the chapter has attempted to avoid, but even the shortest study of a particular area throws doubt on the universality of general principles. Innovative centres survived and prospered only when locations remained industrially or commercially advantageous, not simply because they were innovative centres; and if innovation diffused down a hierarchy it was because that hierarchy already existed and not because the diffusion process structured a hierarchy. All this does not mean that the cyclical and cumulative process of city growth did not operate, but that it was only one of a number of processes of great complexity by which a range of pre-existing and new settlements were sorted out and reached a stage of relative equilibrium.

Figure 13.4 attempts to depict, in an elementary fashion, the forces that shaped the urban system of England and Wales during the period 1730–1900. The inheritance was the system of cities which had emerged into the early modern period. If equilibrium be defined as a minimum of rank change, then it was a system in equilibrium for shifts in rank change had been limited and local for a number of centuries. The onset of a period of rapid fluctuation was characterized by the accumulation and investment

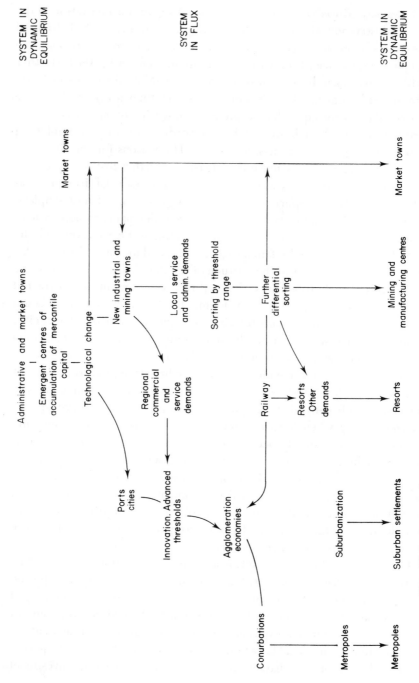

Fig. 13.4. A generalized view of forces shaping the array of towns in the nineteenth century.

of mercantile capital. Growth was fostered particularly where early available capital engendered technical innovation and where economies accrued to the agglomeration process. Thresholds were continuously raised so that innovation became especially associated with the largest centres. A group of regional capitals emerged very different from those of the early eighteenth century. Within the orbit of these leaders a whole range of small industrial settlements came into being, some *ab initio*, others through the transformation of older market towns. If initial size were determined by the sizes of manufacturing and mining enterprises, the need for local government and service provision added an extra basis for discrimination over size. As these administrative and tertiary services became of a more standard character over the century, a countrywide comparative control exerted by thresholds and ranges encouraged the sorting of centres into something approaching a hierarchical order. Within this process the railway had a major impact. Communications are first established where demand is greatest, that is between the largest towns. The result is an addition to that cyclical and cumulative growth which was the basis of the great metropolis. But the railway also created towns such as Crewe and Swindon, and acted discriminately on others. Furthermore, industrial population demanded resorts so that old centres were revived and new ones literally entered the ranks. It is interseting to note that the 1851 census recorded the highest growth rate between 1811 and 1851 in the class called 'watering places' at 254 per cent, as against 224 per cent for 'manufacturing places'.[19] By the latter part of the nineteenth century cumulative growth meant that the largest cities were no longer discrete entities but were associated with a range of separate, satellite suburbs. This extended period of flux and change was approaching its end by the year 1900. It had produced a wide range of settlements, both in function and size, but had now reached a situation where rank change was once again small. In other words it was in a state of dynamic equilibrium with maximum entropy.

Again, this can be illustrated from Wales. Between 1801 and 1901 the number of towns by formal designation increased from 61 to 112, almost doubling in 100 years. Yet only 12 of the 61 settlements of 1801 do not appear in Beresford's gazeteer of Welsh new towns of the Middle Ages. This suggests that periods of maximum flux or change are exceptional for here is not a system subject to minor influences of morphogenesis and morphostasis, but one subject to catastrophic change. Indeed, one is tempted to draw the analogy with the notion of catastrophism in geomorphology and argue that the urban system is subject to short catastrophic periods of change which determine its basic form, and long periods of dynamic equilibrium as the energy injected is dispersed. It might be that much analysis of change in urban systems has not succeeded because of a failure to specify the nature of the time scale being considered. From the broadest point of view the period 1730–1900 can be regarded as one of major transformation as new settlements came into being, interacting with the old and achieving relative equilibrium under the twin controls of threshold and range operating at distinctive levels, with agglomeration economies distorting that simple central place resolution into a more unequal pattern.

The Forms of Towns

The growth of towns has so far been considered in terms of population numbers, but it also involved a vast expansion in the physical extent of the built-up area. Moreover, during the period under review that extension was accompanied by internal restructuring, by the transformation of the so-called pre-industrial city into the modern city. This process of internal restructuring which went along with physical extension was complex, but the critical concept related to it is that of segregation. In land-use terms segregation was the dominant process by which distinctive city areas were produced. What had been a relatively undifferentiated town centre, only distinctively different on market days, was translated into a permanent shopping and administrative area or Central Business District (CBD). Industry and the railway, often in close association, produced their own distinctive city regions. By the end of the century the development of intra-city transportation had metamorphosed the constricted walking city into the extensive tram (or street) car city,[20] thus initiating rapid suburban growth. Suburban growth introduced the second aspect of segregation—social segregation. It is a mistake to envisage the eighteenth-century town as one where there was no spatial manifestation of social class differences; but any such manifestation was constrained by the severe limitations to intra-city movement. With the coming in succession of the horse tram, the tram-car and the suburban railway the constraints were removed and, as the well-off moved out to the new suburbs, social stratification, itself becoming more complex during the century, was mirrowed in spatial segregation; social and physical distance became equated.

It is not possible to deal comprehensively with such major changes in the space available. Accordingly a number of the more critical aspects have been selected for brief review. These are, the evolution of the CBD, the notion of fringe belt development, the character of housing and the development of social areas.

It is unfortunate and surprising that there is no detailed study of a British city which is directly parallel to that by Ward of the evolution of central Boston between 1840 and 1900. [21] Even so, his model of the development of the central area of American cities has a close relationship to the British situation (Fig. 13.5). Ward argues that until the middle of the nineteenth century the functional specialization of land uses was but weakly developed. For example, most of the goods in demand were produced by local craftsmen on the same premises where they were sold and often where the merchants and craftsmen resided. It was the locational separation of these functions of production, storage, distribution and residence which characterized the latter half of the century. Ward proposes that the lead in the break-up of these associated functions was

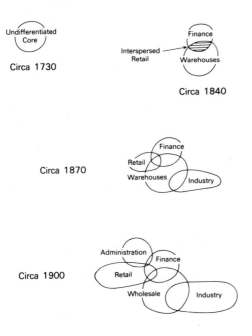

Fig. 13.5. The development of central areas of towns in the eighteenth and nineteenth centuries (based on Ward). [21]

taken by warehousing which created a complex district where both manufacturing and commerce were associated. At the same time, a small but well defined financial area emerged. After 1870 these were progressively sorted out into wholesale, retail, financial and administrative districts, the components of the twentieth-century Central Business District.

A brief study of Cardiff (Fig. 13.6) can be introduced to illustrate the general process at work, if not the precise details which Ward derived from Boston.[22] The core of Cardiff was the area contained within the medieval walls and this, because of the late development already discussed (p. 381), remained functionally undifferentiated to any major degree until well past the mid-nineteenth century. With the growth of coal export and a

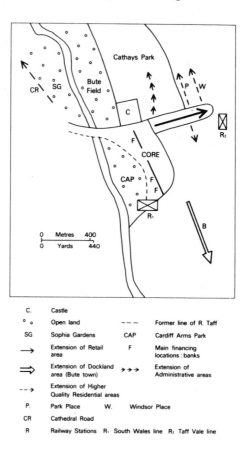

C.	Castle		
° °	Open land	– – –	Former line of R. Taff
SG	Sophia Gardens	CAP	Cardiff Arms Park
→	Extension of Retail area	F	Main financing locations : banks
⇒	Extension of Dockland area (Bute town)	⇥ ⇥ ⇥	Extension of Administrative areas
– – →	Extension of Higher Quality Residential areas		
P.	Park Place	W.	Windsor Place
CR	Cathedral Road		
R	Railway Stations	R₁ South Wales line	R₂ Taff Vale line

Fig. 13.6. The development of central Cardiff in the nineteenth century.

spectacular increase in population after 1860, this core was slowly transformed into a specialized retail and business area. This was not completed, however, until the First World War. The demand for floor space was met internally by the development of arcades, but externally by a clear eastward directed extension which was mainly concentrated in the decade 1880–90, the period when retail trade made a rapid advance with the incoming of chain stores. To the west of the retail core a somewhat inchoate fringe of financial and wholesale institutions represented in an attenuated form those areas which Ward identified in Boston. This poor representation is due to the fact that new docks were developed at the mouth of the river Taff, well to the south of the old town and its medieval riverside quay. It was at this second nucleus that the main financial and warehousing facilities were located, including the Coal Exchange. Cardiff had a further distinctive feature in the Bute estate of Cathay's Park, about the medieval castle, which was kept open until the land was developed by the city and county at the beginning of the present century. It was then transformed into a distinctive administrative area. By the 1870s the segregation of high-class residence was but incipient, producing two closely associated sectors in Park Place and Windsor Place which extended northward alongside the castle land. A parallel development related to the Sophia Gardens which was planned to the west where the open land 'will be skirted by a long line of beautiful villa residences . . .to be formed and called ''the Cathedral Road'' '. [23] It was not in fact completed until the end of the century. At the same time densely built working-class housing filled the central area behind the retail and commercial facade. This brief account must suffice as an indication, and no more, of the way in which, by the end of the nineteenth century, complex central areas had emerged in British towns. Within these areas distinctive functional districts had been created by the segregation of uses as a consequence of physical growth.

What took place in Cardiff at the end of the nineteenth century had taken place in London over a century and a half earlier. The westward extension from the city of London had begun in the 1660s with the development of the Cavendish Harley estate after 1717, and it reached a climax after the Peace of Paris in 1763. The Strand, the early thin link between the Cities of London and Westminster, was backed by an increasing and extensive area of development as the West End was created. The high quality retail area was abstracted from the financial and commercial areas of the traditional 'city'. The development of London's dockland created an extensive low quality East End. By the latter part of the century the highest levels of land-use segregation had become apparent as such areas as 'theatreland' emerged.

In this process of growth, regardless of size, two further elements demanded inner city space, often in close association and with strong repercussions on the central area. These were the railway and industry, the generators of growth. The railways pushed their termini as far as was possible into the town centres, clearing swathes of existing housing, usually of low quality, and creating characteristic sectors. 'Districts divided and confined by the railways tended to be cast finally and irretrievably into the now familiar mould of coal and timber yards, warehousing, mixed light and heavy industrial users and fourth rate residential housing.'[24] Railways themselves took up some 5 to 9 per cent of the central area of the largest British cities.[25] Heavy industry also occupied major extents closely linked to the railway or to rivers or canals. This could be illustrated from almost any British city but a characteristic example is shown in Fig. 13.7. It was especially repellent of high quality residences but, because of the lack of effective mass transit systems, closely associated and shot through with working-class housing.[26] The

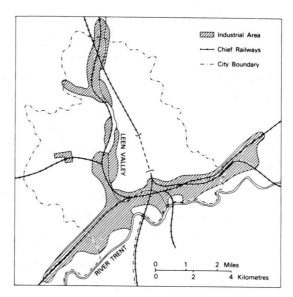

Fig. 13.7. The relation of railways and industrial areas in Nottingham (after K. C. Edwards).

railway termini had a further effect in that as points of maximum entry of population into towns they exerted a major influence on CBD extension. Kellet finds little evidence for this, however, for he writes, 'Only in Liverpool . . . is there any historical evidence of the marked gravitational influence which has been occasionally ascribed to railway stations.'[27] He makes the qualification that his examples are major cities with a century of industrial growth before the arrival of the railway so that its impact would have been less than in smaller places of more recent growth. Certainly many studies have stressed this factor, and Fig. 13.6 shows significantly, whether as cause or effect, the two railway stations in central Cardiff at either extremity of the CBD.

If internal restructuring of the city was a dominant process, its corollary was the outward extension of the built-up area. The critical concept in this process is that of the urban fringe belt, introduced into British historical geography by Conzen[28] and subsequently developed by Whitehand.[29] This concept is based on the fact that towns do not extend evenly and steadily, but by alternating periods of rapid growth and of quiescence or still-stand. This is clearly evidenced by the numerous studies of building cycles during the nineteenth century.[30] As a result there comes about a distinction betweeen an intensively built-up area, the consequence of a growth phase, and a fringing belt immediately about it, which is subsequently only slowly encroached upon. This is most obvious in the contrast between the intra-mural areas of medieval towns where the land was finely divided into burgage lots, and the extral-mural areas where land was usually held in much larger parcels, often by large estates. 'It is', writes Conzen, 'as if such a belt once established created its own environment and imposed its own conditions of further development on its area in terms of shape and size of plots, types of land use, and degree of opening up of streets.'[31] As this statement maintains, the fringe belt differs not only in cadastral but also in land-use characteristics. In simplest terms, the existence of open land, held in large extents, at the margin of the city provides opportunities for extensive consumers of urban land. In the nineteenth century such consumers, greatly enhanced by public health and associated legislation, were the variety of public utilities, cemeteries, waterworks, hospitals, especially psychiatric and isolation hospitals which were carefully removed from residential areas. Public parks, urban-related market gardening and large country houses with extensive grounds can also be included. When extension starts again in a new period of economic growth and housing boom, a further belt of housing will surround the inner fringe belt. Indeed parts of the fringe belt will be 'absorbed', that is engulfed by the new housing demand. The former market garden or large estate built over for housing is a widely recurring feature. But much of the inner fringe belt will remain and give the city an annular structuring as a consequence of the succession of fringe belts which characterize it. Figure 13.8 indicates this pattern as identified by Conzen [32] and Whitehand [33] in Newcastle with the inner fringe belt (IFB) surrounding the medieval town and the middle fringe belt as a distinctive nineteenth-century feature.

> Even before the IFB was enclosed by the residential expansion of the Victorian period, late fringe belts were forming at much greater distances from the centre. The eighteenth and nineteenth centuries saw the building of numerous country houses within a few miles of the city. During the Victorian period in particular, various institutions (notably several isolation hospitals and a lunatic asylum), residences standing in their own grounds, cemeteries and waterworks found sites generally within one and a half miles of the built-up area of the time. Where the geology permitted, quarries and brickworks found similar peripheral locations. During the vigorous residential growth of the late Victorian period some of the less distant plots were swallowed up by the house builder, but the majority survived to form a discontinuous belt of varying width. This belt stretched northward from the riverside in the area of Elswick and Benwell and incorporated the open spaces of the Town Moor and Nun's Moor . . . . In the east the belt followed approximately the line of Jesmond Dene (where the gorge had attracted a number of country houses) down to the Tyne near its confluence with the Ouseburn. The modern representative of this fringe belt . . . is termed the Middle Fringe Belt. [34] (Fig. 13.8)

The structuring principle behind this model of a city composed of a sequence of fringe belts is that during times of economic boom and of an upswing in the building cycle, housing with its greater demand for accessibility and more intensive use of city land will outbid institutions and utilities for urban land and create a ring of residential development, but the reverse will apply in times of economic recession. A characteristic structuring is thus 'written in' to the internal organization of towns.

This chapter has contended that during the nineteenth century there was a growing differentiation of central areas into partly discrete regions and at the same time a structuring of outward growth by a sequence of fringe belts. Into this patterning the development of characteristic nineteenth-century urban housing has to be inserted. Working-class

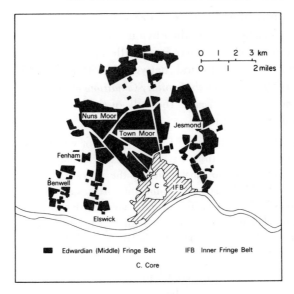

Fig. 13.8: The fringe belts of Newcastle (after J. W. R. Whitehand).[29]

housing has become one of the major themes of urban historical research and a variety of studies exists.[35] Since the major problems became those of sanitation and health the character of housing becomes intricately bound up with public health and related legislation, but there were two critical locational factors. The first was that the demands of town centres remained labour intensive thoughout the period under review, thus requiring large amounts of semi-skilled and unskilled labour. Because of the lack of a transport system, this labour was forced to live within the central area. The same problem of the limited range of journey to work, together with a system of casual employment, meant that where industries were established then housing had to be provided in close proximity, regardless of any environmental drawbacks.

The providers of this central and industrial housing can be grouped into three classes, with an ascending concern with welfare. The first group was the speculative builders whose sole concern was with the immediate profit of the enterprise. The second was the industrial employers whose prime concern was with the creation of an effective housing supply immediately at hand and where profit came firstly from industry. The third group was the philanthropists who were, in a paternalistic fashion, actively concerned in providing housing of a reasonable standard. The second and third group overlapped, as in the obvious case of Titus Salt and his town of Saltaire, [36] and in the creation of Bournville and Port Sunlight at the end of the century. [37] In the period between 1750 and 1842, the date of publication of the *Report on the Sanitary Conditions of the Labouring Population and the Means of its Improvement*, the bulk of the building had been carried out by speculative builders.

> In the manufacturing towns of England, most of which have enlarged with great rapidity, the additions have been made without regard to either the personal comfort of the inhabitants or the necessities which congregation requires. To build the largest number of cottages on the smallest allowable space seems to have been the original view of the speculators . . . . Thus neighbourhoods have arisen in which there is neither water nor out-offices . . . . But more than this, the land had been disposed of in so many small lots, to petty proprietors. [38]

This process described by Edwin Chadwick dominated the city centres and the older industrial areas. Chalklin has outlined these processes in considerable detail, pointing out that development was seemingly never held up for lack of building land. [39] Not only were there the innumerable small sites within existing settlements such as the gardens and open spaces behind earlier houses, but 'the majority of the faster growing towns, such as Liverpool, Manchester, Birmingham, Sheffield, Sunderland, Bath, Bristol and the dockyard towns, housed most of their population by building outward from the early eighteenth century'. In many towns outward extension took place upon large estates which were usually chopped up for purposes of development. Especially important was the achievement of maximum densities, especially on the open gardens behind pre-existing street frontages, often former burgage lots. This was done by building back-to-back houses, or the closely associated tunnel-back or blind-back forms. Beresford has traced the emergence of the back-to-back form in Leeds from the country cottage translated into the city and noted that the earliest forms were not in fact built by speculators but by a building club. 'The argument so far', he writes, 'has suggested how the unventilated, one-up-one-down cottage spread from the innyards into dependent streets, where rows of cottages were thrust so close together that no space remained between each row, and the back walls of adjoining rows were built to touch each other.' [40] Other ways of obtaining high densities were by using cellars, characteristic of Liverpool, and tenements, which were especially characteristic of Glasgow. After the Public Health

Act of 1848 the country was characterized by increasing attempts to regulate building, mainly through the opportunities given to local authorities to establish controlling bye-laws,[41] though it was not until after the Public Health Act of 1875 that improvement became universal. But bye-law housing slowly raised standards so that the three-up-three-down terrace with small back and front gardens slowly became the dominant element of working-class housing.

In the meantime upper-class housing also went through a process of change. Initially terraces or squares of large houses were built relatively close to the city centre using inner fringe belt land. But these locations were often engulfed by the outward spread of the lower orders in the classic invasion and succession sequence. A study of the development of the Calthorpe Edgbaston Estate in Birmingham after 1813 is an excellent example and a necessary correction to the generalization being made here.[42] David Cannadine shows how an attempt was made to create an inner area of residences for 'gentlemen and tradesmen', how the attempt partly succeeded but was compromised by the need to attract a sufficient number of residents, and of how eventually, at the end of the century, deterioration set in. Larger houses, later in the century, could be built on the fringes, that is on middle fringe belt land, although more often than not such developments were based on an inner sector of high quality residences which until very late in the century remained inviolate. But the outward pushing sector, for which perhaps the generic term 'West End' can be used, eventually skipped over any marginal low quality housing, to initiate the new suburbia of the fringe belt. Tarn has admirably sketched the character of the housing.

> Once the ugliness and the cruelty was realised, those who could run away from it not only decamped into suburbs, but at the same time took refuge in a romantic intellectual movement which in architecture took the form of stylistic eclecticism and especially a delight in the revival of Gothic forms. The escape, as a young Pugin so clearly explained, was to a medieval catholic utopia somewhere in the 14th century. What better way could there be of removing the stigma of the industrial age than to recreate the architecture of the idyllic medieval past which he and many others like him began to romanticise and indeed to revive for the nouveau riche and the church?[43]

It is a vast over-simplification to reduce the wide variety of urban housing built between 1730 and 1900 to the terms of the preceding paragraphs (Fig. 13.9). But, even so, the types noted can be used, together with the analysis of central areas and fringe belts, to propose a model of the

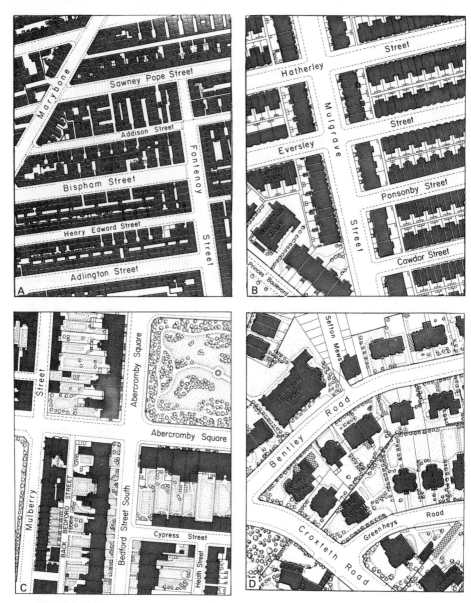

Fig. 13.9. Types of nineteenth-century housing in Liverpool. A, An area of Scotland Road. This is a characteristic inner city area of back-to-back houses at high density, built 1805–15. B, A part of the surround of working-class terrace housing built in the 1870s. Bye-law terraces in Granby Ward. C, Abercromby Square was part of the middle-class residental district developed 1815–35. These were the homes of merchants with a close connection with the city and built near the centre. D, Housing of the 1860s in south Liverpool. These are the large houses of the wealthy, the real beginnings of movement out to the margins. (After J. B. Harley and P. Laxton, in J. A. Patmore and A. G. Hodgkiss (eds.) *Merseyside in Maps* (London, 1970), pp. 18–19.)

development of the industrial town in England and Wales during this period (Fig. 13.10). The most convenient way to discuss this generalized illustration is to arrange the text as a commentary on the figure.

(a) This diagram represents the pattern in 1730 at the beginning of the period, with a regionally undifferentiated kernel surrounded by a fringe belt (eventually the Inner Fringe Belt, IFB). The term 'regionally undifferentiated' is used specifically because it is wrong to think of the town as being homogeneous. There was differentiation on two scales below that of the broader regional level in the diagram.

(i) Within the house, between 'upstairs' and 'downstairs', though both extremes, cellar or basement and attic, represented the lowest section in social terms.

(ii) Within the town, between front street and back street.

(b) This represents the pattern about 1850 at the start of the major period of Irish immigration. The segregation of central city uses has appeared and specialized financial and warehouse or wholesale districts have emerged (F and W). These overlap the retail core (R) which was still incipient. The new industrial areas (I) had much in common with the warehouse district and there was considerable overlap. Industrial housing (Ih) of back-to-back character was closely associated with the industrial region itself, and spread onto the estates of the IFB. The core still retained upper class housing (U). But there had been an infill of densely populated alleys and courts. Some estate land, like the Calthorpe estate at Birmingham, was also devoted to upper class housing. Vance argues that the merchants still retained a close link with the city centre,[44] whereas the non-working élite could move further out.[45]

(c) The town about 1880 is represented in this diagram. By this time a clear retail core had emerged. Dyos has given a detailed picture of the emergence of retail areas in Camberwell beginning with the development of small shops about 1845–50, followed by a rapid acceleration in the 1860s in spite of the continued existence of itinerant vendors of a large variety of commodities.[46] By the 1880s, however, the chain grocery and boot and shoe shops were making their appearance. By this time also the very wealthy were beginning the push out from the town centre, creating a distinctive sector of development. This, in turn, was exerting a pull on the retail area, creating a zone of assimilation as it took over part of what had been the Inner Fringe Belt. Part of that belt, however, was sometimes preserved in the form of an urban park, usually named after the Queen (Victoria Gardens), or the

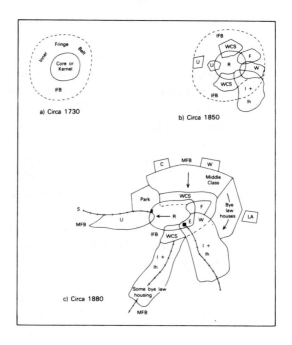

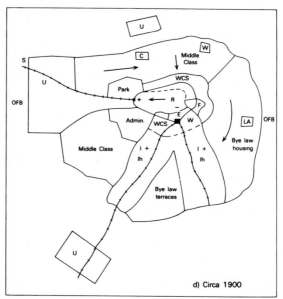

Fig. 13.10. A suggested generalization of the development of the industrial town, 1730–1900. For explanation of the abbreviations, see text pp. 395, 397.

owner of the land. By this time the industrial areas had become more complex and had extended in sympathy with railway development. The associated housing was now subject to some bye-law control and was better in quality. The result was that the inner older areas had become the location of the poorest class of town labourer (working-class slum, WCS) and of the ethnic minorities (E), especially the Irish. The inner areas were dominated by these groups. Away from the industrial parts a middle class area (MC) had developed but one which deteriorated in quality as it approached both the city centre and the industrial sectors. A Middle Fringe Belt (MFB) had come into being with public utilities— cemeteries (C), waterworks (W), lunatic asylum (LA)——located within it.

(d) The city at the end of the nineteenth century is virtually the modern city before post Second World War destruction and renewal. The retail area, as already indicated in (c) was now a clearly distinct centre, still tending to migrate towards the higher social class residences and therefore displaying higher and lower quality parts, and zones of assimilation (+) and zones of discard (−). The upper class had now transformed its residential area from an outward pushing sector into a number of distinctive marginal areas. These appeared in a variety of locations but were especially related to the suburban railways. In these areas the Gothic style houses in their own extensive grounds were built. The central areas remains much the same in character with financial and wholesale areas little different. There is now, however, an extensive surround of intermediate class housing, taking over the Middle Fringe Belt, which however is still apparent in the series of cemeteries (C), waterworks (W) and asylums (LA) which are found within it. A great deal of bye-law infill has followed the 1875 Public Health Act. Part of the remaining section of the Inner Fringe Belt has been taken over for administration following on the re-organization of local government in the 1880s. An Outer Fringe Belt (OFB) has been created.

No one town conforms to this model and it represents a compromise in size between the large scale and distinctive segregation of areas in London and the patterns of the small industrial town. The principles[47] and the processes are the same. Out of the segregation of land-uses and social classes and the development of a variety of housing styles, the modern city emerged at the end of the century. The processes which created it were the consequence of that great and rapid growth which the first part of this chapter considered.

References

1. G. Robert Stange, 'The frightened poets' in H. J. Dyos and M. Wolff (eds.) *The Victorian City : Images and Reality*, (London, 1973), pp. 475–94.
2. A. F. Weber, *The Growth of Cities in the Nineteenth Century*, (New York, 1988).
3. H. C. Darby (ed.), *A New Historical Geography of Engalnd*, (Cambridge, 1973).
4. B. T. Robson, *Urban Growth: an Approach*, (London, 1973).
5. P. Clark and P. Slack, *English Towns in Transition*, (Oxford, 1976), Chapter 1, pp. 1–16 and Chapter 6, pp. 82–96; C. W. Chalklin, *The Provincial Towns of Georgian England*, (London, 1974), pp. 4–31.
6. J. Adams, *Index Villaris or an Alphabetical List of all Cities, Market Towns, Parishes, Villages and Private Seats in England and Wales*, (London, 1680).
7. C. M. Law, 'The growth of urban population in England and Wales, 1801–1911', *Transactions, Institute of British Geographers*, Old Ser., **41** (1967), pp. 125–43.
8. Chalklin, *Provincial Towns of Georgian England*, p. 5.
9. H. Carter, *The Towns of Wales: a Study in Urban Geography*, (2nd edn,), (Cardiff, 1966), pp. 29–68.
10. For example, H. C. Darby, 'The age of the improver: 1600–1800', in Darby (ed.), *A New Historical Geography of England*, p. 381; Chalklin, *Provincial Towns of Georgian England*, pp. 13–17.
11. H. C. Prince, 'England *circa* 1800' in Darby (ed.), *A New Historical Geography of England*, pp. 458–64.
12. Robson, *Urban Growth*, pp. 98–127.
13. *Ibid.*, pp. 16–127.
14. *Ibid.*, p. 38.
15. P. Haggett, A. D. Cliff and A. Frey, *Locational Models*, (London, 1977).
16. *Ibid.*, pp. 123–24.
17. The most useful summary of this contribution is in A. Pred, *City-systems in Advanced Economies*, (London, 1977).
18. For a review of the problems of Cardiff in the nineteenth century see M. J. Daunton, *Coal Metropolis. Cardiff 1870–1914*, (Leicester, 1977), pp. 15–71.
19. *Census 1851*, Vol. 1, p. xiix.
20. D. Ward, 'A comparative historical geography of streetcar suburbs in Boston, Massachusetts and Leeds, England: 1850–1920'. *Annals of the Association of American Geographers*, **54** (1964), pp. 477–89.
21. D. Ward, 'The industrial revolution and the emergence of Boston's Central Business District', *Economic Geography*, **42** (1966), pp. 152–71.
22. H. Carter and G. Rowley, 'The morphology of the Central Business District of Cardiff', *Transactions, Institute of British Geographers*, **38** (1966), pp. 119–34.
23. Daunton, *Coal Metropolis*, p. 80.

24. J. R. Kellett, *The Impact of Railways on Victorian Cities*, (London and Toronto, 1969), p. 293.

25. *Ibid.*, p. 290.

26. J. E. Vance, 'Housing the worker: determinative and contingent ties in nineteenth century Birmingham, *Economic Geography*, **43** (1967), pp. 95–127.

27. Kellet, *Impact of Railways*, p. 311.

28. M. R. G. Conzen, 'Alnwick, Northumberland; a study in town plan analysis', *Transactions, Institute of British Geographers*, **27** (1960).

29. J. W. R. Whitehand, 'Fringe belts: a neglected aspect of urban geography', *Transactions, Institute of British Geographers*, **41** (1967), pp. 223–33. The most useful summary is J. W. R. Whitehand, 'The changing nature of the urban fringe: a time perspective', in J. H. Johnston (ed.), *Suburban Growth. Geographical Processes at the Edge of the Western City*, (London, 1974), Chapter 3, pp. 31–52.

30. J. Parry Lewis, *Building Cycles and Britain's Growth*, (London, 1965).

31. Conzen, 'Alnwick, Northumberland', p. 81.

32. M. R. G. Conzen, 'The plan analysis of an English city centre', in K. Norborg (ed.), *Proceedings of the I. G. U. Symposium in Urban Geography*, Lund 1960, (Lund, 1962), pp. 383–414.

33. Whitehand, 'Fringe belts, a neglected aspect of urban geography'.

34. *Ibid.*, pp. 224–6.

35. Apart from the large number of Public Health reports, the oldest and most well known of these is Engels, *The Condition of the Working Class in England*, first published in 1892. A good modern edition is F. Engels, *The Condition of the Working-Class in England from Personal and Authentic Sources*. Introduction by E. Hobsbawn (2nd edn.) (London, 1969). Three well known modern studies are: S. D. Chapman (ed.), *The History of Working-class Housing*, (Newton Abbot, 1971); J. N. Tarn, *Five per cent Philanthropy. An Account of Housing in Urban Areas between 1840 and 1914* (Cambridge, 1973); A. Sutcliffe (ed.), *Multi-storey Living. The British Working-class Experience*, (London, 1974).

36. C. Stewart, *A Prospect of Cities*, (London, 1952), Chapter VIII. 'A pillar of salt', pp. 148–67.

37. Most histories of town planning include accounts of these towns, examples are: C. and R. Bell, *City Fathers. The Early History of Town Planning in Britain*, (London, 1969); G. Burke, *Towns in the Making*, (London, 1971).

38. E. Chadwick, in M. W. Flinn (ed.), *Report on the Sanitary Condition of the Labouring Population of Great Britain, 1842*, (Edinburgh, 1965).

39. Chalklin, *Provincial Towns of Georgian England*, pp. 57–139.

40. M. W. Beresford, 'The back-to-back house in Leeds, 1787–1937', in Chapman (ed.), *The History of Working-class Housing*, Chapter 3, pp. 104–5.

41. C. A. Forster, *Court Housing in Kingston upon Hull. An Example of Processes in the*

Morphological Development of Nineteenth Century Bye-law Housing, (Hull, 1972), University of Hull, Occasional Papers in Geography, No. 19.

42. D. Cannadine, 'Victorian cities: how different', *Social History*, 1 (1977), pp. 457–82.

43. Tarn, *Five per cent Philanthropy*, p. xiv.

44. J. E. Vance, *This Scene of Man: the Role and Structure of the City in the Geography of Western Civilization*, (New York, 1977), p. 244.

45. J. E. Tunbridge, 'Spatial change in high class residence: the case of Bristol', *Area*, 9 (1977), pp. 171–4.

46. H. J. Dyos, *Victorian Suburbs. A Study of the Growth of Camberwell*, (Leicester, 1961).

47. For a general review of theoretical possibilities, see J. W. R. Whitehand, 'The basis for an historico-geographical theory of urban form', *Transactions, Institute of British Geographers*, New Series, 2, (1977), 400–16.

14
Transport 1730–1900

A. Moyes

Transport is possibly the most crucial agent which man uses to organize the earth's surface. If movement cannot occur between places, then neither can interaction. Areal specialization, complementarity and trade are impossible without transport to lubricate the space separating the interacting areas.

Nevertheless, the precise importance of transport change to the process of economic growth has been debated vigorously. Such are the disagreements in this debate that the savings brought to society even by the railways have been questioned. [1] However, it is an incontrovertible fact that transport changes profoundly affected the spatial structure of economic change, simply because the creation of new transport systems, and therefore the distribution of their effects, invariably took a linear rather than a continuous form. In terms of viability, a minimum threshold of flow can be envisaged for each new medium of transport. Cost restraints cause the network builder to construct the most elemental network possible, onto which this threshold of flow can be attracted. The user, meanwhile, seeks a network which allows his personal profile of trips to be made without disruption. Out of the resultant compromise, there emerge networks of widely differing utility that confer accessibility in discriminating fashion to nodes and lines. Herein lies transport's impact on the structure of economic growth.

Network builders, operators and users are fallible human beings, bounded in their behaviour by imperfect abilities and often conflicting goals. In practice, the first of these interest groups, or the network builders, exercised choice over transport technology, a choice that was reflective of route location. The second group, or the transport operators, exercised choice through their control over levels of service, tariffs, and even between possible routes *within* a network. Lastly, the third group, or users, exercised choice between alternative modes of transport. However, despite the deviations introduced by the exercise of these choices, simple models of network growth can be employed to make sense of transport changes over the eighteenth and nineteenth centuries, though it would be unduly optimistic to expect a single deterministic model to explain more than a fragment of each transport system.

Most models of transport network development have been devised for the developing world, where overseas, subsistence economies are steadily drawn into a pre-existing imperial economy. [2] Ports represent the points of contact between the economies. Some ports gradually supplant others; possibly one has better command over what emerge as the best lines of search into the interior. The earliest penetration lines attract the first strategic long-distance network limbs. Their end-points and intermediate staging-points become important collection and distribution points for the flows of commercial, agricultural or mining products being carried. The network develops as a channelling device, feeding exportable surpluses down to the ports, and receiving and distributing commercial, social and political imports and innovations from the outside world. Gradually, more and more centres or nodes are connected to the network as it expands. Ultimately, each node has direct contact with every other node on the pioneer network.

Economic changes, such as the redistribution of population and economic activity, affect the levels of interaction between places. The resultant changes in flows of people and goods may place parts of the network under increasing stress. This can be countered in three ways: by locally increasing network capacity; by evolving new routes; or by developing alternative, superior, forms of transport. As regards the latter, innovation usually stems from, and is most eagerly applied to, the weak links in earlier networks; these are often where flows are high. As the innovation is tried and tested, acceptance grows cumulatively. As it does so, its initial effect may be to reinforce the 'main streets' of the space-economy, before invading the lesser axes and gaining competitive strength as connectivity rises. Network growth, new transport technologies, economic growth and spatial shifts in economic growth are thereby systematically and circularly related. [3]

The temporal spread of transport innovations characteristically takes the form of a logistic curve (Fig. 14.1). Early adopters test the innovation. If successful, a rapid diffusion follows, fed by an exponentially-increasing 'demonstration' effect. Eventually, only the most recalcitrant areas remain unaffected; in transport terms these are where the relative merits of the innovation are weakest, or where the innovation failed to reach

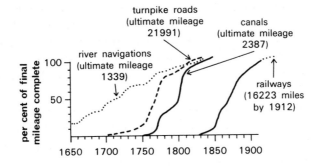

Fig. 14.1. Progress towards completion of the networks of four transport media, England and Wales, to 1900.

before a superior innovation superseded it. Figure 14.1 shows, for instance, that canal expansion did not halt growth of the turnpike network; in contrast, railways brought these two media's expansion to an end. The diffusion process has some spatial coherence in that general rules seem to determine the probability of a new network limb being formed. The rules may include the nearness of the new limb to the point where the network began, the shortness of the link, the importance of the nodes being connected, and the potential amount of *local* and *regional* interaction along it.[4] These conditions conspire to make the formation, and persistence, of disconnected network limbs or sub-graphs rare. These sub-graphs cannot participate in the more brisk levels of interaction possible on highly connected networks. Contagious diffusion is the more likely.

Of course, eighteenth-century Britain was no *tabula rasa*, nor was its land–sea interface as simple as that in the Taaffe-Morrill-Gould model. Willan would argue that, by the seventeenth century, a substantial level of inter-regional trade was being conducted around England at least, largely by coastal shipping, but helped by a limited but important mileage of navigable rivers. In functional terms, England's east coast generated most of the waterborne traffic; its ports owned two-thirds of the provincial tonnage of coastal shipping.[5] London was the single largest consumption point for foodstuffs, fuels and industrial raw materials, sucked in from other areas largely by water transport. As an entrepôt, it was the supply source for lesser distributary ports such as Bristol, Kings Lynn and Hull, controlling the Severn, Ouse and Humber-Trent waterways respectively. Significantly, of the top eight provincial ports in coaster tonnage, the first four were largely involved in the coal trade from Tyneside to London

(Newcastle-upon-Tyne, Sunderland, and, like limpets hanging on to the sea-lanes, Scarborough and Whitby). The next four, namely Hull, Kings Lynn, Yarmouth and Gloucester controlled the major river basins, and the chief penetration lines to the interior. The 'main streets' of the space-economy, at least of eastern, maritime England, were already apparent.

In aggregate, intra- and inter-regional overland trade was probably more important than water-borne trade, though much of it was short-distance. There was, however, an important network of overland, long-distance, London-focused commodity flows, using a sophisticated complex of goods carrier services, by both pack animals and waggons. [6] In 1665, regular passenger coaches were linking London with Exeter, Chester and Newcastle-upon-Tyne. By 1715, even the northern region had six regular carrier services to London per week. The very magnitude of road traffic, and its steady growth during the seventeenth century, was the necessary stimulus to road improvement. Although new river navigations had succeeded in connecting more and more places to a national low-cost circulatory system for freight, [7] the further inland they reached, especially from the south and west coasts, the more circuitous and protracted the journeys from London became compared with overland transport. Water-borne distance was almost 3 times the overland distance to Portsmouth, 3·7 times to Liverpool, 4·7 times to Bedford, 5·2 times to Bristol, and 6·5 times to the mid-Severn valley. Predictably, the turnpike principle was first applied to a meaningful extent on the routes permitting interaction with London, on which water-borne movement was substantial and/or difficult.

The Changing Structural Characteristics of the Transport Networks 1730–1900

Prelude and Preconditions

In itself, the year 1730 has no particular significance in transport terms. Two-thirds of the 1350 miles of rivers eventually made navigable had already been dealt with. Sixty-seven years had elapsed since the first, though short-lived, turnpike gates had been set up, to administer a 45-mile stretch of the Great North Road, leading north from the limits of the Lea navigation. Pound locks had been applied on the pioneer Exeter canal in 1564. Rudimentary horse-worked railways had been recorded in the early seventeenth century on Tyneside and near Nottingham. But as Fig. 14.1 shows, new transport innovations had made little impact, and 1730 forms a realistic point to intercept their subsequent gestation and growth.

Investment in river navigations had already begun to shift northwards. [8] Before the lull in navigation promotions between 1680 and 1700, almost all such schemes had been applied to the rivers of lowland, agrarian England—those of the London basin, those focusing on the Wash, and the Wiltshire Avon. Only Andrew Yarranton's improvement of the Worcester-shire Stour between 1662–5 had been overtly planned to meet industrial needs. The new century brought more deliberate attempts to facilitate growing industrial traffic. By 1730, river navigation reached, or nearly reached Leeds, Wakefield, Derby, Burton-on-Trent, Manchester, York and Sheffield. [9] Although the London-centred river navigation systems were strengthened during this period, to link Newbury to the Thames, and Sudbury to the North Sea, only the Medway was to receive much attention subsequently. Interest now centred more on northern rivers like the Weaver, to cope with the growing mid-Cheshire salt trade, the Dee, to try to recover Chester's loss of trade to Liverpool, and the Douglas to connect the Wigan collieries to tidewater and thus to Liverpool. However, it became no easier to defeat the many opponents of navigation schemes—millers, bridge-builders, downriver traders, or riparian landowners. The short Stroud-water navigation materialized only after 75 years of local and parliamentary haggling. Nor were river navigations guaranteed success. Floods on the Wiltshire Avon, made passable from Christchurch to Salisbury in 1684, swept away the locks irredeemably in 1700. The Yorkshire Foss, rendered navigable a century later, led nowhere and was a financial disaster. [10] By the mid-eighteenth century, the scope for meaningful expansion of river navigations was almost gone.

In the ensuing discussion, it is proposed to analyse separately the advance of each transport medium towards its climax. However, local development of one medium often occured in liason with, or in response to, development in another. Some road improvements were triggered by new river wharves, canal termini or railway stations; early railways were usually designed as feeders to water transport, and ultimately most canals were connected to the open sea.

The Turnpike Age

By the late seventeenth century, the increasing volume of intra- and inter-regional commodity flows had begun to exert pressure on the road network of the country. Transport systems responded by replacing the pack-horse with the more capacious waggon, and by introducing the principle of turnpiking. The latter countered the failure of traditional parish-based road repair systems to keep pace with the growing use of roads. It involved the establishment of a turnpike trust to administer a particular road. The trust was empowered to charge tolls and to use the money so raised to maintain and improve the road. Although not intended to be profitable, relatively little turnpiking was carried out without some prospect of a fair return on capital. Most turnpikes were designed as simple links between pairs of end-points, such as between a town and its source of coal or limestone, rather than as elaborate cross-country networks. As such, most were the product of local initiative and enterprise.[11] A few, particularly in rural Wales and the northern Pennines, were sponsored by local authorities, but these were the exceptions. Significantly they were mostly formed late in the development of the turnpike system, after private enterprise had shown itself unwilling, or unable, to act. Broadly speaking, turnpikes met with no institutional or sectional barriers in their diffusion, other than those posed by the lack of local initiative or the finance needed to fund the Act of Parliament necessary and to carry the costs of the Trust during its early days.

During the leading sector phase in the period up to 1750, the diffusion of turnpikes followed a definite pattern.[12] Stated simply, those routes that led to London and those closer to it were turnpiked first. By 1750, a coherent network of upgraded roads had emerged along the eight main radial routes leading out of London; on the Great North Road, turnpiking had almost reached the Scottish border. Elsewhere, the trusts formed by 1750 tended to discharge either a specific function, or to provide better access to regional centres of trade and industry. Illustrating the former were trusts like that which linked the Droitwich salt works to the navigable river Severn, or that which connected north Staffordshire pottery and iron works to the Mersey. The latter can be illustrated by flurries of regional activity which successively affected towns in the west of England in the 1730s, the West Riding of Yorkshire in the 1740s,[13] and south Durham in the 1750s. Such activity established radial systems of turnpikes around regional nodes, nodes which were themselves connected by turnpikes with London. Altogether, it was a system that, even at this early stage, had derived a remarkable coherence from the way it enhanced accessibility to London. Indeed, apart from simple outliers in the west Cumberland coalfield, around Hull, in East Anglia, and in Wiltshire and Somerset, there were surprisingly few sub-graphs.[14]

Between 1750–70, a veritable turnpike boom occurred. Strategic routes were rapidly completed, and prolonged towards the very tips of Cornwall, South and North Wales. Inter-town links in the already affected areas were intensified, and disconnected sub-graphs attached to the main network. The diffusion wave, speeding from its origins in metropolitan England, left the southern and eastern counties with elaborate networks, but produced its densest coverage in a broad belt from Somerset through the West Midlands to the southern Pennines. By 1770, almost three-quarters of the eventual mileage of 22,000 had been turnpiked. The only major untouched areas were in parts of Wales, and in waterside areas of England such as lower Thames-side, coastal Suffolk, Norfolk and Lancashire, where water transport remained supreme well into the railway age. The last 7000 miles of turnpikes, approved between 1770 and 1836, mainly comprised short infillings to cater for new industrial traffic, especially in the Midlands and north, providing the first wheeled access to isolated waterpower factory sites (as in north-west Derbyshire in 1811 and 1832) or catering for increasing inter-urban flows, as between Oldham and Rochdale (1825). Piecemeal improvements of existing alignments and gradients were also widespread. Strategic links completed included those along the Kent and Sussex coasts under the stress of the Napoleonic wars, and the unprecedented direct government investment in the Shrewsbury-Holyhead and North Wales coast roads, to cater for increased passenger traffic with Ireland following the Act of Union of 1800.

Despite all this activity, turnpikes never accounted for more than one-fifth of the total road mileage. After the last turnpike Act (1836) the network still contained local shortcomings, particularly in peripheral Cornwall or East Anglia, or in nascent industrial areas. In Low Furness, coach access to Lancaster was still via the sands of Morecambe bay (tide willing) in 1851.[15] The South Wales valleys were almost road-less, though the neighbouring Vale of Glamorgan was extremely well covered. The mileage of other, parish roads grew a little over this period, largely in association with enclosure schemes, and added links whose width was often appropriate to their status as routes between villages, towns or regions.[16]

Physical extension of turnpiking did not necessarily increase the effectiveness of roads. Some turnpikes, as between Kendal and Ulverston, were little more than formalized pack-tracks. Not until the early nineteenth century did the road-building principles of Metcalfe or McAdam spread widely from their areas of first application, in west Yorkshire (from 1755) and around Bristol (1816) respectively. Ironically, this proved possible in some areas only with the extension of canals, and a consequent cheapening of road materials. [17] Before 1815, canal companies hardly ever complained about road transport competition, whereas references become numerous after that date. But turnpikes were sufficiently reliable to allow the development of long-distance road hauliers like Pickford by 1760, and for the Post Office to begin its own mail coach network in 1783. This stimulated a rapid growth of the hitherto limited but widespread stage-coach sector, such that road passenger travel probably increased 16-fold between 1790 and 1835. [18] The stage network lagged behind the completion of turnpiking, so that places like Penzance were not regularly served until 1820. Even in better connected areas, the coach network did not flower until after 1820 (in south Hampshire) or after 1830 (West Riding). [19] Travel speeds increased unevenly; carriers' waggon schedules between Manchester and London were halved in an orgy of competition in 1776 and were thereafter little changed. [20] Roads on this route were good enough by 1814 to permit use of elliptical steel springs. But stage-coach speeds in Hampshire seem to have slowed after 1827, as if the technical, if not physiological, limits of horse-power had been reached. [21]

As the turnpike network became more fully connected, it presented new opportunities for users to cut costs, increase speeds or visit new destinations. The carrier Pickford could readily re-route his through Manchester–London waggons via Ashbourne, Derby, Leicester and Northampton in 1790, when canal competition killed trade on his existing route. By 1830, this haulier could exploit short-term gaps in the rail network, using the rich coverage of inter-urban turnpikes. [22] Despite the increasing range of routes possible, it is significant that most stage-coach proprietors in west Yorkshire swarmed onto a very few axes, on which they could maximize traffic if not minimize mileage; the numerous other links being thinly served. [23] By 1850, the opportunities to fill gaps were much reduced. Turnpike revenues had fallen by one-third since 1835, coach services on routes with a rail equivalent had been decimated, and their integration with canal or river passenger services largely abandoned. [24]

The Canals

As a network, the canal system developed less coherently. Its peak mileage was to be only 11 per cent of that of turnpikes, reflecting the much higher capitalization necessary per mile. [25] Some canals took so long to build that their initial spatial logic was blurred by the time of completion. Also, many short dead-end canals were built to slot into existing river navigations or ports without the need for other canals. Such canals peppered the coasts from Carlisle through Cardigan to the Tamar, then more thinly around the south and east coasts, where river navigations were relatively plentiful (Fig. 14.2). Localized application was followed by rapid imitation of the first inter-regional canal, so linking the Thames, Humber–Trent, Mersey and Severn basins with each other. The canal 'mania' of 1792–4 not only led to a duplication of the arms of this 'cross' but also triplication of the first Thames-to-Severn and trans-Pennine canals. Concurrently, lateral branch canals multiplied, as did up-valley extensions of river navigations, and downstream supplanters of them, particularly in highland England. The new medium at least halved the cost of freight movement compared with road transport, and at most cut it by three quarters. But the canals' sensitivity to topography created irregular barriers to the diffusion of the network, and the penetration of its cost advantage. [26]

Behind the municipal promotors of the pioneering Sankey Brook navigation were Liverpool salt-refiners. They stood to benefit from the cheaper delivered prices of water-borne coal from the St Helens area, than could be offered by the nearer but land-locked Prescot collieries. [27] The short, initially isolated Bridgewater canal, opened eight years later in 1765, was likewise to cheapen coal costs in Manchester. Soon it expanded to make a 25-mile link to the sea-going section of the Mersey at Runcorn, avoiding the shoals of the upper Mersey and Irwell. This early stress on the Mersey basin inspired Potteries' industrialists to promote, in 1766, the first English canal to breach a watershed, that between the Trent and the Mersey. The lower reaches of these rivers were already used to carry materials and products to and from the Potteries, but the turnpikes towards the Weaver and Derby which industrialists had already set up were inadequate. The connecting Staffordshire and Worcestershire canal, crossing the much easier Trent–Severn watershed, opened in 1772. In turn, it met the Wolverhampton–Birmingham canal, which had been planned in anticipation. With its eventual three winding routes at

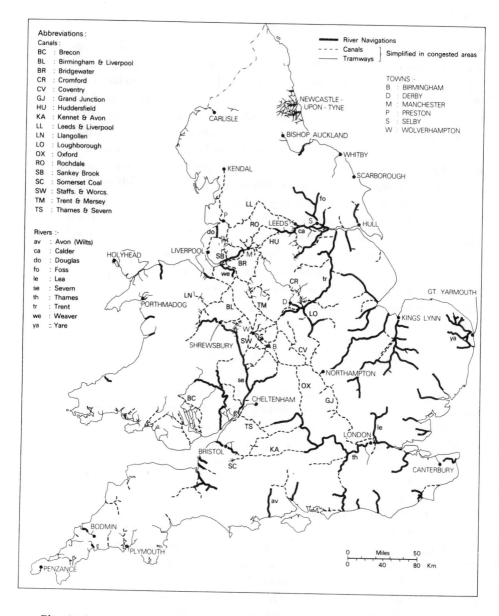

Abbreviations :
Canals :
BC : Brecon
BL : Birmingham & Liverpool
BR : Bridgewater
CR : Cromford
CV : Coventry
GJ : Grand Junction
HU : Huddersfield
KA : Kennet & Avon
LL : Leeds & Liverpool
LN : Llangollen
LO : Loughborough
OX : Oxford
RO : Rochdale
SB : Sankey Brook
SC : Somerset Coal
SW : Staffs. & Worcs.
TM : Trent & Mersey
TS : Thames & Severn

Rivers :-
av : Avon (Wilts)
ca : Calder
do : Douglas
fo : Foss
le : Lea
se : Severn
th : Thames
tr : Trent
we : Weaver
ya :: Yare

River Navigations
Canals
Tramways } Simplified in congested areas

TOWNS :-
B : BIRMINGHAM
D : DERBY
M : MANCHESTER
P : PRESTON
S : SELBY
W : WOLVERHAMPTON

Fig. 14.2. River navigations and canals in England and Wales with their feeder tramways.

different levels on the Black Country plateau, it was to provide intricate accessibility to 550 private basins at iron and other works, and to ironstone, coal and limestone mines within a 100 square mile area.

Though instigated in the provinces, the canals now sought contact with London. The short and tempting 30-mile gap between the navigable upper Thames near Lechlade and the Severn was the first attacked. It was completed by 1789, tunnelling through the almost waterless Cotswold scarp to meet the Stroudwater navigation. Bristol-to-London traffic generally was furthered, but potentially more significant was the facility it now offered for coal from the Forest of Dean, Bristol and even the West Midlands to be sold on the London market. [28] Soon, however, the West Midlands secured better links with London. When the Coventry canal (originally intended as a mere feeder to the Trent and Mersey) and the winding Oxford canal opened, they met end-on. The latter, as with the Thames and Severn, connected into the upper Thames. Canal communication was now possible, albeit indirectly, from London to Liverpool, Manchester, the Trent system, and to Severnside. However, it was crucially dependent on the erratic navigability of the Thames. [29] Not surprisingly, much through traffic chose to use the new canals only north of Braunston, and rely on swifter road haulage between that point and London. [30]

On the increasingly important trans-Pennine axis, the superficially easiest route was similarly chosen first, and shorter, more difficult ones later. Brindley's first survey in the 1770s for Liverpool and Bradford businessmen used the lowest watershed, between Aire and Ribble, although producing a tortuous through route from Leeds to Liverpool via Skipton. The advantages of being first were lost in vacillation over the route in east and mid-Lancashire, due to uncertainty over whether to serve limestone areas or not, established towns or growing ones, and whether to jeopardize water supplies by risking a short summit level. [31] Financial crises and the pre-empting of some sections by newer canals all delayed completion till 1806, when it had become 20 miles longer than when first planned. The shorter, costlier Huddersfield canal had meanwhile been open for five years, linking Manchester with the industrial West Riding through the three-mile Standedge tunnel, and the topographically less brave, if longer Rochdale canal between Manchester and the upper Calder, for twelve.

There followed an investment boom in canals. From 1792 to 1795 alone, 51 canal Acts were passed, authorizing expenditure of £7½ million, and attracting investment not just from local sources, but countrywide. The early canals were encouragingly profitable. Industrialists were now prepared to support canals to underpin their expansion plans. Canals also aided agriculture in its gearing-up to a war economy. With this boom, the network became topologically complex. Along with coastal shipping, it now formed more than one fundamental circuit;[32] the first inter-regional canals increased connectivity more than would later schemes, and allowed a new scale of interaction. Of the consequent reinforcements to this 'cross', the most important was the Grand Junction, providing, with associated ventures, a broad, more direct canal from London's dockland to the West Midlands, and, *inter alia*, from Birmingham to Worcester, further down the Severn than previous connections. Dependence on the unsatisfactory Thames was reduced further by the construction of a link between the navigable Kennet at Newbury and the Avon at Bath. The tributary Somerset Coal Canal could now feed useful traffic from the Radstock mines, to London and intervening markets.

Away from the 'cross', most of the 'mania' canals were less important. Often, they comprised local culs-de-sac probing up valleys to tap or distribute coal and limestone. During the Napoleonic Wars, several strategic canals were conceived, to by-pass dangerous stretches of coastline. As with that built to link London with Portsmouth, they were commercial failures in peacetime. The last major barge canal completed (1834) was symbolically audacious. Built in defiance of the impending railways, the terrain and even of intervening settlements, the Birmingham and Liverpool Junction shortened the distance between the two cities by 15 miles, and obviated as many as 45 locks compared with the pre-existing canal route. Thereafter, canal building occurred only at the economic or geographical edges of the country, especially in the west, or as improvements where traffic held up well against the railways, such as in the Black Country or on the Yorkshire port-feeders.

The more highly connected the canal network became, the more its weak links were exposed, such as the condition of the Thames and the high charges on the Oxford canal. Nevertheless, high profits and vigorous interaction were possible on local sub-sections of the network like the connecting Loughborough and Erewash navigations.[33] However, traffic levels bore no direct relationship to profitability. The early canals, though not always cheap to build, at least borrowed cheaply. Later ones usually saddled themselves with heavy interest payments, or compensation to earlier canals for traffic abstracted. However, irrespective of profitability, canals conferred advantage on the areas they served. In particular, for many areas, they opened up the prospect of a coal-fired economy. But ironically, they furthered the spread of waggonways, which, in a refined form, were later to supplant them.

Tramways and Early Railways

Tramways were locally significant even before the canal age. Riverside coals near Newcastle-upon-Tyne were exhausted by the early eighteenth century, and horse-worked wooden waggonways (tramways) were serving mines as far as eight miles inland by 1723.[34] By the end of the century, two main tree-like sub-graphs of waggonways, built by the coal-owners with varying amounts of co-operation, were evident on south Tyneside. On the north bank, and on Wearside, the plethora of separate, often parallel waggonways suggests less co-operation despite constructional costs of up to £1000 per mile.[35] When the Newcastle–North Shields railway opened in 1839, it intersected nine separate waggonway sub-graphs making for the riverbank within three and a half miles of each other.[36] In the north-east coalfield, rapid development of waggonways, and the difficult topography of the lower Tyne and Wear valleys, stifled canal building completely.

Most canal Acts after 1760 permitted tramways to be built as feeders, thereby enabling the influence of the canal to be extended beyond the strict limits imposed by terrain, water supply or traffic thresholds;[37] indeed, without feeder tramways, and their self-acting inclined planes, some canals had no chance of reaching their goals. Most feeders were short; the Cromford canal in Derbyshire inspired 16 feeders, of which only two were more than two miles long. But a 16-mile tramway in effect prolonged the Stratford-on-Avon canal to Moreton-in-Marsh from 1826, a 33-mile link was opened across the Derbyshire limestone plateau between the Cromford and Peak Forest canals in 1831, and a 38-mile connecting trio of tramways tied Kington to the canal head at Brecon by 1825. Of about 1400 miles of tramways built, slightly under half were built in liason with canals, and almost half of these were in the South Wales coalfield.[38] Growth of iron-smelting on the coalfield's northern rim had outrun the capacity of the turnpikes and the lock-ridden canals from Cardiff to Merthyr and Newport to Crumlin. Intended first as feeders, tramways were by 1800 duplicating long stretches of these canals. Thirty years later, inland industrialists' cheapest routes were often a judicious mixture of both media.

As Fig. 14.2 shows, substantial mileages of tramways were linked not with the canals but with harbours or navigable rivers. The 220 miles of tramways in the north-east were the most notable cluster, far larger than the next longest, in the Forest of Dean and Coalbrookdale, both of which led down to the river Severn. But elsewhere, tramways tended to be simple in layout, and isolated. Tramways allowed more economical use of horse power than road transport, and accordingly were widely adopted during the Napoleonic Wars when horses were scarce and expensive to operate.[39] By the 1830s they could be as ambitious as that built from Whitby over fearsome inclines to the Vale of Pickering. But fundamentally they remained feeders; their last essay, as late as 1863, connected the Croesor slate quarries with Porthmadog harbour, on the western edges of the space-economy.

By 1830, the canal and associated tramway network was nearly complete. Forty-five per cent of the direct links that could have been made between 115 key nodes on the canal and navigable river network of England and Wales had in fact been made, offering four times the connectivity of a century before.[40] New inter-regional freight links had been formed. Manufacturing and mining had sited themselves preferentially along the network. But territorial weaknesses in coverage remained, particularly outside a quadrilateral bounded by London, Hull, Preston and Bristol, and some overprovision within it. Incomplete coverage led to transhipment, delay, and cost increases; coal priced at 7s 6d per ton at the pithead in the Forest of Dean cost 9s 2d more at Cheltenham, 25 miles, two tramways and a riverboat away.[41] Railways, often cheaper to build, would soon exploit such deficiencies.

The Railway Age

The slender distinction between horse-worked tramways and locomotive-worked railways was essentially one of axle loads, carrying capacity and strategic achievement. Wooden tramway tracks had already been replaced by 1800 with cast-iron rails and flanged wheels (in the north-east) or flanged plates (in other districts). As better-wearing, less brittle iron rails came into increasing use in the 1820s, steam locomotion became more feasible, offering far greater productivity at the price of heavier track and works.[42] In many respects, the opening of the Liverpool and Manchester railway (1830) more clearly marks the start of the railway era than that of the Stockton and Darlington line in 1825. The latter was an upgraded waggonway, linking the outcrop coals of Bishop Auckland with the hitherto little used Teesmouth. It was happy to mix steam- and horse-haulage for some years. The Liverpool and Manchester was to be exclusively locomotive-worked. Unlike the canals or turnpikes, it provided and ran all the rolling stock and motive power on its line. It was an arrow-straight and, despite intentions, passenger railway carrying by 1835 three and a half times the expected numbers. It was virtually oblivious of water transport or intervening traffic. But soon it sent out minimum-length branches to Wigan, and the Bolton and Leigh railway. Its mid-point at Newton-le-Willows was to form the natural point of attachment for railways to link London and the two main centres of the north-west, which in the decade 1821–31 had experienced their fastest-ever rate of population increase.

At the end of 1835, 269 miles of railways authorized by Parliament were open.[43] South Lancashire had a tight knot of 65 interconnected miles, and was ready to spawn a St Helens–Widnes line to rival the Sankey navigation. Northumberland and Durham had 121 miles, in effect six sub-graphs, which would eventually fuse by 1850. The rest lay in scattered, local lines, mainly feeding water transport. Some would expand vigorously, like the Leeds and Selby; others like the remote Bodmin and Wadebridge would remain solitary for many years. Meanwhile, a substantial wave of promotions began. It started with two interlinking companies which, by 1838, linked the Liverpool and Manchester line to London via Birmingham. Onto this stem, most of the early trunk lines north and west of the capital were grafted, reaching out from Birmingham to Derby, York, and soon as far as Tyneside. Radial links promoted from London to high-order central places like Southampton (1834), Bristol (1835) and Brighton (1837) emphasize the importance of passenger traffic in expectations. Twenty-nine new railway companies were promoted in 1836,[44] and although promotions slowed thereafter, there were 100 nominally separate companies on the eve of the railway 'mania' in 1844, worked in effect by 41 concerns.[45]

During this initial phase, several main lines had evolved haphazardly by the end-on linking of companies which had not always worked in concert. Nevertheless, the inter-urban network was not topologically inefficient. Only 14 of the 41 towns in England with more than 25,000 people at the 1841 Census were not yet rail-connected. Of these, Exeter, Halifax and Macclesfield were imminently anticipating connection, Norwich and Yarmouth were soon to be connected to each other, but not yet with other lines; the Potteries, Bradford, Blackburn, Dudley, Huddersfield and Worcester had not long to wait. Only Ipswich and Plymouth/Devonport were far from the network at this date. In mileage, the links between London, Birmingham, the north-west, west Yorkshire and the north-east of England were only 6 per cent longer than the theoretical minimum-mileage network connecting these areas,[46] and the Pennines can be blamed for much of that excess. Direct alignments between chosen objectives were usual. Intermediate traffic was often ignored, and left to locally-promoted branches or road feeders. Like the Grand Junction canal before it, the London and Birmingham railway baulked at the descent into the Nene valley to serve Northampton, but it carefully skirted the central army depot at Weedon, to curry government support.[47] Topographical obstacles meant different things to different schools of engineers; the Stephensons would initially tolerate no ruling gradient steeper than 1:330, whereas Joseph Locke would accept 1:120 on the London and Southampton, and Moorsom an audacious 1:37 on the Birmingham and Gloucester. At a local level, land ownership and the patchy distribution of support for or antagonism against railways could be equally powerful distorting influences.[48]

Despite fragmented ownership and control, inter-company planning was frequent in this first railway boom. Second-stage lines were usually planned to be of minimal length, and to maximize the use of existing routes, if their owners agreed. Thus the South-Eastern attached its route from Dover to the existing London–Brighton line at Redhill, rather than pursue an independent, costly route into London. The same distance-minimizing principle applied to the lowest-order branches which bifurcated from the main lines at right-angles to serve such places as Aylesbury, Leamington, Maidstone, Nottingham, Oxford and Peterborough.

Cost-minimizing principles were aired during Parliament's considera-tion of the possible routes to Scotland and Ireland. If the Board of Trade had had *carte blanche*, it would have preferred a London–Edinburgh line via Cambridge, Peterborough, Lincoln, York and Tyneside. But since west coast rails reached as far north as Preston, their continuation to Carlisle and Glasgow made more sense, especially given the increasing interaction between Lancastria and central Scotland. Similarly, a link to Dublin via Chester and Holyhead was preferred because it made use of existing lines as far as Chester, whereas the alternative route via Worcester would have required new and more expensive construction.[49]

In sum, hardly fewer route-miles could have been used to connect the places served by the railnet in 1845, than the 2000 miles used. The network bore an uncanny resemblance to the centrally-planned motorway network of a century later. Ignoring the fact that each radial route from London except one had separate termini, remarkably few sub-graphs existed; only two port-feeders in South Wales and one in Furness were of any substance. Nevertheless, from the user's viewpoint, the level of connectivity was more apparent than real. Physical connections in many towns were absent or poor, as in London, Manchester, Sheffield, Birmingham and Gloucester; through booking facilities were rare, and bodily transhipment of goods and passengers from system to system common.[50] Branch connections could be so indirect that rail had little advantage over road for passenger movement, as between Maidstone and London. Finally, the medium had diffused little away from the 'main streets' as yet. Given the latent demand for travel which the railways unleashed, the next railway boom had the effect of swamping the topological virtues of the early network in an indiscriminate attempt to connect everywhere directly with everywhere else, including as improbable a pair as Manchester and Bordeaux.[51]

The Railway Mania and After

In 1845, England and Wales' railway mileage was 11 per cent towards completion; by 1852, the percentage was almost 40. The 'railway mania' of 1844–7 was largely fuelled by cheap money, and fanned by fear that railway promotion was soon to be strictly controlled by Parliament. Abandonment of tight control in 1845 caused an even greater promotional fever. At the mania's crest in 1846, 272 Bills received parliamentary assent, authorizing 4540 miles of lines; another 620 companies had been incorporated, and 643 more were proposed but had yet to register a prospectus.[52] As money supplies dried up, the mania subsided. Had all approved lines materialized, 12,000 route-miles of railway would have been operating by the 1850s, instead of the 7500 miles completed. Many proposals, however, were imitative rather than pioneering; in Bedfordshire alone, 20 of the 24 'mania' lines proposed, but not built, duplicated or presaged main lines already or eventually built.[53] Proposals to carry the network further into rural western Britain usually foundered.

Comparing the post- with the pre-mania densities, the network had thickened within a quadrilateral bounded by Liverpool, Scarborough,

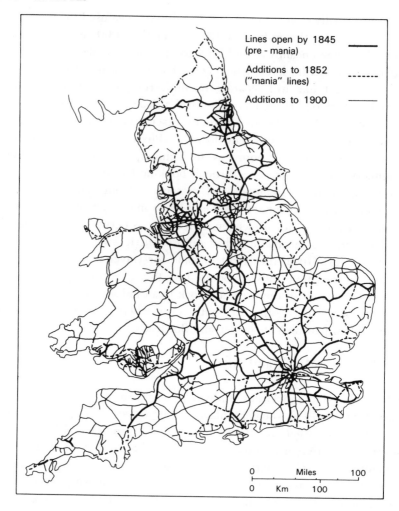

Fig. 14.3. The railway network in England and Wales, *c.* 1900, identifying dates of completion of lines.

Dover and Brighton. Alternative inter-city routes were emerging. As before, the network was spreading by contagion. New connections were often cheap, short branches, as to Salisbury or Bedford, leaving further dead-ends for later lines to manipulate. Lines had spread coherently eastwards into East Anglia and Lincolnshire from the newly completed London–Doncaster main line. Apart from ignoring peripheral Britain, the 1852 network was perhaps not as disastrous as the term 'mania' might imply. Many links would have materialized even in a more sober era—such as to serve the Denbighshire or Potteries coalfields, or to make the cut-off from Rugby to Stafford. Few sections of lapsed lines were not picked up and re-incorporated in later lines. Only in the Vale of York was there blatant excess, thanks to the territorial designs of promoter George Hudson.

As Fig. 14.1 shows, mileage increased strongly again in the 1860s, more through contractors' speculation than by local trading interests. [54] Empty spaces in mid-Wales were well filled, those of Devon and Cornwall less so. Feeder agricultural branches of marginal profitability were continually forming. [55] More clear-cut rivalry built up between companies, expressed not in rate-cutting but in overlapping facilities, and speed; hence cut-offs to accelerate travel between London and, for example, Liverpool and Hull. Expansive, newly amalgamated companies, prevented from building territorial monopolies by parliamentary distrust, drove ambitious and unremunerative lines through gaps and obstacles which their predecessors had avoided, [56] and all ended up with octopoid networks. The Midland company, for example, rooted in the north Midlands, had interests at Swansea, Bournemouth, London, Great Yarmouth, Carlisle and Manchester by the 1880s. Yet, as towns grew, and industrial technology and society changed, so new axes of interaction emerged, and the railway companies understandably raced to trap them: flows of passengers between towns, between conurbations and resorts, London and speculative surburbia, freight flows between developing coalfields and ports, orefields and smelters. [57] Gaps in coverage were gradually filling, with north Devon, Cornwall and Norfolk finally being reached in the 1890s. With more financial teeth, the Light Railways Act of 1896 could have brought plans for lines to furthest Hartland, St Davids and Aberdaron to fruition.

Perhaps the most meteoric build-up of lines in later years was in the South Wales valleys. Cautiously awaiting the proving of the coalfield, nine locally inspired companies evolved between the 1830s and 1890s, some from earlier canal or tramway concerns, and often with their own dock schemes, to move increasing amounts of coal to tide water. By 1900, 85 per cent of the coal leaving the area was doing so by sea, either coastwise or for export. Three English main-line companies were also present, filtering off coal for landward distribution. Of the 810 miles of routes within the coalfield, one-tenth were duplicative, though there was traffic and profit for all. [58] The opening of the Severn tunnel in 1886 laid the way for the South Wales main line to become a 'main street' of the British space-economy in the twentieth century.

Other Media in the Railway Age

The South Wales experience emphasizes that the railways' growth could bring repercussions for other media. Shipping became more efficient and cheaper as the use of steam-power grew, as dock utilization improved, as the lower reaches of rivers like the Tyne were deepened, and as dock-building moved steadily downriver. Although the railways lost some coal movement to coastal shipping after the 1870s, they gained new traffic from maritime trade. They built their own docks, especially for coal shipment, at Hull, Grimsby and even at the canal port of Goole.[59] Intense competition for the growing cross-channel and international passenger traffic belatedly thickened the railnet on both banks of the lower Thames. The railways' port interest was increasingly, and in some quarters unpopularly, used to trap seaborne imports of foodstuffs and manufactures into favoured ports, and then offer cheaper bulk overland transit to final, even coastal, markets than would apply to home products.[60] At large ports, railways courted shipping, but the arrival of railways at small ports usually robbed them of incoming seaborne coal, unless return cargoes of building materials or metalliferous ores were available to keep port installations busy and tramping freight rates low.[61]

The railways' impact on the canals could be equally selective, though usually destructive. Short-distance rail freight traffic built up slowly, while passenger traffic was fast-growing, profitable and better balanced. In 1850, the Bridgewater canal was still (by agreement) carrying more than two-thirds of the freight between Liverpool and Manchester.[62] But 40 years later, railways were carrying eight times as much tonnage as the canals. A haphazardly distributed third of their mileage was now railway-owned, and generally left to die. Even where traffic held up well, receipts fell because of the need for price-cutting; on the Grand Junction, they were halved within six years of the London and Birmingham railway's opening.[63] In the absence of canals, rail freight rates were generally higher, but in turn, rival railways might materialize.[64] Some canals were tactically useful to their railway owners; rates on the Black Country canals were pitched to keep short-distance mineral traffic on the canals, out of the way of long-distance rail traffic.[65] In the case of many rural canals, their swan-song came in ferrying construction materials for the railway that would usurp them. [66]

Road transport too was unevenly hit by railway encroachment, particularly in the short-term. Traffic on turnpikes paralleled by railways could be decimated, and total all-medium connectivity often fell for a while. [67] But growing feeder traffic ultimately led to a far larger road transport industry. The number of horses used for commercial purposes was little higher in 1851 than 1811 but probably quadrupled in the next 50 years, for short-distance distributive work, and in urban public and hackney transport. [68] The village carrier system, formalized by the late eighteenth century, expanded as a multi-purpose link between country and town. Hinterland boundaries between towns were well-defined by 1815; services within these gradually intensified in frequency and coverage, especially around major market centres like Maidstone, Newark and Leicester. [69] In the last quarter-century, daily omnibus services were hiving off from freight. Around lesser market towns, multi-purpose carrier services kept a more market-day character; at Devizes in 1865, 70 per cent of incoming carriers ran on only one day per week. [70] Within urban areas, short radial horse-bus and (after 1870)—tram systems developed. In cities they grew into large businesses; Liverpool's 380-odd buses and trams required a stud of 3007 horses in 1879. [71] In London, pedestrian circulation was locally so vigorous as to merit the first underground railway in 1863, though the system made little progress until electric traction materialized in the 1890s. Elsewhere, steam locomotion was permitted on street tramways from 1879, unleashing an expansion of short-distance urban systems. The increasingly local character of road traffic, even if of greater intensity, gradually allowed acquiescence in a reversion of turnpikes to local authority care, though the process of disturnpiking was not complete until 1895.

Transport and the Changing Form of the Space-economy

Because each transport innovation bore fruit at a different time, each left a slightly different matrix of nodes and connections for its successor to manipulate. But the role of transport change as a whole to the development of the space-economy can be treated as two-fold: as a contributor to that space-economy, and as a consumer within it.

Transport as a Contributor

The mere structure of connections within a transport network causes the constituent nodes and links to be differentiated from each other. Some links appear more often in best routes between pairs of places than others; they command more flows, and gather more equipment to deal with them, such as inns, coach builders, farriers and goods agents in the pre-railway age, arranged along the trunk routes in rhythmically spaced clusters.[72] Railway companies favoured highly accessible points within their networks for their repair facilities; ship-repair yards were widely, if less evenly, spattered over the coasts.[73] The network was acting as an allocative device, and helping the more highly connected nodes to grow at the expense of the poorly-connected.[74] Around them, an embryonic Von Thünian landscape might be evident, culminating in a national space-economy whose yardsticks and values were set by the metropolis. These values, or prices, minus transport costs to the metropolitan market could fix the maximum level of prices at the farm gate or the pithead.[75] Changes in transport costs or accessibility allowed new areas to enter the national space-economy, as with Dorset or the Staffordshire Moorlands in the London milk market.[76] But not all opportunities were grasped.[77]

Given its incomplete coverage, transport served to warp Euclidian space into more complicated, discontinuous forms. Networks constituted the search environment for those seeking to use them. Highly accessible areas like the West Midlands had a wider range of resources and options available to them than peripheral, poorly connected industrial areas; suppliers could also be played off against each other to better effect. If industrial technology changed, adaption and survival *in situ* were easier. Secondly, transport charges did not directly reflect Euclidian distance.[78] Turnpikes often discriminated between traffics. Canals' and railways' maximum charges might be fixed by statute, but *de facto* charges could vary greatly between and within companies. Though slow to evolve pricing policies, the railways soon saw the logic of backhaul freight rates, laying the way open for division of production between locations, such as of iron smelting between coalfields and orefields. Tapering freight rates were operated from the early years of the railways, though not formalized until 1891; they encouraged long-distance competition and hence longer hauls. Inferior products could lose their local monopoly as the sales radius of the premium product extended, as with the eclipsing of cheap, poor quality local coal by rail-borne in Ingleton, Yorkshire.[79] Other stratagems wiped out locational advantages; delivered prices of Yorkshire manufactures for export were made identical at any port between Hull and Tyneside by agreement in 1855–6, irrespective of distance carried. [80] Exceptional rates, like those which kept the Westbury iron works in Wiltshire in business, [81] make it difficult to compile space-cost curves for nineteenth-century industry. [82] Finally, the pattern of support for transport improvements shows slight bias towards places near in topological terms to the locale of improvements, but far in Euclidian terms. [83]

The impact of transport change on industrial location is paradoxical. Many features of the spatial structure of the Industrial Revolution are attributed to transport costs. Transport cost-minimizing models of industrial location broadly fit the shift of weight-losing activities from coalfield or orefield to the coast. But these new locational habits stem more from sharp falls in fuel use and in ocean freight rates, than from changes of costs or coverage of inland transport. Industrial agglomeration too is thought to reflect clustering of linked industrial activities so as to minimize the costs of interaction. Yet the most clustered activities in industry are often those like textiles and the small metal trades in which transport costs were very small. If transport has a part to play in justifying these clusters, is it through its helping to define the information networks and action spaces of decision-makers, and in moulding space and distance so that these clusters can be perpetuated? Could it be that without transport facilities the regionalization of the economy would have been impossible, but, having said that, the exact location of many of the various interlocking components was irrelevant?

Transport as a Consumer

In canal- and railway-building, land was perhaps the most obvious resource consumed directly. The impact of railway-building on Victorian cities has been carefully assessed, through demolition in inner urban areas, creation of suburbia, and furtherance of inner urban re-planning. [84] More subtle and less investigated are the ripples induced by transport's purchases from other sectors of the economy. Ephemeral demands for building materials accompanied each canal or railway scheme, needing short-lived quarries, claypits, brick- and mortar-kilns, and longer-term sources of ballast. The relative importance of these demands is problematic; Hawke suggests that the railways consumed about 18 per cent of the national brick production

during the 'mania' but thereafter barely 5 per cent per year.[85] Estimates
for railways' direct demand for iron are similar in proportional terms;
even in South Wales, the area most committed to railway iron production,
only one-sixth of the pig-iron was thus consumed. Rolling mills were,
admittedly, much more dependent on the rail trade, to the extent of 36
per cent in South Wales in 1848, but, again, much less thereafter. Indirect
purchases of iron were undoubtedly made via mechanical engineering, 20
per cent of whose products went to the railways in the 1830s, about one-
third during the 'mania', but much less afterwards.[86] Not until a century
later do industrial censuses become sufficiently fine to allow indirect
transport-induced consumption of other goods, such as timber, vehicle
parts, glass and rubber, to be estimated. Even the importance of their fuel
requirements is uncertain; the railways directly consumed 2 million tons
of coal in 1869, rising to 6·2 million in 1887, but the energy inputs to
horses working in transport remain speculative.[87] Indeed, perhaps more
can be deduced from studies of gross change in economic activity at the
local level—the rising importance of hay as a cash crop for farms on north
Thames-side to feed London's horses; the growth of iron-smelting at
Wednesbury thanks to backward integration by a coach- and railway-axle
maker; the waxing and waning of steel rail manufacture at Sheffield;[88] the
Great Western Railway's buying its own colliery at Tonyrefail—than
merely by estimating miniscule shifts in national economic variables
which were irrelevant to most people on the ground. Even so, the
significance of transport as a creator of local, or even national,
employment opportunity is difficult to chart. Employment in transport,
and in making products for transport industries, occupied at least one
person in thirty at work in England and Wales in 1841. Surges in
employment in railway building were to be experienced soon after. But by
1901, the proportion was more than one in eight, as the railways' direct
employment rose, and the vehicle trades grew.[89]

Conclusions

Some spatial and temporal order can be perceived in the development of
transport networks in England and Wales. Emphasis has ebbed and flowed
between maritime and land-based circulation systems. Extension of the
river navigations and turnpikes followed broadly similar lines: early
application in metropolitan England, then quickening adoption

progressively further from this birthplace over time. In the growth points of industrial England, transport stress led to the germination of rival technologies—the canal, the tramway and the railway—whose diffusion paths each took, or tried to take, similar trajectories. Localized testing and proving was followed by strategic linking with London, thence radial expansion to high-order central places. From all these axes, links, often of the shortest possible distance, sought to tie progressively lower-order centres to the network. Increasingly, however, transport's role in economic growth seems to have been redistributive. Symbolically, the urban creations of the transport media—the canal ports, the coaching and the railway towns—caused no major overturning of the urban hierarchy, although they have undoubted intrinsic interest. Transport change was the handmaiden, rather than the midwife, of the Industrial Revolution.

References

1. G. R. Hawke, *Railways and Economic Growth in England and Wales, 1840–70*, (Oxford, 1970).
2. E. J. Taaffe, R. L. Morrill and P. R. Gould, 'Transport expansion in underdeveloped countries: a comparative analysis', *Geographical Review*, **27** (1963), pp. 503–29.
3. E. Pawson, *Transport and Economy: the Turnpike Roads of Eighteenth Century Britain*, (London, 1977), p. 12.
4. W. R. Black in P. Haggett and R. J. Chorley, *Network Analysis in Geography*, (London, 1969), p. 265.
5. T. S. Willan, *The English Coasting Trade 1600–1750*, (Manchester, 1938), Appendix 7.
6. J. A. Chartres, 'Road carrying in England in the seventeenth century: myth and reality', *Economic History Review*, 2nd ser., **30** (1977), p. 74; G. L. Turnbull, 'Provincial road carrying in England in the eighteenth century', *Journal of Transport History*, New ser., **4** (1977), p. 37.
7. W. T. Jackman, *The Development of Transportation in Modern England*, (2nd edn.), (London, 1962), p. 209; P. S. Bagwell, *The Transport Revolution from 1770*, (London, 1974), p. 13. Bagwell presents useful comparisons of the effectiveness of horse-power in different transport applications: pack-horse load 2 to 3 cwt; heavy waggon team on soft road 1 ton; horse with chaldron on waggonway (iron) up to 8 tons; on river towpath 30 tons; on canal towpath 50 tons. Charges were not commensurate with these differences, however.

8. A. W. Skempton, 'The engineers of the English river navigations 1620–1760', *Transactions, Newcomen Society*, **29** (1953), p. 53.

9. T. S. Willan, *River Navigation in England 1600–1750*, (2nd edn.), (London, 1964).

10. J. Tann, 'The Yorkshire Foss Navigation', *Transport History*, 3 (1970), p. 90.

11. G. T. Unwin *et al.*, *Samuel Oldknow and the Arkwrights*, (Manchester, 1924), pp. 222–35; E. Beazley, *Madocks and the Wonder of Wales*, (London, 1967), pp. 69–77.

12. Pawson, *Transport and Economy*, p. 138.

13. R. G. Wilson, 'Transport dues as indices of economic growth 1775–1820', *Economic History Review*, 2nd ser., **19** (1966), p. 111.

14. W. Albert, *The Turnpike Road System in England 1663–1840*, (Cambridge, 1972), p. 122; Pawson, *Transport and Economy*, p. 150.

15. L. A. Williams, *Road Transport in Cumbria in the Nineteenth Century*, (London, 1975), p. 126.

16. J. Appleton, *The Geography of Communications in England and Wales*, (Oxford, 1962), p. 150; W. G. Hoskins, *The Making of the English Landscape*, (London, 1955), p. 154.

17. G. J. Fuller, 'The development of roads in the Surrey-Sussex Weald and coastlands between 1700 and 1900', *Transactions and Papers, Institute of British Geographers*, **19** (1953), p. 45.

18. Bagwell, *Transport Revolution*, p. 43.

19. M. J. Freeman, 'The stage-coach system of South Hampshire 1775–1851', *Journal of Historical Geography*, 1 (1975), p. 266; G. C. Dickinson, 'Stage-coach services in the West Riding of Yorkshire 1830–40', *Journal of Transport History*, 4 (1959), p. 3.

20. G. L. Turnbull, 'Pickfords 1750–1920: a study in the development of transportation', Ph.D. Thesis, University of Glasgow, 1973, p. 43.

21. Freeman, 'Stage-coach system', p. 278.

22. Turnbull, 'Pickfords', p. 185.

23. Dickinson, 'Stage-coach services', p. 9.

24. H. J. Dyos and D. H. Aldcroft, *British Transport: an Economic Survey from the Seventeenth Century to the Twentieth*, (Leicester, 1969), p. 223.

25. Bagwell, *Transport Revolution*, p. 38 provides data suggesting that in 1838, about £51 was spent on each mile of turnpike, and £11 on each mile of parish road. About £7,500 was authorized for each mile of canal eventually built.

26. Appleton, *Geography of Communications, passim.*

27. T. C. Barker, 'The beginnings of the canal age in the British Isles', in L. S. Pressnell (ed.), *Studies in the Industrial Revolution*, (London, 1960), p. 12.

28. H. Household, *The Thames and Severn Canal*, (Newton Abbott, 1969).

29. C. Hadfield, *British Canals*, (London, 1959), p. 188.

30. Turnbull, 'Pickfords', p. 82.
31. J. H. Farrington, 'The Leeds and Liverpool Canal: a study in route selection', *Transport History*, **3** (1970), pp. 52–79.
32. Haggett and Chorley, *Network Analysis*, p. 35.
33. T. J. Chandler, 'The canals of Leicestershire: their development and trade', *East Midland Geographer*, **10** (1958), p. 27.
34. C. E. Lee 'The world's earliest railway', *Transactions, Newcomen Society*, **25** (1946), p. 143.
35. B. Baxter, *Stone Blocks and Iron Rails (Tramways)*, (Newton Abbott, 1966), quotes costs ranging from £440 per mile excluding land, in 1797, to £1000 in 1799 (p. 34); however the Kington Railway, completed in 1825, cost £2700 per mile. The terms tramroad, tramway and wag(g)onway are synonymous.
36. C. E. Lee, 'Tyneside tramroads of Northumberland', *Transactions, Newcomen Society*, **26** (1948), p. 202.
37. V. H. Coleman, 'The Kington Railway', *Transactions, Woolhope Naturalists' Field Club*, **38** (1965): p. 23 indicates an average traffic of only 10 tons per day in 1839, although the concern was not loss-making.
38. Baxter, *Stone Blocks*, p. 34 and 'Gazetteer', pp. 146–226.
39. A. Harris, 'The Tindale Fell Waggonway', *Transactions, Cumberland and Westmorland Antiquarian and Archaeological Society*, **72** (1972), p. 236.
40. B. Fullerton, *The Development of British Transport Systems*, (Oxford, 1975), calculated from data on p. 13.
41. D. E. Bick, *The Gloucester and Cheltenham Railway*, (Lingfield, 1968), p. 38.
42. J. Simmons, 'For and against the locomotive', *Journal of Transport History*, **2** (1955), pp. 150–1; Baxter, *Stone Blocks*, p. 84.
43. H. G. Lewin, *Early British Railways 1801–44*, (London, 1925), p. 37.
44. Bagwell, *Transport Revolution*, p. 93.
45. Lewin, *Early British Railways*, p. 182.
46. Calculated using procedures in C. Werner, 'Networks of minimum length', *Canadian Geographer*, **13** (1969), pp. 47–69.
47. P. S. Richards, 'A geographical analysis of some of the surveys made for the London to Birmingham railway line', *Birmingham Archaeological Society Transactions and Proceedings*, **80** (1962), p. 17.
48. J. T. Ward, 'West Riding landowners and the railways', *Journal of Transport History*, **4** (1960), p. 242; J. R. Hepple, 'Abingdon and the G. W. R.', *Journal of Transport History*, New Ser., **2** (1974), p. 155.
49. Lewin, *Early British Railways*, p. 123.
50. Board of Trade, *Railway Gauges: Report of the Commissioners with Appendix*, H.C. 684, (1846), p. xvi.
51. D. J. Rowe, 'Southampton and "Railway Mania" 1844–7', *Transport History*, **2** (1969), p. 230.

52. H. G. Lewin, *The Railway Mania and its Aftermath 1845–52*, (1st edn.), (London, 1936), p. 115.
53. F. G. Cockman, 'The railway age in Bedfordshire', *Bedfordshire Historical Record Society*, Publication No. 3, (Bedford, 1974), p. i.
54. P. L. Cottrell, 'Railway finance and the crisis of 1866', *Journal of Transport History*, New Ser., **3** (1975), p. 22; A. G. Kenwood, 'Railway investment in Britain 1825–75', *Economica*, **32** (1965), p. 318.
55. C. L. Mowat, *The Golden Valley Railway*, (Cardiff, 1964), p. 11; H. W. Parris, 'Northallerton to Hawes: a study in branch line history', *Journal of Transport History*, **2** (1955), p. 235.
56. G. Channon, 'A nineteenth century investment decision: the Midland Railway's London extension', *Economic History Review*, 2nd ser., **25** (1972), p. 451.
57. B. J. Turton, 'Traffic on the Midland Railway in the late nineteenth century,' *East Midland Geographer*, **5** (1970), p. 113.
58. Dyos and Aldcroft, *British Transport*, p. 194.
59. J. D. Porteous, *Canal Ports: the Urban Achievements of the Canal Age*, (London, 1977), pp. 177–84.
60. P. J. Cain, 'Railways and price discrimination: the case of agriculture 1880–1914', *Business History*, **18** (1976), pp. 190–204.
61. P. J. Perry, 'Return cargoes and small port survival: two Dorset examples', *Proceedings, Dorset Natural History and Archaeological Society*, **89** (1968), p. 315.
62. Bagwell, *Transport Revolution*, p. 157
63. Hadfield, *British Canals*, p. 215.
64. Hawke, *Railways and Economic Growth*, p. 321.
65. M. Le Guillou, 'Freight rates and their influence on the Black Country iron trade 1850–1914', *Journal of Transport History*, New Ser., **3** (1975), p. 112.
66. C. Hadfield, *The Canals of South West England*, (Newton Abbott, 1967), pp. 82, 111.
67. Freeman, 'Stage–coach system', p. 274.
68. F. M. L. Thompson, 'Nineteenth century horse sense', *Economic History Review*, 2nd ser., **29** (1976), pp. 79–80.
69. A. Everitt, 'Country carriers in the nineteenth century', *Journal of Transport History*, New Ser., **3** (1976), p. 188.
70. A. Greening, 'Nineteenth-century country carriers in North Wiltshire', *Wiltshire Archaeological and Natural History Society Magazine*, **66** (1971), pp. 169–71.
71. J. B. Horne and T. B. Maund, *Liverpool Transport: Vol. 1: 1830–1900*, (London, 1975), p. 79.
72. J. A. Chartres, 'The place of inns in the commercial life of London and western England', 1660–1760, D. Phil. Thesis, University of Oxford, 1973, p. 138.

73. B. J. Turton, 'The British railway engineering industry', *Tijdschrift v. Economische en Sociale Geografie*, **48** (1967), p. 195; M. E. Hughes, 'The Historical Geography of the Seafaring Industry of the coasts of Cardigan Bay during the 18th and 19th centuries', M.A. thesis, University of Wales, 1962, Appendix 8.

74. Freeman, 'Stage-coach system', p. 273.

75. A. M. Hay, 'A simple location theory for mining activity', *Geography*, **61** (1976), pp. 65–76.

76. E. H. Whetham, 'The London milk trade 1860–1900', *Economic History Review*, 2nd ser., **17** (1965), p. 369.

77. D. W. Howell, 'The impact of railways on agricultural development in nineteenth century Wales', *Welsh History Review*, **7** (1974), p. 40.

78. Hawke, *Railways and Economic Growth*, pp. 317–61.

79. A. Harris, 'The Ingleton coalfield', *Industrial Archaeology*, **5** (1968), p. 319.

80. D. Brooke, 'Railway consolidation and competition in North East England 1854–80', *Transport History*, **5** (1973), p. 6.

81. Hawke, *Railways and Economic Growth*, p. 329.

82. D. M. Smith, 'A theoretical framework for geographical studies of industrial location', *Economic Geography*, **42** (1966), pp. 95–113; P. W. Lewis, 'Measuring spatial interaction', *Geografiska Annaler*, **52(B)** (1970), p. 28.

83. For examples, *vide* Household, *Thames and Severn Canal*, pp. 34–8; H. Pollins, 'The Swansea Canal', *Journal of Transport History*, **1** (1953), pp. 135–8; T. S. Willan, *The Early History of the Don Navigation*, (Manchester, 1965), p. 10.

84. J. R. Kellett, *The Impact of Railways on Victorian Cities*, (London, 1969).

85. Hawke, *Railways and Economic Growth*, p. 200.

86. B. R. Mitchell, 'The coming of the railway and economic growth', *Journal of Economic History*, **24** (1964), p. 326.

87. Thompson, 'Horse sense', p. 77.

88. K. Warren, 'The Sheffield rail trade 1861–1930: an episode in the locational history of the British steel industry', *Transactions and Papers, Institute of British Geographers*, **34** (1964), p. 131.

89. Great Britain, Census of Population, 1841, *Occupations*, Preface, pp. 53–7; 1901, *General Report with Appendices*, Table 34, pp. 256–69.

Subject Index